From Auster to Apache

From Auster to Apache

The History of 656 Squadron RAF/AAC 1942–2012

Guy Warner

Guy Warner
June 2013

Pen & Sword
AVIATION

First published in Great Britain in 2013 by
Pen & Sword Aviation
an imprint of
Pen & Sword Books Ltd
47 Church Street
Barnsley
South Yorkshire
S70 2AS

ISBN: 978-1-78159-098-0

Typeset in 11pt Ehrhardt by
Mac Style, Beverley, E. Yorkshire

Printed and bound in India by Replika Press Pvt. Ltd.

Pen & Sword Books Ltd incorporates the Imprints of Pen & Sword Aviation,
Pen & Sword Family History, Pen & Sword Maritime, Pen & Sword Military,
Pen & Sword Discovery, Wharncliffe Local History, Wharncliffe True Crime,
Wharncliffe Transport, Pen & Sword Select, Pen & Sword Military Classics,
Leo Cooper, The Praetorian Press, Remember When, Seaforth Publishing
and Frontline Publishing.

For a complete list of Pen & Sword titles please contact
PEN & SWORD BOOKS LIMITED
47 Church Street, Barnsley, South Yorkshire, S70 2AS, England
E-mail: enquiries@pen-and-sword.co.uk
Website: www.pen-and-sword.co.uk

Contents

Foreword

By

General Sir John Learmont KCB, CBE

It is always a privilege to be invited to write a Foreword and it gives me great pleasure to do so for Guy Warner's timely book on 656 Squadron. It is timely in the sense that although the Squadron is far from being the oldest Army aviation squadron, it is unique in having a near continuous operational record and it reaches the milestone of celebrating its 70th anniversary in early 2013.

The Air Observation Post (Air OP) concept was contentious when advocated by its pioneer, Captain Charles Bazeley RA in 1938 and was fiercely resisted by the Air Ministry. The idea of Royal Artillery officers flying rudimentary, unarmed aircraft to control artillery fire was inspired, but took until 1941 to be realized with the first Air OP Squadron, No 651. Yet the practice worked even better than the concept and by the time 656 Squadron formed up at RAF Westley in early 1943, the squadron establishment and concept of operations had been tested, by 651 Squadron, in North Africa. However, 656 Squadron's first Officer Commanding, Major Denis Coyle DFC, MBE, RA, with whom, in later life, I was privileged to serve in the 1950s, was made aware that his command would not be deployed close to home, but in the more distant and uncertain environment of the Burma Campaign, in support of 14th Army. On arrival in the Far East, he was immediately faced with two major problems. Firstly there was a complete lack of comprehension on how to deal with an RAF/RA aviation unit, by both the Army and RAF administrations, which led him to make farsighted, unilateral decisions. Secondly, whereas in other theatres, Air OP squadrons were able to deploy a flight in support of a division, Denis Coyle's only option was to place his flights at the disposal of a corps, while sections of a single Auster and pilot and his four man joint RAF/RA support team were regularly detached to support divisions. Such was the effectiveness and popularity of these self-sufficient sections that they became a *modus operandi*, and led to a close trust and loyalty between pilots and divisional commanders.

Acts of great heroics and airmanship were conducted in the harshest of conditions. Two pilots were to receive both the MC and DFC – which remains unsurpassed – while nine DFCs were awarded in total. Towards the end of World War II the Squadron deployed to Malaya, where it was to remain for the next twenty-five years, providing intimate aviation support throughout the Malaya Emergency and Indonesian

Confrontation. During this period the Squadron successfully dispatched sub-units/support to Java, Hong Kong, Korea, Brunei and Borneo.

In 1957 the Squadron transferred to the newly formed Army Air Corps (AAC), when it was retitled 656 Light Aircraft Squadron AAC. Gradually, 'light blue beret REME' replaced RAF technicians, and airtroopers took over ground crew duties. While there were major changes of personnel, the ethos and spirit engendered by Major Coyle was retained. By the early 1960s the Squadron was equipped with the wholly unreliable Scout helicopter – providing a challenge for pilots and technicians alike – while it also retained a fixed wing capability with the robust Beaver aircraft. In preparing to leave Malaysia, the Squadron Report stated:

"So 656 Squadron flies out of Malaysia's history. We are sad to be closing down, for after all, this is the Aviation unit with the longest record of active service; twenty-three out of twenty-seven years have been spent on operations, from the Arakan to Imphal and on to Rangoon, from Java and Sumatra to the Thai Border and all over East Malaysia – flying a total of over 250,000 hours on operations. All of us who served with 656 in any capacity are proud to have done so."

The Squadron's total flying hours in an operational theatre is a record not matched by any RN, AAC or RAF squadron to this day. From Malaysia the Squadron moved to Hong Kong, where, for the next eight years, it was well prepared to support operations to identify and capture illegal immigrants.

In 1978, 664 Squadron based in Farnborough was retitled 656 Squadron as part of a larger AAC reorganization. Shortly afterwards it was deployed on Op AGILA to support the Commonwealth Monitoring Group in Rhodesia/Zimbabwe, in the build-up to free elections. I was the Deputy Commander, so came into contact with many of the Squadron personnel on a daily basis, and was a regular passenger in their Scout and Gazelle helicopters. The Squadron's contribution to the Operation was immense and I believe that without the skill and professional expertise of the pilots, and the positive leadership shown by those in command, the Operation would not have succeeded. This was my first experience of working closely with Army Aviation, prior to being appointed Colonel Commandant of the Army Air Corps in 1988, a position which I was honoured to hold for the next six years.

In early 1982, the Squadron was tasked as the only AAC squadron to deploy on Op CORPORATE to recover the Falkland Islands from the Argentinian Forces. This operation provided no precedents, where innovation and courage were essential to success. The Scout and Gazelle flights operated in the harshest of conditions, providing close support – often under fire – to the advancing forces. Their determination to recover casualties, regardless of the time of day or night or weather conditions, is a testament to their sense of duty. Two pilots were awarded the DFC.

During the 1990s, the Squadron continued to be deployed on operations, particularly in Bosnia-Herzegovina and Croatia in support of the Cessation of Hostilities Agreement.

In 2003 the Squadron was selected to be the first AAC squadron to convert to the Apache. the deployment of the Attack Helicopter was to be a severe test and a major step-change which was critically observed by the RAF. Captain Piers Lewis, later to become OC in 2012, found that the conversion was: 'a real change in gear, going from 2nd in a Gazelle to 5th in the Apache.'

The Squadron has subsequently deployed on three operational tours of Afghanistan, and in 2011 operated five Apaches from HMS *Ocean* off the coast of Libya during Op Ellamy. The Apache chapter reads like an adrenalin rush of acronyms and with a pace of support and 'kinetic' operations which lends itself to a generation which readily embraces modern digital technology and personal challenges. Two MCs were awarded to aircrew which points back to similar awards in 1945.

What this book brilliantly illustrates is that those with an intimate understanding of operations on the ground are well placed to extend their skills to become Army pilots. The story starts with young Royal Artillery officers flying unarmed fixed wing aircraft in Burma, and brings us to the present Apache Attack Helicopter operations flown by both genders. Yet the primary task remains essentially unchanged; the direction of fire in support of ground operations. At the time of this book's publication, the Squadron has assumed the role of national Transitional Intervention Capability in any future global intervention. The story is far from over.

Such a history would not be complete without recognizing the sacrifice paid by the twenty-five members who died on operations. They are recorded at Appendix 1 and remembered with honour. The memory of those that have served in the Squadron is preserved through its innovative Association, which instigated this book project. It takes pride in being the only AAC squadron association in existence. One of its members, and a former Officer Commanding, Lieutenant General Sir Gary Coward KCB, CB, became the first Army Air Corps officer to reach the rank of Lieutenant General and has recently been appointed President of the Air OP Officers' Association.

None of this would have been possible without the close support and understanding of the technicians and ground crew. This bond was established in Burma with the single aircraft sections and has been maintained through all subsequent operations. What this book shows is that the Squadron's successes are not so much about the aircraft but about the soldiers. In all Army units there are notable characters and 656 Squadron is no different. The first Officer Commanding, Major Denis Coyle DFC, MBE, RA, engendered the ethos of the Squadron, and although only twenty-five years old when he took command, he displayed exceptional qualities of leadership and sheer steadfastness. His legacy is immense and lasting. Others in an elite band of the most decorated Army aviation pilots include Captain Ted Maslen-Jones MC, DFC, RA and Captain (later Brigadier) Jimmy Jarrett, MC, DFC, RA (both Burma), Major 'Warby' Warburton DFC, MBE, CdeG, RA (Java, Korea and Malaya) and Captain (later Lieutenant Colonel) Sam Drennan DFC, AFC, MBE, AAC (Falkland Islands). Their professionalism, humour and companionship transcend the generations. The full list of awards received by squadron personnel can be found at Appendix 2.

I commend this book to a wide audience, as it tells the story of a small but very proud and distinguished aviation unit from Auster to Apache. I congratulate Guy Warner on writing a compelling history encompassing seventy years of dedicated service to the Crown by the air and ground crews of 656 Squadron. This book is recommended reading for both the specialist and the general reader.

Glossary

AAC	Army Air Corps
AC	Aircraftsman
ACSEA	Air Command South-East Asia
AFNEI	Allied Forces Netherlands East Indies
AGRA	Army Group Royal Artillery, a formation consisting of a number of artillery regiments, usually four, commanded by a brigadier and usually under corps command, or one of varying type and number forming a reserve of firepower in the hands of the Army Commander.
ALFSEA	Allied Land Forces South-East Asia
ALG	Advanced landing ground
AOC	Air Officer Commanding
AOP	Air Observation Post
AQMS	Artificer Quartermaster Sergeant
Basha	A wooden hut made from bamboo and roofed with jungle foliage
BGS	Brigadier General Staff
BMA	British Military Administration
BRA	Brigadier Royal Artillery – the artillery adviser to an Army Commander and commander of that Army's artillery.
Bren Gun	Standard British light machine-gun from WW2 to 1950s (first designed in Brno and later manufactured in Enfield – hence the name)
CBAS	Commando Brigade Air Squadron
Chaung	A stream or river (Burma)
Chinthe	A Burmese mythological lion-like creature (or leogryph), symbolizing divine power over land and air. A stone Chinthe stands guard over the entrance to every Burmese temple, and its head is on the 656 Squadron badge
CO	Commanding Officer
CRA	Commander Royal Artillery – the artillery brigadier at an AGRA HQ or one who commands the artillery of a division and who advises the divisional commander on its employment.
CCRA	Corps Commander Royal Artillery – the artillery commander at a Corps HQ and who advises the corps commander on its employment
CT	Communist terrorist

ENSA	Entertainments National Service Association (not Every Night Something Awful)
FARELF	Far Eastern Land Forces
FEAF	Far East Air Force
FTX	Field training exercise
GOC	General Officer Commanding
GPMG	General purpose machine-gun
HLS	Helicopter Landing Site
HMIS	His Majesty's Indian Ship
The Hump	The nickname for the eastern end of the Himalayas that lay between Allied air bases in Assam and China.
IAS	Indicated airspeed
IMC	Instrument meteorological conditions
Kampong	Malay term for a village or hamlet
LAC	Leading Aircraftsman
LAD	Light Aid Detachment REME
LMG	Light machine-gun
LCT	Landing Craft Tank
LSL	Landing Ship Logistic
LST	Landing Ship Tank
MCP	Malayan Communist Party
MGRA	Major General Royal Artillery, the senior gunner at command or Army Group level.
MPAJA	Malayan People's Anti-Japanese Army
MRLA	Malayan Races Liberation Army
MT	Mechanical transport
NCO	Non-commissioned officer
NEI	Netherlands East Indies
Netting	Use of common radio frequency for passing information from AOP to units on the ground.
OC	Officer Commanding – commander of a sub-unit below battalion/regimental level: infantry companies, artillery batteries or an AAC squadron.
OP	Observation post
OR	Other rank
OTU	Operational Training Unit
QFI	Qualified Flying Instructor
RA	Royal Artillery (also known as "gunners")
RAAF	Royal Australian Air Force
RAF	Royal Air Force
RASC	Royal Army Service Corps
Ranging	The process of firing a considerable number of shells solely in order to establish the correct line and range to the target.
RCT	Royal Corps of Transport
Register	To adjust with precision. One gun firing trial shots, corrected by an OP or Air OP, could ascertain the range of a target or prominent landmarks

within the target area. From this information the range of other targets could be judged with considerable accuracy and other guns in the vicinity of the registering guns could make use of the same data and so allow a greater concentration of artillery.

REME	Royal Electrical and Mechanical Engineers
RMAF	Royal Malayan Air Force
RNZAF	Royal New Zealand Air Force
SASO	Senior Air Staff Officer
SEAC	South-East Asia Command
SEATO	South-East Asia Treaty Organization
SO2	A Staff Officer Grade 2
Sten Gun	9mm automatic carbine – with a nasty habit of going off unexpectedly.
u/s	unserviceable
USAAF	United States Army Air Force
WASB	Women's Auxiliary Service (Burma)
2i/c	Second in command

Acknowledgements

David Amlôt, Philip Barak, Darren Bloomfield, Gavin Bosher, Tony Bourne, Peter Capon, Andy Cash, John Charteris, Sir Gary Coward, Neil Dalton, Dickie Dawes, Tim Deane, John Dicksee, Laura Dimmock-Jones, Sam Drennan, Malcolm Fleming, Simon Fogden, Héloise Goodley, John Greenhalgh, Richard Grevatte-Ball, Paul Hayhurst, Chris Hearn, John Heyes, Sylvia Heyes, Michael Hickey, Spencer Holtom, Jeff Jefford, David Joyce, Sarah Joyce, Valerie Joyce, Garry Key, Jonathan Knowles, Sir John Learmont, Piers Lewis, Susan Lindsay, Crispin Lockhart, Tim Lynch, Dame Vera Lynn, Jim Lyons, Iain Mackie, Simon Marsh, Steven Marshall, Ted Maslen-Jones, Ken Mattocks, Tony McMahon, Mark Meaton, Graham Mehaffy for the splendid maps, Wayne Middlemiss, Keith Millsom, Bill Morgan, Giovanni Morini, Johnny Moss, Stephen Nathan, Mike Neville, Jack Nicholas, Mike Painter, Chris Pickup, Philip Piper, Bernard Redshaw, Matthew Rogers, Martin Sawyer, Tim Sharp, Marcus Sharpe, Peter Short, Colin Sibun, Andrew Simkins, Ross Skingley, Donald Smith, John Stirk, Mike Subritzky, David Swan, Alex Tucker, Derek Walker, Ron Ward, David Westley, Dick Whidborne, Peter Wilson, Lee Wright.

I am very grateful to all those named above who have assisted me with this most enjoyable, though, at times, daunting and challenging task. In particular I would like to thank Lieutenant Colonel Andrew Simkins OBE, the President of 656 Squadron Association, who asked me if I would like to write the history of the Squadron and who has been a constant source of advice and encouragement. Other members of the Association's committee whose help has been invaluable include Mark Meaton, for his exhaustive research in the archives at the Museum of Army Flying, Ron Ward, for his work on the Roll of Honour and Honours and Awards appendices and Major Derek Walker for his view from the REME perspective. All four have also been diligent proof readers and have also been of immense help with regard to the selection of appropriate photographs from the many thousands held within the Association's archive, which is also held at the Museum. All illustrations, except where attributed otherwise, are from this collection. Major Piers Lewis AAC, the OC of 656 Squadron, has been of tremendous help, as have many other past and present members of the Squadron, whose names are included in the list above. Finally, sincere thanks to my editor Ken Patterson and to all the staff at Pen & Sword, especially Laura Hirst and Charles Hewitt.

Introduction

Wat follows is a unique history. 656 Squadron is not the oldest squadron in the Army Air Corps, but it has the distinction of having operated in more theatres, over extended periods, than any other squadron. It seems that whenever there was a new role or emergency the Squadron was there. What is it that makes this Squadron unique? Many who have served in the Squadron cite its first Officer Commanding, Major Denis Coyle, as setting just the right balance of leadership, vision and compassion. His abiding influence has endured during the many changes of personnel, aircraft and theatre that have occurred in the past seventy years. When starting this book I thought that Afghanistan would be the last major operation before publication. Yet a 656 Squadron Group deployed with five Apaches and crew in HMS *Ocean* during Operation Ellamy, the liberation of Libya, in 2011. Yet again acts of great courage, initiative and humour were in plentiful supply. Perhaps the essence of the Squadron is that it recognizes the achievement and contribution of all its personnel, which is why this history embraces the recollections – from across the full range of ranks and specializations in the air and on the ground – of many of those men and women, who have served with it over the last seventy years. It is the story of what a small unit, with a strong esprit de corps, can achieve.

On 10 January 1943, a talk was given to the early arrivals of the newly-formed 656 Squadron RAF by Major Denis Coyle RA. His theme was 'an outline of the history, achievements and functions of Air OP squadrons.' At that time six Air Observation Post (Air OP) squadrons, of which the most recent was 656, had been formed. The first, 651, had been on active service in North Africa since November 1942, where it would be joined in March 1943 by 654 and five months later by 655. Two other squadrons, 652 and 653, were engaged in training and exercises in Scotland and England respectively. They too would go to war, but not until after the invasion of occupied Europe in June 1944. Between January 1943 and March 1945, ten more Air OP squadrons would be formed (657 to 666), all of which would serve in Italy, France, Holland or Germany.

The role of the Air OP has been summarized by one of 656's pilots, Captain Frank McMath,

'Our operational role was primarily to observe for, and to correct the fire of, the Artillery, and secondary to carry out all kinds of reconnaissance which might, under ideal conditions of terrain, have been allotted to an Artillery Observation Post. In other words we were an organization for obtaining complete Artillery observation over a battlefield, whether in the desert, the flat fields of Europe, or the jungle. Our aircraft were Austers, piloted by Royal Artillery captains flying alone and serviced by RAF ground crews. All the rest of the work was divided between Army and RAF personnel. Although this sounds a most complex affair, comprising as it did twenty-two Army officers, all pilots, three RAF officers, no pilots, ninety soldiers and eighty airmen, in fact it always worked smoothly and with no trace of inter-service friction.'

656 Squadron would be, however, unique, in that it was the only Air OP squadron to support 14th Army – the 'Forgotten Army' – in India and Burma. As such it would face particular challenges of climate and terrain, which would create extreme difficulties for men, machines and the supply of all essential items to maintain these. Moreover, as a single squadron providing the Air OP requirement of an entire army, operating independently, and without higher echelon support (a squadron was normally allotted to a corps, of which there were three in Burma) and therefore one pilot would often be responsible for the demands of a division, it can be asserted with some confidence that it was not over-resourced and that its young pilots, fitters, riggers, drivers and signallers would be stretched to the very limits of their endurance and ingenuity. Major Coyle

No 3 Air OP Course

14 Jul 41   23 Aug 41

Back Row: Lt J K Thompson RA: Lt P H Dowse RA: Capt D W Coyle RA:
            Capt T W Lewis RA(TA):

Front Row: Lt I G Neilson RA(TA): Sqn Ldr J R Davenport RAF(CO):
            Sqn Ldr E D Joyce RAF(Instr): Capt D P D Oldman RA.

Denis Coyle is shown here as a Captain, while he was a student on No 3 Air OP Course at Andover. He would subsequently command 656 Squadron, in the rank of Major, from its formation in 1942, throughout the campaign in India and Burma.

concluded his talk by 'sketching the probable scheme of training for the next few months.' It was, perhaps, fortunate that he did not have a crystal ball which would have enabled him to foresee the challenges which lay ahead and which as OC, he would have to overcome.

Six months later, on the evening of 31 July 1943, Captain Rex Boys of C Flight took off in the Auster III, MZ224, to give an air experience flight to an unnamed passenger. He landed back at the airfield some fifty minutes later, after what would be the last flight made by 656 Squadron from home soil for almost thirty-five years. During this time it would complete in excess of 250,000 operational flying hours from bases in India, Burma, Java, Malaya, Borneo and Hong Kong. Following its re-establishment in the United Kingdom in 1978, its travels were far from over and it would add further operational laurels in Rhodesia, the Falkland Islands, Bosnia, Kosovo and, most recently Afghanistan and Libya. This, therefore, is the story of a quite remarkable military unit, one of the most 'operational' squadrons in any air force or corps in history.

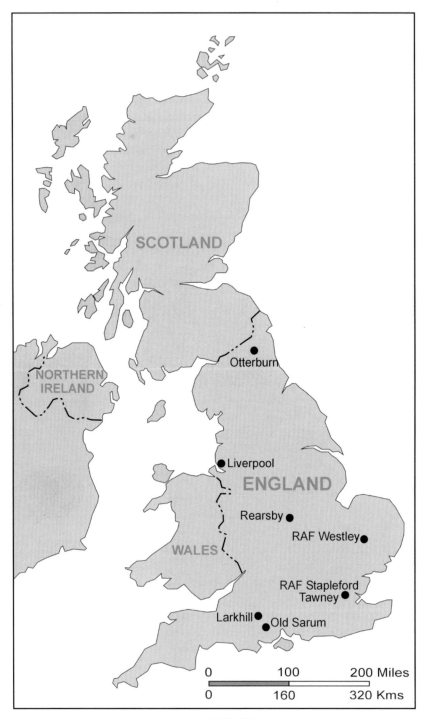

England 1942–1943.

Chapter 1

England 1942–1943

To the west of Bury St Edmunds in Suffolk lay the small grass airfield of RAF Westley, which was established in 1938, with two small hangars, as home for the West Suffolk Aero Club with its Taylorcraft Model A, B and Plus C monoplanes. Those who learned to fly there included some twenty or so members of the Civil Air Guard, a voluntary scheme which offered subsidized flying training. It was too small to be taken over by RAF Volunteer Reserve, so private flying was allowed to continue until the outbreak of war.

It was reopened in 1940 as a base for the Westland Lysanders of No 268 Squadron, which was followed by No 241 Squadron in 1941. After its departure the next to arrive was 652 (AOP) Squadron in August 1942. It in turn moved to Dumfries at the end of the year but left behind two young Royal Artillery officers, Captains Denis Coyle and Ian Shield. On 31 December, they were joined by AC2s Sid Peel and Arthur Windscheffel, the first RAF ground crew to arrive. At the striking of the clock to herald the start of a new year the nucleus of 656 Squadron consisted of two officers, three Army ORs and four RAF ORs. Gunner Pete Dobson later recalled that the highlight of those first few cold and rainy days was the bacon sandwiches served in the nearby Coronation Café.

On 5 January 1943, the administrative burden was eased by the arrival of the Adjutant, Pilot Officer Arthur Eaton (later Flight Lieutenant) and on the following day the formal notice of posting was received, transferring Coyle and Shield from their parent unit, 652 Squadron and confirming that Denis Coyle was to be the Commanding Officer, in the rank of Acting Major. The critical importance of Coyle's approach to command can scarcely be over-estimated – it was he who would set the tone of the Squadron and the standards which it would adopt. He was a young man, only twenty-five years of age. He was a regular soldier, having been commissioned into the Royal Artillery from the Royal Military Academy, Woolwich (known as The Shop) in 1937. His first posting was to 22 Field Brigade; one of the last to be horsed rather than mechanized. Following the outbreak of war he served in 2nd Field Regiment with the British Expeditionary Force in France and Belgium and after being evacuated from Dunkirk he volunteered for Air OP training. He attended No 3 Pilot Training Course at Andover in December 1940, was a founder member of 651 Squadron in August 1941 and served as a Flight Commander with 652 Squadron between April and December 1942. It may be thought that he was still a fairly inexperienced officer to take on the duties of OC, but Air OP was a nascent part of the Order of Battle, which offered opportunity to those who showed initiative and

Taylorcraft of the West Suffolk Aero Club at Westley in 1939 (Eugene Prentice via Frank Whitnall).

talent. There is no doubt that he was an impressive figure, being described by Frank McMath as,

> 'That fairly rare person, a much loved Commanding Officer; tolerant, forbearing, even patient; he knew everyone and no one feared him, but all were proud to take his orders.'

Fellow pilot and member of A Flight, Ted Maslen-Jones added,

> 'Denis Coyle was exceptionally well-equipped for emergencies, having a cool head and an abundance of energy. He had an extraordinary ability to assess a man's character and to work out what made him tick. He was a great innovator himself and knew when to give people their head. Quite simply, he was also a good bloke.'

The first aircraft for the new squadron had not as yet arrived. However, a DH82 Tiger Moth biplane, T6897, had been left behind by 652 and with the approval of Army Cooperation Command; this was taken over by 656, allowing the commencement of flight training. It was involved in a landing accident due to fog and had to make a forced landing in a field near Buntingford in Hertfordshire on 24 January but was soon back in service. It was joined by the first of the Squadron's proper establishment three days later – the Auster I, LB379, which was flown in by a ferry pilot from the manufacturers at Rearsby in Leicestershire. This high-wing, single-engine, monoplane type was a development of the Taylorcraft. The Mark I would soon be replaced by a slighter better version, the Auster III.

Westley had its rural charms but there was no Sergeants' Mess, canteen or NAAFI; the officers were accommodated in Westley Hall, while most of the men had been found billets in private houses scattered around the district. A night out at the Athenaeum in Bury St Edmunds was a welcome diversion, as was an ENSA concert starring the celebrated jazz trumpeter and bandleader, Nat Gonella. By the end of the first month

Denis Coyle was able to write in the Operational Record (OR) Book, describing how his command was evolving,

'Personnel posted in :- Army 76, RAF 58. [Out of a total complement of 196 men] About 50 per cent of the authorized RAF equipment has been received, but very little army equipment. No transport has been received in spite of action taken to secure vehicles from Eastern Command. Lack of transport proved a serious handicap both to training and administration.'

The division of administrative responsibility between the RAF and the Army was always to provide something of a headache as it seemed to generate twice the amount of paperwork. The first job was, however, to start to turn the Squadron into a potential fighting unit. Its establishment comprised four flights, HQ, A, B and C. The Officer Commanding, his 2i/c and the five pilots in each flight were all Royal Artillery officers; the Adjutant, Equipment Officer and Administration Officer were RAF. To the gunner NCOs and ORs fell the duties of motor transport maintenance, driving and communications, while the RAF's aircraftsmen maintained the Austers. The basic unit within a flight was the section, of which there were four, each commanded by the pilot, who would normally be a captain. Each section consisted of two RAF ORs, an engine fitter and an airframe rigger and two RA, a signaller and a driver-batman. Each section had a jeep and a three-ton truck and therefore could be very flexible and entirely self-supporting in the field. Communication within the section, flight and squadron (and also with other ground units) was maintained by the standard Army Wireless Set No 22, which was bulky, heavy and notoriously temperamental. For such a small unit the establishment was to prove remarkably suited to the harsh environment of Burma, when the Squadron would find itself spread over hundreds of miles, with atrociously poor lines of communication. Even the Set No 22 would perform well beyond its design specifications. By the end of February, eight more aircraft had arrived, four Auster Is and four Auster IIIs, as well as seven additional pilots, the Squadron Engineering Officer, Flight Sergeant McCarthy (later Warrant Officer) and an assortment of vehicles – three-ton trucks, motorcycles, jeeps, wireless trucks, an office lorry and the OC's car. An unfortunate accident occurred when AC2 Windscheffel was hit on the hand during prop-swinging and was admitted to hospital at Ipswich where, after surgery, he recovered the use of his hand and rejoined the Squadron in due course. Training began in earnest in March when B Flight was sent to take part in Exercise *Spartan*. Frank McMath, of A Flight, recalled a lesson learned at that time which he later put in to practice in Burma,

'Diving low over the heads of the marching troops with engine throttled right back so as to reduce the noise, I pointed in the direction of the airfield and shouted out of the window "Turn left here", and then was relieved to see them set off the right way. I had learnt this shouting trick years ago from the OC when, as a very new officer, I had led the Squadron HQ convoy to an exercise in Norfolk. Halting a few miles from the destination in the hope that a driver, whom I had lost, would catch up before we turned off the main road, I was a bit disconcerted to see the OC fly over very low and shout "Get a move on" – in very clear and angry tones.'

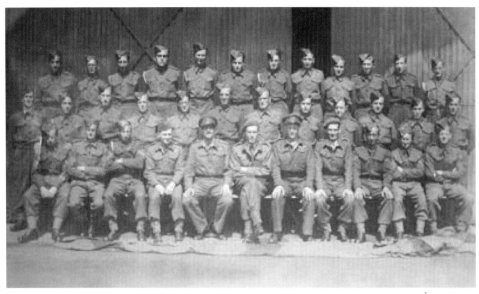

A Flight, 656 Squadron, at RAF Stapleford Tawney in 1943.

Names to go with the above photograph.

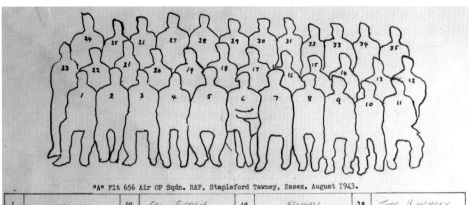

"A" Flt 656 Air OP Sqdn. RAF. Stapleford Tawney, Essex. August 1943.

#	Name	#	Name	#	Name	#	Name
1	WALLACE	10	CPL GERRY	19	EDWARDS	28	JOHN HUMPHREY
2	J LARSON	11	TONKISS	20	JACK JONES	29	RAY PETT
3	BOURNE	12	READ	21	(THE COOK)	30	"TAFFY" ERIC HOSKINS
4	CAPT R.D HENSHAW	13	LIGHTFOOT	22	ARTHUR BAINBOROUGH	31	VIC GREEN
5	CAPT P'LINSDEN	14	HALLAM	23	"PEACHY" FOSTER	32	JOHNNY WHITE
6	CAPT IAN SHIELD	15	EMBRY	24	TONY PAGLIA	33	MICHIE
7	CAPT MOSELIN-JONES	16	HILL	25	E. BUTLER	34	VINCE WEAVER
8	CAPT RALPH HADLEY	17	JEFFREY	26	BUDDIMAN	35	NIXON
9	MIDDLE	18	JACK COTTON	27	ARTHUR MAYCROFT		

It had been decided that the ever expanding Squadron's needs would be better met by moving from Westley to a larger RAF airfield, Stapleford Tawney, near Romford in Essex. Stapleford opened in 1933 as an operating base for Hillman's Airways – a charter company formed three years earlier by businessman Edward Hillman. In April 1933 he started a scheduled service to Paris, France, using his newly acquired DH 89 Dragon Rapides at a return fare was £5.10s.0d. Stapleford was known in those days as Essex Aerodrome. Sadly, Hillman died at a relatively early age in 1934 and this far-sighted and enterprising pioneer of British civil aviation is now all but forgotten. The airfield was requisitioned shortly after the start of World War II as RAF Stapleford Tawney. A long perimeter track and dispersal points were built and some accommodation buildings were erected. By the end of March 1940 the airfield was ready to become a satellite station for North Weald. In March 1943, Stapleford was transferred from Fighter Command and placed within No 34 Wing, Army Cooperation Command. As for Westley, it welcomed two more Air OP squadrons before the end of the war; 657 Squadron for eight weeks from May 1943 and in February 1944, 662 Squadron began a stay of four and a half months.

Corporals Derrick Beard and Alfred Howard were the first RAF personnel to join the Squadron at Bury St Edmunds, having spent two weeks at the Taylorcraft factory in Leicester where they, 'had to work on the construction of the aircraft from start to finish,' this in-depth knowledge would prove of considerable assistance in the months ahead.

By the middle of March the Squadron had relocated successfully and a further seven pilots had arrived, shortly to be followed by a batch of sixteen new Auster IIIs replacing the original aircraft (though the Tiger Moth was also retained). It was now possible to establish the regular three flights, A, B and C and to embark upon a series of training exercises with a variety of army units around the country. This would often require the flights to operate detachments away from Stapleford and independently of SHQ.

Ted Maslen-Jones, also of A Flight, remembers live shooting in support of artillery regiments in Wales and the North Country and particularly valued a special permit,

'During this period I carried with me in the aircraft a form of authority allowing me to carry out low flying and to land virtually anywhere in the country. This was a tremendously valuable privilege in terms of gaining experience and developing these essential skills, which would stand us in such good stead later and we were encouraged to make full use of it, particularly on journeys to and from exercises. The opportunity to make short landings in unfamiliar places was really useful. Manoeuvrability at low-level was really our only defence against enemy fighters, at the same time helping us to avoid detection from the ground as well as in the air. We carried no armaments and no parachute. When in trouble there would be no alternative to forced landing. In such a situation the relatively slow speed of the Auster was a great advantage.'

He enjoyed certain other aspects of Exercise *Border*, which took place in June 1943, on the artillery ranges at Otterburn in Northumberland, recalling,

'I operated with my section from a landing ground that was normally a field full of sheep and was adjacent to the Percy Arms. This was most convenient and gave rise to several enjoyable evenings after flying had finished.'

Some idea of the intensity of the preparation may be gathered from the fact that – to take a not untypical day – on 1 June, the Squadron was spread around half a dozen different locations; SHQ and one section of C Flight were at Stapleford Tawney; A Flight was at Bramford in Suffolk; B Flight at Redesdale in Northumberland, attached to the Guards Armoured Division; while the three remaining sections of C Flight were detached to 145th Field Regiment, 120th Field Regiment and 61st Recce Regiment. SHQ also practised deployment, while training took place in night flying, map-reading (not only for pilots but also for the drivers, commencing with expeditions by bicycle, a section at a time), cross-country flying, short field landings at advanced landing grounds (ALGs), testing the radios and microphones and on 25 June, weapon drill and the firing of rifles, Bren Gun, Sten gun and Tommy guns. On 19 June, Major Coyle had made what must have been a very useful visit to Old Sarum for a Squadron Commanders' Conference, which was addressed by Major 'Jim' Neathercoat, the OC of 651 Squadron, on the experiences of 651 and 654 Squadrons in Tunisia. Ten days later the Squadron received its Mobilization Order from the War Office – it was to be ready to deploy to a tropical theatre by 1 August. In July, all personnel were inoculated and vaccinated and took it in turn to have a fortnight's embarkation leave. Much effort was devoted to packing, as the C Flight diary noted,

> 'Inter-flight rivalries develop as packing continues! A Flight pride themselves on their speed, but C Flight prefers the security of the finished product. B Flight made a corner in wood wool [packaging material made from slivers of wood], which would have put maintenance out of business if we hadn't gone to their aid with all available reserves. C Flight stopped work at 1945 hours, just in time for the ENSA show.'

Many years later, the prevailing mood within the Squadron at that time was described by Bombardier Ernest Smith,

> 'We were about half-and-half Royal Air Force and Royal Artillery and we got on together wonderfully – a bit of banter, naturally, about Brylcreem Boys and Brown Jobs – but we lived together, messed together and went out on the town together. The officers, with the exception of the Adjutant and the Equipment Officer, who were RAF, were all Royal Artillery and young. The whole outfit was informal, cheerful and matey.'

Towards the end of July the issue of tropical kit started, this included pith helmets or solar topees. Few were impressed by these relics of earlier Imperial times, indeed Ted Maslen-Jones recalled that, some weeks later, he and several others threw them overboard into the waters of Bombay Harbour and watching a 'strange-looking flotilla' bobbing away.

Denis Coyle later summed up the first few months of the Squadron's life as follows,

> 'The formation of 656 Air OP Squadron RAF went very much the same way as for all the other squadrons in this era. It was a matter of collecting together pilots, aircraft, soldiers, airmen and vehicles and turning them into a flying and fighting unit. One had the impression that the soldiers and airmen were a trifle suspicious of each other

until they found that they were both exactly the same without their uniform on and although the airmen were essentially the technicians looking after the aircraft and the soldiers were the drivers and signallers, many firm friendships quickly developed. By mid-August, after some fairly intensive training, we were warned for an unknown tropical destination and spent the last month in collecting all the aircraft spares that we could possibly lay our hands on and packing them up as securely as possible in thousands of packing cases. Included amongst the packing cases but in very specially constructed containers were the instruments of our dance band which had been formed earlier on and which had already earned a lot of money for PRI by playing in the local village halls near Stapleford Tawney in Essex where we had been based.'

Before saying farewell to Stapleford Tawney a cocktail party was held in the Officers' Mess, as well as parties in the Corporals' Club and Sergeants' Mess and an Airmen's dance with free beer provided by the Station and the Squadron.

Chapter 2

India and Burma 1943–1945

The Squadron main party departed from Theydon Bois Railway Station at a quarter past midnight on 12 August for an unknown destination and after a cold but comfortable journey were surprised at dawn to find themselves de-training in Liverpool and then proceeding by tram for the journey to the docks. C Flight's diary noted, 'No arrangements were made to transport the ammunition which was much too heavy for individual Bren Gunners. So Captain A.T. Cross pinched a trolley, took it on the train with him, put all the Flight's ammunition on it and wheeled it triumphantly to the quay over very rough cobblestones.'

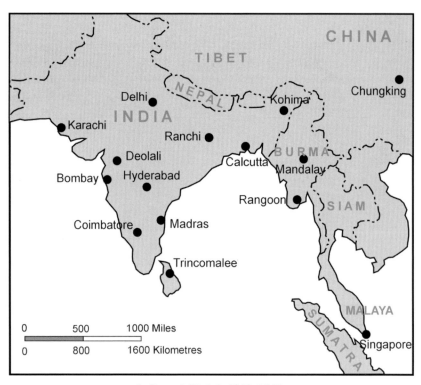

India and SE Asia 1943–1945.

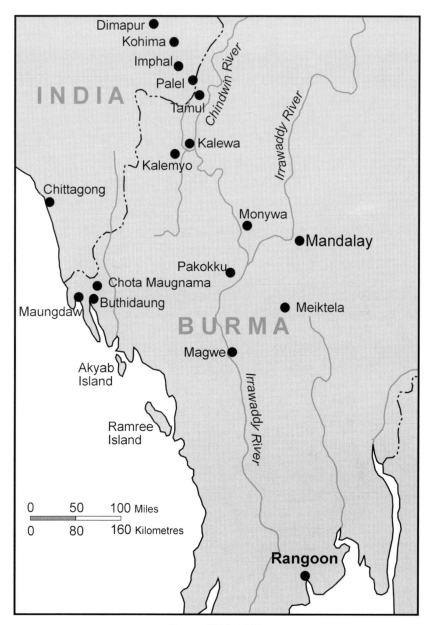

Burma 1943–1945.

At the quayside they encountered their first clash with authority because the RAF embarkation staff, seeing the mixture of uniforms, tried to separate the soldiers and airmen. Major Coyle thought otherwise and insisted that the Squadron should fall in by flights. However, the movement staff finally won because, when they boarded the 24,000 ton SS *Monarch of Bermuda*, a former luxury liner, they were split up into penny packets in three separate parts of what was also discovered to be a 'dry' ship. After twenty-four hours in the mouth of the Mersey, during which time, 'the men experienced their first problems with climbing into hammocks amid great amusement', they sailed for the Clyde, where a convoy was assembling and eventually proceeded to sea on 16 August. The voyage is very well described in the Squadron diary,

'The ship set sail again at about 1800 hours, passing the Isle of Man and Ireland into the open sea. The convoy was large, about twenty ships (apparently all troopships) and including an escort of HMS *Shropshire*, one aircraft carrier and at least six destroyers.

17 August:	Seafires and Swordfish from the aircraft carrier demonstrated aerobatics, formation flying and very short landings.
18 August:	The convoy passed well into the Atlantic (presumably to avoid U-boats).
19 August:	The first depth charges were dropped by a destroyer in the escort. Some Squadron officers attended the first Hindustani lesson by Pilot Officer Singh. The course lasted the whole voyage, but Squadron officers soon gave it up in despair.
21 August:	We turned east in region of the Azores. The escort was increased by one anti-aircraft cruiser.
22 August:	More depth charges were dropped by an escorting destroyer. HMS *Shropshire* came in close in a farewell salute, as she was going on via the Cape to Australia. Tropical kit was worn for the first time.
23 August:	The convoy passed through the Straits of Gibraltar at dawn and saw the lights of La Linea on starboard side. Most of the escort and part of the convoy left here. Gunfire from all ships was directed at an enemy aircraft at 1000 hours. In the afternoon we passed a large convoy of seventy ships.
24 August:	In sight of the North African coast all day, we passed Algiers at 1700 hours.
25 August:	Passed Bizentia and Cape Bon in the evening. Air escort of P-39 Airacobras. And also saw an Italian cruiser which was ablaze following an RAF attack.
26 August:	Just glimpsed Malta on port side in the morning, temperature beginning to warm up. The men were informed that this was the first convoy through the Mediterranean since Italy joined in the war and the Germans blocked the Suez Canal. [Axis forces in North Africa had surrendered on 13 May]
27 August:	Approximately twelve depth charges were dropped very close to the ship at 0435 hours. Sighted a large convoy on its way to invade Italy.
28 August:	In the evening we saw the lights of Alexandria. Ship's concert this evening starring Squadron Band under Captain Moffat's leadership at the piano, with Pilot Officer Oliver Wakefield (of BBC fame) as compère. The band members were Sergeant G.G. Moss – saxophone, Gunner P.G. Dobson – guitar, LAC R. Limbert – trumpet and Gunner Eddie Stannard – drums. (The concert was actually repeated on three nights, with one matinee, so as to give everyone a chance of seeing it).'

Professional entertainment had also been provided on the voyage by the well-known entertainers Cyril Fletcher and Vic Oliver and as an additional bonus, 'We found we were accompanied by two RAF field hospitals complete with their quota of nursing sisters.'

Bombardier Ernest Smith also had very fond memories of the voyage,

> 'The ship's kitchens were geared to catering for passengers who had paid a lot for their journey and the grub was wonderful – they baked beautiful bread daily, we had real butter (strict rationing in Blighty, remember) and eggs for breakfast every day. The sea was quiet, dolphins and flying fish intrigued us and the men of the South Wales Borderers sang to us beautifully on the main deck in the evenings.'

But returning to the official diary,

29 August: The convoy reached Port Said at 0930 hours but did not stop and entered the Suez Canal. Spent the day going through the Canal and we all thanked our Gods we weren't stationed on a gunsite there. Anchored overnight at Bitter Lake. Lights on the shore were a lovely sight – no blackout from now on until we reach Aden.

30 August: The convoy reached Suez at 1000 hours, where passengers for the Middle East disembarked. The Squadron baggage party, under Captains Jones, Moffat and Maslen-Jones, were working hard all day. They took all Squadron hold baggage ashore in lighters and spent the night with the baggage at Port Tewfik.

31 August: Squadron personnel were transhipped from the *Monarch of Bermuda* to HMT *Ascania* 11,000 tons, a converted merchant cruiser and former Cunard liner, a dry and incidentally, very dirty ship, sailing without escort. The move went off very smoothly.

It went off slightly less smoothly for one Squadron member, Arthur Windscheffel, 'The small ferry boat was going up and down quite a lot and we had to get off at its highest point and jump on to the *Ascania* with my full kit on my back, Bren Gun in one hand and box of 28lb spare ammo in the other. I misjudged the timing to get off one boat and onto the other but two safe hands grabbed my arms and pulled me aboard. My thanks to Captains Fowler and Jarrett for saving me from a watery end.'

At this time Major Coyle made firm representations to OC Troops that the Squadron should be treated as a single unit, with the result that all personnel were accommodated on the one mess deck. This was the only good news, as the voyage down the Red Sea was 'incredibly unpleasant' in the extreme heat and with many personnel affected by mild dysentery, which caused considerable overcrowding in the ship's sick bay. The cabins were fitted with hot pipes and heaters, rather than the more desirable fans, so many opted to sleep on deck. They arrived in Bombay on 14 September and disembarked on the following morning, to the considerable surprise of Movement Control, who were not prepared for this much earlier arrival, thanks to the convoy making its passage through the Mediterranean and the Suez Canal rather that the much longer route round the Cape of Good Hope. They did not know what to make of such a peculiar RAF unit with mixed personnel and asked whether they would like to lodge in an Army or RAF transit camp.

Enquiries elicited that the RAF camp at Worli was more comfortable and so this was the one that was chosen and it was certainly more suitable because it had a 'very nice little' airfield at Juhu, 'on the sea, lovely beach, bathing and palm trees.' First impressions of India were mixed with 'a hair-raising ride in lorries driven by Indians to Worli. Everybody eating lots of fruit – issued with mosquito nets.'

Once unpacked, Major Coyle lost no time in allocating responsibilities to his officers, which gives an excellent example of his leadership, drive and focus, as recorded in the OR book,

'Captain Kingston to obtain particulars of new identity cards to be issued to RA officers. Captains Day and Moffat to obtain details of Army organization in India and locations of HQ.
Captains Fowler and Price to obtain similar information concerning the RAF.
Captains Boys and Jarrett to obtain information concerning SS *Delius*, carrying unit equipment.
Captains McMath and Deacon to obtain information of unit transport – from where it would be available.
Captain Henshaw to obtain clothing scales applicable to India.
Captain Cross to obtain unit censor stamp if possible.
Captain Shield to contact Army Pay Officer for details of Officers' pay and allowances.'

Gradually, the manifold problems were overcome by dint of, 'improvising, legitimate borrowing, scrounging and diplomacy.' One of the major difficulties was, of course, the complete lack of aeroplanes, which they were advised had only left England on 12 September. The OC decided that he needed to visit the MGRA in Delhi and flew there by RAF Lockheed Hudson on 22 September. He came back with the news that the Squadron would move to the School of Artillery and airfield of Deolali and had been ordered to be ready for jungle warfare by 31 December. As Denis Coyle well knew, the Squadron was to move as swiftly as possible to India to join 14th Army and help push the Japanese out of Burma.

C Flight's diarist noted,

'This is good news. This is what we came here for, but we will have our work cut out to be ready in time. All officers went over to Juhu, a suburb of Bombay, for the OC's conference at which he gave out a lot of information, much of it too secret to go in this diary. The gist of it was that India wanted us, and has been asking for us for years. There is definitely a job for us.'

As a consequence, the Squadron made preparations to move to Deolali, by rail. SS *Delius* had been located in Bombay harbour and arrangements were set in hand to unload the many crates of carefully packed Squadron stores and transport them to Juhu. An inspection was made of Deolali by the OC, four officers and two ORs. The C Flight diary for 1 October recorded,

'The main body of the Squadron moved to Deolali; entrained at 1200 hours with officers travelling Second Class and ORs Third. Tiresome journey – train seemed to stop for hours at every station. Arrived at 1830 hours and transported by truck to camp. ORs in huts and officers in tents.'

Training recommenced almost at once, covering such topics as small arms drill, toolkit maintenance, map-reading, radio operation, first aid and field engineering, as well as lectures on 'Hygiene in the Jungle' and 'The Japanese Characteristics.' Time was also set aside for swimming, football and cricket. On 28 October news of a considerable setback was received from Juhu. A disastrous fire had consumed much of the Squadron's equipment stored there. However, there was also some good news, as with much effort Denis Coyle had managed to obtain four Tiger Moths on loan from two Indian Air Force Elementary Flying Training Schools. So early in November, the Squadron's pilots could at last take to the air again for some much needed flying practice. The Tiger Moths were joined by the first Auster III on 21 November, four of which had arrived on board the SS *Behar*. Training continued with all personnel spending time attending the jungle school at Vada, 'living rough, making a landing ground, jungle training, swimming etc. Conditions are very similar to the Arakan, Burma, and everyone loves it.' Denis Coyle made the first landing on the new strip at Vada in an Auster III on 3 December.

Further reinforcements were obtained in the shape of some fifty non-combatant locally enrolled followers who proved an invaluable labour force. However, their administration and discipline almost made them more trouble than they were worth when the Squadron finally got into the field because, 'they not only spoke many different languages but insisted on eating different food and had different religious prejudices.' As the OC later noted,

'It is liable to be very disconcerting when the otherwise excellent mess waiter goes off to pray halfway through serving the evening meal. Finally, we were obliged to dispense with the services of all those who would not eat British rations and it was encouraging that many of the better ones changed their eating habits in order to stay with us throughout the campaign.'

Within a few weeks he was able to summarise the progress made as follows,

'By the end of the year we had completed our "theatre conversion" including some very useful practice in observation of fire at the School of Artillery at Deolali. Our oldest pilot, Captain "Daddy" Cross, who had flown with the Royal Naval Air Service in the First World War, ran a first class jungle camp which accustomed everyone to the problems of living rough in their new environment. Meanwhile, there were signs that our Austers were about to arrive and we arranged for one flight's worth to be offloaded at Bombay while the others were taken to Calcutta in order to save us having to fly them all right across the continent. Our work-up period had undoubtedly been a great success, with the exception of the fact that all the aircraft spares which we had so carefully accumulated before leaving UK, were destroyed by fire under rather mysterious circumstances.'

On 27 November, Sergeant 'Tug' Wilson, with AC1 'Nobby' Clark and two others, set off for Calcutta in a Chevrolet 15 cwt truck to blaze a trail for the Squadron. They arrived on 9 December, having covered 1,480 miles in nine days and the next morning began work at Barrackpore racecourse on reassembling nine Austers, which had been brought to Calcutta by the SS *Mohaut*. Meanwhile, Frank McMath was engaged in experimental work fitting a long-range fuel tank to an Auster, which doubled its range from 150 to 300 miles. The OC retained the use of his Tiger Moth for the Burma campaign, preferring its superior performance to the Auster.

Into Battle 1944

At this stage in the story it would be appropriate to pause and examine briefly the background to the campaign in India and Burma which the Squadron was on the point of joining. Following the attack on Pearl Harbour on 7 December 1941, the armed forces of the Japanese Empire launched a series of highly successful campaigns throughout South-East Asia and the Pacific. The invasion of Burma by the 33rd and 55th Divisions of Lieutenant General Shōjirō Iida's 15th Army resulted in a fighting and painful retreat by the under-prepared and hastily assembled Anglo-Indian and Burmese forces. It must also be admitted that the ability of the Japanese forces had been underestimated by the British C-in-C, General Sir Archibald Wavell. By May 1942 and the onset of the annual monsoon rains, all of the country was under Japanese control, with the weary Allied troops back in India.

An explanation of this devastating state of affairs was given by Manbahadur Rai, one of the Gurkha soldiers who fought in Burma,

'The Japanese soldiers we encountered were well equipped and trained and had mastered the art of jungle warfare. They were disciplined with superhuman endurance and fought with ferocity and courage. They didn't understand the meaning of the word surrender and would fight to the last man. They prided themselves on being the invincible warriors of the emperor. They had come – as they saw it – not as conquerors, but as liberators, with a divine mission to defeat the western colonial powers in Asia. The British defeat in Burma by the numerically inferior Japanese was the result of the Europeans' tendency to fight from static positions. Their strategies were road bound and depended on surface lines of communication. The highly mobile Japanese troops, guided by native scouts along jungle trails, would infiltrate the British positions, forcing them to retreat. The British forces in South-East Asia, at first, were not prepared or equipped for such warfare.'

The next Japanese target would be India. There were two alternative invasion routes; via the western coastal strip – the Arakan, or through the much more difficult hill country to the north. Following the costly and bloody failure of 14th Indian Division's First Arakan Offensive in 1942–43 and, during the rest of the year, there was a fair degree of hard fighting and an expanding programme of 'Tiger Patrols' into Japanese held territory but no definite move by either side. The Allies were able to use this time to organize defences, digest the hard lessons learned, regroup, retrain, improve their battle techniques, further develop a jungle health and hygiene regime and experiment with innovative means of warfare – Brigadier Orde Wingate's 'Chindits' operating behind enemy lines between February and April 1943, and the extensive use of air power – particularly transport aircraft. On New Year's Day 1944, Lieutenant General Philip Christison's 15 Corps of 14th Army (which itself had been formed in November under the command of Lieutenant General William Slim) began an offensive into the Arakan from the north.

On 12 January 1944, the Squadron (less B Flight, which was left behind at Juhu to take part in a planned amphibious landing in South Arakan with 33 Corps, which was later cancelled) left Deolali for the Arakan front south of Chittagong, at Chota Maungnama. The road party, under the command of Captain Rex Boys, performed wonders in arriving on time to catch the SS *Ethiopia* at Calcutta on 23 January. Two of the vehicles were sent on, and covered 660 miles in thirty-three hours over the most appalling roads in order to deliver the wireless sets and cradles to Barrackpore to be installed in the Austers. Rex Boys later wrote about the journey,

> 'As I was in the lead Dodge command car of a convoy of between twenty and thirty vehicles, others received the benefit of my dust. I had time to drink in the novelty of the sights and sounds of the Indian countryside. We passed through everything from semi-desert to near jungle, we saw hundreds of holy but hungry cows, hundreds of coolie women, with children at their breast, humping baskets of earth to make up the road; all the commonplace sights of India. We also saw some beautiful scenery and the occasional palace.'

Despite the novelty of the situation, it was deadly serious and Rex Boys was keenly aware of the trust which had been placed in him and the responsibility that rested on his shoulders. He recalled one particular moment when he walked back down the halted convoy, which was taking a rest in a coconut grove. One of the men called out in jest, asking the Captain to shoot down a coconut so that he could slake his thirst. Boys pulled out his pistol and fired in the right general direction and to his amazement a coconut fell down at his feet – to cheers from his hot and dusty troops. Details of another means of diversion were provided by Bombardier Ernest Smith,

> 'The other thing was that someone had got hold of an Indian-produced copy of *The Adventures of Fanny Hill* which was passed from vehicle to vehicle for the man who wasn't driving to read.'

They disembarked at Chittagong on 26 January and drove a further 156 miles to their destination, which was only three miles from the Japanese front. It was not long before they had their first encounter with the enemy, again Ernest Smith recalled,

> 'At Bawli Bazaar I seem to remember a bridge over a river and an open space in which a number of vehicles were drawn up. In front was a dirt road stretching ahead, blocked by stationary vehicles, some were on fire and one was an ambulance from which men were rescuing casualties. Suddenly, as we came to a halt, there appeared at the far end of the road a Japanese aircraft, seemingly at head level, flashes from its gun muzzles flickering along its wings. This was 656 Squadron's baptism of fire and we did what seemed natural – out of the vehicles and down on the ground!'

Meanwhile, Frank McMath had already flown the Squadron's first operational sortie on 25 January,

'The aircraft flew from Calcutta (five hours flying with stops at Jessore, Dacca, Fermi and Chittagong) with the exception of one, which I took in 200 mile hops over the 1400 miles which separated Deolali from our destination. As this meant that I might be expected to arrive at the war several days ahead of the rest of the Squadron, Denis Coyle had appointed me recce officer, with the tasks of meeting the senior gunner officers of the Corps HQ and the two Divisions which we would be supporting and also deciding on the position of a Squadron landing ground reasonably close to the guns.'

He went on to tell the story of the Squadron's first action,

'Reporting that afternoon to Brigadier Bob Mansergh, who was the CRA (the chief gunner of the 5th Indian Division); he was delighted with my news of the Squadron's imminent arrival and told me of plans for launching an offensive southwards down the coast, starting the next morning. Ground observations would be difficult, so could I be airborne at 0900 hours to observe progress of the tanks' attack and report to him? "I haven't got any wireless, Sir. The sets are still on the road somewhere," I said.

"Never mind, fly and look and get your report to me as quickly as possible," was his order.

That night I slept in the Auster, and was up at dawn tinkering with the engine and filling up the tank from the spare cans I had carried. This wasn't difficult with an Auster as the tank carried only ten gallons anyway. At about quarter to nine it started like a bird and I was soon up in the clear morning air identifying the different features on the ground – strange to me then, but soon to be so well known. At about 1000 feet I saw the low round hill called Tortoise, on top of which at that moment our tanks should have been perched triumphantly. Nothing! Then I saw them, barely advanced from their start lines and evidently under heavy fire. Not that I could hear anything above the noise of my engine, but little puffs of smoke and dust could mean nothing else. This was to be almost the first use of British tanks in Burma, and as they were still so pitifully scarce, no doubt orders were to keep losses down to a minimum. I could just see infantry in one or two places waiting for the tanks to make the first progress, but still sheltering beyond rifle range. Here was a disaster. Infected by the confidence of everyone I had met so far, nothing had prepared me for witnessing failure. How could I get a message quickly to my Brigadier? Obviously the only way was to write a report and drop it. Now what to put a message in with enough weight to be aimed accurately, but not enough to do any damage? Brainwave! Heading back towards the HQ, I unlaced one of my Army boots, took off a sock, to which I judged the past two days of use would have given a good damp weight, put the message in and replaced the boot, which made controlling the aircraft rather easier. I soon identified the Commander's tent at HQ, flew in low and pitched my sock out of the window, to land – as I learned later that day – right in the doorway at the feet of the astonished Brigadier.'

The Squadron was placed under command of 15 Corps, with A Flight supporting the 5th Indian Division on the coastal plain and C Flight supporting 7th Indian Division, which was moving south down the Kalapanzin valley. Within twenty-four hours of the ground party joining up with the aircraft, a full-scale surprise Japanese attack by the 55th Division under Lieutenant General Hanaya Tadashi was launched, which cut off the two leading divisions and with them the Squadron. Its aim was to prevent any reinforcement of the Imphal front. The Squadron's base was located at the very spot at which the Japanese had decided to cut the road to 5th Division, so everyone took the opportunity to dig in earnest and occupy a defensive position. After a few days the road back to Corps HQ was cleared and they were ordered back to a safer position alongside the HQ, the move being accompanied by very intense Japanese air activity, mainly aimed at a very flimsy bridge which they luckily failed to hit. Meanwhile, C Flight was cut off for a further two weeks and spent an exciting and very frightening time guarding an ammunition dump which was frequently under shellfire, of which more later. The Squadron suffered its first casualty on 4 February, when Rex Boys was shot down and badly wounded whilst on a reconnaissance flight. He described his experience as follows,

'I suppose what happened to me was part of the body of experience that led the Squadron to its subsequent successful operations throughout the campaign. It would certainly have been bad for our reputation and our morale to have turned away from danger. Anyway, I took off for the river, which was quite close, and flew up and down the banks seeing nothing. For the first time, I realized how little one could observe through dense forest, even at low altitude. The whole area could have been teeming with Japs for all I could tell. Then I flew south to Taung Bazar. At once the Japs came swarming out of the village huts and began to shoot at me. I tried to count. Impossible. There were groups of men everywhere and flashes of small arms fire. Splendid targets, but I had no guns to call on. I saw no signs of vehicles or artillery. I was about to turn back when I realized I had lost control of my aircraft, which went crashing into the ground from about 500 feet. It happened very suddenly, no time to think. I should have been dead, except that my guardian angel was watching over me and has continued to do so ever since. His main achievement was to put me down in a small clearing in the forest and prevent the aircraft from catching fire as it might well have done. I do not know how long I was unconscious, and the first thing I dimly realized was that I must get out quick. I opened the door and tumbled out bottom first, dragging my broken legs after me, and lay beneath the wing, losing consciousness again.'

His life was saved by the local Burmese who carried him through the Japanese lines to safety. He was to spend the following ten months in hospital, in India, Egypt and, finally, London.

C Flight took part in the famous battle of the 'Admin Box' – an isolated, defended perimeter in which troops would dig in and force the enemy to take the initiative. They were part of a very mixed garrison of 8000, mostly rear area troops – including the staff of the Officers' Clothing Shop. Wisely and presciently, Slim had insisted that all soldiers, whether they were support staff or not, should be trained to fight. One of those surrounded by Japanese attackers was Gunner Reg Bailey, who would live for a fortnight on, 'two hard biscuits a day and a tablespoon of mushy bully beef,' with a daily routine which included, 'shelling, and strafing by aircraft in the daytime, and attacks by Japanese infantry at night.' His location was Ammunition Hill,

> 'It was perhaps 150 yards long, 30-40 foot high with steep sides and very narrow on the top, almost like a ridge. It was covered with trees and thick jungle. When we got to the top we found that slit trenches had already been dug right along the ridge by previous occupants, either Japanese or our own. For those of us on the top of the Hill it was rather like sitting on top of a fire on Guy Fawkes Night – flames everywhere and bursting shells and shrapnel screeching through the trees. It was here that Sergeant R.A. Roe set a fine example and did what he could, probably more than anyone, to try and put out the fires, but was hit by a piece of flying shrapnel and injured in the throat. With great courage he dressed this serious wound himself and was later to receive a Mention in Dispatches.'

If it was unpleasant in the daytime by night it was much worse,

> 'The Japanese came out of their hiding places in the jungle on the hill opposite and streamed across the plains towards our positions. Of course, we could not see them in the dark but the noise was dreadful, their shouting and screams as they were hit by the machine-gun fire. In this respect we were very, very fortunate in having the tanks with us. They were stationed around us in the form of pillboxes. They did not normally move at night but with their heavy machine guns directed towards the Japanese positions, supported by infantry dug in around them with Bren Guns, they were able to lay down a curtain of fire, which was well-nigh impenetrable. I think very few of the Japanese actually got through, and the scenes the next morning of Japanese bodies strewn all over the plain bore witness to the carnage of the night before. However, those that did get through wreaked a fair bit of havoc when they could. One party actually broke into the 'Field Hospital', which was no more than stretchers laid under trees, and bayoneted all the patients. [They also used the medical staff and patients as "human shields" and slaughtered the remaining doctors after they had tended the Japanese wounded.]'

During the battle for the 'Admin Box' some of the Squadron's technicians and drivers were cut off from their unit, and served as infantry. At one stage during a lull in the fighting they were bathing in a river when they were strafed and bombed by Japanese Zeroes. Fortunately there were no serious casualties.

On 18 February, the OC, flying an Auster III, NK128, led 'Coyle's Circus' (as he described it in his log book), a dozen US L-1 and L-5 light ambulance aircraft, into the 114 Brigade Box. Ted Maslen-Jones, who also flew casualty evacuation sorties with the Auster, comments,

> 'Denis Coyle knew his way into this difficult LG and had also been made aware of the build-up of casualties in the 'Admin Box'. He felt he was in a position to do something to relieve the situation. After this initial sortie the task of evacuating

wounded from the forward areas was carried out by pilots of the US Army Air Force, flying Stinson L-5 Sentinels, an aircraft which was similar to the Auster, but more powerful, and adapted to carry up to three stretchers. These pilots were dedicated and fearless in their work. Theirs was truly a mission of mercy throughout the campaign.'

It reminded one of those on the ground of the arrival of Sir Alan Cobham's 'Flying Circus' to his home town before the war. Denis Coyle later noted that this exploit had proved that any formation that could make a small landing strip would not be completely isolated and, as soon as the news spread around, every brigade produced a strip without being asked, which had the benefit of making the Squadron's everyday job much easier.

After this rather spectacular beginning, the Arakan battle settled down to a slogging match while the enemy were winkled out of their well-prepared and heavily defended positions and this period gave pilots a chance to settle down and learn the real art of observation. They were also able to fly at night, as although there were no navigational aids, one flank was on the sea, which provided an excellent natural substitute, while the beach provided extensive ALGs. It was during this period that the Squadron's pilots first realized that they were having an effect on Japanese artillery activity, the infantry were convinced that their presence in the air gave them peace to move around above the surface and Ted Maslen-Jones also noticed that the Japanese guns did not fire when his aircraft was facing towards them and that the best way of spotting their position was to turn away and look in the rear-view mirror, which was actually provided to help spot any hostile aircraft sneaking up on one.

As Ted Maslen-Jones explains,

'The procedure was for our pilots to visit Divisional or Brigade HQ in order to establish codes and frequencies so that we could tune our wireless sets to individual units. We could, while in the air, change frequencies at will, so we were able to call on the most suitable guns depending upon the type of target. We also adapted the drill and techniques of OP work to the situation and type of country we were operating in. One was not only above the target area and able to vary height at will, but ground positions could be viewed from different angles, even from behind, where camouflage perhaps had not been thought necessary. The height of the jungle canopy and the wind direction at the time were also important factors. Our eyes got used to the challenge of looking for Japs through the foliage, unusual tracks or signs of disturbance, discarded equipment and movement of any kind.'

A considerable quantity and variety of artillery was available for direction – Heavy Regiments with 7.2 inch howitzers, Heavy Anti-Aircraft Regiments with 3.7 inch guns, Medium Regiments with 5.5 inch guns and Field Artillery Regiments with 25-pounders. Additionally, targets could also be identified for air strikes by fighter-bombers, or light bombers, or indeed the 3 inch mortars belonging to patrols. A rather more unorthodox form of target marking was pioneered by Ted Maslen-Jones by the simple expedient of flying very low and firing a Very pistol flare cartridge into the thatched roof of a native basha. There is no doubt that as the pilots gained in experience they became very effective observers. The artillery certainly needed all the assistance it could get, as ground observers were greatly hampered by the poor visibility afforded by the thick jungle, making targets hard to identify, observing the fall of shot very difficult, and accurately adjusting the range and bearing a considerable challenge.

As a consequence of the experience gained, the Squadron Newsletter dated 1 April clearly highlighted the major lessons learned, as well as the innovation and initiative shown,

'We have learnt more in the last three months than in all previous training which, due to being a new type of unit, has been very theoretical. I wish we had more time to digest it. We have carried most things in our Austers from time to time, captured documents and equipment, money for local purchase, casualties, medical supplies and all the serviceable parts of Rex Boys' aircraft. In general we need more time to decide exactly what our capabilities are out here. One thing that has most definitely been proved is that light aircraft for inter-communication are essential to this type of warfare.

Aircraft
Up to date we have been very lucky in that there have been no minor flying accidents so serviceability has been fair. Spares are, however, urgently needed. The Auster III is a most uneconomical aircraft for the type of work required of it in this country. Different aircraft have to be used for passenger carrying work, and work which requires wireless, because the removal and replacement of the wireless installation takes too long. The Auster IV will carry both and I think that a case could be made for this Front to have a priority for them. They should certainly be obtained for next season as they are the answer to the long-range problem as well. The Squadron suffered a serious setback shortly after arriving in India when all the stores of Squadron HQ, Maintenance Flight and Equipment Section were destroyed in a fire. On moving to the Arakan, a proportion of the deficiencies caused by the fire had been made up, but none of the aircraft spares which had been brought out from England with the Squadron were obtainable in India. One Maintenance Unit goes as far as to employ an NCO who specializes in the purchase of items in the black market. The deficiency of aircraft spares has been made good by the cannibalization of aircraft and by the salvage of everything possible from crashes. [This was to remain a major problem throughout the campaign – when available, technical stores and spares had to be flown to the various flights by SHQ.]

Vehicles
The new vehicles stood up to the cross-India journey very well considering the forced marches. There is no doubt that every Jeep must have a trailer, or else it is a most uneconomical vehicle. I do not consider that a motorcycle is of any use on this Front.

Layout
One of the biggest problems seems to be to get the correct layout of the Air OP Squadron on the ground. Conditions in the Arakan have not permitted us to keep

Flights detached out to the Divisions, because landing grounds in Divisional areas are too vulnerable to keep aircraft on at night. The general principle therefore, has been to keep a Section manning landing grounds as required and to concentrate the bulk of the Squadron on a landing ground as near as possible to Corps HQ.

Landing Grounds

Although there are no natural landing grounds except the beach in this part of the world, they take very little making. With the aid of a bulldozer and a grader, one can be made in four to six hours. This produces a very level strip, but it is liable to be soft and it shows up very easily from the air. A strip made by hand usually takes about two days, but as long as the paddy fields are the same level the results produced are better than the machine made one and as the lines where the bunds have been remain, it is very difficult to see from the air. As yet we have had no experience of wet weather but we have two experiments in hand to deal with this. One is a bamboo matting surface which would be laid over a prepared strip. This I think will prove very slippery and we may have trouble with the tail skids catching in the bamboo. The other is a coconut matting strip on the same lines as those used in Italy.

Method of Operation

The only difference in our method of operation from the standard one is in the heights at which we fly. The 600 feet rule does not appear to apply to this type of fighting. It is preferable to fly over doubtful country at 1000 feet rather than at tree-top height: shoots can be done at 3000 feet sometimes flying directly above the target. It has been impossible to lay down any hard and fast rules about this, but every sortie has to be judged on its merits. The factors to be considered are, the position of the target, the position of the sun, and the resultant danger of being shot down by hostile aircraft, or ground fire from possible small pockets of enemy which may have infiltrated. On the whole we have found that it is safer to fly high, but this is purely because up to now, enemy air activity has been negligible.

We have tried to stick very rigidly to the rules of not being misused and this has been helped by the fact that we cannot carry both a passenger and a wireless set.

Communications

The No 22 Wireless set has worked very well indeed both for ground-to-ground communications within the Squadron and air-to-ground for carrying out shoots. Even at night, with conditions at their worst, we

The Squadron's "Radio wizard", AC1 Nobby Clark, in Burma, 1944. Many years later he was the mainspring for the formation of 656 Squadron Association.

have had twenty miles air-to-ground, the reception in the aircraft being the weaker of the two. Night flying has been carried out initially from a beach landing ground and later from a forward RAF strip. It has been found completely practicable and I hope that during the next period of moon we shall be able to take some shoots.'

Communication between SHQ and the other flights always presented a problem, simply due to the distances involved, as the nearest flight could be 100 miles away and the most distant up to 250 miles. The Squadron 'wizard' with the radio equipment was AC1 (later Corporal) 'Nobby' Clark who spread his knowledge and understanding of the No 22 set to all personnel, with the result that even when fully deployed the Squadron was comprehensively netted with HQ and all flights in contact with each other. This was a remarkable achievement when one considers that the No 22 set was designed to work over only a fraction of the distances achieved. He later designed a simple modification to the No 22 set, allowing it to be used as an intercom between pilots and observers in Mk IV and V Austers (who up until that point had to shout at each other). In December 1944, Denis Coyle sent the details of this mod in a secret message to several Corps and Army HQs, suggesting it might also have a useful application in armoured vehicles.

A Flight would soon be on its own for several weeks in the Arakan at Bawli Bazar, as, in the middle of April, SHQ and C Flight were ordered to proceed the 900 miles to Dimapur to assist 33 Corps in the Battle for Kohima, in the princely state of Manipur, where B Flight had been working with 4 Corps at Imphal since the beginning of the month. A formidable Japanese offensive by its 15th, 31st and 33rd Divisions had been launched with the aim of:

(a) Crossing the frontier of India and seizing the main Allied advanced bases at Imphal and Dimapur, along with the immense stockpiles of stores and equipment held there.
(b) Cutting the Bengal to Assam railway, which was the lifeline for General Joseph Stilwell and his American and Chinese forces.
(c) Overrunning the Assam airfields from which the airbridge over the 'Hump' to China was mounted.
(d) Advancing as far as possible into India in the hope of fomenting a popular uprising against British rule.

General Slim, the GOC-in-C, decided to allow the enemy to cross the border and to fight it out on the high Imphal Plain, thereby lengthening the Japanese line of supply and shortening his own. The pleasant hill town of Kohima and the larger town of Imphal, key road junctions about 100 miles apart, were both surrounded and besieged and so began a fierce and desperate defence.

In the meantime, A Flight, with Captains Deacon, Henshaw, Gregg, Maslen-Jones and McMath, carried on its valuable work until the onset of the monsoon at the end of May, the pilots averaging five sorties per day. On 27 April both Ted Maslen-Jones and Frank McMath flew as many as eight sorties on either side of the Mayu Range, with a combined total of some sixteen hours in the air. McMath operated from the east side and lived on a very unpleasant strip which had been built in the old 'Admin Box' and rejoiced in a furious crosswind during the hours of daylight. He flew continually in search of enemy guns and also undertook the Squadron's first night shoot to cover the withdrawal of the 4th Indian Brigade. Maslen-Jones, on the coastal plain, carried out several deep reconnaissance missions and also gave close support to Royal Marines Commando operations behind enemy lines. On a lighter note, Frank McMath later recalled the culinary highlights of this period being firstly, the ability of Gunner Ray Pett to produce delicious bacon and eggs in the most unpromising circumstances and secondly, the unrivalled hospitality and standard of cuisine of the 8th (Belfast) Heavy AA Regiment, which was based, so they said, on the level of service provided by the Grand Central Hotel in their home city. The Regiment's personnel appreciated the Squadron's efforts, as Gunner Tom Reynolds recalled,

'This spotter plane was on a landing strip and was surrounded entirely with four guns and also the command post, the predictors and everything else. The pilot was a big Scottish bloke with a black moustache [Captain Pat "Black Mac" McLinden]. His job was to take off from this strip, fly over the Mayu ridge, identify targets and then radio back to our command post whatever height or distance was required. And he told us that on one occasion about eighty odd Japs were killed, lining up at their cookhouse for their bowls of rice. Another time he actually pinpointed a barge coming up river and we got direct hits on it.'

This photograph from Denis Coyle's log book of the Tamu Road in 1944 gives a graphic impression of "the hair-raising mountain paths with a sheer drop to one side" with which the Squadron's road convoys had to cope.

Through the mighty efforts of the defending forces, the Japanese invasion through the Arakan was utterly thwarted and 'the triumphant 14th Army, having inflicted its first big defeat on the hitherto invincible Japanese, stood poised and ready to reconquer the whole of the Arakan.'

During the first week of June, A Flight withdrew and made its way to Ranchi which was 250 miles north-west of Calcutta. Ted Maslen-Jones' trip was given added interest when he landed at Dacca to wait for a storm to pass, where he was greeted by three jeeps, from which emerged a number of rather grim looking US Military Police. He was escorted to a dispersal bay, where he learned that the arrival of a bomb group of Boeing B-29 Superfortresses from one of the first raids mounted on Tokyo from India was expected imminently. As this involved a round trip of 6000 miles and several of the huge bombers were limping home, he could understand that he was low down the list of priorities.

Turning now to the rest of the Squadron; as mentioned earlier, B Flight had already moved to the Kohima – Imphal area after a marathon tactical deployment right across India, in which they covered 1500 miles without seeing a recognized landing ground. The road party started out at 0900 each morning, followed two hours later by the Austers flying in pairs with a half hour interval between. The leading pair would overtake the convoy to look for the next landing site and it would then guide the next pair towards it. One of the four aircraft would then return to drop instructions to the lead driver below. From Calcutta to Imphal they travelled firstly by train, but completed the final 120 miles along hair-raising mountain paths with a sheer drop to one side. They arrived in Imphal and settled in on the main airstrip just in time for the Japanese attack. The airfield was very crowded and the Flight was located amongst a number of dummy fighter aircraft which the camouflage officer had hoped would attract enemy attention and he was not to be disappointed in this wish as B Flight was greeted on its first morning by a couple of Mitsubishi Zeros carrying out low-level strafing. The Imphal siege, which lasted eighty days, was a period of intense activity for the Flight, which had an excellent concentration of guns and plentiful enemy targets to engage. Each section flew in support of one of 4 Corps' brigades. There were four divisions in the valley, each with its own strip which was liable to be overrun at night, so the Flight remained based on the intensely busy main airfield which was operating up to 300 C-47 Dakotas, C-54 Skymasters and Vickers Wellingtons, as well as No 11 Squadron of Hawker Hurricane IIC fighters. There was something of a dispute with the airfield control staff at first, who saw no need to make any allowances for the Austers' limited fuel reserves while they waited for the green landing signal. Nor were they in any hurry to let them take off again, until it was pointed out to them that the artillery of an entire division – seventy-two guns – was awaiting the return of the Auster in order that they could get on with the war. Higher priority was allocated from that time onwards. In another incident on 21 March, Captain A.V. Cheshire crashed on coming in to land and in the words of Arthur Windscheffel, 'the kite went completely for a Burton. I'm pleased to record that Captain C came out alright and unhurt.' A week later he reported, 'Captain Cheshire missing, but found later that he had crashed again but was OK.' Cheshire was rescued by another pilot and his Auster, MT369, was salvaged by an enterprising REME Lieutenant Colonel and a three-ton truck.

The strain on the ground crew was immense, in the words of Arthur Windscheffel again,

'Feeling terribly tired after so much guard duty – every other night and long working days from 5am to 5pm. Only time to clean up and have tea and change for guards these days. Have to stand to in the bunker or trench at all hours, even if we're not on guard night. Nearly dropped off to sleep two or three times after 2am this morning but managed to keep awake somehow. Rained all night and everywhere a veritable sea of mud and slime this morning. Spent an uncomfortable night when off guard, as six of us were huddled in the dug-out which is about 7 feet x 5 feet and 7 feet deep. Debate – presided over by Captain Fowler – on the food problem – too much damned Soya Link – a spiced (heavily spiced I should say) form of pork and soya bean sausage – they're worse than terrible. No wonder the Yanks refuse to have them as rations.'

The two crashed aircraft were cannibalized and the Flight's airmen kept four Austers operational. Many and varied tasks were undertaken, from air drops of supplies to OPs on mountain tops, to scattering thousands of propaganda leaflets inviting the enemy to give up, as well as map-making trips, with the pilots' sketches being copied and mass produced for use by the infantry. The regular shoots continued – including Lee-Grant M3 tanks with their 75 mm guns being used as static artillery. A particularly successful shoot resulted in a bridge over a ravine being knocked down by the guns of the 8th Medium Regiment.

There were a number of narrow escapes during this period, one of which occurred on 21 May when Captain Eric Southern set off one morning to land on an outlying strip, which had been surrounded by the Japanese who had infiltrated, dressed as civilian refugees, during the night. Southern landed and taxied with no undue hurry into the temporary shelter of the splinter pen. He was somewhat surprised that LAC Jack Nash and Gunner Ronnie Greaves were not there to welcome him (they were in fact trying to warn him not to land by firing flares which he failed to notice), but as he wandered over to the telephone, which should have connected him to HQRA, he gradually became aware that all was not in order. Lee-Grant tanks of the 3rd Carabiniers started firing into the wood alongside the strip, while grenade discharge and mortar bombs began to fall on the strip itself and small arms fire rippled from the wood. Southern dived for the Auster, swung its tail around and pushed it onto the strip. Poking his head into the cockpit he flicked the petrol and switches on and in his haste put the throttle setting at about half open. Luck was still with him for the engine fired at once, but being at half throttle the Auster moved off on its own in a hurry. He ducked under the wing and dived in and if the spectators watching from the safety of their slit trenches are to be believed, the aircraft took off with his feet still hanging out of the door. He made his getaway untouched, with a take-off run parallel to Japanese positions 100 yards away, mainly because the strip was just in dead ground to anyone in a prone position on the front edge of the wood.

The lead elements of SHQ and C Flight having arrived at Dimapur, began operations on 17 April, then did their best to support 33 Corps in the Kohima Battle, in which it strived manfully to prevent the Japanese 31st Division from reaching the Assam Valley and also to keep open the road link with 4 Corps on the Imphal Plain. However, their activities were limited not only by the performance of the Auster III, which had an absolute ceiling of 7000 feet, but also the need to operate from the nearest airfield, which was half an hour's flying time away from the battle. During this time Denis Coyle managed to pay one visit to B Flight at Imphal and to do this he had to use the Squadron's one and only Tiger Moth, which was the only aircraft available with the range and ceiling to get through, but was, of course, entirely lacking in armour or armament. A description of a typical day's activity is given by the C Flight diary for 7/8 April,

'Captain John Day 'pranged' one mile from Bawli Bridge. After crossing the Goppe Pass he opened up the throttle with no effect, and successfully landed without undercarriage into a paddy field. Captain Day was OK but [Auster III] MK132 was u/s. Captain Peter Kingston did a sortie over the battle area and did corrections for 30 Medium Regiment who were firing smoke just in front of our own troops. Tanks, dive-bomber Hurricane strikes were all very spectacular and successful. After the Fire Plan was finished, Captain Kingston had two Batteries of 30 Medium Regiment on tap for opportunity targets but nothing was seen. Successful infantry attack for eighty-five dead Japs and two guns were found on the feature. Our own casualties were fifteen killed and about thirty wounded. Captain "Black Mac" McLinden carried out four Counter Battery sorties ... but the Japs did not fire when we were up, which is most annoying (for us).'

Remarkably, even in the thick of battle, entertainment was provided by the redoubtable British stars who had bravely volunteered to travel to India, including, as the Squadron diary notes on 16 May,

'Some of the Squadron saw an ENSA show starring Gert and Daisy (Elsie and Doris Waters).' [Very popular stars of the inter-war period, they were the sisters of another well-loved performer, the actor Jack Warner]

By the end of May the monsoon had broken and there was very little more that could be done, so most of the Squadron emulated A Flight and withdrew to Ranchi for a refit and to replace the Auster III to the Auster IV. The return flight was not a complete success for all pilots, especially two of the trio who, after one and a half hours flying through cloud, emerged over the flood waters of the Brahmaputra River. When on the point of despair, they saw a little village at the edge of the water with a dry football pitch. The first pilot, Captain John Day, undershot, hit a bank, and finished in the villagers' lotus pool. The second, Captain Ralph Hadley (who in civilian life had been a sports reporter for the *News of the World*), overshot and went straight into the floods, which taught the rest of the Squadron a useful lesson, because they thereby discovered that it was possible to get out of an Auster under water. The third pilot, Captain McLinden, came in downwind and landed safely. All three were entertained royally for the next few days by the hospitable villagers and then rescued by motorboat patrol.

Some words of explanation about the monsoon may help to explain its considerable influence on aerial activity, military operations and indeed life in general in the region. Stoked up by the great heat of early spring, it is born each year in the Bay of Bengal in May. It moves towards the great mountains of north-east India and Northern Burma and on encountering these, it sheds vast quantities of torrential rain on to their windward slopes. It brings with it swirling cloud, into which the jagged mountain tops rear and also violent atmospheric disturbance. These hazards make flying not only highly unpleasant, but also very dangerous. Some 200 inches of rain will fall in an average monsoon season.

By October, the monsoon wanes and finally dies, leaving the weather clear and pleasant. In June 1944, the Japanese were hoping that the onset of the monsoon might bring them some respite on the Imphal – Kohima front, where, by the beginning of July, their army was in full retreat back into Central Burma, after the most intense combat which resulted in the heaviest defeat ever suffered by a Japanese army.

In order to ensure that the enemy would suffer an unambiguous defeat on the battlefield and did not simply slip away back to Burma, General Slim pressed on with his counter-attack in the teeth of the monsoon. Conditions at Imphal were dreadful, as Arthur Windscheffel's diary records,

'The beds are saturated and we are soaked to the skins – scarcely a chance to dry ourselves out in these downpours, let alone the beds. I wrung my trousers out before putting them on this morning. Heavy rain fell all day and everywhere a sea of mud, mostly knee-deep.'

There was some welcome relief for the hard-pressed fitters when, in the third week of July, Denis Coyle managed to organize three replacement machines to be sent up inside three C-47 transports. He wrote in the Squadron Newsletter,

'I travelled to Imphal with one of the C-47s and spent four days with B Flight. Flying conditions within the Imphal Plain were surprisingly good and even the rain storms were insufficiently heavy to curtail flying. The cloud on the surrounding hills, however, cut down our possible use to a minimum and a waiting list of artillery registrations was mounting up. Only on the Tiddim road could we be used to full extent. By now the Jap will be beyond our reach.'

B Flight remained there until 6 September, when it too withdrew to Ranchi for a much needed rest and refit, arriving there on 22 September. By this time and having worked through the monsoon period, they had to abandon their aircraft as their fabric was rotted through. Denis Coyle estimated that in normal conditions fabric would last four months, despite the best efforts of the RAF to prolong its life by producing a more durable dope. The wooden propellers and the perspex cockpit canopies fared little better.

The CCRA of 33 Corps had a fearsome reputation and rejoiced in the name of Brigadier 'Hair Trigger' Steevens, who would arrive unannounced, 'in his usual flurry of dust and screech of brakes.' The Squadron and A Flight in particular, never had a moment's trouble, finding him to be at all times supportive and indeed almost paternal in his attitude to them. Indeed, while at Ranchi the Squadron received the following letter from Brigadier Steevens, which was one of several appreciative notes sent by CRAs or CCRAs,

HQRA 33 IND CORPS
15 ABPO 11 JUN 44

656 Air O.P. Sqn R.A.F.

I should like to thank you for the excellent work you have put in for us up here. We have both, I think, learned a lot during the period you have been with us, and so

Lance Corporal Jones of Dad's Army would have approved of the unofficial badge of 1587 Flight.

should be ready to start again at high pressure as soon as the monsoon shows any sign of finishing.

You have been most useful in carrying out accurate registration which we would not have been able to do without you. In addition to this your recce sorties have been of great value. The fact that you have had no accidents, in spite of the very bad flying conditions here, shows that your maintenance must be of the highest order.

I consider that your pilots have shown great skill and keenness in the number of flying hours they have managed to put in lately. I hope that we shall have C Flight again when we next co-operate together.

Ranchi was a pleasant and well-equipped garrison with hangarage for the aircraft and an artillery firing range on which to exercise with gunner regiments also on rest. Local flying included wireless practice and live shoots on the range. Off-duty hours could be filled with sport, visits to one of the three local cinemas and, for the more broad-minded, a fairly risqué stage show. Medical needs could also receive attention, even though the dentist was 'pleasant but positively horrific.' The taking of some well-earned leave was also a priority. Ted Maslen-Jones combined a visit to Calcutta with a chance encounter with Vera Lynn at the Calcutta Swimming Club and an impromptu 'joy-ride' over the 'Hump' to China in a USAAF C-47, flown by two pilots whom he had also met at the Club.

During the period in Ranchi the Squadron also received its first reinforcement of Indian trained pilots via 1587 Flight at Deolali, which included its only Indian pilot, Captain F.S.B. Mehta, who hailed from Bombay and on whom was accordingly bestowed the nickname 'Duck'. He later went on to retire as a Brigadier in the Indian Army. Other new pilots included Captains Pip Harrison and Ian Walton. The Flight had been set up by Denis Coyle on 16 October, 1944, and placed under the command of Captain R.T. Jones (who was succeeded by Captain Bob Henshaw in July 1945), with Captains Cross and A.W. Cheshire as the other instructors. One of the trainee pilots, Captain Harry Groom, has fond memories of his period with the Flight,

'Our posting was to Deolali where there was a Maidan (a municipal open area used for sports and parades) used solely by 1587 Flight as a base for flying training in tropical conditions. One of the instructors was Captain Cross RA whom we called "Daddy Cross", he must have been at least forty-five. Without labouring the point, it is relevant to record that there were no navigational aids, no wireless contact, and no contact with control towers. Flying was 'by the seat of the pants' over the Western Ghats, (coastal mountain ranges) in local storms, over the jungle and in the foothills for low flying, but it was so absorbing. We were given practice in short landings and on the clear maidan into strong wind with full flap it was possible to put down in twenty yards.'

Aircraft operated included a Tiger Moth and five Auster Mk IIIs, which were replaced by three new Auster Mk Vs in September 1945. The Flight was disbanded on 31 December 1945, having trained a total of thirty-one pilots.

The much anticipated Auster AOP IV was something of a disappointment at first in that it suffered from severe over-heating problems. Its 130 hp Lycoming engine had not been designed for aircraft, but was intended for use by farmers to drive water pumping machinery. This no doubt accounted for its very crude carburettor. Restarting a heated engine was extremely difficult. It was also discovered that the engine cowling had been wrongly designed and required a simple modification entailing the use of a pair of tin-snips to increase the airflow available for cooling. On the positive side, it had longer endurance, the capacity to carry both a radio and an observer and enhanced visibility from the cockpit fore and aft. Denis Coyle was rather proud of the fact that the conversion to the new mark was made 'without the benefit of any QFI.' Frank McMath wrote of his early experiences with the Auster Mk IV,

' An advance party consisting of the OC, George Deacon and myself, with two RAF fitters Corporals Brown and Quinn (both of A Flight), flew from Calcutta in three brand new Austers on the first leg of the 400 mile journey into Manipur. We landed first at Jessore, a heavy bomber station, where we had to search through the petrol dump ourselves to find 75 octane petrol.

As the weight of an Auster had to be kept to a minimum they carried no self-starter, and so the engine could be started only by swinging the propeller by hand. Now, in the glaring heat of the mid-morning sun Corporal Brown started swinging the OC's and Corporal Quinn, George's, while I, being the junior member of the party, swung my own, with chocks in front of the wheels and the throttle set half open. Twenty minutes later not a sound had come from any of the engines, so George and Quinn changed over jobs, Brown had a go at mine, and Denis set to work on his own. Suddenly George's started and then, almost immediately, the OC's, whereupon Brown and I made supreme but quite useless efforts to get some life out of mine. We began to see ourselves left behind for ever at Jessore, when, to our great relief, the other two made a glorious sacrifice, switching off their own aircraft to come and help us. From then on we kept up a series of swinging relays, punctuated only by taking the engine to bits and putting it together again, and by occasions when all five of us were so worn out that none could move from the burning ground on to which we had collapsed. "What would you do, Mac, if this happened when you were going up on an op?" Denis asked casually.

"Oh, we shall have to teach the Japs to wait for us," I replied.

After about three hours we had been swinging right through the heat of the day, and felt too exhausted to do anything but flop. George, however, reckoned he was primarily in need of food, so off he went towards the airfield buildings to return a little later triumphantly bearing the unwanted remains of the Watch Office lunch. With a slice of bully inside us we thought we might have enough strength to tackle the propeller again, so off we went sucking-in and blowing-out well into the afternoon. Suddenly, without any warning, the engine fired and purred away happily, whereupon a great cheer arose and I taxied off joyfully round the perimeter track while the others worked on the two which had previously shown themselves rather more reasonable. Sure enough, they both started with only a few swings, and by about half-past three we resumed our great flight for another 150 miles to Comilla, where we arrived at five o'clock.'

Into Action Once More 1944-45

With the ending of the monsoon in October 1944, SHQ and the individual flights could recommence operational flying. In the Imphal area, A and B Flights worked with 33 Corps and 4 Corps respectively and accompanied the troops as they advanced through Central Burma, while C Flight had already begun activity in the Arakan in September at Cox's Bazar with a forward strip at Maungdaw, supporting 25th Division. The two areas were very different; the central front starting as dense jungle with few breaks in the canopy and the great teak trees rising to more than 100 feet, with high mountains on the right flank. Whereas the coast strip was a series of islands with a great deal of mangrove swamp and many beaches which could be used as ALGs.

A Flight moved back into Burma on 5 November, working down the Kabaw Valley with the 11th East Africa Division as it advanced on Kelewa. This brought an unforeseen minor problem. As aircraft were operated a considerable distance from units being supported and radio sets were frequently in short supply on the ground, message dropping came into its own. Unfortunately, the Africans loved the highly coloured message bags and the only way of getting them back was to visit the units concerned and collect them from the entrances to the men's tents and dugouts where they were hanging, presumably as a deterrent to evil spirits. Some 90,000 men from Britain's West and East African colonies fought in Burma, including troops from The Gambia, Sierra Leone, the Gold Coast, Nigeria, Kenya, Uganda, Tanganyika, Nyasaland, British Somaliland and Northern Rhodesia.

More life threatening issues were the extreme humidity, which could bring on severe heat exhaustion, the prevalence of a particularly virulent strain of malaria and also of Tick or Scrub Typhus.

A Flight had moved from Palel (where SHQ would remain for several months) to Yazagyo, where they witnessed an appalling accident on their first night. A US Noorduyn C-64A Norseman carrying L-5 Sentinel reserve pilots, ran into a parked Tiger Moth after touch down, spun round and caught fire. Only one occupant managed to get out, but he died from his injuries, the other seven passengers perished in the flames.

A little later in the month supply problems led to a shortage of fuel for the aircraft at Honnaing. George Deacon sent a truck with his batman/driver, Gunner Embley and another soldier back to Yazagyo to collect as much fuel as possible. Their epic overnight trip along unmarked tracks, through an area known to be used extensively at night by small parties of Japanese left behind in the retreat, who were bent on sabotage as they made their way back to their own lines, produced 200 gallons of petrol before first light in time for the dawn sorties.

'A' FLT STRIP IN KABAW VALLEY

MAJOR, R.A.
Cmds. 656 (Air O.P.) Squadron, R.A.F.

A photo taken by Denis Coyle of A Flight's landing strip in the Kabaw Valley, later pasted into his log book and shown here with his signature and the Squadron stamp.

By the end of November, the Flight had moved to the head of the Kabaw Valley, towards the western end of the Myittha Gorge. Frank McMath described the life of an Air OP flight in the jungle at Hpaungzeik,

'We dug our holes and pitched our tents over them within thirty yards of the strip, but unfortunately this put us within ten yards of the road, and the road was the usual track covered in six inches of fine brown dust. The fog was sometimes appalling; aircraft running up their engines on the dusty strip and a convoy moving along the road would stir up so much choking dust that one could see barely five yards. Poor LAC Whitlock had his cookhouse almost in the thick of it and how he kept the food as clean as he did was a miracle. But then he was always performing miracles. Sometimes, in the morning, we couldn't see anything at all when this awful dust mingled with the early mists to create a real London pea-souper, which would show no sign of clearing whatever until the sun climbed quite high and got really hot. Then suddenly, the cold damp fog vanished and the full mid-day heat took its place with the temperature rising to as much as 100 degrees Fahrenheit. Between 10am and 4pm the air conditions were very turbulent, with constantly veering winds. Although flying was restricted until about 8am by these fogs, we soon found that life at Hpaungzeik was going to be very hectic indeed as the leading East African Brigade forcing its way through the Myittha had been meeting stiff opposition.'

The Flight was used for two main tasks, firstly maintaining contact and communications with the gunner officer in the leading infantry company, searching for any sign of the enemy. In order to locate the foremost friendly troops, they habitually raised a great orange umbrella, which showed up perfectly amid the dense green foliage. The second job kept a couple of pilots fully occupied from the time the mist cleared until dusk, ranging artillery on likely enemy observation posts, gun positions or bunkers.

Ted Maslen-Jones had a very singular experience when he nearly succumbed to 'friendly fire' from a flight of Dakotas dropping supplies. He was crossing a supply dropping zone in a jeep driven by Gunner Vic Foster. Foster's forage cap blew off so he stopped the jeep and reversed to go and pick it up. Just at that moment the Dakotas arrived and began unloading heavy bags of rice. Ted sprinted for safety and watched in horror as a falling bag took the front nearside wing off the jeep. A nearby African collection party was highly amused and one was heard to shout, 'Near miss, Sah!'

Frank McMath also had a brush with death when he borrowed Ted Maslen-Jones' Auster for a shoot with one medium battery and two field regiments, giving him control of eight 5.5 inch howitzers, twenty-four 3.7 inch mountain guns and thirty-four 25 pounders. This was very successful, but involved so much flying that by the time he turned for home he was down to his last gallon of petrol. The engine stopped and he had no choice but to make a forced landing, fortunately into a patch of elephant grass which was 12 feet high and cushioned the impact. In the meantime, his worried colleagues decided that Ted should take off on a search mission – despite the fact that the light was fading fast. He returned to make a difficult night landing with the aid of a flare path provided by the headlights of the Flight's vehicles. Frank turned up unscathed an hour or so later. By good fortune he had landed close to the Medium Gun battery which he had been directing, who provided him with refreshment and a lift back to base.

Kalewa fell in early December and by the middle of the month the advancing forces were across the Chindwin, which was bridged for the first time in its history by means of the longest Bailey bridge in the world, built by British and African engineers. Now, with the open plains of Burma in sight – at least from the air – Frank McMath wrote a very evocative description of life in camp in Burma in 1944,

'We managed to make ourselves reasonably comfortable everywhere we went. The formula was always the same; one tiny 40lb tent for each officer to sleep in, with odd bits of tent, camouflage nets and tarpaulins strung together to make a blacked-out officer's mess, which measured about 12 feet by 8 feet and contained one extremely collapsible table and a few canvas folding chairs. We had all our meals in there, served by two of the five Indian enrolled followers on our establishment, one of whom was an excellent cook. We always had dinner at about half past six and then got down to discussing the day's work and making out detailed reports, then planning the flying and other odd jobs for the next day. We also used to indulge in some line-shooting, no doubt in an RAF Mess the same thing would have happened – because of the exhilaration of the day's flying – but it was notable that our yarns told always of shooting prowess, for we regarded the flying part of our job as no more than the means to better Artillery observation.

This used to take about an hour, so that by eight the maps were away, and we settled down to get a little amusement. George and Ted (Maslen-Jones) seemed to write quite a lot of letters as they had both been married fairly recently and must have felt the separation far more than the rest of us gave them credit for doing. We single fellows read a bit, wrote an occasional, not very enthusiastic letter – for what on earth could one write about when everything had to come under the censor's pencil? And then sometimes we would get together for an hour or so of poker until bedtime around ten o'clock. As the school never changed we had to play for pretty small stakes, but if there was precious little excitement about it at least we got some fun. Later on, a craze developed for a game with poker dice called Liar Dice. I don't remember anyone ever suggesting bridge, nor one attempt at intelligent recreation of any sort at all. Admittedly, none of us was the intellectual type, but the day-to-day existence and complete absorption in the battle left just no room for incentive towards brain work.

With the necessity for blackout and absolute silence, we naturally never had anything like a party, which would have been ruled out anyway by the liquor ration of one bottle of whisky or gin per officer – very occasionally one of each – and two or three pint bottles of American beer for each officer and man per month. Of course, none of us kept his own bottle of liquor to himself, and most evenings a bottle would appear on the table after dinner and we would have one or two tots during the evening. Looking back, it seems amazing that we lasted so long without ever letting our hair down, though I honestly believe, even if it does sound a bit of a line-shoot, that we never gave a critical thought to our monastic existence.

The men, I am afraid, lived worse than we did. They slept about eight together, in tents the size of our mess; fed in the open, as all meals were taken in daylight; and had no place where they could all get together in the evening. As a result they used to gather in little cliques in each other's tents, where they played much more intellectual card games than their officers, chatted a little, and always about the

Friends and comrades in A Flight, Captains Ted Maslen-Jones and Frank McMath, shown here in Burma.

old days, listened to LAC Tony Paglia's fantasies, which rolled off his tongue in a never-ending stream, and wrote their letters, dropping off one by one to bed any time after about eight.'

On Christmas Day Auster IV, MT313, landed, and out climbed Denis Coyle and Mike Gregg from SHQ. They had come down to spend a few hours with A Flight and also to fly over the forward troops trailing behind them a home-made banner made from twenty feet of aircraft fabric, saying in huge letters 'Merry Christmas'. The gesture was much appreciated by the soldiers crouching in their weapon-pits, as also were the packets of cigarettes and sweets which Mike hurled out of the side window. They then flew off to repeat the process with B Flight. Higher command also approved, as a 'nice' signal was received from 14th Army in recognition of the sortie. A Flight also received a gift hamper dropped by a Dakota, containing cigars, cigarettes, sweets, biscuits and other assorted Christmas fare, which was accompanied by a card bearing the message,

'Happy Christmas to A Flight 656 Air OP Squadron from A Flight 62 Squadron RAF. Good luck.'

After spending a short period with the 5th Indian Division at Tiddim, B Flight was allocated to 4 Corps at the end of November and moved out with 19th Division at the start of its trek from the Chindwin to the Irrawaddy. They received the very sad news that Captain Cheshire had died at the age of twenty-four in hospital at Deolali on 29 November of polio which he had contracted while on leave and also of the death of Gunner "Tubby" Cherrington of C Flight, who was only twenty-one, of burns received during a refuelling accident.

On 9 December, Arthur Windscheffel and his section were the first RAF personnel to cross the Chindwin River and as he remarked with laconic humour, 'Quite an honour in its way for the Section I suppose – though one I'd rather do without.' They reached Pinbon on 19 December, after which the Flight was ordered to rejoin HQ 4 Corps at Kalemyo. Christmas Day was spent at Tonhe without much enthusiasm from the men, 'although there was Christmas cake and pudding and a beer issue,' according to the Flight Diary. By the end of the month it had covered some 700 miles by road in December alone and all personnel were relieved to be back in action rather than being engaged in ferrying aircraft and long-distance driving.

C Flight had recommenced operations on 28 September, in the Arakan, where Captain McLinden carried out a reconnaissance and a battery shoot from Cox's Bazaar. Soon, the entire Flight was working at full stretch from Maungdaw in support of 25th and 26th Indian Divisions, the Commando Brigade on the coast and 81st West African Division working down the Kaladan Valley. Shoots were carried out with all units of the Divisional Artillery, many on supply dumps and buildings in the Buthidaung area. It also observed for warships; the Flight diary made mention of the first instance on 13 December, 'Captain W. Boyd did two shoots with an Australian destroyer – the first active "Combined Ops" by 656 Squadron – and was very successful.' This was a fairly extensive operational portfolio and although additional pilots could be made available, the ground crew had simply to absorb the extra work required. There was no let up on Christmas Day as the Flight diary recorded,

The landing strip on the Irrawaddy River, where B Flight spent Christmas 1944.

Another photo from Denis Coyle's log book illustrates a river crossing as mentioned by Arthur Windscheffel. This one is on the Tiddim Road

'Captain Jarrett took the CRA to Kwazan strip, flew a Yorks and Lancs casualty to 'Bella', took a crashed Hurricane pilot to 'Julia', went back to Kwazan to pick up the CRA, having to fly round for over thirty-five minutes while Dakotas persisted in dropping supplies all over it. Later, with Captain Hadley he flew down to 74 Brigade and back. Lieutenant Hutt flew the Brigadier 51 Brigade on a contact sortie over Pt.1296. Captain Boyd did numerous contact sorties and shot a troop of 8 Medium Regiment on Pagoda Hill, Rathedaung. Captain McLinden looked for three guns marked on captured Jap sketch, saw none, but he shot up trenches and did two registrations. Captain Day landed at Kwazan and flew on a search for a second Hurricane pilot. Despite the activity, over seventeen hours flying time in twenty-one sorties, a good Christmas was had. Our scrounging and the rations, combined with the skills of LAC Scaife and Gunner Michael, producing prodigious platefuls of goose, duck, plum pudding etc. and the Flight lay about in bloated heaps all afternoon.'

The third and last offensive in the Arakan had begun in earnest on 14 December. The coastal strip was narrow and the guns kept to the shoreline. The beach was wide and firm and stretched the whole length of the coast from Cox's Bazar to Foul Point at the tip of the Mayu Peninsula, making perfect ALGs above the high-water mark for the Auster IIIs which C Flight preferred. The job of the ground crew was not made any easier by the sand, which got in to the petrol systems and the wheel bearings. Despite their best efforts, on 28 December, Captain Boyd suffered engine failure when flying NJ777 on an artillery shoot against an enemy line of supply and had to make a forced landing five miles inside supposed hostile territory. When he made his way to a settlement, he was greatly relieved to find out from the villagers that the Japanese had departed. They escorted him to the coast where he was met by an Air-Sea Rescue Hurricane, which directed a patrol to pick him up in a Bren Gun carrier. He returned to the Flight none the worse, but rather tired after a lot of walking. When the Flight Commander, Captain Jimmy Jarrett, set out with a repair and salvage party a few days later, he found that most of the fabric had been stripped off and recycled as clothing by the very satisfied and cheerful Burmese.

At the end of December 1944, with SHQ at Palel, the three flights were spread over a front of 320 miles; from B Flight in the northern area of the Chindwin with 4 Corps, to A Flight which was 150 miles to the south at Kalewa with 33 Corps (both with Auster IVs) and C Flight (still operating Auster IIIs) in the Arakan alongside 15 Corps.

The activities of SHQ included cable-laying, photography and a certain amount of transporting senior officers, but its main purpose was to supply the outlying flights with all they needed in terms of support for men and machines. The installation of long-range tanks, when required, made visiting C Flight a much more feasible proposition. A story is told of a SHQ aircraft, commuting between Flights about 100 miles across jungle and mountains, which landed on an abandoned strip in the jungle to liaise with an independent unit. At that time, Auster IVs were continuing to have overheating trouble, which made restarting a hot engine a chancy business. Returning to his machine after a long walk along a deserted track, the pilot saw a sinister-looking African nearby, equipped with rifle and machete. The pilot swung his propeller for a very long time without success. At last the silence was broken by the African who uttered the terse but telling comment, 'Bad maintenance, sah.' Some idea of the level of support given by SHQ can be gathered from this description by Frank McMath,

'No sooner had George Deacon sent his requirements to SHQ through on the wireless than they provided an even prompter answer than usual, for the sky suddenly filled with Austers which landed and disgorged the OC with his entire HQ staff, including the Engineer and Equipment Officers who normally worked strictly in camera. We were delighted to see them all, of course; and getting down to business found that most of our urgent needs could be met. Spare sets of aircraft plugs, new tyres, more fabric for patching fuselage and mainplanes, more wireless sets and accumulators, and even fresh clothing for officers and men were promised, and duly delivered by air the next day. Finally, Denis reassured us on the question of reinforcement pilots: "Don't have all your pilots killed off, George; though I shall have some new chaps ready when you want them."'

However, SHQ was not the sole repository of technical expertise, as noted by McMath again,

'Another problem was our MT, which had begun to show unmistakable signs of disliking the Burmese road surfaces, but which we knew well, would have to be coaxed through several thousand more miles before the grave. We were lucky here in having a couple of excellent fitters, Lance Bombardiers Tom Topliss and J.G. Wiggins, who individually had their faults, but together produced a mixture of caution and daring, of technical skill and enthusiasm which overcame all mechanical troubles and very soon had the Section vehicles ready for anything.'

Trials of cable-laying in an operational area were begun by SHQ near Mutaik in December 1944. A cable winding machine and a satisfactory means of mounting a cable container inside an Auster were devised. Tests were first of all conducted at ground level using a jeep travelling at 40–50 mph. On 15 December, two miles of telephone cable were laid from the air, flying at a steady speed and an altitude of 100 feet. It was found that the average pilot, with very little practice, could lay a cable in a line of trees along a road, or make a road crossing using two selected trees. Up until this point, laying telephone cable on the ground was slow work, and it was laid next to tracks and subject to cutting by vehicles tracks and artillery, as well as interception by the enemy.

The campaign moved on to a much more free flowing stage before this successful experiment could be exploited operationally. Aerial photography was shown to be a useful adjunct and SHQ was authorized to indent for K.20 cameras and film. They tried to keep passenger flying to a minimum, or it would have become a full-time job. One such mission was, however, accepted with some alacrity in November, as it involved taking a party of nursing sisters from Imphal to Tiddim, to join 5th Indian Division which had been smitten by scrub typhus. The flight took an hour over some of the most inhospitable country in the world, but the girls, who were novices in the air, did not even turn a hair when they saw where they had to land. The Tiddim strip was at about 6000 feet and consisted of 300 yards bulldozed off the top of a mountain spur, with a nearly sheer drop of about 3000 feet at each end. The take-off in particular was very spectacular as the aircraft would sink out of sight after leaving the ground and take at least a minute of hard climbing to regain the level of the strip.

In late1944 the Squadron carried out trials of cable-laying from the air. Denis Coyle designed the apparatus which was used to wind the cable prior to loading it in an Auster.

The much desired and appreciated mail from home was delivered weekly by an Auster 'milk run' and once a fortnight the Adjutant, Flight Lieutenant Arthur Eaton, made his rounds with the pay.

SHQ also noted in the OR Book that Flight ALGs had been visited in January by Lieutenant General Sir Oliver Leese, C-in-C ALFSEA and also by the newly-knighted Lieutenant General Sir William Slim. General Leese remarked,

'I want to congratulate you on the magnificent work you fellows are doing on all fronts. Everywhere I go I hear praise from everyone on the work Air OP is putting in. Please pass on my thanks and those of Lieutenant General Slim to all ranks.'

It was well-merited praise, in December alone the Squadron's ten Auster IVs and eight Auster IIIs had flown 898 operational sorties and had accumulated 722.30 flying hours. There would be no slackening of pace, as this would increase by 25 per cent in the following month.

1945

A Flight was now in open country and learned from Brigadier Steevens, when he paid a visit on New Year's Day, that its workload was to increase, as was recorded in the Flight diary,

'As well as the British 2nd Division, we were now to support the 19th Indian Division, which after a prodigious march across North Burma had now turned south and was about to take up position on the left of the 33 Corps advance. On the right, between 2nd Division and the Chindwin, the 20th Indian Division was moving into place and had already contacted the enemy. So, instead of supporting one Division along one axis of advance (which was the correct function of an Air OP Flight), we were henceforth to observe for three Divisions, covering a battlefront of a hundred miles in length.'

On the same day back at SHQ, as the OR Book reported,

'Today the OC inaugurated the Squadron "Hump run" by flying from Gangaw across the Chin Hills to Chittagong flying MV352 in five hours with one stop. Pilots who have done the same trip since quote variously from 6800 to 10200 feet as minimum height to clear the hills and/or clouds. A well-loaded Auster IV usually makes very heavy weather of any height above 7000 feet.'

The start of the New Year for B Flight was a little more mundane and homely but none the less welcome as Arthur Windscheffel noted,

'2 January: A WASB mobile canteen came round and there was a mad rush by the men to get to the head of the queue and stock up on luxuries like a lot of high-balling jackasses, but I was the first one there. I bought myself Kelloggs cornflakes, custard cream biscuits, a tin of Horlicks milk powder, a tin of unsweetened milk, a box of sugar cubes, a tinned Christmas pudding, some beech-nut chewing gum, some Sharp's toffees and some Bourneville chocolate. I set about the Horlicks, Christmas pudding and milk tonight!'

The Women's Auxiliary Service (Burma), which had been established in 1942 and was known colloquially as the 'Wasbies', consisted of intrepid and dedicated ladies who saw it as their duty to press as far forward as possible in their self-propelled mobile canteens to bring a degree of home comfort to the men. They ran dances and other entertainments and also operated static canteens, such as the Elephant Arms at Imphal. As its official history stated, 'They took with them wherever they went an atmosphere of home and a concern for welfare of men that only women can give.'

In contrast, C Flight began 1945 with a really noteworthy exploit; the capture of Akyab Island, which had been heavily defended by the Japanese and which it was planned to recapture by a major combined operation including bombardment by a considerable force of land based artillery; one 15-inch gun battleship (HMS *Queen Elizabeth*), three 6-inch gun cruisers (HMS *Newcastle*, HMS *Nigeria* and HMS *Phoebe*), six destroyers, forty-eight B-25 Mitchell bombers, seventy-two P-47 Thunderbolts, thirty-six Hawker Hurricane IV 'Hurribombers', forty-eight Bristol Beaufighters, twelve P-38 Lightnings, twelve B-24 Liberators, and two dozen Supermarine Spitfires. Forty-eight hours before the assault was due it was discovered from observation by Captain 'Black Mac' McLinden that the enemy had left and the local inhabitants were waving white flags and had cleared an area to land on the main airstrip. Captain Jimmy Jarrett was ordered to go and see if any of the local inhabitants, who were known to be

Pilots of C Flight are shown here relaxing during the Arakan campaign in Burma. Standing is Pat "Black Mac" McLinden. Then from L-R are Jimmy Jarrett, John Day, Wally Boyd and Ralph Hadley.

pro-British, were in the target area. On landing, he found them busy making haystacks and in a very cheerful state of mind because they said the Japanese had finally gone. Having reported to Corps HQ he was somewhat bewildered by the statement that the assault must take place as planned and, because he had some suspicion that his evidence was doubted, he returned to Akyab to collect the Headman and took his batman, Gunner Carter, with him to help control the crowd. On landing, after being wished a happy New Year and given three cheers, along with similar salutations for the British Empire, King George VI, and Winston Churchill, he called for the Headman and about ten rushed forward and tried to get into the Auster at once. The result was quite considerable damage to the fabric and at least one foot through the tailplane of the machine. He pointed out that, while their enthusiasm was all very gratifying, they were spoiling his aeroplane, and if he didn't get back, their liberation would be delayed or possibly postponed. Finally, he selected the largest, toughest and noisiest headman, who also sported a smart blue blazer with a magnificent gold crest and Gunner Jimmy Carter was left as Military Governor of the island. The Headman, late of Rangoon University, was interrogated at Corps HQ and as a result it was agreed that the landing should go on as an exercise with fire 'at call' only. However, it was not until H minus 1 on 3 January, when Captain 'Wally' Boyd made contact over the wireless with the invasion fleet twenty miles out at sea, that the naval bombardment from Force 61, of three cruisers and three destroyers, was withheld and even then he had the greatest of difficulty in persuading them not to fire. The landing went smoothly and the movie cameraman, who was being flown overhead by Captain John Day, had a field day taking impressive shots of Commandos storming up the beach. The Royal Marines had not been told of the change of circumstances and were somewhat surprised to find a battalion of the York and Lancaster Regiment resting under the trees half a mile inland, having already made their way by river. When everyone was firmly established Lieutenant General Sir Philip Christison, GOC 15 Corps, landed in an L-5 and took over the Military Governorship from Gunner Carter, who meanwhile had been royally treated by the village elders and plied with coffee and fried chicken. This was the start of a period of intense activity for the Flight, flying no less than 145 sorties in seven days.

The next target for the advancing troops on A and B Flights' fronts was the Irrawaddy River – the greatest river barrier faced by any Allied army in the entire war. In a move of brilliant daring 4 Corps had marched in total secrecy 100 miles around the rear of 33 Corps with the aim of crossing the Irrawaddy further south and seeking a decisive encounter with the enemy at Meiktela – the main enemy administrative and supply centre, while 33 Corps pressed on to the city of Mandalay. The two flights supported 33 Corps and 4 Corps in their crossings of the Irrawaddy. Numerous airstrips were used and the flights changed locations nearly every day. Once out of the jungle and on to the central plain around Mandalay the battle moved much more quickly and the Japanese presented many more worthwhile targets for the pilots to engage. Ted Maslen-Jones remarked to his CRA that a blackboard would be useful in explaining the state of play around Monywa. On returning from a sortie, he was somewhat astonished to find that not only a board but also coloured chalks had been provided and that his Divisional Commander, Major General Douglas Gracey, his CRA, and the Brigade Commander were waiting, sitting on the ground for Ted to begin his exposition. He thought of asking for an easel but decided not to push his luck. The level of appreciation of the work of the Air OP pilots may be deduced from, the then, Captain 'Wally' Hammond, who was Gun Position Officer of 34 Battery, 16 Field Regiment RA,

'On the ground in Burma we eagerly looked forward to the two to three sorties per day and the cheerful "no nonsense" voice of Pip [Captain S.N. Harrison] as he joined the net and made his report; maps were updated, information noted and any fire orders answered with alacrity. He was a first class shot. The Air OP/Artillery co-operation by this time was near perfect: gun response was quick, communications excellent and misunderstandings very few and far between. There is no doubt that 656 was a great help to us on the ground during the advance. A good, regular flow of excellent, up-to-date info – not otherwise available – allowed us to follow progress on our immediate front. Early target registration anticipated possible problem areas. Pip was a much-respected addition to the Regimental family and I am sure he was equally appreciated by the other two Regiments (10th and 99th). I recall that, on occasion, he would be registering guns from three or four units at the same time, ordering corrections for one gun, while the shell from another was on its way.'

Not long afterwards 'Duck' Mehta had a very fortunate escape when a bullet or piece of shrapnel passed through the door of his Auster and out the roof, via his cap, forcing out a large piece of lining which stood out like a Fusilier's plume.

Troops crossed the two miles wide Irrawaddy on 14 February and on 19 February, with George Deacon being posted home to take up duties as an Air OP instructor; Frank McMath succeeded him in charge of A Flight. The flying effort intensified, with all five pilots and two additional reserves being fully occupied, flying thirty hours in a day to create a new record. Captain Mike Gregg was particularly busy with the advance down the east bank, carrying out fifteen gun registrations on one sortie, during a day when he completed five and a half hours flying.

SHQ had a visit from Lieutenant Colonel John Merton at the end of January. He was the originator of the Merton Oblique Photography technique, first used by 651 Squadron in North Africa. He gave the Squadron a glass which could be fitted over the lens of the K20 camera to produce gridded photographs. In 1944, he had been appointed assistant to Lord Mountbatten's scientific advisor at Kandy, where he devised a method of measuring, from high altitude, the gradient and depth of water on beaches, helping to assess their suitability for landings by troops.

The OC visited Delhi in early February for an Air OP Conference where it was proposed that an AOP Wing of three squadrons should be formed – as soon as additional personnel, aircraft and equipment could be made available. In the meantime 656 would soldier on alone and indeed would continue to do so for the rest of the war.

The first Auster Mk V, RT537, had been collected on 9 February by Denis Coyle from 134 Repair & Salvage Unit. The journey from Calcutta was made via C Flight and with the long-range tank it did the hop from Comilla to Akyab in three hours and fifteen minutes. While there, he carried out a couple of reconnaissance flights in the new aircraft with Jimmy Jarrett. The Squadron was now operating, simultaneously, three Marks of Auster and by the end of the month had three Auster Mk V, ten Auster Mk IV and seven Auster Mk III. At first, the Vs were retained by SHQ but as more were delivered, they were issued to the Flights. Some pilots thought that it was the best operational aircraft and most versatile of all the Austers – it was more refined in that it had a tab trimmer on the elevators and a full blind-flying instrument panel, but still no self-starter, which meant that trying to start the Lycoming 130 hp engine under hot conditions could still be a wearisome struggle. Interestingly, when the Taylorcraft representative in India visited C Flight in April, he advised them that the Lycoming overheated, even in Leicester, which no doubt cheered them up a lot.

From January to the first half of February, B Flight continued its peregrinations, racking up another 200 road miles as 4 Corps manoeuvred into position for the surprise armoured thrust that completed the disintegration of the Japanese armies in Burma. Some idea of the conditions during the journey can be gained from this extract from a contemporary account,

'The road had vanished beneath a foot or more of the usual fine dust; it had never been better than a dirt track, but it was now the only line of communication for a complete Division. Moving slowly through the dense, choking fog of dust the drivers had to follow the many bends of the track as it wound along the valley of a dry river, frequently crossing it by flimsy wooden bridges whose loose planks cracked like a machine gun underneath the wheels. The cheerfulness of the drivers in these awful conditions was a never-ending miracle, especially as the dust covered them from head to foot so that it was almost impossible to tell whether the light brown face and body behind the steering wheel belonged to an Englishman, an Indian or even an African.'

Yet they were ready to go into action when required. In March, supporting 17 Division, B Flight took part in a combined armoured and airborne thrust for Meiktela, thus cutting off the remaining Japanese forces defending Mandalay. This caused a vigorous Japanese reaction and the largest concentration of Japanese artillery which the Squadron was to encounter. The battle for Meiktela was one of the most fiercely contested of the entire campaign.

One of the Squadron's regular tasks was to search for gun positions, some of which may be seen in this photograph.

B Flight set themselves up initially on a strip on the edge of the town which came under observed artillery fire and they were forced to withdraw into a very congested area on the edge of the lake. They were at full stretch supporting two Divisions without the benefit of reserve pilots. Denis Coyle flew in to visit them and was rather horrified to find that their new strip was marked by a fuel dump on the water's edge and a line of tanks being maintained on the other side of the strip. There was just sufficient width for an Auster, as long as the tanks were kept in line, but the tank crews did not seem to understand that it really was not ideal for an aircraft landing or taking off to be suddenly faced with a tank in its path.

Coyle found that the Flight had had all their aircraft damaged, but had managed to produce three serviceable machines out of their original five (due to the Herculean efforts of the ground crew and Corporal Sam Ford in particular) and at the same time dig themselves in like fury so that the desultory harassing fire from the Japanese artillery produced the minimum damage. With the aid of an extra aircraft and the necessary spares to repair the others, plus photographic sorties undertaken by SHQ to aid in the location of hostile guns, B Flight was rapidly back in business with good targets and participated in the advance on Rangoon, following the capture of Mandalay on 20 March and of Meiktela a week later. They accompanied 4 Corps down the Rangoon Road in April, the Flight being split with one section working with the forward HQ, until they joined again at Toungoo.

It is noteworthy that A and B Flights took part in every important battle of 14th Army's victorious campaign, from Palel to Rangoon, as the Japanese put up a grim and ruthless resistance to the now irresistible Allied progress.

By the third week of March, the Japanese defensive positions had been broken and a speedy Allied advance began, with the result that the need for Air OP temporarily lessened. This was fortunate, in that the hard-used Austers had begun to develop engine trouble. However, such was the rapidity of progress, that on several occasions A Flight pilots flew sorties simply to establish the forward position of the advancing troops and the pace of activity picked up once more. Denis Coyle was recalled to the UK at the end of March for a series of conferences and discussions on the proposed Air OP Wing. Captain Shield assumed command until his return a few weeks later.

The weather was becoming an ever more important factor for both A and B Flights. By the middle of April the approaching monsoon, 'seemed to build warning shadows in the western sky, for each afternoon great clouds towered above the mountains, dazzling white at first but gradually darkening into a threatening grey. At night-fall they would disperse rapidly and by seven or eight o'clock the sky would again be radiant with a million stars stretching from horizon to horizon. Regular furious thunderstorms with lightning, wind, dust and rain rolled down from the western hills.'

The speed of their approach constituted the main danger to flying, for a pilot got ample warning from the vertical development of the cumulus clouds, but he might easily over-estimate the time which he could spend finishing off his task before heading for home. Captain Pip Harrison of A Flight flew straight into one such storm and found that his Auster could make no progress, so he had to turn and flee downwind to an old landing ground, where he hurriedly landed and tied the aircraft down until it had passed.

C Flight had a particularly busy time in the first quarter of 1945 as Allied troops island-hopped along the west coast, landing on the Myebon Peninsula on 12 January and on Ramree Island ten days later. The only fatalities directly due to enemy action suffered by the Squadron occurred on 25 January, when the vehicle carrying Lance Bombardier Dougie Gibbons, AC2 H.E. 'Taffy' John and AC2 R.J. 'Mac' McCauley struck a landmine, killing all three. They were twenty-one, twenty-three and twenty-four years old respectively. C Flight's diary described 12 Section's heavy loss in Captain Bob Henshaw's own words,

'We were driving down the alleged de-mined road and came to a flimsy wooden bridge over a dried up river bed. As we seemed to be the first four-wheeled vehicle to cross the bridge I told the driver to wait whilst I checked the bridge supports and made sure the bridge itself was not mined. All appeared to be in order, although the bridge supports looked weak. I then walked across the bridge and told the driver of the Jeep to follow me, as I intended to get into the vehicle once we had crossed the river bed. There was a tremendous explosion. They were all blown to pieces along with their Jeep and trailer. A crater about eight feet wide and six feet deep appeared. The explosion was so intense that there was virtually nothing left. I was walking about six feet in front of the Jeep, and although I was covered from head to foot in debris I escaped serious injury. I had a small cut on my hand, and suffered shell shock. The Jeep had set off an anti-tank mine connected to a 250lb RAF bomb which had been buried by the Japs. I staggered back and came across Captain John Day, having closed the road to further traffic.'

C Flight became very accustomed to working with seaborne forces and also to flying in the face of small arms fire and a new weapon, an airburst mortar bomb. Lieutenant Hutt encountered this phenomenon on 28 January on a shoot with HMIS *Narbarda*. He was at 2000 feet when he felt the force of an explosion about 200 feet below. Following a 'polite enquiry', he was assured by the ship's crew that they were not responsible. After Akyab, the Flight directed fire support for at least six assault landings and carried out shoots with a considerable assortment of naval vessels.

On one of these sorties, Captain Boyd became embroiled in a dive-bombing raid by eight Japanese Oscars. While netting in to the Black Swan Class sloop HMIS *Narbada*, he was surprised to see two large splashes straddling the ship. The ship started putting up a heavy ack-ack barrage and he wondered whether an Auster should carry out 'evasive low flying' when at sea off a hostile coastline. Consequently, he decided to make for the dry land in the hope that it was uninhabited and he was horrified to see an Oscar diving straight towards him. However, it had already been hit by ack-ack fire and dived into the sea with a splash 400 yards ahead. When the raid was over, his friends on the ships looked around for the Auster and were amused to see what they described as, 'Wally Boyd flying tight circles at wave level, round and round inside a small cove with his eyes tight shut.' *Narbarda's* CO was Captain M.H. Nott RIN, the uncle of the future Secretary of State for Defence, Sir John Nott.

On a lighter note, on 4 March, George Formby, the very popular comedian and songster, gave an ENSA Show and most of the Flight attended.

C Flight's last act in the campaign was to take part in the seaborne assault on Rangoon and here they were able once again to be greeted in an enthusiastic manner by local residents, who were pleased to report that the Japanese had gone, but on this occasion they were also welcomed by ex-prisoners of war. Having carried out some deck landing practice ashore at the end of April, they landed on their Ruler and Archer Class Escort Carriers on 29 April. The aircraft were flown off as follows: HMS *Khedive* (Lieutenant R.J. Hutt), HMS *Emperor* (Captain 'Wally' Boyd), HMS *Hunter* (Captain John Day), HMS *Stalker* (Captain 'Black Mac' McLinden), on 4 May about fifty miles off Rangoon, escorted by a Supermarine Walrus, with orders to head for the main airfield unless they made contact with their own ground party which had gone ashore in landing craft. In fact, the members of the landing party were up to their waists in mud on the banks of the delta, south of Rangoon. To further complicate the situation, after releasing them from the carriers, the Senior Naval Officer realized that he did not know whether the airfield was, as yet, safely in Allied hands, but since he had no means of recalling the aircraft there was nothing he could do about it. As they flew over the city they were among the first to perceive that the enemy had indeed moved out when they saw, on the roof of the gaol, the famous message written by the prisoners-of-war, 'Japs gone extract digit.' Inevitably, the pilots failed to make contact with the ground party, finally landing at Mingladon airfield and entering the city from the north in rickshaws, while the assaulting troops were still making their way up the river from the sea.

The inordinate demands being made of the Austers, their pilots and the ground crews were recognized in a letter from the Air C-in-C, Air Chief Marshal Sir Keith Park, in

April, which stated that, as they had been exceeding maximum effort for several months and that there was no possibility of reinforcement until August at the earliest, with spares also being in short supply, present resources had to be used as sparingly as possible in order to eke them out. Meanwhile, the Acting OC, Captain Ian Shield, also put pen to paper to complain about the lack of cigarettes for the men, which he described as being due to the 'inexcusable incompetence and inefficiency' of the supply chain.

Victory in Europe, VE-Day, was proclaimed by Winston Churchill and the new US President, Harry S. Truman, on 8 May. A Flight listened to the announcement on Frank McMath's radio with a slightly jaundiced air,

'We heard on the wireless that Germany had surrendered, and that the long-awaited Victory Day would be celebrated in England next day with a holiday and merry-making. Nothing could have seemed more remote from the actuality of our own war. Hemmed in for months past by the jungle, with the enemy on all sides, we had never been able to rouse more than a technical interest in the other war, and now that it had finished we felt little more than the anticipation of reinforcements and equipment for our next and harder battles towards the "Land of the Rising Sun". On the evening of VE-Day the whole Flight gathered round our one wireless set to listen to the broadcasts from London streets, which were relayed from Delhi. Relief and triumph, and gaiety could be read into every word of the programme, but we, crouched in darkness in a crude dugout, lest a flicker of light should bring a shell whining across the river, felt no response to the mood of our country. We had never known Flying Bombs and V2s and the devastation which they wrought, so we could only realize, selfishly, that the "Forgotten Army" that night was banished from English minds in their joyous celebrations. It was better not to listen for fear of growing envious, so I switched the set off and we all turned our minds back to the problem of the moment.'

This picture from Frank McMath's photo album shows an A Flight landing ground possibly at Kuala Lumpur at the end of the Burma campaign. The two aircraft closest to the camera are the Auster Vs RT538 and TJ192.

Following a very gracious thank-you and farewell from Brigadier Steevens, A Flight arrived at Mingladon on 13 May, SHQ followed on 19 May, with B Flight not far behind. SHQ and Denis Coyle had 'tackled prodigious feats of organization' to keep the Flights fully operational and in fighting trim. It had moved with the most advanced elements of 14th Army HQ, with whom it had to keep in touch to obtain supplies, remain up to date about the Army Commander's future intentions and to receive orders from the BRA, under whose command the Squadron was operating. Moves were as infrequent as possible to allow the workshop and equipment sections to get on with their jobs. In the advance from Imphal, SHQ had established itself in turn at Palel, Kalemyo, Monywa, Meiktela and, finally, Rangoon. Denis Coyle wrote a letter from Monywa in February 1945, to Lieutenant Colonel Terry Willett, at 43 OCU at RAF Andover,

'Everything continues well on the whole, though the aircraft spares situation is intolerable. Our present HQ location is the best since leaving England. Right on the bank of the Chindwin with bags of bathing at the end of the day to wash the sand and dirt off. So excellent that we shall probably become a rest camp for tired staff officers.'

The war was not yet over, the Japanese forces in Burma had not given up and they regrouped for several months of ultimately futile, but nonetheless fierce resistance. 4 Corps and 33 Corps were now incorporated in the newly created 12th Army, while 14th

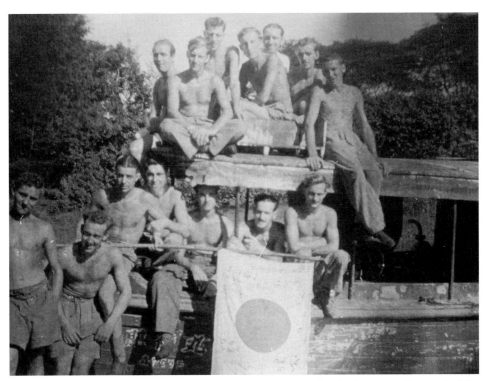

C Flight ground crew pose with a Japanese trophy on the Royal Lake, Rangoon, Burma, in May 1945.

Army was reconstituted back in India for the planned invasion and liberation of Malaya and Singapore. It was not until August, after the final significant battle at Sittang in July, that the formal surrender was concluded.

Yet, within three weeks of its arrival in Rangoon, the Squadron was once more at sea on its way back to Madras to get ready for the invasion of Malaya. However, they made their mark in Rangoon by unpacking their dance band instruments and throwing the first dance to be held after the release of the city from the Japanese. Denis Coyle wrote in the Squadron diary,

> 'This marks the close of the Squadron's second operational season and the unit can justly be proud of the results achieved. That no less than 5708.30 operational hours have been flown since the Squadron resumed operations at the end of September 1944 is in itself an achievement, especially in view of the extensive troubles experienced with the Lycoming engine. For prolonged periods the Squadron operated at above maximum scale of effort and this, at a period when Flights moved frequently, in close touch with the Army formations for which they worked, reflects great credit on pilots and ground personnel alike. The season's work has, however, imposed great strain on aircraft and personnel, and renewal of the former and a proper period of rest for the latter is essential before further operations can be undertaken.'

Frank McMath calculated the total number of sorties flown during the Burma Campaign as 6712, from more than 200 airstrips, most of which were less than 400 yards long, with only four accidents on take-off or landing. Many years later Ted Maslen-Jones wrote,

> 'Up to July 1945, 656 Squadron had been awarded two MCs, nine DFCs, two MBEs and many Mentions in Dispatches. There is no record of an award being recommended for any of the ORs and it therefore should be recorded that the list of awards made to pilots was due entirely to the skill and dedication of the ground crew – airmen and soldiers alike. Their performance in keeping the aircraft flying and communications open in such difficult and hazardous conditions, was quite exceptional over such a sustained period. Of the nine DFCs awarded, five had originally been recommended as MCs. These were changed to DFCs after a directive from London to HQ South-East Asia. However, as both Jarrett and Maslen-Jones had already received immediate awards of the Military Cross in the field, these were not changed.'

This is a characteristically modest statement by Ted Maslen-Jones, as he and Jimmy Jarrett were the only Army pilots, in all theatres, to be awarded both the MC and DFC.

The aircraft were dismantled and shipped to Madras aboard the SS *La Pampa* and the remainder of the equipment on the SS *Empire Beauty*, both ships arriving in port on 27 June. The Squadron was based for the time being at the Royal Naval Air Station Coimbatore and could attend to such urgent matters as leave, maintenance and replacement of vehicles and, by no means least, the complete overhaul of the aircraft. The RN was most helpful in every way, although the airmen found the business of having to fall-in at the main gate and be inspected before 'going ashore' was a trifle irksome after many months in the jungle. By this time Denis Coyle was in need of a rest which was reflected in his slightly tetchy monthly summary,

'Although the results of the month's work have been amazingly good, the methods used to achieve the results were far from satisfactory. Personnel who more than deserved and required a good rest and an absolute minimum of fourteen days at a Hill Station have had their leave cut short; some have had none at all, while others, who just started to taste the ripe fruits of various Hill Stations, were dragged away to collect stores or drive vehicles from the most distant depots to Coimbatore. Everyone accepted these various setbacks very well and made my unpleasant tasks of curtailing leave much easier.

Elsewhere it has been normal for a single Air OP Squadron to support a Corps of three Divisions. In supporting the whole of the 14th Army on our own, we have effectively been reduced to just one Flight to a Corps of three Divisions. Hence, each of our Sections (one pilot, one aircraft and four men) has been allocated a Division to itself!

The Squadron has undertaken the work of three for the last two years, with the result that we have had less than the bare minimum of rest. Nominally we have had two rest periods, this being our second, but both have been so short and the re-equipping so difficult that the personal effort during the rest period has been as great or greater than when in action. It is apparent that we should never have shouldered the task of supporting the whole of ALFSEA single-handed, for now, when Air OP Squadrons are ten-a-penny in Europe we are still left to hold the fort by ourselves. There have been rumours of more Squadrons for eighteen months now, but they never arrive.

The reasons for non-arrival of reinforcement Squadrons are legion but the prime factor is undoubtedly, lack of the necessary element of co-operation between ALFSEA and ACSEA and the War Office and Air Ministry. Being nominally an RAF Unit, the RAF insists on having the last word, but as we operate solely with the Army they are not really interested. The future of Air OP lies in an Army Air Arm where we shall cease to fall between two stools for the first time in our history.'

Such a sentiment was to prove prophetic, though it took another twelve years of determined campaigning by Denis Coyle and others to bring this about.

He had been told that despite the Squadron's manifest need for an extended period of Rest and Recuperation, it would very shortly be at the forefront of the battle again, accompanying the spearhead troops in the planned full-scale, seaborne invasion and reoccupation of Malaya and Singapore – Operation Zipper. This involved much additional work, including the waterproofing of all MT.

It did not proceed quite as planned, for with the dropping of atom bombs on Hiroshima and Nagasaki on 6 and 9 August, the Japanese Emperor, Hirohito, came to the conclusion that his Empire could no longer carry on the fight. Unconditional surrender was offered and accepted on 14 August; the Imperial Rescript telling his people to 'endure the unendurable' was signed the next day and was followed by the formal ratification of this on board USS *Missouri* in Tokyo Bay on 2 September. Operation Zipper would still go ahead, but as an unopposed landing, though nobody could be sure that there was not going to be a hostile reception.

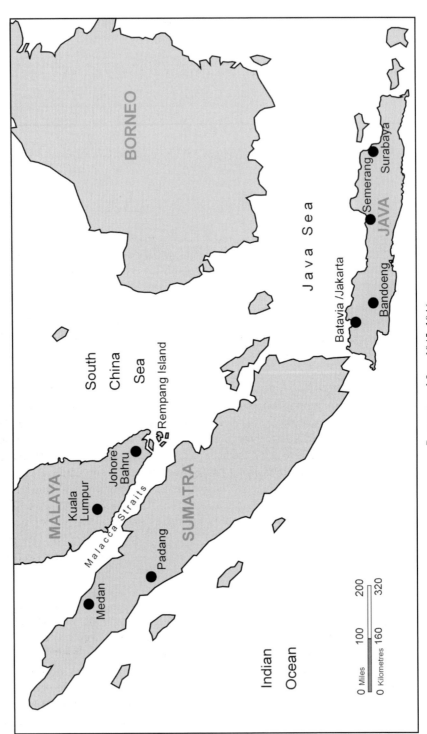

Sumatra and Java 1945–1946

Chapter 3

Malaya, Java and Sumatra 1945–1947

The Squadron set out with the aircraft being loaded onto the Escort Carriers HMS *Smiter* and HMS *Trumpeter*, the ground party sailing in LSTs, (Landing Ships Tank) with fully waterproofed vehicles. Gunner Ray Pett wrote of his experiences at this time,

'Having driven to Bombay to get vehicles waterproofed, we then returned to Madras, where Captain Bromwich, Gunner Vin Weaver and I embarked on one of three LSTs, with a mixture of Gurkhas, Infantry and a few vehicles including our 15 cwt. We were informed we would be landing two or three days before the main landing: we were going ashore just below Port Dickson as a decoy for main landing. After a few days at sea we were told the war was over but we were to continue. We were just the three LSTs – no convoy: one of the LSTs had no bow door but not ours, thankfully. The three boats beached, I think early morning, and we came ashore in assault craft with the Gurkhas. The landing took all day as the first truck slid sideways blocking the ramp and on the second LST they had great difficulty in releasing the ramp. Eventually we managed to regroup and entered Port Dickson with the Gurkhas, etc. The Japanese had not been disarmed as we were the first troops in. We were told of a POW camp outside Port Dickson and took some Gurkhas with us to the camp to find fully armed Japs were on guard at the main gate, much to the annoyance of the Gurkhas. It was mostly Indian and Chinese civilian and military, the sight and smells were horrific.'

It was fortunate that Zipper was not opposed by defenders on the shore, as the beaches had been inadequately surveyed and many of the heavily laden vessels ran aground on sandbanks and would therefore have been sitting ducks for enemy fire.

On 9 September, Squadron personnel landed on the beach at Morib (near Port Dickson) – possibly the first airmen ashore in Malaya. A Flight, with 37 Brigade, landed at Sepang and the OC and C Flight landed in the Morib area. The following day two aircraft arrived, having taken off from HMS *Trumpeter*. A Flight was established at Port Dickson. As had been the case at Rangoon, radio communication between the ground party and the aircraft failed, but once again the aircraft landed safely. On 11 September, a day ahead of the rest of the Army, Denis Coyle and Jimmy Jarrett flew to Kuala Lumpur in Auster V, TJ215, to be waved in and parked by the 'Nip duty crew', who tried to

Some of the Squadron's ground personnel travelled to Malaya in September 1945 in an LST and took part in the Morib landings, codenamed Operation Zipper.

surrender to them, which they found somewhat embarrassing. They flew in the Victory Parade on 14 September, which was an honour, but no less than the Squadron deserved. Denis Coyle did not think much of the main airfield which he felt sure was going to be rather crowded, but found a very fine strip on the golf course which 'the Japanese had kindly constructed but never used,' this was where the remaining eight Austers from HMS *Trumpeter* landed on 24 September. In the somewhat ironic words of Denis Coyle,

'Having established a main base the flights proceeded to get as far away from Squadron Headquarters as possible, C Flight going to lpoh where they were based on the racecourse, A Flight to Johore Bahru, where they also were on the racecourse, while B Flight, having been retained at Kuala Lumpur until October, found a very comfortable billet on the golf course at Trenganu on the east coast.'

Frank McMath, who would assume command from Denis Coyle on 10 November, added,

'In spite of the disappointment over missing our first large scale combined operation, the month proved to be one of the most interesting in Squadron history. As soon as the landing shambles had been straightened out and all Flight and Squadron Advance Parties were complete, the organization of a Tactical SHQ and independent and detached flights proved capable of working extremely smoothly. Throughout the Squadron morale was very high, due to the pressure of work and also to the

Japanese troops surrender to the Squadron in Malaya, September 1945, or as Denis Coyle annotated this photograph in his log book, "Jap tries to hand over K-L to 656".

unexpectedly pleasant climate and country. All ranks were unanimous in wishing that the Burma campaign could have been fought in Malaya.'

The duties that fell to the Squadron during this period – covering the whole of Malaya – included flying passengers and mail, as well as reconnaissance sorties looking for bandits, photographic work, 'roads, railways, sea lanes, estuaries, rivers, mines, factories, plantations etc.' They also assisted the work of the British Military Administration (BMA) – which was an interim body established by Proclamation No. 1 (September 1945), of Admiral Lord Louis Mountbatten, the Supreme Allied Commander of South-East Asia Command, giving it, 'judicial, legislative, executive and administrative powers and responsibilities and conclusive jurisdiction over all persons and property throughout such areas of Malaya.' The Federated Malay States, the Unfederated Malay States, as well as the Straits Settlement, including Singapore, were placed under temporary British military rule. Despite the vast responsibility give to the BMA, the time was described in the C Flight diary as, 'a fairly gentle existence.' Such was its reputation for quiet efficiency and a 'can do' attitude, that it was even requested to transport 20,000 tons of stores to Siam – which was politely declined. Captain Harry Groom recalled that period with great pleasure,

'We also had the task, immediately after reoccupation, of flying diplomats and Force 136 personnel to various Sultanates to negotiate Treaties. Landing on their front lawns was a great convenience. On one occasion, having photographed Chendorah

The Squadron was based on the golf course at Kuala Lumpur before its flights dispersed to other locations in Malaya, this aerial view was taken by Denis Coyle.

Dam, I exceeded my brief and flew below rooftop level to take a photograph of the Sultan's palace, which upset him a bit, causing a complaint to be raised through British Headquarters. There was no difficulty in tracing the miscreant and I was duly carpeted. My Flight Commander knew the power of photographs and asked if the photo was any good, which it was. He took it to a Chinese technician in Ipoh and had it enlarged and framed and sent to the Sultan with the Squadron's compliments. The Sultan was a well-educated man and replied with thanks and a request for the pilot's name, that of his observer and details as to lens, aperture, exposure, light setting, date and time, which I was pleased to provide. Ten years later, I had a neighbour, a British Diplomat, recently retired from Malaya, who told me that the Sultan still kept the photograph on his chimney piece.'

Java and Sumatra

This pleasant interlude was not to last, as in November A Flight was given twenty-four hours' notice to prepare for operational deployment to Java in the Dutch East Indies. The Japanese surrender had left behind a power vacuum which the Dutch authorities, weakened by five years of occupation at home and abroad, were contesting with the Indonesian Nationalist movement. The country was in a state of chaos, with little viable transportation and severe food shortages. It had a population of an estimated 50 million in an area about the same size as England and was probably the most highly cultivated and productive area of its size in the world; more than a quarter of its surface being given over to rice growing alone. The Republic of Indonesia had been proclaimed on 17 August 1945 by Dr Achmed Sukarno and was the prelude to 'an unpleasant little war' which was to last for five years and cost thousands of lives, until the Dutch somewhat reluctantly conceded to Indonesian independence in December 1949. In the autumn of 1945 the British and Indian Armies were therefore obliged to send forces to 'maintain law and order and save human life' – not least the lives of thousands of prisoners-of-war and internees, who were in urgent need of rescue and repatriation. A booklet was issued by SEAC giving helpful information and advice, including the following,

> Much of the success, or otherwise, of our occupation of the Indies, rests on the impression you succeed in making on the native. There are between 40,000,000 and 50,000,000 in Java alone and that's not a number to be regarded lightly. You're in his country. He knows all about it. Don't be too proud to learn from him. Make a friend of him. You will find it well worth the trouble.

Allied Forces Netherlands East Indies (AFNEI) was assembled under the command of Lieutenant General Sir Philip Christison and sent with all haste, the 23rd Division to Java and a Brigade Group of 26th Division to Sumatra. Shortly before A Flight arrived a battle had taken place at Surabaya, a major port and naval base in East Java, on 10 November, in which at least 6000 Indonesians died and perhaps 200,000 fled the devastated city. British and Indian casualties totalled approximately 600.

It is therefore understandable why A Flight set sail 'with mixed feelings' from Singapore for Java on 20 November. The Flight was travelling by LST at assault scale – four aircraft, six vehicles, five officers and seventeen other ranks. The men were nearly all founder members of the Flight, but only two of the officers had been with the Flight more than a week. Its role would be to undertake Air OP duties in the Surabaya area in support of the forces on the ground.

They soon had a foretaste of what conditions were to be like, as the local Indonesians had several field guns covering the town and throughout the night of A Flight's arrival they harassed the dock area at irregular intervals. On the morning of 24 November, the Flight disembarked and the aircraft were towed up to the airfield behind Jeeps. As was noted somewhat caustically in the Flight diary,

> 'Of course, no adequate arrangements for our reception had been made, and the billets allotted by HQRA were poor in the extreme. This was soon remedied, for a recce was immediately carried out, and we moved the next day into five excellent bungalows on the edge of the airfield. The first night ashore was rudely disturbed by Indonesian shells and mortar bombs landing in the vicinity; one of our own 25 pounder shells also came down in the back garden, but luckily did not explode.'

As soon as the aircraft had been assembled flying started in support of operations to clear the rest of the town. Neither of the two Field Regiments (3rd and 5th Indian) had much experience of AOP, and, indeed, for the first fortnight the biggest task was to find some work. Life was at first far from comfortable, water was rationed to one gallon per man per day and every night the airfield was harassed by the Indonesian artillery. In the air too, life had its dangers, as Captain R.T. Roberts found out on his second sortie, when he was engaged by a Bofors anti-aircraft gun. On 30 November, two shoots were observed for the Navy. HMS *Cavendish*, a War Emergency type destroyer, was due to celebrate her first birthday in the evening and as she had never fired a round in anger it was arranged that an Auster should go up and look for opportunity targets. Captain R. Trevor-Jones went out in the morning and found,

> 'A wood with some trenches on one side, but not a soul for miles, this was a good enough excuse and he fired some sixty rounds of 4.5 inch shells into it.'

Early December was marked by a considerable increase of flying. Everyone was beginning to realize how much could be seen from the air. The town was cleared completely and company patrol bases established three to five miles outside the perimeter. The military situation remained the same from then onwards, with patrols daily sweeping the area about the town. Trevor-Jones became the first to have his aircraft damaged by enemy fire, when his sternpost was hit by a single shot. The new OC, Major Frank McMath, paid a visit and was even more unfortunate, being,

> 'Fired on by an Indonesian when Jeeping from SHQ, the only British unit in the Batavia Red Light area, to the airfield. A burst of tommy gun was let loose at his feet and several pieces of metal lodged in both of his eyes. However, in a trip in a Dakota with a Dutch stewardess he made vast improvements and he was able to fly to Kuala Lumpur as passenger.'

Meanwhile, back in Malaya SHQ, B and C Flights began making extensive reconnaissance and photographic sorties aimed at opening up the difficult terrain around the Siam border. Ted-Maslen Jones had a most unusual and interesting experience on 25 November, taking the Japanese General, Seishirō Itagaki, from Johore to reconnoitre Rempang Island, where some 300,000 Japanese prisoners-of-war were being interned. The General arrived in a convoy of three Jeeps, each flying a mandatory white flag and was escorted to the strip by eight of his staff, including the Air Commander Malaya. A beautifully drawn map signed by Itagaki was handed over with the written instructions,

> 'Over the spots marked X, kindly swing your wings to show the General your position. Thank you very much for flying me over Rempang Island, and bringing me down safely.'

Maslen-Jones was all too well aware that the General was a strong candidate for execution for war crimes in Manchuria and also for later inhumane treatment of Allied POWs (he was hanged on 23 December 1948, at Sugamo Prison, Tokyo) and did not wish to participate in a pre-emptive act of hara-kiri, so he was on his guard and made a 'rather flamboyant' show of the revolver tucked into his belt. The flight was duly carried out; Itagaki sat stiffly to attention the whole time, except when the aircraft hit a violent bump and he rather 'lost face'. On return there was a certain amount of bowing and standing to attention as the civilities were observed, but the General could not resist

Early in 1946 C Flight went to Bandoeng, in western Java, which had a cool and pleasant climate.

having the last word, as his interpreter hurried back with a final rather unhelpful and totally inaccurate message,

> 'The General wants to say one thing. The war is not over – it will go on for a hundred years.'

It was decided that, in light of the prevailing circumstances, the rest of the Squadron would join A Flight in Java. On 11 January 1946, SHQ, with A Flight rear party and C Flight embarked on LSTs, while on the same day B Flight arrived at Singapore and awaited passage.

The Squadron was at this stage equipped with a mix of Auster IVs and Vs, several of which were rather worn out. From its new HQ at Batavia, the capital, which had been founded by the Dutch in 1619, the flights were dispersed, C Flight went to Bandoeng, which was situated on a plateau about 2000 feet above sea level and so had a cool and agreeable climate. When it arrived, B Flight was sent to Semarang, a pleasant residential town, which was some 300 miles to the east. Various types of sorties were flown – shoots, road convoy escort, casualty evacuation, photographic, mail and passenger flights. The C Flight diary muses on the rather anomalous situation in which they found themselves,

> 'We did not have to provide our own guard as the airfield was splendidly guarded by our gallant collaborators the Japanese. This, however, was not without its drawbacks. Every now and then the Jap Liaison Officer would respectfully ask if we could spare the Nips employed in the Flight on cookhouse fatigues, dhobi etc., for a couple of hours, as they were required on arms drill. However, since the Indonesians were scarcely of a friendly disposition and since the Japs periodically dispersed

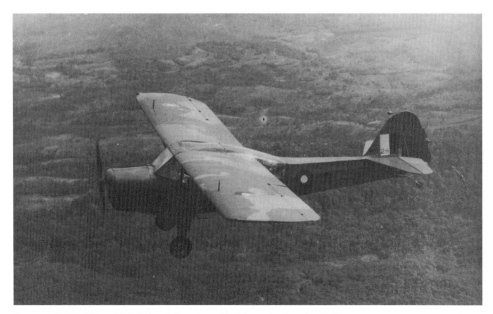

Auster IV MT288 of C Flight flying over the jungle in Java in 1946.

unpleasantly large numbers of armed belligerent youths in the unpleasantly near proximity of the Flight lines, we suffered these disruptions to our domestic economy.'

Captain Harry Groom, by then the Flight Commander, found much to enjoy,

'By way of temporary 'loot', each member of 'C' Flight acquired an American car from the fifty or so left on the strip. Of course there was nowhere to go, except for racing up and down the concrete runway, until the Civil Authorities became aware and the vehicles were impounded. I was able to acquire, for a few days, the General's horse, which was brought out each morning by three or four Japanese 'sais' faultlessly groomed and accoutred.'

In April, Frank McMath spoke at some length on Radio Batavia, describing the Squadron's activities in India, Burma, Malaya and the NEI. From May, B Flight ceased to function as an operational Flight and was renamed B (Holding) Flight, to be attached to SHQ as a training flight for new intakes, while C Flight arrived from Bandoeng to join SHQ in Batavia. Towards the end of the month A Flight, commanded by Captain Russell Matthews MC, moved 1000 miles by LST from Java to Medan on the island of Sumatra to support 26th Indian Division. He was accompanied by Jock, his white English Bull Terrier, who enjoyed flying but absolutely hated cats and was not very friendly towards the Japanese, Indonesians or his master's lady friends. The area abounded in tobacco plantations, as pre-war Medan had been famed for the quality of its cigars. One section was based at Padang on the Indian Ocean coast, with the rest of the Flight on the Strait of Malacca coast between Sumatra and Malaya. It is interesting to note that one of the first occasions on which the Squadron's flight safety radio net was actually used for rescue purposes, was when a lone LST, carrying Flight transport from Java to Sumatra broke down, with the result that the vessel was drifting out of control off the normal shipping routes and with a non-functioning naval wireless. Communications were established between Flight personnel and SHQ on its Army radio, SHQ telephoned the RN and a rescue was set in motion. On 10 June, due to the effects of his wounds, Frank McMath handed over command to Major H.B. 'Warby' Warburton, who later had much to say about the Squadron's involvement in this conflict,

'The scale of operations in the Netherlands East Indies after the ceasefire in the Far East was deliberately played down for political reasons. Operations were being continued, not against pockets of isolated Japanese resistance in Java and Sumatra, but against a well-equipped and well-organized Communist directed terrorist organization. Their aim was simply to unbridle Indonesia from the Dutch yoke, and they used the short period, between the war ending and the occupying forces arriving, to help themselves to vast dumps of military equipment, and to start organized training on a strict military basis.

I took over at the end of May with hostilities in full swing. I had left the Squadron in Malaya less than a year before, and in this time there had been almost a complete change of pilots. Morale in the Squadron was high, and a swashbuckling atmosphere prevailed amongst the pilots, who were allowed their head to great advantage. The aircraft, however, were rapidly becoming tired, having withstood the harsh weather and heavy utilization of the Burma campaign. Most of the airframes needed re-covering, the fabric having rotted and become brittle; after stripping off the fabric, several aircraft had to be written off as it was found that the airframes had not been sufficiently protectively treated and had corroded to a dangerous degree. Some newly-coated reserve aircraft were called forward, but the inspection of these became critical when it was discovered that one aircraft had a large and unexplained hole in the fabric; when this was stripped back, a large chunk was found to missing from the main spar – a hungry rat had made its nest in the wing, chewing its way, bit by bit, into the main spar, putting it beyond repair. Our main tasks were: Air OP; Visual Recce; Photo Recce (PR) and Casualty Evacuation.

The RAF was not able to finish PR cover of strategic targets, owing to lack of spares for PR Spitfires. The Squadron took over the completion of 4500 pinpoint obliques, along a coastline of 900 miles, within a target time of three months and before the monsoon broke. Some of these pinpoints involved a round flight of 450 miles and five hours duration; this was achieved by the Squadron Engineer Officer fitting a second tank behind the pilot with a manual rotary pump in between the seats to effect the fuel transfer; this arrangement gave the aircraft a safe five hours endurance with a bit to spare. Captains Tommy Tommis and Mike Cubbage were the two officers who took on this task, much to the amazement of Air Force HQ, as the task was given to us rather tongue in cheek. Given also the fact that the Photo Section consisted of one LAC photographer and one gunner amateur enthusiast, the processing of some 13,000 prints in total was a remarkable feat.

As our operations progressed, we found that the terrorists were becoming an increasing menace in taking pot shots at us: they were effective and all our aircraft were hit from time to time. Things came to a head when one of our aircraft, flying out of Medan, took a 0.5-inch cannon shell through the main spar; we now decided to take our own countermeasures. Pilots had their own choice of weapons – some chose the Sten Gun, others preferred the Bren Gun, fired through the camera port; one pilot, Dickie Parker, always used a long-barrelled Mauser pistol, with which he was a good shot! It was not long before the opposition were treating our Austers with more respect. One very dramatic success was scored by one of our RAF corporal cooks who was acting as observer to Captain Ken Litt. An Indonesian staff car, resplendent with flag, was engaged; the car ran off the road, hitting a tree, the radiator blowing up in a spectacular cloud of steam. This little action had an immediate effect on the occupants of the cookhouse, the food being better than ever and from then on we had a constant flow of volunteers from the erks to ride as observer. One Auster we fitted with a light-series bomb rack and only the lack of 20lb GP fragmentation bombs prevented the "Auster Cloth Bomber Mk IV" from going into action before we left Java. An unusual but pleasant feature of operations in Java was the existence of an unofficial truce, which was observed on Sundays at nightfall or during heavy rain; this at least allowed us to relax and enjoy the lavish entertainment which was offered by the various Service Messes and Embassies; when this palled we could always enjoy the piano playing in our own Mess by Mike Cubbage or Bill Eastman. The Dutch were most generous and living conditions were considerably eased by the gift of several refrigerators and electric fans; our Mess was comfortable and the food was cooked by an excellent Chinese cook. One asset was a permanent tailoress who was employed doing repairs and making excellent sports jackets out of lightweight blankets. Two Japanese infantry subalterns kept the garden tidy and the drains clear, and there was an ample number of Javanese batwomen to look after us.

The Squadron Mess, which was situated in one of the more doubtful areas of Batavia, was prone to raids by the light-fingered gentry, who completely cleared the Mess of all eating irons, pots and pans three times, in spite of the fact that the Mess was wired in by triple Dannert wire, and booby-trapped each evening with trip wires and grenades – it was distinctly dangerous to venture out to obey the calls of nature after bedtime, as the slightest movement in the garden would bring forth a fusillade of Sten Gun bullets from the bedroom windows.'

'Warby' would become a legendary name in Army aviation circles – he completed operational AOP tours during the Second World War in North Africa, Italy, North-East Europe and the Far East, before returning to Andover and then being summoned to Java. Stories concerning Warby are legion. In Indonesia, he was known to raise morale by declaring a weekly 'Swiss Navy' day, when officers were obliged to wear their headgear back to front and on returning from the local fleshpots, to drive their Jeeps in reverse. In Malaya, where 656 was at one time sharing an airfield with a Spitfire squadron, he was somewhat annoyed by the bragging of a young fighter pilot who claimed that soldiers flying Austers would not stand a chance against a well handled fighter. Warby challenged the young man to a 'duel' and in a 'dazzling display of evasive flying' made a complete fool of him in front of an appreciative crowd of spectators on the ground. That night he ostentatiously wore spectacles and fumbled his way to the bar where drinks were on the RAF. While in Indonesia, Warby also wrote a letter to Squadron Leader P. Gordon-Hall, the Chief Flying Instructor at 43 OTU RAF Andover, with details of some lessons learned,

'We are carrying out a lot of shooting and the country is much easier to map-spot than Salisbury Plain. We usually fly at 1500-2000 feet, at which observation is perfect and we either fly behind or above the target. We don't fly lower, as the Extremists are good rifle shots and also have LMGs. On the other hand, somebody dumped our armour plating in the sea before our entry into Malaya. There is not enough emphasis on photography in the present OTU programme – at present photography is a very close second to our primary task of Gunnery. Pupils must be taught to fly absolutely accurately over long distances at heights from 50 to 5000 feet and I can say from experience that a sortie of an hour and a half at 50 feet does take a hell of a lot of concentration. Our longest projected photographic sortie up to date is 270 miles, 250 miles of this over occupied country; this necessitates a long-range tank, as our aircraft only do 80 mph IAS. (The long-range tank is our own modification, of which we will send you photographs; it is 100 per cent better than the official Taylorcraft mod). We still have a few tricky ALGs to deal with – the pathetic take-off performance of our ancient aircraft making things dicey at times. The standard of flying is quite satisfactory, but airmanship generally bad. In conclusion I should like to add that we have flown 110 operational sorties in the first ten days of this month and considering we only have eleven old aircraft, nine serviceable at the moment and nine pilots below establishment, you can guess we are all very busy.'

There were also some exciting moments for A Flight in Sumatra,

'Life on the ground at this time became considerably more dangerous than life in the air. Double guards on the billets were essential as there were no troops between them and the Indonesians. One night, Gunner Jimmy Wyatt, made his first attempt at winning a VC: in the early hours he observed two characters creeping inside our defended locality. He challenged and then fired five rounds at the offenders; to conserve ammunition he fixed his bayonet and charged three others who were hiding in the bushes. No hits were observed, but later in the morning two Indonesian ambulances visited the adjacent kampong.'

The Flight was called upon to perform a most unusual duty on 10 August, being requested to participate in a Gymkhana which was held on the Manggalaan sports ground,

'We were asked to provide an aircraft to drop packs of playing cards on the crowd; the person who picked up the lucky card would be given a bottle of brandy. Captain J. Baker flew Captain R. Matthews on this strange sortie. Both doors were removed and four runs were made over the assembled populace, Matthews leaning out in the slipstream on one side, with a foot on the strut, dealing out cards to the crowd, Baker leaning out the other side, the better to judge his approach. The official RAF comment on this feat was, "It was a bad show; it made flying look too easy." Tailpiece: the bottle of brandy was won by a four-year old.'

C Flight transferred from Java in September, reinforcing the A Flight detachment at Padang. In October, an Auster Float Plane trial was carried out at RAF Seletar by Squadron Leader A.M. Rushton, DFC, 209 Squadron RAF (which was equipped with Short Sunderland Mk V flying boats) and Major Warburton. After one flight and one take-off aborted following a loud bang from an undercarriage strut breaking, the trial was called off on the reasonable grounds that the aircraft was underpowered, the floats were not adequate and the undercarriage not strong enough. A and C Flights were recalled from Sumatra in November, with the last operational task being carried out by C Flight on 26th and they were pleased to receive a valedictory letter from Major General R.C.O. Hedley, DSO, Commander, Allied Land Forces, (Sumatra),

'Before you leave Medan and Padang, I want you to know how much I appreciate all the splendid work which you have done for 26th Indian Division. You have earned the gratitude of all our fighting troops for your willing, cheerful and efficient co-operation, which has so materially assisted them to carry out their tasks. Thank you all very much. Goodbye and good luck.'

Then on 28 November 1946, the Squadron handed over its commitments to 17 (Dutch) Air OP Squadron and began to move back to Malaya, but not before a very appreciative letter was received, from the AOC, Air Commodore C.A. Stevens, CBE, MC,

The pilots of 656 Squadron under the command of the redoubtable "Warby" at Kuala Lumpur in December 1946.

'My Dear Warburton,

It is with very great regret that I write to say goodbye to No 656 Squadron, who, starting with the arrival of A Flight in Surabaya at the end of November 1945, have been under my Command in NEI for almost a year. You have been fortunate in being selected as the one Air OP Squadron to continue on active operations for a full year and more after the defeat of Japan.

Your work here has been difficult and often dangerous, but you have completed all you have been called upon to do with skill, initiative and enthusiasm. From the troops on the ground, with whom you operate in such close contact, I have heard nothing but praise. I would like also to mention your invaluable photographic reconnaissance work and the exceptionally long-range flights you have undertaken in this connection.

I would like to thank you personally and all past and present members of No 656 Squadron for the truly excellent job you have done in the NEI and I hope you will enjoy life at your new home at Kuala Lumpur when you foregather there next month. Goodbye and good luck to you all wherever you may go.'

Warburton held his AOC in high regard and appreciated his support and encouragement. He also enjoyed the company of Stevens' SASO, Group Captain Hughie Edwards, VC, DSO, DFC, with whom he flew in his Auster many times. The praise was well-deserved, as during its period of service in the Netherlands East Indies, the Squadron had completed 2300 sorties in 2310 flying hours, without the loss of a man or aircraft. Some 1200 British and Indian military personnel were killed or posted missing in just over a year; the RAF sustained relatively light casualties, with forty killed or missing and the loss of two DH Mosquito Mk VIs, three Republic P-47D Thunderbolt IIs and two C-47 Dakotas.

Chapter 4

Malaya and Korea 1948–1960

By the middle of December the Squadron was once again concentrated at Kuala Lumpur, where in its absence, on 1 April 1946, the BMA had been dissolved and replaced with a confederation named the Malayan Union, the first governor of which was Sir Edward Gent. It was regarded by the Colonial Office in Whitehall as a first step towards independence, but was unpopular in Malaya, as it had been imposed without sufficient local consultation. Singapore was separated from the confederation and made a Crown Colony in its own right, with its own governor – the aim being to preserve its status as a developing free port, air and naval base, while also marginalizing the impact of Singapore's one million ethnic Chinese on Malayan politics as a whole.

The Squadron Disbanded

The New Year, 1947, was to bring a very significant change as, on 15 January, the Squadron was disbanded, with the exception of one flight, which became No 1914 (AOP) Flight, remaining at Kuala Lumpur under the command of Captain Russell Matthews, MC. Many of the officers and men returned to the UK and the majority of the Auster IVs and Vs were sold to local scrap dealers – a sad end after such loyal and groundbreaking service. However, as the OC wrote,

'The Flight is in good spirits and once it is fully equipped and sorted out it will be champing at the bit.'

The Air OP Officers' Association Review gave a very brief and not very prescient report on the Flight's activities during the first half of the year,

'As trouble appears at last to have died down in South-East Asia, the Flight's tasks will be limited to training with the Regiments and to communications work.'

In fact it was kept quite busy with reconnaissance, mapping, photography and swamp clearance – whatever that was. Some useful credit was obtained by offering flying instruction to the GOC, Lieutenant General Galloway and the BGS, Brigadier Wilkinson. Group Captain Hughie Edwards, VC, was the Station Commander at Kuala Lumpur and he also availed himself of the opportunity to fly an Auster when the opportunity arose. In April, the Flight was tasked to carry out leaflet dropping over the

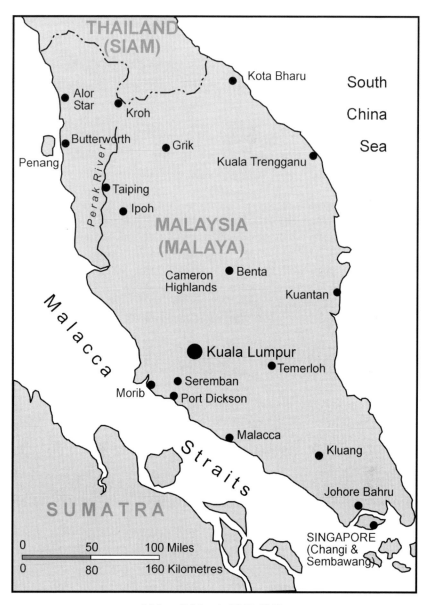

Malaya/Malaysia 1945–1969.

city – advertising the forthcoming Army Week Tattoo. Perhaps more in hope than in expectation, a practice strip was marked out on the runway in May to enable carrier landings to be simulated and preparations began for the King's Birthday Parade. Five aircraft practiced 'The Gaggle', what was believed to be the first Air OP formation display team and duly performed to great acclaim on 12 June. Captains J.R. Webb and P.N.H. Jebb, had a most enjoyable experience in August, flying a long recce sortie with the GOC and BGS, investigating campsites at Kluang, Changi and Malacca, while being provided with 'an excellent picnic lunch' by the senior officers. The first hint of more serious business to come arose in the same month, when aid was given to the local police CID, searching for Chinese bandits who had murdered several Malays. There was time for some traditional Air OP work in September – a practice shoot with 26 Field Regiment RA and also the chance to offer some hospitality to a pair of naval aviators who arrived in a Supermarine Sea Otter amphibian. Later in the month, Captain Collins crash-landed TJ276 in the jungle near Kluang, luckily without serious injury to himself.

The next Air OP Officers' Association bulletin was a little longer and noted that the Flight was kept busy in October with a major photographic task. It changed location 190 miles to the south-east, to Singapore, firstly to Changi on 15 November, and then again to Sembawang in January 1948, when a new OC, Major J.R.S. Elmsley, assumed command. The first Auster AOP 6s had been reassembled and flown just before the move. Living conditions at Sembawang were described as 'rather spartan, living the outdoor life in two 30 cwt trucks, converted for use as offices, with old caravans as stores.' Operational duties increased considerably in early spring, with aircraft being detached to North Malaya to assist the local police once more in hunting what were described as 'bandits.' It was noted that banditry was on the increase from their bases in jungle clearings. Indeed, in April, assistance was given to regular troops from the King's Own Yorkshire Light Infantry. Supply dropping was judged to be a success – apart from a two-gallon can of rum, 'the home-made parachute of which failed to open, with disastrous results.'

Back in England the Squadron's name and spirit had been maintained by two well-attended Annual Reunion Dinners in 1947 and 1948. Denis Coyle was able to bring those present up to date on events concerning 1914 Flight, noting that their new Auster AOP 6 had been in crates for one and a half years before being assembled, whereupon, it was discovered that their engines were heavily corroded and required much remedial attention. (This latest version of the Auster had flown for the first time in May 1945 and received a rather mixed reception, being well-liked by some for its ruggedness and reliability and hated by others, who still preferred the Mk V. Its main difference from the Auster V was that it was powered by a 145 hp Gypsy Major, had new type aerofoil flaps and an electric self-starter.) Denis Coyle went on to note that faulty bungee undercarriage elastic was causing a problem for both types, but that all pilots had been issued with hand-held 8–inch cameras, as aerial photography was regarded as a major requirement. As will be seen, the Auster V would soldier on for several more years.

The Squadron Re-formed

656 Squadron was reformed from 1914 Flight at Sembawang on 29 June 1948, still under the command of Major J.R.S. Elmsley. As it was to spend the next twenty years serving in Malaya, it would be as well at this stage to pause and examine the historical

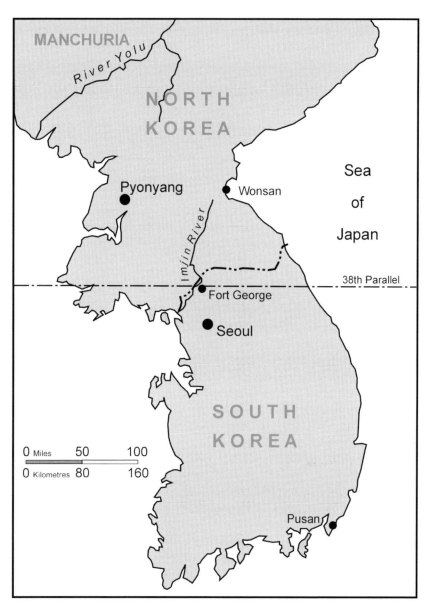

Korea 1951–1955 *(1903 & 1913 Flights)*

and geographical background which would henceforth shape and influence the Squadron's activities.

When India attained independence on 14 August 1947, the importance of Malaya and Singapore to Britain increased as the main military base and centre of Commonwealth influence in the Far East. The long association between England and the Malay Peninsula had begun in the seventeenth century, when the East India Company had set up a trading post at the mouth of the Kedah River. During the succeeding two centuries the link between the British Crown and the princely rulers of the Malay states had deepened and prospered. In 1867, Singapore and the Strait Settlements on the west coast became a Crown Colony. In later years, British Residents were appointed to the Malay States to assist with modernization and development. By the late 1930s, the relationship between the Federated Malay States and the British Empire was based on two very prosperous native industries – the production of rubber and the mining of tin. After 1945, Britain still regarded the production of these commodities as very important to the national interest, as the export of tin and rubber was the largest single source of US dollar earnings.

The peninsula stretched some 500 miles from the border with Siam (Thailand) in the north, to the Johore Strait, which separated it from Singapore Island. It was 200 miles wide at its maximum extent. Four-fifths of the land area was covered by jungle, with a central backbone of mountains rising to 7000 feet. Primary jungle was made up of continuous forest, with an average tree height of 180–200 feet, forming a canopy which cut out the sun, apart from the odd shaft of light, while secondary jungle consisted of extremely dense undergrowth up to 60 feet deep. As a rough guide to the challenges this presented; a foot patrol could expect to average about three miles per day in primary jungle, while 500 – 1000 yards per day in secondary jungle was a more realistic expectation. It has been described as, 'an evergreen world' of luxuriant foliage, where 'elephants, tigers, bears, pigs, buffalo and deer roamed the thick undergrowth,' and 'flying foxes, monkeys and parrots chattered and screeched in its high places,' while snakes, leeches and mosquitoes awaited the unwary or unprepared. The remaining fifth of the land was devoted to rubber and coconut palm plantations, tin mines, rice fields, native villages and towns. The climate was hot and humid throughout the year, the monsoon was less intense than that experienced in Burma, but frequent and prolonged tropical storms brought more than sufficient low cloud, heavy rain and turbulence to render the whole business of flying more challenging.

The population was split between the indigenous Malays who mostly worked on the land, the Chinese who were urban traders and also had arrived to work in the tin mines and those of Indian and Ceylonese origin, who had originally been imported to work on the rubber estates. The Malays and Chinese distrusted each other profoundly; there was little or no intermarriage. The British tended to be the planters, engineers, civil servants and doctors.

Communist infiltration of South-East Asia began in the 1920s at the instigation of the Soviet Union, with the Malayan Communist Party (MCP) being formed in 1929. This attracted the Chinese, but not the Malays, Tamils or Indians. The MCP was declared illegal in 1937. After the fall of Singapore in 1942 and the invasion of the Malay Peninsula, it was decided that a network of locally recruited agents was needed to provide the nucleus of a resistance movement to the Japanese occupying forces. It was deemed expedient to make use of some 200 MCP members, who along with their British instructors, retreated into the jungle. From these beginnings grew the Malayan People's Anti-Japanese Army (MPAJA), which by the end of the war numbered 4000 highly organized and well-armed guerillas. In theory the MPAJA disbanded and handed in its weapons to the BMA in December 1945, but in practice several hundred did not and went back to their jungle hideouts under the control of the MCP. They were also influenced by the success of the communists on mainland China under the leadership of Mao Tse-Tung. An attempted coup d'état failed in 1947, but by 1948 subversive activities had expanded from organizing strikes and infiltrating public organizations, to the commencement of a programme of intimidation and violent demonstrations, followed by a carefully planned series of murders and sabotage, designed to cause terror and economic disruption in rural areas. A number of planters and government officials were brutally slain. The Malayan Union was replaced by the Malayan Federation on 2 February, with Sir Edward Gent becoming the High Commissioner. It was not popular with the Chinese and Indian communities as it was perceived by them to be biased in favour of Malays. On 16 June, emergency powers were invoked by the Federal Government and the military was called in to assist with the restoration of law and order. This would become known as the Malayan Emergency (Operation Firedog) and would last for the next twelve years. The opposing forces at the start of the Emergency consisted of about 12,500 MCP members, about 2300 of whom were actively engaged in terrorism, against which were ranged 9000 Malay Police and ten British Army infantry battalions, of which seven were from the Brigade of Gurkhas. The numbers on both sides would rise considerably over the next few years as the conflict intensified. The role of military aircraft was defined in Emergency Directive No 2, 'to operate in conjunction with and support of the ground forces.'

On the outbreak of the Emergency an immediate request was made by the Army for the establishment of a squadron of five flights of Austers to be deployed at strategic points throughout the Federation. The reformed 656 Squadron was supplied with aircraft by 390 Maintenance Unit (MU) at RAF Seletar – twenty-five Auster Vs, which had been held in store since the end of the war and were about to be 'flogged to the locals at 200 dollars apiece.' Due to the diligence of the MU, all the aircraft arrived in a very serviceable condition, the main problem being the almost complete lack of spares. The MU broke up eight old Auster Vs to provide some, but it would only be a question of time before these were exhausted as Mk V spares, especially for the engines, were unobtainable from the UK. The MT was in much poorer condition as the vehicles had been left out in the open for the best part of two years and it was remarked that, 'they are not reliable, to put it mildly.'

Within a short period from the Squadron's re-birth at Sembawang, where SHQ would remain, three detached flights had been sent to work in support of the various Sub-Districts: 1902 (Captain R.H. Matthews) with North Malaya Sub-District at Taiping in the State of Perak, 1903 (Captain M.A. Pritchard) with Central Malaya Sub-District at Seremban in Negri Sembilan, and 1914 (Captain J.B. Chanter) with South Malaya Sub-District at Kluang in Johore.

As an odd anomaly, a fourth flight was constituted, the Communications Flight, sent to work with Malaya District at Kuala Lumpur in Selangor, manned entirely by RAF pilots. This would be disbanded within a couple of months, with its duties being assumed by 1907 Flight (Captain A. Noble) which arrived at Kuala Lumpur at the end of August. 1914 Flight had the only Auster 6s, which was of dubious benefit to it. The distances between SHQ and the outlying flights were as follows: Sembawang to Kluang 50 miles, to Seremban 160 miles, to Kuala Lumpur 190 miles and to Taiping 320 miles.

The flights that went up country found plenty of work to do. Flying about 200 hours per month, their main roles were reconnaissance, oblique photography and support of ground troops sweeping a suspected area. The old No 22 wireless set had been replaced by the No 62, which proved its worth, as the Squadron Newsletter reported,

> 'The No 62 sets worked well with No 38 sets on the ground. As company and platoon 38 sets were masked by the thick jungle trees and did not communicate very well with each other, so an Auster overhead often retransmitted for them. Again, sections frequently lost their bearings in thick country, and an Auster was invaluable for either telling them where to go next, or, alternatively, where they were now. Many recces were carried out with officers of the resident battalions. To start with, far too many of these recces were abortive, because the infantry being carried had no real idea of what they were looking for. Later on the standard improved greatly and now recces are conducted correctly, with specific laid-down objects in view.'

It was reported that 1902 Flight, on at least one occasion, fired on bandits on the ground with a Bren gun, 'No definite casualties were seen, but the party moved smartly in every direction, and it is hoped that at least their digestions were upset.' Searching large areas of jungle for camps was carried out, but with little success, and it was noted that, being largely new to AOP, the pilots found it very difficult to spot small clearings. 1914 Flight carried out some supply dropping to jungle patrols, 'including beer and cigarettes, rations, medical supplies, wireless spares and plastic explosive.' As well as,

> 'Getting down to a considerable amount of training: Officers were able to do low flying, forced landings, strip landing and map-reading practices. Also, ground lectures on navigation and meteorology, gunnery, and signals. Gunners and airmen received instruction in map-reading, use of small-arms, ALG drill, prop-swinging and refuelling, and aircraft recognition. Also, practical instruction in rear-observer's duties and in MT driving.'

The aim of the police and soldiers on the ground was to harass and contain the terrorists (CTs), arresting suspects, seizing arms, ammunition and subversive literature and seeking out jungle camps. However, the lack of a sufficient quantity of trained jungle troops meant that the MCP was by no means defeated. Furthermore, the death of Sir Edward Gent in an air crash on 4 July, while he was visiting the UK, deprived the campaign of an experienced leader. His 99 Squadron RAF Avro York took off from Northolt and collided with a Swedish SAS Douglas DC-6 airliner over Northwood. This was the worst mid-air collision in British aviation history, resulting in thirty-nine fatalities. It was not until October that Sir Edward was replaced by Sir Henry Gurney, who had been the Chief Secretary in Palestine during the last two years of the British Mandate, so was well acquainted with the effects of terrorism. Indeed, towards the end of the year, the CTs carried out a number of vicious and successful attacks on plantations, villages, troops and transport.

Jack Elmsley left the Squadron in November 1948, on being posted to England on a Long Staff Gunnery Course. He was replaced by Major Stuart Gates, who was able to report a couple of novelties in the December Newsletter,

> 'Several sorties were flown on Christmas Day, much to the disgust of the pilots concerned and we hope to the consternation of the bandits [as the CTs were still referred to at this point]. 1902 Flight still maintained the detachment at Sungei Patani for most of the month and concluded Operation *Albatross*, which commenced last month. The final air strike in this operation was led by a Bristol Beaufighter Mk X of No 45 Squadron, with an Air OP pilot [Captain C. Surgeon] standing behind the pilot directing him onto the target. Needless to say the strike was a great success.'

In his normal robust fashion, Denis Coyle was able to sum up the progress made in his address at the Squadron Reunion Dinner,

> 'The problems that the Squadron has had to contend with are legion. They started with a rush when they were pitchforked into action with untrained sections, ropey equipment and no spares. They have met with red tape, obstruction and interference and overcome the lot. Their aircraft troubles are not new to most of us – bungees, rotting, rust, rats and overheating. Their record in the field of sport is remarkable for a small unit and shows that there is nothing wrong with their spirit. I would like to suggest that we send them a telegram in the name of all those present tonight, wishing them well for the future and congratulating them on past efforts. Gentlemen, I give you the toast of 656 Air OP Squadron.'

On 1 February 1949, the CTs restyled themselves as the Malayan Races Liberation Army (MRLA) in an effort to encourage popular support for their cause under the guise of nationalism. This force was divided into ten regiments that were deployed approximately on a state basis, each of which contained between 200 and 500 terrorists divided between four or five companies and ten or twelve platoons. In addition, an Independent Platoon of sixty or seventy terrorists was attached to each regiment. The strongest regiments were deployed in the western states of Malaya where the main inhabited areas were located. The Security Forces mounted a series of offensive operations which achieved a large measure of tactical success.

As well as engaging in the normal reconnaissance, communications, casevac, supply, road and railway patrol, mail run, leaflet dropping and photographic tasks, the Squadron was able to apply its specialized Air OP skills in the direction of mortar (quite successful) and 3.7 inch howitzer (less so) shoots on suspected terrorist camps in the jungle and also shore bombardment from the 4.5 inch guns of the destroyer HMS *Consort*, which fired 216 rounds at a CT camp during a three hour shoot. The main object of visual reconnaissance sorties was to spot signs of cultivation where the CTs would be supporting their camps and of any unusual movements, or of any object with a straight edge – which therefore was unlikely to be the product of nature. These flights could be of several hours in duration at heights down to 100 feet above the canopy, but often at higher level to allay the suspicion of those being observed and to avoid creating predictable flying patterns. After about six months intensive flying, pilots had generally acquired the highly specialized skills needed to find camps and cultivations, some of which were no larger than tennis courts, plot these on a one-inch jungle map and participate in their destruction by infantry assault or airstrike. It was reported that the highlights of one operation were,

> '(a) the successful air drop in the jungle to a Squadron Commander of the 4th Hussars of his red carpet slippers and (b) the report of a pilot that on requesting a location from a ground party, he received a reply in all seriousness in the fashion as taught in Infantry Training manuals "Reference Green Bushy topped tree etc, etc." Most helpful in the jungle we feel.'

Direction and observation was also given to airstrikes by Spitfire PR.19s and Beaufighters, while smoke flares were adapted and designed by 1902 Flight to assist supply dropping Dakotas. It was noted that the dropping of rations by Air OP could be achieved for up to fifty men in one sortie per day, regardless of the thickness of the jungle. VIP transport flights by 1907 Flight were usually routine in nature, with the odd unfortunate exception,

> 'A large number of communication sorties were flown. Passengers included Mr Anthony Eden [the Deputy Leader of the Conservative Party], the GOC, the Commissioner of Police, the Chief Engineer, War Office, and the usual Battalion

The Deputy Leader of the Conservative Party, Anthony Eden, addresses 1914 Flight at Paroi, in 1949.

Commanders etc. While engaged with Mr Eden an unfortunate incident happened. Mr Eden was safely carried by one pilot and his luggage was due to be delivered by another. Unfortunately, the Shell Company let the flight down, a very rare occurrence, and was late in delivering petrol to the strip and consequently the luggage was delayed. The aircraft finally arrived just as Mr Eden was scheduled to face a cocktail party and the clothes were rushed to King's House by a very agitated ADC. However, it is learnt that the clothes arrived just in the nick of time and saved Mr Eden from appearing in a bath towel and a straw hat.'

1903 Flight moved from Seremban to Hong Kong in April, under the command of Captain M.A. Pritchard. Its Auster V aircraft were handed to 1914 Flight and it was re-equipped with Auster 6s. The whole Flight, complete with stores, was embarked on a LST at Singapore on 12 April and reached Hong Kong on 21 April. It was located on the main Kai Tak airfield and as this airfield was a very busy one, it was hoped that it would soon have its own strip in the New Territories (which was provided in June at Shatin, 'in the idyllic Shatin Valley beside the beautiful cove of Shatin Hoi, 350 yards of tarmac airstrip raised above the level of the surrounding paddy'). The advances made by the communists in mainland China had persuaded the authorities that the Hong Kong garrison needed reinforcement and a greater degree of aerial surveillance capability. One of its roles would be to work in close liaison with the Hong Kong Police on preventing incursions of illegal immigrants from China and also in curbing smuggling. It was reported that,

'We are settling in very well generally but it has been found that living is more expensive than was anticipated. The station has its own cinema, yacht club, playing fields etc., and even goes so far as to have ONE HORSE! There appears to be plenty of scope for Air OP in Hong Kong and intensive training has already been commenced by the Flight.'

The next few months saw a very tense stand-off between the Royal Navy and the Chinese Communists, the famous 'Yangtse Incident' involving the frigate HMS *Amethyst*. In August, 1903 became an independent flight, with the result that 656 Squadron was reduced to three flights. In the same month SHQ moved from Sembawang to Changi, on the eastern corner of Singapore Island. Sadly, on 29 August, Captain Ken Wilson was killed in a flying accident. His AOP 6, VW989, collided with the US Navy Martin PBM-5 Mariner flying boat, 84079, while on approach to Kai Tak. The OC wrote,

'The Squadron sends its deepest sympathy to the flight on the death of Captain Ken Wilson. He was well liked and respected by the whole Squadron and we are deeply sorry to hear of the tragic accident.'

The September Squadron Newsletter drew particular attention to the efforts of Captain G.F. Duckworth of 1902 Flight to find a downed aircraft,

'The Flight was requested to search for a Dakota which had crashed whilst searching for a Spitfire that was missing. Captain Duckworth finally located this aircraft in the hills west of Lenggong, and flying almost continuously for two days, guided a rescue team to it. In all, he flew ten sorties, mostly in bad weather in narrow valleys and just above the trees.'

Captain John Churcher of 1907 Flight lost his life in another crash on 27 October. He had been detailed to fly Brigadier M.D. Erskine from the airstrip at Seremban to a jungle strip. While the Brigadier was about his business the weather had closed in and Churcher advised him that it would be sensible to stay the night. According to the late Colonel John Moss (who was at the time a young, Air OP qualified RA captain in Malaya and was maintaining his skills by flying for 656 on an opportunity basis and was actually on foot patrol in the same area that day and who recalled thinking it was lousy weather for flying) the Brigadier pulled rank and insisted that they should depart forthwith. Accordingly, Auster AOP V, TJ674, took off and disappeared. Despite extensive aerial searches by Austers and Dakotas, nothing was found – until nearly five years later, when a foot patrol came upon some scattered wreckage and some human bones. From a few fragments of medal ribbon, they were able to ascertain that one of the victims had held the DSO – which the missing Brigadier had been awarded. The OC wrote of John Churcher as follows,

'This officer will be greatly missed. He was very efficient, hardworking and greatly liked and admired by all ranks. He set a magnificent example by his attention to duty and unfailing cheerfulness. Although there is little hope now of him being found alive we all sincerely hope that by some lucky chance he is still alive and will be found.'

Captain John Churcher and Brigadier M.D. Erskine, CBE, DSO, who lost their lives in a jungle air crash on 27 October 1949.

The year concluded with what must have been a rather frustrating, not to say dizzy spell inducing, task for a pilot from 1907 Flight,

'An operation on the Batu Caves. One aircraft was detailed to circle the area and observe bandit movements while the ground troops attacked with tear gas and flame-throwers. The operation was fruitless, although a good time appeared to have been had by all, except the pilot who was getting giddy going round and round in circles.'

At the start of 1950 the authorities could look back on eighteen months in which the CTs had been resisted but not crushed. The total death toll had mounted to over 350 members of the Security Forces, 700 civilians and 1000 CTs, with a further 900 captured or surrendering. The MRLA had formed smaller cadres, which were harder to track down and had refined their ambush techniques. Until April 1950, control of offensive operations by police and troops had been vested in the Commissioner of Police. It was decided that this lacked sufficiently strong direction and a Director of Operations was appointed in order to seize the initiative and devise a scheme to clear Malaya of the terrorists. The first Director was Lieutenant General Sir Harold Briggs, who had commanded 5th Indian Division in Burma and was highly recommended by the Chief of the Imperial General Staff, Field Marshal Sir William Slim. The Briggs Plan, as it came to be known, would be the blueprint used by the Security Forces for the duration of the Emergency. It involved greater co-ordination of civil and military efforts to defeat the CTs, the realization that the collection of intelligence to disrupt the CTs' supply lines and locate their jungle camps was essential, as also was the establishment of protected settlements for the Chinese squatter population, to deny the CTs their passive or active support. This last initiative had the effect of forcing the CTs to start feeding themselves through the cultivation of clearings in the deep jungle – which would then be sought out by the Austers and their crews.

The year began for 656 Squadron with a modern twist on a very traditional Scottish activity on Burns Night, or thereabouts,

'It has been found, by actual experiment, that airborne bagpipes can be heard on the ground. Two pipers of a certain Scots Regiment were flown over members of their battalion who were highly delighted to hear the skirl loud and clear. The effect on the pilot is not recorded.'

In March, Major Gates returned to the UK and was succeeded in command by Major D.P.D. Oldman, DFC. A record number of sorties were flown in May, 854 in a total of 646.20 flying hours. At last, the Squadron was fully re-equipped with the Auster 6, with the elderly, if not positively geriatric, Mk Vs being handed in as they became due for major inspection. In the same month, Lieutenant General Sir Harold Briggs was carried as a passenger for the first time. SHQ, less the Mobile Servicing Section, moved from Changi to Noble Field, Kuala Lumpur, in order to be nearer the centre of operations. 1907 Flight moved location twice, first to Seremban and then to Changi, from where they were better able to cope with their work for 26 Gurkha Infantry Brigade.

One of the most significant developments for the Squadron was the establishment of a new role to add to its already ubiquitous presence. In May 1950 the Far East Air Force

Casualty Evacuation Flight was formed at Changi. It consisted of three Westland Dragonfly helicopters and four pilots. It was a fairly ad-hoc arrangement as the helicopter was very much in its infancy at this stage. One of the pilots, Flight Lieutenant John Dowling, writing many years later, paid tribute to the invaluable assistance given by 656 Squadron. It should be said that Dowling was a somewhat gruff character and not easily impressed or given to fulsome praise,

'The presence of the Auster flights of No 656 AOP Squadron (RAF) on airstrips throughout the peninsula was of very great assistance. Not only did they have RAF ground crews and static, if not permanent, domestic accommodation; more importantly they had Army pilots, who were thoroughly trained as professional aviators. They had an absolutely expert knowledge of their local area and what was going on within it. Best of all, they had ground stations, through which voice communication was possible between all the Flights as well as any Auster, whether airborne or not, throughout the Federation. They could also talk to the troops on the ground.'

When an incident occurred in the jungle which required medical evacuation by helicopter, an Auster would be tasked to investigate the area and assess if the nearest clearing was suitable as a helicopter landing site. If not, the pilot could either advise the troops on the ground what was needed to bring the clearing up to a suitable condition, or how to move to a better position nearby. The Casualty Evacuation Flight soon came to rely on the Auster pilot's judgement and to trust it implicitly. While this was going on the Dragonfly would be making its way to the site at about 60 – 65 knots, escorted by another Auster, which could not only fly slowly enough, but also was flown by a pilot who was much more familiar with the territory, therefore saving valuable time looking for the clearing. Alternatively, the helicopter pilot would arrive at the strip and hop into an Auster for a preliminary look at the site. On one occasion, the Auster was used by the helicopter pilot to provide him with a horizontal datum in conditions of poor visibility. The first casualty evacuation was performed on 14 June 1950 (a few weeks before the first American operational helicopter sorties in Korea). By the end of the year twenty-nine casualties had been uplifted and an official statement had been made to Air HQ, praising the vital assistance of the Air OP Austers.

Also in June, the Squadron was augmented by the addition of seven more Austers and the creation of an extra flight, No 1911 at Changi (and which deployed to Seremban in August). Other items of interest included a five aircraft turnout by 1907 Flight to take part in the King's Birthday Fly Past at Singapore and a two aircraft contribution from SHQ to participate in a similar event in Kuala Lumpur. A new record total of flying hours was achieved in August, 745.25. The Squadron also welcomed the first draft of Glider Pilot Regiment Officer and NCO pilots, as well as non-technical ground crew, who would eventually man the first Army Light Liaison flight when it was formed. They were distributed to the flights to gain operational experience and to become familiar with the 'vagaries of the weather'. It was also noted that,

'The highlight of the month's operations was two naval bombardments carried out with the frigate HMS *Cardigan Bay* on bandit resting areas east of the Jenaluang –

Mersing road. The ship was at anchor, and its shooting very accurate. This short taste of the Squadron's "proper role" pleased the pilots greatly.'

The new OC had a taste of action in August,

'Following a chance sight of a clearing in the Batu Rawang area from the aircraft in which the GOC [Major General R.E. Urquhart of Arnhem fame] was being flown by the OC, information from other sources indicated that occupants were about to quit the camp, so a strike was laid on of four Bristol Brigands with a Dakota to act as marker. Major Oldman went up to direct the marking, and had a happy hour flying in the Dakota after the Brigands had finished their runs, dropping twenty-two fire bombs.'

However, the Auster 6s received a less than glowing report in the October Newsletter,

'On the whole the performance of the Auster 6 was disappointing; at full load, in the heat of the day, it took all of 300 yards to become airborne at a safe speed for climbing. Confidence was growing as the various snags were worked out of the engines, but there was a long way to go before they reached the standard of serviceability of the Auster Mk Vs.'

Despite this less than satisfactory state of affairs the total of flying hours achieved each month continued to climb, rising to 859.50 in November. The delivery of the first Auster T7 (which was essentially a dual control version of the Mk 6) to SHQ brought a mixed reaction,

'It was used for the important passengers who found the task of climbing over the wireless in the Auster AOP 6 a little awkward. While the tail weight was in position the flying characteristics seemed to be those of a well-balanced brick, in the tail down position. Removal of the weight much improved the handling and the motor seemed to give more power than the Mk 6. The Squadron was disappointed to find that the engine was the same as the Mk 6.'

While some old friends departed,

'Two Auster Fives have left the Squadron after giving sterling service for a long time. There are, however, still a number of strips that have not been lengthened to the Six standard, for which we have been allowed to retain three. We shall indeed be sorry to see the last of them.'

With nearly 1000 CTs killed, captured or surrendering, set against 393 Security Force fatalities and 496 wounded, as well as 646 civilians killed, 409 wounded and 106 missing, 1950 had been a challenging year. There was still time, however, for traditional Christmas festivities,

'Christmas was celebrated in style by all the Flights and Squadron HQ. All had their parties, most of them apparently on Christmas Eve, when the festival was given a good start and the members of the Squadron a liberal oiling. The Squadron Commander managed a visit to two Flights and Squadron HQ on Christmas Day. After awakening the Flight, he flew to Temerloh to visit 1914 Flight, who gave him a great welcome and a rousing send-off later. He arrived back at Squadron HQ in time to be escorted into the dining hall for Christmas Dinner, suitably garbed as Father Christmas (aircrew style). At Johore Bahru and Seremban the Christmas dinners were served in the traditional manner and the holiday was enjoyed by everyone.'

As the MRLA had licked its wounds and was preparing to launch an all-out offensive of violence and intimidation, 1951 was to prove a critical year of the whole campaign. More front-line fighting units would be sent deeper into the jungle to locate and eradicate CT camps with the aid of air support. Initially the cultivated sites in the jungle were quite large and were fairly easily visible from the air. Moreover it took about three months from the initial clearing until the crop was ready to harvest. However, January began at SHQ with an accident, which no doubt the Army pilots found very amusing,

'The AOC's representative, Group Captain Kelly, had his first experience in the Auster T7, which was exciting for all concerned, since we understand that his recent experience has been on transport aircraft of the heavier types. He did however manage to emulate his predecessor, who had the canvas seat of a Mk V collapse under him, leaving him sitting on the outside fabric. Fortunately the aircraft had just landed, and control could still be maintained.'

In order that overfamiliarity with a particular area should not blunt the pilots' critical faculties, it was decided that individual flights should be moved around the brigade areas now and again over the course of the year and this practice was maintained subsequently.

One of 1907 Flight's aircraft was fitted with a loud hailer, for IS duties. It was noted that, 'So far it had not been used in its proper role, but it comes in very handy for ordering transport to the strip, and getting one lined up ready in the mess.' In May the last Auster V left the Squadron, with the farewell tribute,

'They have proved an extremely reliable aircraft, having stood up to very heavy use without giving much trouble. We shall miss their reliability and nice handling qualities, but the reluctance of certain engines to start when hot will be remembered for a long time.'

During the same month, Lieutenant Joe Sellers of 1914 Flight was compelled to force land in Kelantan. He was flying back from Kota Bahru, with Captain Clive Russell aboard, when he noticed smoke coming from the engine. On throttling back this disappeared, so he set course for the nearest strip. On opening up the throttle the propeller flew off. He managed to make a forced landing on part of the east coast railway and was unfortunate to hit part of the fencing alongside the track, severely damaging the aircraft. Both pilot and passenger were unhurt. The value of the trailing aerial was fully shown as he was over 200 miles from SHQ, yet a pilot flying at only 2000 feet managed to pass his location, and details of the occurrence, to SHQ before completing his landing.

In 1951 one of 1907 Flight's Austers was fitted with a loud-hailing speaker, similar to the installation shown on this civil Auster.

The pilot later reported his safe landing by wireless, using the wire from the trailing aerial as a horizontal aerial.

In July, Captain Derek Vaudrey and Lieutenant John Crawshaw departed on the aircraft carrier HMS *Unicorn*, their original destination of Korea being changed to Hong Kong at short notice,

'Reports from them indicate a very easy life for the time being, as there are no Austers available. It is possible that they may go on a Harvard Conversion Course to help pass the time of day. They have, together with Lieutenant Joyce, formed a detachment of 656 Air OP Squadron at Hong Kong. In the meantime their enforced holiday has exhausted their slender finances. [They returned from Hong Kong on the HMT *Devonshire* in September, as their services were not required in Korea at that point, eventually Crawshaw was posted to 1903 Flight in November]'

In August, 1907 Flight reported from Sembawang that it had carried out the casualty evacuation of a Malay policeman who had been savaged by a tiger, while 1914 Flight announced that it had won nine and lost seven cricket matches. In September, the chief item of interest was the celebration which took place on Arnhem Day at 1911 Flight, at which the GOC, Major General Urquhart was the Guest of Honour. The function started with a ceremonial parade of the Flight, drawn up in review order with the aircraft and vehicles on parade. The GOC, flown in by Major Oldman, drew up as the Flight came to attention. He then inspected the parade, and talked personally with every man in the Flight about their jobs.

After the parade, the General then gave a short but most interesting lecture to the Flight about the Battle of Arnhem, with the aid of two wall diagrams. He then met the NCOs in the Sergeants' Mess and talked with Staff Sergeants Gay, Gear and Sergeant Wastell, all of whom had been engaged in the battle.

The OC of 1907 Flight, Captain Tom Lacey, took part in an interesting exercise in September. With the assistance of Lieutenant Commander Norman, the naval test pilot at Sembawang, he practised evasive action against a Hawker Sea Fury fighter. Diving turns to port or starboard proved effective from 800 feet, but ground level evasive tactics were not so successful. The wireless masts at Tebrau gave the best protection, and by agreement this was accepted as unfair to the Fury.

Lieutenant R.J. Farwell of 1907 Flight went missing on 1 October while flying an Auster 6 from Grik to Taiping, in North Perak. While attempting to climb over some bad weather to reach base, he entered a cloud, which was ascending more quickly than he was. Due to the turbulence, he lost control in the cloud, spun, and while recovering from the ensuing dive, crashed into the jungle on the side of a mountain. Although he and his passenger, Lieutenant Colonel Bossard, were considerably shaken, they managed to walk out to the road and returned to Taiping in a lorry belonging to a Chinese. The search was called off and the Flight noted with some relief that their injuries were not serious, consisting chiefly of multiple leech bites. Farwell was the first person to have made a successful forced landing in the jungle and got away with it. Had the aircraft been fitted with a trailing aerial, it is highly probable that it would never had occurred, since the pilot could have been ordered to divert, or return to the strip from which he took off. A number of important lessons were learned about the best method of organizing and controlling a search. The difficulty of locating a crashed aircraft in deep jungle was underlined, since all efforts to find the remains failed.

Most of the flying undertaken by 1911 Flight in the first part of the month was in connection with the operation which followed the murder of the High Commissioner, Sir Henry Gurney, on 6 October and 'consisted of visual and contact recces, leaflet drops, and recces along the roads between Kota Bahru and Raub.' Gurney was ambushed by a MRLA unit forty miles north of Kuala Lumpur. His death was a great setback at such a crucial stage of the campaign and was followed not long afterwards by another blow, the resignation of Lieutenant General Briggs, due to ill health.

The Squadron Newsletter provided some interesting statistics at the end of October,

> 'The Squadron's total hours entered four figures for the first time in its history, a total of 1017 hours 40 minutes being achieved in 1377 sorties. Of this, nearly half was directly concerned with operations. Another reason why the month is of special importance is because No 1911 Flight broke the record for the highest number of hours in any flight, by flying 345 hours in 456 sorties. The previous record was held by No 1907 Flight, at 319 hours. These achievements have given great satisfaction to all ranks in the unit, and reflect credit on all who played a part.'

More challenges were to follow soon. On 3 November, Sergeant E.J. Webb of 1911 Flight, whose passenger was a police officer engaged in a visual reconnaissance of the area, had to make a forced landing in the deep jungle to the west of Gua Musang. The aircraft crashed due to engine failure, but fortunately the wireless remained intact and there was sufficient charge left in the damaged battery for an SOS to reach the Flight. This was made possible because Webb was carrying a wire aerial in the aircraft, which he erected as soon as he landed. They were located after forty-eight hours, following a search by a large part of the Squadron. After receiving a supply drop, they 'sailed happily down the Rivers Perola and Betis on a bamboo raft under Auster escort,' back to the nearest police post. From there they walked twenty-five miles back to Gua Musang, and were then flown home, little the worse for their ordeal, bringing to an end a search and rescue operation which lasted for 'four harassing and difficult days.'

Much less happily, on 11 November, Gunner F.R. Houghton of 1902 Flight, was taking part in a road convoy which was ambushed. He was an old and valued member of the Flight and his death was a great shock to his friends and colleagues.

Demands for trained reinforcements for 1913 Flight in Korea took Sergeant J.W. Hutchings from 1911 Flight,

'He was one of the first draft of Glider Pilots to come to the Squadron, and accomplished an astonishing amount of flying before he left; he was a difficult person to keep out of the air, and he accomplished in a year and two months over 650 hours. [He continued flying to a very high standard in Korea and was awarded the Distinguished Flying Medal for service in Malaya and Korea]'

Towards the end of the month the retiring Director of Operations, Sir Harold Briggs and his successor, Sir Rob Lockhart, were flown by pilots of 1911, 1914 Flights and SHQ, on a tour of the entire theatre. As the year came to a close, the Squadron could reflect on more records broken, with a total of 10,000 hours being flown – an average of 43.5 hours per pilot per month. Passenger flying took up over half of this, with visual reconnaissance flights for company and patrol commanders being regarded as particularly important. The yearly summary also mentioned considerable success in finding CT camps and in directing air strikes against them. When the air effort was a large one, with possibly as many as twenty-five aircraft involved, the pilot who had located the camp, would direct the lead strike aircraft as a passenger in a Bristol Brigand B1 (the successor to the Beaufighter). Small and well-concealed targets, which were all but invisible to the faster types, could be marked by harking back to techniques used in Burma – firing a Very pistol from a low flying Auster and then guiding the Brigands or Vampires onto the mark by radio. It was in 1951 in which the highest number of casualties was suffered, 505 members of the Security Forces killed and 668 wounded, 660 civilians murdered and 1077 CTs killed, 121 captured and 201 surrendered.

Korea

Though, strictly speaking, not part of 656's story, events in Korea cannot be overlooked, not least because many reinforcements to the two flights supporting the 1st Commonwealth Division were provided from the Squadron and many pilots undertook a spell of operations for a 'change of air' before returning to complete their tour in Malaya. Canadian and Australian pilots also served with the Flights.

The war had begun in June 1950 with a surprise attack from the Soviet-sponsored People's Democratic Republic of North Korea on the American-backed Republic of Korea in the south. The United Nations responded and an international force was sent to Korea under US leadership. The Red Chinese Army entered combat in November 1950. The following year would see much fierce fighting.

1903 Flight was sent from Hong Kong and 1913 Flight from the UK. 1903 Flight was conveyed to Iwakuni in Japan, on board the aircraft carrier HMS *Unicorn*, in July 1951. Permission was sought to fly off but was not granted, so the aircraft were unloaded by lighter. Before long, the five Auster 6s were escorted across the Korea Strait from Ashiya to Pusan by a Short Sunderland flying boat of No 205 Squadron, thus the Flight had the distinction of being the first RAF unit to be based in Korea, commencing operational flying at the start of August. The first flight over the front line was made by the OC, Major Ronnie Gower, taking the CRA, Brigadier W.G.H. Pike, DSO, up for a 'general reconnaissance' on 2 August. There was a gap of about 1000 yards between the opposing forces, bisected by the Imjin River. By the end of its first month the Flight had carried out thirty-four shoots with the artillery of 1st Commonwealth Division. A new airstrip was made by Canadian Sappers on paddy fields just south of the Imjin River and was dried out by the application of napalm to the surface, which was later acclaimed as one of the best light aircraft strips in Korea. The OC welcomed Captain Peter Downward, who was in command of 1913 Flight, on a preliminary visit in September. He was taken up on a typical two hour AOP sortie over enemy lines and, on landing, was interested to find that the loud bang which he had heard was indeed caused by an anti-aircraft shell, which had left a large hole in the starboard flap, a few inches from his head. 1913 Flight joined 1903 at Fort George early in November.

The Flights' primary tasks, working with Commonwealth and US forces, were observing enemy movements and gun positions, directing counter battery shoots and giving early warning of enemy attacks. Prior to offensives, battalion and company commanders were taken aloft to examine the areas over which they intended to advance. It had been intended that, as a Light Liaison Flight staffed by six pilots from the Glider Pilot Regiment, 1913 Flight would confine its activities to air-taxi work. However, its OC made strong representations to his GOC, Major General C.A.J.H. 'Jim' Cassels, with the

1903 and 1913 Flights were based at Fort George in Korea from the autumn of 1951 onwards.

result that the two Flights shared much of the work, which allowed 1903 to concentrate on its primary duty of directing the fire of 14 Field Regiment RA, 16 New Zealand Field Regiment and 2 Royal Canadian Horse. The UN forces had total air superiority over the battlefield, but there was still the ever present danger from anti-aircraft fire, as Peter Downward had discovered. The Korean winter was harsh, but special clothing, engine heater tents and flameless heaters ensured that flying continued – though sleeping bags were not issued to all ranks until September 1952. Before the advent of winter clothing, pilots resorted to stuffing their flying kit with newspaper. Most sorties were flown above 5000 feet out of consideration of light flak. It was also necessary, in any case, to fly high in order to keep clear of the path of friendly shellfire. Precautions notwithstanding, the aircraft were frequently rocked by shells and one pilot who underestimated the power of a US 155mm 'Long-Tom' found his Auster nearly inverted. When ranging and registering these guns they sometimes had to fly on winter days at over 13,000 feet, where the cold in the unheated cockpits was numbing. In contrast, during the hot, humid summer weather, the pilots often flew dressed in vests and PT shorts. One of the pilots was Captain Gerry Joyce, who in later years would recall his time spent in the 'Land of the Morning Calm.' As the Flight's role involved taking reconnaissance photos of enemy encampments and troop movements, they were required to know the terrain intimately. The Flight was based immediately behind the front line with its 'office' being an underground bunker. Nor were the living quarters any more attractive. He later wrote, describing general infantry conditions in Korea,

'There was often six inches of water underfoot in the underground living quarters and ice or snow in the winter. We lived in these conditions, below ground, for two and a half years. The contents could be summarized as oil stove, bed and grocery box furniture. The worst part of it was the rats which would sometimes crawl across the men's faces. Second to this was the constant threat of enemy patrols attacking the underground bunkers at night. These stealthy patrols would run silently in rubber running shoes and regularly infiltrated at night – hence everyone slept with a carbine in hand. The Officers' Mess was a wooden hut named "Casa Mitty", where we learned to play chess by the light of a lantern.'

His description of the flying conditions is equally succinct,

'Each pilot completed two sorties a day and round the clock sorties if attacks were mounted by either side. We flew from an airstrip that had been bulldozed along the River Imjin. I habitually flew low and fast, twisting and turning in and out of the mountainous terrain. The enemy tended to fire directly at the Auster and, having no knowledge of making allowance for deflection, the bullets usually passed harmlessly behind. For added security and just in case a stray bullet might find its mark, I always sat on my logbook!'

He also flew out to the aircraft carriers HMS *Glory* and HMS *Ocean* for special operations up the coast. Gerry flew hundreds of hours over enemy territory in the course of a continuous tour of duty lasting some eighteen months on operations. One night in particular his luck nearly ran out,

Left to right: Major "Warby" Warburton, Captain Peter Tees RCA, Captain John Crawshaw, Captain Gerry Joyce and Captain Brian Forward RAA at Fort George.

'I became lost over enemy lines at night. Exhausted, I grew more disoriented and the fuel gauge of my Auster fell lower and lower. I felt that now I had finally "bought it". I was twenty-eight – I had a lifetime before me. Then – suddenly – just as I thought that this was "it", a full moon emerged from behind the clouds. Far below, snaking away and lit by the brilliant moonlight, I was able to make out the familiar twists and turns of the River Imjin. My heart leapt; I knew every inch of this terrain and now that I could see the Imjin I was able to re-establish my position and make my way back to base and to safety. Moonlight over the River Imjin had saved my life.'

Gerry Joyce was also accorded a high degree of praise by his OC, Major Hailes, writing in December 1952,

'The provision of winter clothing, materials for building etc. to guard against the severe Korean winter has been excellent. Section huts, messes etc. are now very warm and for this a great deal of credit must be given to the Flight QM, Captain G.W.C. Joyce RA, whose energy in obtaining these commodities, not always by "honest" means, has been continuous.'

1913 Flight was also equipped with Auster 6s, to which was added a T7 in November 1952 and also, from January 1952, a US Army Cessna L-19A, reportedly as a result of the Corps Commander, Lieutenant General John W. 'Iron Mike' O'Danniel's, 'concern at the discomfort the GOC, Major General Cassels suffered when travelling about in an Auster.' The GOC had endured an unfortunate upside-down landing in an Auster flown by his Canadian ADC. It was rumoured that the deal was sealed with a case of Scotch. The L-19 'Bird Dog' was improved by the addition of RAF roundels and red plates with two stars attached on both sides of the engine cowling. Captain Tony Brown was appointed the 'chauffeur' of GOC's 'staff car'. Flight Commander Peter Downward later commented, 'Army 754 was truly a very comfortable kite to fly in and handled beautifully.' However, for a number of years afterwards he was pursued by MOD accountants as, due to the unorthodox nature of the transaction, the correct paperwork could not be found to decommission an aircraft which had never actually been formally part of Her Majesty's forces. Interestingly, in a letter written in 1977 to Brigadier Peter Mead, Colonel Bob Begbie, who was then a young captain flying Air OP sorties in Korea with the 3rd US Light Aviation Section, noted that the Flight had 'inherited his plush, new L-19.' Begbie not only flew the Bird Dog operationally, but also the Stinson L-5 Sentinel, Aeronca L-16 Grasshopper, Ryan L-17B Navion and North American T6F Texan; being awarded the US Air Medal for his efforts. In the 1960s he achieved further distinction when he became OC 656.

Downward was succeeded as OC 1913 Flight by Captain Peter Wilson in 1952, while in the same year Gower was followed by Major Jim Hailes. Peter Wilson's memories of Fort George include the abundance of golden-plumed pheasants in the vicinity. Shotguns were borrowed from the Americans and the rations were duly supplemented.

Another unorthodox arrangement was made on 6 February 1952, when the death of King George VI and the succession of Queen Elizabeth II was announced. The Divisional Artillery fired a 101 gun salute – with a live shell every fifteen seconds into the Chinese lines, following the order, 'The King is dead, long live the Queen. One hundred and one gun salute, begin!' A certain degree of black humour was the rule, as is evident from the following entry in the Operational Record Book of 26 October 1952,

'Major H.B. Warburton, DFC, RA took a bath, a hazardous and unpleasant business at this time of year and Captain Tees RCHA washed what was left of his hair. Warby celebrated his 1903rd hour in the air before heading off to Malaya as OC 1907.'

During two years of operational service in Korea, Flight personnel from both flights were awarded one DSO, thirteen DFCs, two DFMs, one AFM, two BEMs, four US Air Medals and fourteen Mentions in Dispatches. It was not without cost in human life; on 5 June 1952, Captain B.T. 'Joe' Luscombe of the Royal Australian Artillery was shot down by anti-aircraft fire. The rudder cable of his Auster 6 was severed, the aircraft stalled and he flew into a small cliff just near the landing strip as he tried to land. Early in August, American backpack type parachutes were issued and a week afterwards Captain Joe Liston, of the Royal Canadian Artillery, was shot down while flying VF561, baled out and was taken prisoner. He was eventually released at the end of hostilities. Towards the end of that year, on 9 December, Gunner Alan 'Nobby' Bond died at the age of only twenty, when a store hut caught fire. On 12 May 1953, LAC K. 'Tubby' Goodfield, who was just nineteen, went up with Captain Ken Perkins on a regular sortie in an Auster 6, but on their way back hit a low slung cable and came down in the swollen Imjin River, the aircraft flipping over onto its back. Perkins managed to get clear but despite his best efforts, Goodfield became tangled up with some flotsam, was carried downstream and drowned. Only five days later, Sergeant Cameron and Craftsman Duffy of 1913 Flight were carrying out a dawn recce sortie when the aircraft was damaged by a shell exploding just below, they both baled out and became prisoners of war. They were released three months later.

Coronation Day, 2 June 1953, was also the day when the news of the conquest of Everest by Edmund Hilary and Sherpa Tenzing was announced. The OC 1903 Flight, Major Wilfred Harris MC, was busy organizing the Flight's celebrations and, having got them underway in the Officers' Mess, jumped into a Jeep to drive round to the Sergeants' Mess to do likewise. This entailed crossing the airstrip. It is not altogether clear what happened but it seems that two American fighter aircraft came in over the strip waggling their wings. Whether Harris thought this was some kind of acknowledgement

Major Wilfred Harris MC, who sadly was killed in an accident on 2 June 1953.

of the celebrations going on will never be known. It appears now, that they were in fact trying to warn of the imminent attempt by another of their pilots to land a badly damaged Republic F-84 Thunderjet. Upon touching down, its undercarriage collapsed, the aircraft slewed and careered off the runway into the path of the Jeep. It was completely destroyed and Major Harris died instantly. However, the Thunderjet pilot survived. Peter Wilson also had a dangerous encounter with an out of control aeroplane when a badly damaged T6 Texan attempted a forced landing at Fort George. The pilot's vision was obscured by engine oil covering the canopy and he did not realize that he was in fact chasing Peter down the adjacent vehicle track as he bounced along the strip. The danger was not over even as it came to rest, as a malfunction caused its underwing rockets to fire. Peter fell and cartwheeled into the paddy, which was also a minefield. He was rescued by Ken Perkins and spent the next week in hospital with severe cuts and bruises.

Naturally there were lighter moments as well and some of these were recalled by National Serviceman and aircraft mechanic, Clive Howe,

'Entertainment came from the UK and the USA and at 'rear div' which had an ideal open air auditorium that could hold over 1000 sitting on a hillside. I met Danny Kaye and Ted Ray personally. Kaye flew with Major Gower in my aircraft, VF582, after his show. He did not enjoy the trip! I enjoyed three R & Rs in Tokyo, arriving at Ebisu Leave Camp, getting de-loused and kitted out with fresh kit, then off to the Ginza for five "lost days", what an experience for a nineteen year old. Money was no object as we spent no money in Korea and the rate in Japan at that time was 1000 yen to the pound. The Ginza Beer Hall was the Commonwealth Division's drinking den and every serviceman who ever went to Tokyo came away with a picture taken there.'

He remains deeply proud of his service with the Flight and of its contribution to the war,

'It was a small, very efficient unit which at any time only comprised about fifty servicemen who, despite horrendous weather conditions, lack of proper clothing, housing and heating, survived, and all aircraft were operational except when extreme weather prevented. The Flight flew some 3000 AOP sorties. Captain Derek Jarvis alone flew 639 operational hours in Korea, which included 306 operational sorties, 304 air shoots and 60 night landings.'

An armistice was signed on 27 July 1953, and an uneasy peace has prevailed over the following half century and more. Most of the flying for the last eighteen months or so in Korea involved patrolling the Demilitarized Zone (DMZ), which entailed flying six hours per day in sorties of one or

18 March 1954 – A member of the US Special Forces practices on the ground before his parachute drop from Auster AOP 6 VF516.

two hours in length, up and down the divisional boundaries at a height of above 5000 feet and 1000 yards back from the southern edge of the DMZ. A considerable amount of time was also devoted to photographic sorties and to conducting practice artillery shoots. One activity which gave the pilots considerable pleasure was a fighter evasion exercise with the Gloster Meteor F.8s of No 77 Squadron RAAF, which showed that the Austers were 'surprisingly capable, under most circumstances, of avoiding an attack by up to two jet fighters.' Another interesting exercise sortie was carried out by 1913 Flight on 18 March 1954, which involved US Special Forces parachuting from the Austers over the Han River north of Seoul. Both Flights returned to the UK early in 1955.

Malaya Part II

Following a fact-finding visit by the new Conservative Secretary of State for the Colonies, Oliver Lyttelton, it was decided that the posts of High Commissioner and Director of Operations would be combined, and on 5 February 1952, this appointment was taken up by General Sir Gerald Templar. Given supreme and unified control, he would prove to be a dynamic leader, sweeping aside the complacency which still manifested itself in some parts of the administration. He was vested with wide powers with the aim of defeating the CTs utterly and gave assurances that Britain would not quit its responsibilities until Malaya was a stable self-governing nation. To a large extent he refined and improved the Briggs Plan. The Security Forces had been greatly expanded with more than 16,000 police and 47,000 auxiliaries, supported by up to 23 infantry battalions from the UK, Nepal, Australia, New Zealand, Fiji and East Africa. During the course of 1952, slowly but surely, the tide began to turn against the CTs.

One of the most significant improvements for 656 Squadron concerned communications. Several aircraft were fitted with VHF radio sets. These were deemed a great success, giving improved communication over a large area and also access to homing facilities, with good cover from Singapore to Taiping via Kuala Lumpur, and in the centre, cover from a relay station over a smaller area. Individual aircrew and Austers co-operated successfully with Bristol Brigands in target identification using VHF communications. Full authority was obtained 'after a long hard battle' for fitting the trailing aerial modification to all aircraft. This may well have been considered something of a mixed blessing for Captain Peter Wilson, who landed at Kuala Lumpur one day, only to be told he had blacked out 'the whole of KL' by forgetting to wind in his aerial, which he had managed to drag through a power line.

The Squadron suffered a fatality on 13 March, when Staff Sergeant Dennis Gay of 1911 Flight spun in on approach to Kulai Besar, about twenty miles from Johore Bahru, while flying Auster 6, VF576. The aircraft impacted in a rubber plantation, sadly Gay was killed and his passenger, Sergeant Hill, was injured. David Oldman had a fairly fortunate escape when testing out a new airstrip. He did a low-level run over the strip and when turning on completion of the run his propeller disintegrated. He had no option but to land straight ahead in a swamp. The aircraft came to rest upside down and he described himself later as, 'a very muddy officer.' The three most experienced pilots were the OC, the indefatigable 'Warby', who had returned for another operational tour and Captain L.J. Wheeler, DFC, the OC of 1914 Flight. Warby had a lucky escape a little later in the year when his engine lost power and eventually failed some fifteen miles inland from the East Coast, giving him 'an unpleasant ten minutes.' He managed to maintain sufficient height to make a forced landing. It did not curb his enthusiasm, as he volunteered for a short spell in Korea, from whence he returned 'having completed his third row of medal ribbons.' Other postings to Korea during the year included Captain J.M.H. Hailes, who assumed command of 1903 Flight.

A more serious accident was experienced by 1914 Flight's Sergeant J. Rolley in Auster 6 when, on 3 June, he became overdue on a reconnaissance flight with a police officer. He had taken off with an unserviceable wireless set so that no contact could be made with him throughout his sortie. A search was instituted and the position of the survivors was spotted. The ground forces who went in to meet them never actually found them, but they turned up on their own forty-eight hours later. Sergeant Rolley was able to report that he had been 'out climbed by a mountain' after having flown up a valley in which he was unable to turn.

David Oldman's time as OC expired at the end of June, returning to the UK for 'no doubt a life of ease if not glory, on the staff.' He was replaced by the newly promoted Major Wheeler. Oldman was a real AOP veteran, having first learned to fly on No 3 Course with Denis Coyle in 1941. He was accorded the following valedictory remarks in the Squadron Newsletter, written in a more innocent age,

'The Squadron lost the guiding hand of its Commander since March 1950. There were a series of farewells throughout the Federation culminating in a gay week-end in Kuala Lumpur. His influence, and figure, will be much missed in Malaya.'

It was reported that a safe and successful target marker had been produced to replace the faithful old Very cartridge, made from a No 8 Smoke Generator, ignited by a No 4 Pull Switch and a small piece of safety fuse, the whole being held together by a locally produced bracket. It produced smoke for three minutes and became known as the Hawkins Marker, as it was invented by a captain of that name. Its only limitation was that it had to be released at a height great enough for the device to ignite before it hit the ground. This proved to be between 300 to 500 feet.

A not so successful experiment was the 'crop-spraying Agricultural Auster, VF560.' The aim was to spray diesoline and destroy vegetable crops grown by the CTs in small clearings of five to ten acres, normally surrounded by tall jungle. It was noted that, 'mechanically, the machine has been made to work: that is to say, drops of water do come out of the spreader or boom. It also flies – just.' The estimated flying height was not less than 250 feet above ground level. Most of these clearings were on very steep mountainsides, which must have served to concentrate the mind of a spray-equipped pilot. The crop spraying machine was finally returned to 390 MU for reconversion. The trials proved that under ideal conditions the maximum liquid output was 42 gallons per acre which was too small a volume for the task.

By the end of June the Squadron announced that it had achieved a grand total, since 1948, of 20,000 hours in 27,000 sorties, which represented,

> 'Much hard, sometimes exciting, but all too often, monotonous routine flying on the part of the pilots, many sun-scorched hours of maintenance by the airmen and great numbers of miles, signals, and letters chalked up by the remainder.'

A signal of appreciation was received from the GOC,

> 'The GOC Malaya wishes to congratulate No 656 Air OP Squadron on having completed twenty thousand hours of flying. This is a considerable achievement and is even more impressive when considered with the number of sorties flown and the infinitesimal accident rate. The figures demonstrate the efficiency and keenness both of the pilots and the ground staff who carry out the maintenance. Please pass on my congratulations to all ranks on this first class record.'

It was felt that the Squadron Newsletter should add a few thoughts on those 20,000 hours, in the shape of a letter from 'Banger' [Major Wheeler] to 'Dick' [possibly Captain R.D. Wilkinson],

> 'The flying roles have varied but slightly. In the early days, much emphasis was placed on air recces after incidents, searches for patrols out of contact and supply drops. With the overall change in the role of the security forces generally (The Briggs Plan), the emphasis now is upon visual recces for ground troop commanders and to locate food producing areas, photo recce, casualty evacuation in conjunction with the helicopters and, oddly enough, shooting the field battery. Recently, 1914 Flight flew fifteen hours Air OP, Lieutenant Joe Sellers completing ten shoots in a morning, an unusual number in Malaya. [As the 1950s wore on many thousands of rounds were

fired as they were approaching their "fire-by" or expiry date and it seemed a shame to waste them by dumping them in the sea.]

There is always an element of doubt about a CT camp. Not only are they difficult to find but having found them one has to convince the local units or formation that they are a worthwhile target. This reluctance may be forgiven when one remembers that, depending upon the position, it may well take anything up to a week for the troops to walk there. The simplest answer always is an airstrike, but some advantage of this is lost if no troops are immediately available to follow-up. One of the camps found by 1902 Flight was such a target. It was subsequently discovered that the camp was not only much larger than first thought, but that it was occupied by about sixty men at the time of the strike.

These roles of course are divorced from the communication work which in fact still makes up the greater part of the flying. Wearisome though this may be, it is undoubtedly worthwhile, as its saves not only time, but also allows manpower to be used for operational tasks rather than on road convoy duties.

The development of airstrips has gone on throughout the whole three years. Quite apart from those on the West Coast which are now to be found in almost every town of any size, in North Johore and Pahang, Kampong Baapa, Kampong Aur, Gambir, Temerloh, Jerantut, Bentong and Raub have all been opened up. South Kelantan began to be opened up, but owing to lack of demands and shortage of bandits, is reverting again, except for Gua Musang which has been extended to Beaver specifications. Altogether there are now about eighty landing grounds in constant use.

The most important advantage the AOP 6 has over the Mk V is that we are able to carry a wireless set at all times and with the production of a trailing aerial the pilot is in constant touch on the Squadron Command Net. You will probably readily agree that this can be most comforting. It has also the added facilities of longer range, a self-starter, better vision and so on. It is, however, unquestionably more troublesome technically and not nearly so efficient and reliable as the Mk V. The Gipsy VII engine is most unpopular. During the Emergency almost every single VIP who resides in, or has visited Malaya, has been carried in an aircraft of the Squadron and also officers from the American and French Armies, the Military Attaché to Siam and US Military Attaché.'

In fact the Squadron was underselling itself – it celebrated 50,000 hours in 1953 and had actually completed nearly 35,000 hours by the end of 1952. The Squadron monthly record by then stood at 1320 hours and the Flight monthly record achieved by 1914 Flight was 373 hours. It was thought worthy of special note that Captain R.J. Farwell, 'be it known a married officer,' in August achieved a personal total of ninety-three hours.

Another important issue was the provision of an adequate and comprehensive jungle survival kit which included,

'On the one hand every conceivable device for making signals, including all types of smoke and marker balloons, and on the other equipment for survival, marching compasses, self-heating soups, rations and warm clothing.'

In support of this, the example was cited of a DH Hornet F3 from No 33 Squadron which disappeared on a strike only 500 yards from 1911 Flight Airstrip at Seremban. The sudden break in radio contact made it almost certain that it had crashed near the target area. Despite the following factors, namely a helicopter was nearby and listening out when the crash occurred, two Austers and a Sunderland were airborne near the target area, they all failed to locate the crash. It was eventually found by ground troops, after which a few broken branches became apparent from the air.

However, it was not all hard work and no play, there was plenty of time devoted to a wide variety of sporting activities, both organized and rather more informal, as towards the end of the year the Newsletter reported,

'Op Copley for us [and one section of 1914 Flight in particular] is extremely popular. It should be explained to those unfamiliar with Malaya that Kota Bahru, the capital of the somewhat remote, predominantly Malay, and very colourful state of Kelantan is, especially in the minds of those who listen to travellers' stories, a sort of South Sea island paradise. It is in fact the nearest thing one can find in Malaya to the popular conception of a South Pacific scene. It has a silver beach (called the Beach of Passionate Love), it has a tropical moon, it has waving palm trees and it does have dancing girls. In this kind of atmosphere CTs are seldom found, and at present few operations requiring air support take place in that state. Those that are mounted are in Ulu Kelantan some fifty miles south of the capital. Op Copley was one such. The keenness of the bachelor pilots to be sent on any tasks to Kota Bahru is quite astonishing and only exceeded by the enthusiasm displayed by soldiers and airmen.'

To be fair, it was later recorded that by the time the Auster returned to Taiping it had flown 184 hours in a little over six weeks. Some thousands of square miles of the remoter regions of Malaya were covered during this period and much useful information was produced. In November, 1914 Flight, which was, of course, the link with the original 656 Squadron, completed 10,000 hours flying since the declaration of the Emergency. Two pilots in particular were mentioned, Captain Bruce Venour, who, in February 1950, became the first pilot serving in Malaya to complete 1000 hours and Lieutenant Joe Sellers, who in three years had flown more than 1400 hours in Malaya alone. In the same month the Squadron said goodbye to the largest batch of National Servicemen ever sent off at one time, nineteen in all,

'All these soldiers have served with the Squadron for eighteen months and we have been proud of their achievements. Some during this time have reached the exalted grade of Driver/Operator Class II. About half will serve their part-time service with Auxiliary Squadrons and we wish all of them the best of good fortune.'

A new air route for communication was opened during December by Major Wheeler, who, 'after much careful thought and preparation,' took a policeman from Alor Star in Kedah, to Songkhla in Siam.

It was decided that the operational emphasis had changed sufficiently to alter the designation of two flights, 1907 and 1911, from Air OP to Light Liaison and that of the unit as a whole to 656 AOP/LL Squadron. The fact that this implied a reduced scale of

The Squadron practices formation flying above Kuala Lumpur. Seen here are a pair of AOP 6s.

MT was not looked upon with any favour. Such was the increasing scale of demands on the Squadron's services that a case was made for the raising of the second section in the Light Liaison Flights, with an addition of four aircraft to be distributed one per Flight. It was anticipated that the arrival in theatre, early in 1953, of the Sikorsky S-55 Helicopters of 848 Naval Air Squadron and the increase in the number of RAF S-51s [now of No 194 Squadron] might on the one hand give the Squadron some further interesting flying and on the other, relieve it of some communication work, 'We await the developments with interest.'

At the start of the first Newsletter in 1953, the OC described the various types of duty that the Squadron was required to undertake,

'Firstly, the square by square search by flights of their entire areas to provide such up to date information on terrorist activity as can be seen. These recces are done as and when possible, the aim being to cover the whole area about once a quarter. For specific large operations reconnaissance of a selected area is often made about a month in advance. Alternatively, we may be asked to find some particular piece of information, or to fly a battalion or company commander over his area for a general look/see. It also includes flights for specialists like the Protectors of Aborigines, who can estimate the number of Sakai living in any particular valley from the amount of visible cultivation. Other important tasks include vectoring patrols into camps or clearings, looking for patrols out of wireless contact, selecting landing zones for casualty evacuations and a most important and popular task, the marking of occasional targets for air strikes. The other familiar tasks, communications, Air OP, supply dropping, PR and leaflet dropping, continue in much the same proportion. Each flight now has a fairly comprehensive intelligence organization where all the information which they have collected is recorded.'

The leaflet dropping was part of a very significant psychological warfare operation, normally large transport or bomber aircraft were used, but the Austers came into their own when accurate drops of limited quantities of leaflets were needed, often when the requirement was to exploit rapidly a local success achieved by security forces on the ground. The OC continued with some remarks about target marking and how it had been improved and refined,

'After some trials with an Avro Lincoln B1 heavy bomber squadron from Singapore it was eventually decided that a normal No 80 phosphorus grenade, operated by a static line and using bomb safety wire in lieu of the normal pin, was the best answer. The duration of smoke is short but the technique allows the bombers to attack one minute after the Auster has marked. To allow for errors in timing, for operations, the Hawkins and the 80 grenade have been combined. It is said that the use of this marker materially assists the accuracy of the Lincolns when bombing in formation.'

Colonel Michael Hickey commented on this aspect of operations in an e-mail to the author,

'Until then the RAF, lacking good marking, were simply unloading FEAF's huge stocks of iron bombs onto designated jungle areas; once 656 developed reasonably reliable markers it was possible to attack precision targets by day and then night, with spectacular results; the major developer of the refined technique was Captain Colin Pickthall, who got a DFC for it. Our liaison with the heavies (Lincolns) and the fighter bombers of 33 and 45 Squadrons (Hornets) was very close.'

The OC then moved on to a description of a contraption which had been designed to assist supply dropping,

'1914 Flight has produced a small hook and spring device known as the Selrick Dropper (specifications by Captain Sellers, design and prototype by Corporal Rickards and execution by No 1 Station Workshops) which enables supply dropping to be done entirely by the pilot. Not only can this be done with much greater accuracy than before, but the absence of a dispatcher enables a much greater load to be carried. The articles to be dropped are suspended outside the aircraft, dropped, and the next lot hung outside, all by the pilot; 216lbs of rations i.e. forty-eight men for one day, have been carried and despatched by the pilot.'

Concluding his final Newsletter with some statistical gems,

'During this quarter all our previous records were surpassed by a margin which one would have thought scarcely possible. The total flying for the quarter was 3989 hours of which 1574 were flown in March. 1902 Flight now holds the monthly record with no less than 483 hours and Captain F.C. Russell holding the individual monthly record with 103 hours. He was closely followed by Captain C.H.C. Pickthall of 1907 Flight, with 101 hours. After March it was suggested that 1902 Flight might find it simpler to record the hours spent on the ground.'

He also found the time to write a letter of appreciation to the Auster Company which was reprinted in its house journal,

'A letter we have recently received from Major L.J. Wheeler, OC 656 AOP/LL Squadron operating in Malaya, reveals the high serviceability that can be obtained from an Auster, he writes, "a new T7 aircraft (WE 610) issued to us in December last year flew over 300 hours to first minor inspection and was not unserviceable for a single day during the thirteen week period. This is a very praiseworthy performance especially when one considers the climatic conditions in which the aircraft are parked".'

Back in England the seventh annual Squadron Reunion Dinner was held on 21 March, at the Lotus Restaurant in the Haymarket in London at a price per head of 11s : 6d. It was decided that the Squadron's 10th Anniversary should be celebrated by the presentation of a plaque, with a suggested subscription of five shillings a head. This was to be the last such Newsletter for almost fifty years. Sadly, Arthur Eaton, who was the driving force behind the Reunions, died in 1955.

At the end of June 1953, Major L.J. Wheeler left the Squadron to take over 1903 Flight in Korea following the tragic death of Major Harris. He was replaced by Major A.F. 'Sandy' Robertson, who wrote,

'Banger has been with the Squadron in Malaya for three years and was Commanding Officer during the last twelve months. His efforts were untiring in maintaining its

Starting the engine of Auster T7 WE614 by 'prop-swinging' at Noble Field, Kuala Lumpur.

The 7th Annual Squadron Reunion Dinner was held on 21 March 1953 at the Lotus Restaurant, Haymarket, London.

efficiency in the war against the terrorists. The high reputation enjoyed by the unit at the moment is a tribute to his energy and efficiency.'

The promised Fleet Air Arm helicopters had indeed arrived at Sembawang, courtesy of the ferry carrier HMS *Perseus* on 8 January 1953, and under the command of Lieutenant Commander S.H. Suthers, DSC. The pilots carried out theatre familiarization by means of individual attachments to an 'ever helpful' Air OP flight. After they had worked up in February, March and April, the helicopters took part in their initial operations alongside 1914, 1907 and 1911 Flights respectively. The Sikorsky S-55 was a more capable machine than the S-51, it could carry four or five fully armed troops, depending upon the size of the clearing into which it was operating, or alternatively, three stretcher cases and two walking wounded. By means of a quid pro quo, a deck landing exercise took place in May with HMS *Unicorn*. Eight pilots took part, each doing three or four carrier landings. It was noted that,

'A wind speed of 15–17 knots over the deck seemed to be very adequate. As each fresh pilot landed on, the Captain came onto the flightdeck and shook hands with the pilot in the aircraft. His greeting may have been mingled with relief.'

In August, the first large-scale spraying operation with S-55s (HAR 21s) took place in Johore. This was known as *Cyclone*, and 1902 Flight provided the up-to-date information on thirty clearings. In order to safeguard the spraying helicopters, all clearings were marked by Auster and strafed by Hornets before the S-55 arrived with the defoliant to begin its work, which would otherwise certainly have been vulnerable to ground fire. The majority of these operations took place between late 1953 and early 1954.

Further in-theatre help and instruction was provided to four RAF officers who were earmarked for the newly formed Scottish Aviation Pioneer CC1 element of 1311 Transport Flight at Seletar. Each was attached to a flight for three weeks and flew a number of hours in Austers. Members of 656 Squadron devoutly hoped that they would take a considerable load off its communication flying. The Pioneers could carry four passengers, or up to 1000lbs of freight, and had a remarkable short field performance, being able to take-off in 75 yards and land within 66 yards.

It was noted that the number of terrorist provoked incidents had dropped from a total of about 6000 in 1951, to some 1100 in 1953, and that the average monthly terrorist elimination rate for 1953 was 110 (including kills, captures and surrenders). It was thought that the decrease was due to the fact that a good deal of CT effort had been diverted from provoking incidents, to existing in the jungle. With the increase of food control and pressure by the Security Forces, CTs have had to retire into deep jungle areas and grow food in order to live. The Squadron flew a total of 16,665 hours during the year, including its 50,000th Firedog hour on 5 October,

'And in case we are accused of hour bashing, it was not a case of looking for work, but turning down many of the less important demands. The importance of the Austers to Security Forces operating in the jungle has been realized to an increasing extent. Flight Commanders have worked hard to educate units in obtaining the best results from light aircraft and it is true to say that no military operation now takes place without the information and support of the Squadron. The advent of helicopters in Malaya has transformed many operations which previously would have entailed hours of hacking through jungle. Troops are easily lifted in a matter of minutes to within striking distance of their objective. Much of our work consists of co-operating with the helicopters in both troop lifting and casualty evacuation.'

In 1954 the aircraft establishment was raised by five, making a total of thirty-one Austers. After a certain amount of debate, the proposal of a fifth flight was turned down and it was agreed to absorb the extra aircraft into the existing flights, with the intention of positioning aircraft as follows; Taiping, Benta, Noble Field (Kuala Lumpur) eight each, Seremban and Sembawang six apiece. However, this was still an aspiration as the supply of new Austers was unable to fulfil the demand. The utilization rate was also increased to seventy hours per aircraft per month.

Writing many years later, Colonel Michael Hickey described life at Benta,

'All who served at Benta airstrip will remember it as long as they live. Hacked out of a rubber plantation during the Japanese occupation as an emergency landing ground, and guarded by a company of infantry (for it was in the heart of a "black" area), it boasted a few palm-thatched attap huts and a clutch of tents. The aircraft lived in the open, exposed to the worst the Malayan climate could provide. Dense mists enshrouded the treetops and prohibited early morning flying. By 0900 the first Austers were about their business; by noon, the daily build-up of cumulonimbus thunderheads was looming in all directions; in the mid-afternoon, torrential rain, fierce electric storms, high winds and extreme turbulence made light-aircraft flying a hazardous pastime.'

Sadly, a fatal accident took place on 21 January 1954. Auster 6, VF604, with Sergeant J. Perry as pilot and Flight Lieutenant Jack Maulden of 194 Squadron as passenger, took off to carry out a weather reconnaissance in the mountains east of Kuala Lumpur. Despite a very large-scale search no trace of the aircraft or its crew could be found. At the time of the accident the aircraft was carrying a number of No 80 Grenades to mark clearings during a *Cyclone* operation and it was thought that the latter may have caused the accident. [The jungle was once more reluctant to give up its secrets and the wreckage was not found until March 1957, when a Gurkha patrol came across it covered in creepers; also lying around were a rifle, a compass, eight hand grenades, a wristwatch and other personal effects.] Another crew was fortunate not to suffer a similar fate, on 31 March, Staff Sergeant R. Skinley, in Auster 6,VF560, with Lieutenant Michael Hickey as observer, was nearing Kroh while flying beneath low cloud. In attempting to clear a ridge he failed to

When moving from one base to another, the pilots repositioned the aircraft, while the rest of the personnel and equipment had to travel by road, escorted by the Squadron's own Dingo scout cars.

appreciate that he was in a downdraught and the aircraft crashed into the jungle. The Auster went through the jungle canopy and slid down a large tree. On hitting the ground it caught fire and was totally destroyed. Remarkably, Skinley and Hickey were able to emerge from the crash and walked out of the jungle onto the Baling-Kroh road. A third accident was rather more self-inflicted, Captain D.W. Smith was flying Auster 6, WJ378, in Johore on 2 July, to mark a target for an airstrike. In order to attract the attention of the Hornet leader he fired a Very pistol through the chute provided. The bomb rack, loaded with flares, obstructed the exit and the aircraft caught fire. The fire extinguisher lever was extremely stiff and could not be operated with one hand. The pilot then landed in a swamp without damage to himself but with considerable damage to the airframe. The Hornets provided top cover until the pilot was rescued by helicopter. As the OC later wrote,

'The lesson from this accident would appear to be the necessity of mechanical safeguards to prevent pilots doing silly things in moments of stress. It was well known that bomb racks, when fitted, obstructed firing chutes and a flying order was issued. Intense concentration on marking the target caused the pilot to forget the flying order and react automatically to previous training.'

An interesting operation was subsequently reported on in the Auster News,

'It is worth placing on record the facts of a unique operation carried out in Malaya early in March by a destroyer and a military Auster. The destroyer was the 2600-ton HMS *Defender*, one of Britain's most modern warships. Slowly sailing up the Johore River and avoiding the many sand-banks and reefs: the *Defender* passed through many miles of uncharted waters and finally arrived at a position from which she could bombard Communist guerrilla hideouts. As the *Defender* dropped anchor and opened fire with her six 4.5 inch guns, an Auster arrived overhead and proceeded to direct the fire by radio. Soon after the bombardment had finished Gurkha troops moved in on the shattered jungle hideouts and mopped up any survivors.'

Some technical advances were noted, firstly regarding target marking, 'in fact, after years of experiment we think we have the answer.' A number of aircraft were modified with the Light Series Bomb Carrier mounted on a metal frame under the fuselage. It was manually operated by means of a Bowden cable mounted to the right and just aft of the pilot's seat. The actual marker was a Flare Reconnaissance No 2 Mk 1, with a double parachute. Each weighed about 18lbs and a total of four were carried in the rack. Lincoln and Hornet crews were reported to be pleased with the volume and duration of smoke. The number of strike missions flown peaked in 1954, with a total of 426 during the year. The Avro Lincolns were from No 83 Squadron RAF and No 1 Squadron RAAF. In order to allow the CTs the minimum amount of time to run for cover, the gap between the Austers and the bombers was often as little as ninety seconds. Typically, five Lincolns would drop sixty-five 1000lb bombs, which made a devastating impact, though later assessment by foot patrols of the damage caused was difficult, as, understandably, they did not care overmuch for patrolling though tangled undergrowth choked with splintered bamboo.

Eleven VHF wireless sets had been installed in the aircraft and the air wireless fitters and mechanics struggled manfully to sort out the snags despite a lack of proper publications and test equipment. It was noted that generally, transmission was a lot better than reception. The performance of the PTR 61 did not match that of the Ecko CE1140 sets which, unfortunately, seemed always to be fitted to aircraft which subsequently suffered an accident. The lack of trailing aerials was regarded with great disfavour,

'One third of the Squadron aircraft are without trailing aerials – a serious matter when one considers that 4/5ths of Malaya is jungle. The new Auster 6s that reach us are fitted with Mod 355 (a hole in the floor!) And the complementary mod (the winch drum and bits and pieces) are not available in the country. Our five T7s are also without trailing aerials. We made our own at one time but were told we mustn't and are now waiting for somebody else to do it.'

However, the delivery of a more modern version of the Auster was keenly awaited,

'We have been promised two dual Auster Mk 9 aircraft in March 1955, and a further five non-dual machines in June 1955. These aircraft are awaited with eager anticipation, although the promised dates are treated with a certain amount of scepticism!'

In June, General Sir Gerald Templer left Malaya and the functions of High Commissioner and Director of Operations were split. Sir Donald MacGillivray was appointed civil High Commissioner and Lieutenant General Sir Geoffrey Bourne, in his capacity as GOC Malaya (renamed Malaya Command), became Director of Operations. General Templer, General Bourne, and Air Vice-Marshal Sherger visited Noble Field in May. General Templer congratulated SHQ on its layout, although 'nothing could persuade the distinguished visitors to enter the OC's newly decorated and adorned office which had had a special sprucing up for the occasion.' Sir Gerald talked with all the pilots and most of the soldiers and airmen; before leaving he said the Squadron was doing a first class job of work, its efforts being appreciated by everybody. By then the aircraft strength had reached its complement of thirty-one and not entirely tongue in cheek, the following comment was offered, but probably not directly to the VIP guests,

> 'With a monthly task of over 2000 hours we wonder if this is not the largest and most flown Squadron in history and if the title of Wing (with appropriate promotions) would not be more fitting. The fact that the pilots fly between 75 and 100 hours a month and the aircraft, which when not actually flying, stand out in the open in a rigorous climate, achieve 100 hours per month, is a very great tribute to pilots, ground crew and aircraft alike.'

In July the Director of Operations was able to announce without fear of contradiction that, 'the threat of armed revolution is now broken.' These regular Newsletters are such a valuable source of contemporary information to the historian that it is of interest to include a few words from Major Robertson on the rationale behind their production,

OC, Major "Sandy" Robertson, General Sir Gerald Templer, Flight Lieutenant Niven, Captain Bath, Captain Ken Perkins and Captain G. Refoy on the occasion of the Director of Operation's visit to SHQ, Noble Field in 1954.

'It is perhaps necessary to restate the aim of this, and perhaps other, AOP newsletters. The original idea was to exchange news and views with other Squadrons and the Light Aircraft School at Middle Wallop. Due to popular demand however, the distribution list has assumed formidable proportions, but it must be stated that the quarterly Squadron newsletter in no way constitutes an official report of activities. We hope that facts are correctly presented and opinions are personal opinions of members of the Squadron. Should newsletters be bound by the rules relating to official documents much of their value would been lost.'

In the December Newsletter he provided this summary of the Squadron's recent achievements,

'From our point of view, 1954 was a year of greatly increased effort. The total number of *Firedog* hours flown to the end of December is now 77,591.55 and the number of sorties flown, 90,105. The value of Auster support has been recognized to an increasing extent and during the year 23,252 hours were flown. Put another way, this is equivalent to flying an aircraft eighty-three times around the world, or keeping five Austers airborne over the jungle every hour of every day of the year. Hours flown are, of course, only a means to an end and it is the finds which really matter. Our finds for 1954 are not published for security reasons, but in view of the present difficulty in finding CTs from the air, they are regarded as not unsatisfactory, and justify the hours spent on visual reconnaissance at between 1000 and 3000 feet with a pair of binoculars. The excellent serviceability of the Auster 6 and 7 is noteworthy – an average of 78 per cent having been attained. First and second line servicing personnel are to be congratulated on their very fine efforts.'

The first item of note in 1955 was the arrival of the Canberra B6 jet bombers of No 101 Squadron, which was soon working on strike missions with 1902 Flight. One of the first of which gave Sergeant Ken McConnell, in an Auster 6, more excitement than he really needed. He was about to mark a target at night for a Canberra strike, when he was alarmed to see sparks and a glow beneath his aircraft, due to one of his flares hanging up and catching fire prematurely. With a little difficulty he jettisoned his flares and returned to base in good order. This was the first of a series of accidents, which were due to weather conditions, pilot error, or mechanical failure.

The down draught season claimed a victim in February. Captain L.P. 'Mick' Griffiths of 1914 Flight, was attempting to clear a ridge while engaged on a visual reconnaissance in the Kuala Klawang area. Too late, he realized that he was failing to climb and while turning away crashed into primary jungle. The pilot walked out on to a main road where he was picked up by a foot patrol. Then a couple of weeks later, Captain A.B.J. Forman of 1911 Flight, suddenly found his aeroplane had no propeller, five minutes after take-off from Sembawang and at a height of 900 feet over the Naval Base. Despite the rude shock of this discovery, he put down a truly miraculous landing in the ammunition storage area, to be precise, on top of a magazine containing 500 depth charges! Crankshaft failure was the cause of the incident. A hazardous situation which was due to an entirely different cause arose some time later. An Auster 6 of 1914 Flight was seen to carry out a rapid approach and touchdown at Noble Field. Almost before the aircraft had stopped rolling an astonished ground crew saw the pilot leap out of the aircraft. It appears that as the Flight Commander, Captain Pat Musters, was on finals, a snake appeared from beneath the instrument panel and made 'threatening gestures' at him. When asked to give a full description of the close encounter he replied,

'Passing over the ridge that lay between Negri Sembilan and Selangor, I thought for a moment that I had seen a movement somewhere at the bottom edge of the windshield, where two tubular struts ran vertically down behind the instrument panel combing – a cockroach perhaps, but no, nothing. Eyes back on the horizon again – but not for long! There was something behind the instrument panel – for a forked tongue flicked and flicked again, and disappeared – just where one of those struts went down through a hole in the combing. A moment later, waving slightly from side to side, a beautiful large snake came up before my eyes, about three feet in front of face, wound around the left of those two struts, stopped and just looked at me.'

On landing, a spirited chase took place, ending in the port wing, which had to be removed before the six foot long snake was despatched by the versatile ground crew.

Regrettably, another fatal accident occurred on 29 April. Captain M.R. Mather of SHQ, who had only been with the Squadron a few months, was carrying out a leaflet drop in the Jerantut area. It is thought that the aircraft, Auster 6, VJ408, hit a tree on an estate, crashed and burnt out.

It was felt that the sharp rise in the accident rate due to pilot error required detailed analysis. From this it appeared that there was a dangerous period between 200 and 400 hours to which newly joined pilots needed to pay particular regard. It was decided that a greater amount of attention should be paid to continuation training and the first four months of a pilot's tour.

On a happier note, in June, Austers from Sembawang, Seremban and Noble Field took part in fly-pasts to celebrate the Queen's Official Birthday. The fly-past at Kuala Lumpur was a grand affair involving flights of Sycamores, Whirlwinds, Sikorskys, Pioneer CC1s, Harvard T2Bs, Vickers Valetta C1s, Lincoln B1s, Canberra B2s and Vampire FB4s, as well as the Austers.

The arrival of the Auster AOP 9 had been keenly anticipated. The last operational Auster version was considerably redesigned, with a 180 hp Bombardier engine, a full instrument panel, foot brakes and a new undercarriage, fin and rudder. The seating arrangement provided for the pilot was also a considerable boon, being upholstered in comfortable leather rather than the Mk 6's 'thin horsehair-filled biscuit', which according to one pilot was the origin of the saying, 'orficers 'as 'emorroids, sergeant pilots 'as piles.' The prototype had made its first flight from Rearsby in Leicestershire, in March 1954. In July 1955, the first production batch was delivered, accompanied by Les Leetham the Auster Company's 'test pilot, technical rep and general dogsbody,' whose job was to iron out any snags that might arise. He noted that there was some urgency behind his task,

'The Mk 6s and 7s had begun to shed their propeller hubs and as Army pilots were over hostile jungle territory and not Rearsby's green fields, so prop hub doubts were not good news.'

Auster 9 WZ670 dropping leaflets. Some 232 million leaflets were dropped by the Squadron during the Malayan Emergency.

The first Auster 9 to take to the air in Malaya was WZ670 on 14 July. It soon started to exhibit mechanical problems and having attended to these, Leetham was able to begin converting Squadron pilots, with Major Robertson as his first pupil. He was invited to visit some of the jungle airstrips to gain first-hand experience of what the pilots had to contend with on a daily basis,

> 'Perhaps it was in return for my initiation routine that I was taken to some of their "pet" strips – the hairy ones – some literally hacked out of the surrounding jungle with the felled giant trees being used as the foundation for the 400 by 30 yard runway, with a surface of the all-pervading laterite – the local red, shale type deposits with the consistency of crushed brick. With some, I was told that if you could see the strip during the approach you were too high. On one, it was advisable to land uphill and take-off downhill, regardless of wind, and it wasn't unusual to see directions in the Flight's strip manual (essential reading) that certain locations in valley bottoms had offshoot clefts in the valley sides that had to be avoided after take-off, as they quickly became blind alleys, ending abruptly before the aircraft had time to gain height and were too narrow to allow a turn. I wondered how they found out in the first place. After seeing the terrain and the strips, remembering the storms and the down draught season when aircraft could be literally pushed below the tree tops, dodgy engines etc. you could only admire and marvel at the casual professionalism, courage and skill of the Air OP pilots.'

The Squadron Newsletter also had a few comments to make,

'Originally scheduled to arrive in March, they in fact arrived in September. It was also found, that due to possible vaporization in the fuel system, they could not be flown if the ground temperature exceeded 86°F. The first four were therefore based at Noble Field and a comprehensive conversion training programme carried out during the early mornings and evenings for all pilots in the Squadron. This was run by acting Squadron Captain, Captain B.A. Allum, with the considerable assistance of Mr L.A. Leetham of Austers and Flight Sergeant C. Childs, who worked long hours and were handicapped by shortage of spares, ground equipment and publications.'

The opportunity was taken to pay tribute to the retiring types,

'Introduced into the Squadron in July 1950, Mk 6s and 7s have flown 85,372 hours in support of Emergency operations. The aircraft has been made to do a variety of tasks for which it was never designed, and although its performance and handling characteristics have caused many rude comments among pilots, its serviceability record has been excellent. From June 1954 to June 1955, an average of 79 per cent has been achieved. The oldest aircraft in the Squadron, VF626, was recently pronounced a write-off after flying some 3400 hours, using up eight new engines and ten propellers in the process.'

Two events of great political importance for the future of Malaya occurred during the summer of 1955. The first elected Federal Government took up office, and after seven years of fighting, an amnesty offer was made to the MCP. Terrorist activity slackened off, although incidents still occurred, mainly in Johore. The burning of twenty-eight estate lorries proved that the communists had by no means thrown in the sponge. Amnesty day was also the tenth anniversary of the Squadron's landing in Malaya. To mark the occasion, all flights held parties, including a very successful one in SHQ. The amnesty was not a success and the anti-terrorist war would continue into 1956 with the Malayan Government, headed by Tunku Abdul Rahman

Another milestone passed by the Squadron was the completion of its 100,000 flying hour in Malaya, which the OC calculated was nearly the same as flying one Auster around the world 332 times. A new OC arrived at the end of January in the shape of a very familiar figure, Major Wheeler returning for a second tour in command. His first thoughts contained a tribute to his predecessor,

'Major Sandy Robertson RA, returned to UK in February after nearly three years in command. Sandy guided the Squadron at the absolute peak of its efforts, he saw to the perfection of target marking technique and he had the difficult task of converting from the Mk 6 to the Mk 9, both aircraft giving considerable and unexpected mechanical troubles at the time. An efficient and popular commander, Sandy will be missed in Malaya.'

By the end of March 1956 the Squadron was all but completely re-equipped with the Auster 9. It was generally agreed that it was a great improvement on the old Mk 6, despite the fact that during the first nine months of its service, more than fifty major defects due to faulty design or bad workmanship were discovered and rectified, and as the OC pointed out,

The Straits Times celebrated the Squadron's completion of 100,000 operational flying hours in Malaya, with an article and this photograph.

On 15 January 1956 Acting Captain Mike Hickey of 656 Squadron was presented with the Distinguished Conduct Medal (Perak) by the Sultan.

'It is perhaps easy to be critical of the manufacturers, but there are a vast number of glaring faults which ought never to have occurred, or have been discovered early in life.'

The radio fit was more comprehensive, with a 10 channel VHF 1998 set for air traffic, a B47 VHF standard Army radio and an Army 62 set with a trailing aerial, the hand operated winch for which was located in the cabin roof.

Major Wheeler devoted considerable attention to the subject of flying training. The continuation syllabus for newly joined pilots was brought up to date and into line with current practice. In future the pure flying training would be undertaken by a Squadron QFI before pilots joined their flight for operational training. The first QFI was Flight Lieutenant R.S. Cooper. Continuation training exercises for the experienced pilots would henceforth be observed religiously and would be carried out as completely separate sorties, with mandatory Flight Commander's monthly checks.

Unfortunately, there were two more crashes. In the first of these, on 23 May, Sergeant Ken McConnell crashed near Ipoh after he lost control in bad weather. No less than sixty-nine sorties were flown looking for him, but to no avail. Remarkably, Sergeant McConnell survived the crash and spent the next three weeks surviving in the jungle before making his way back to civilization. He had crashed on a mountainside in thick primary jungle and had suffered injuries to his head, ribs and legs. He had the bare minimum of rations and hobbled, stumbled and crawled to a Malay village. It was quite a miraculous feat and for many years was quoted as an example of survival by sheer willpower at the Jungle Warfare School.

The second had a less happy outcome on 26 June in Negri Sembilan, when Captain Mick Griffiths of 1914 Flight hit a tree while he was in the process of making a low turn. Both the pilot and his two passengers, Majors Truss and Pahamain Gurung were killed. It was thought that a contributing factor might have been the fact that the aircraft was flying at close to maximum permitted all-up weight.

An incident on 25 October, gave ample evidence that the CTs had not yet been entirely defeated, when J.B.D. Edwards, the Assistant Manager of the Sungei Kruda estate and his escort were ambushed and killed. A search for the perpetrators on the ground and from the air was ordered. Later that morning WO2 G.D. Jenkins, the SSM, was flying low along the northern boundary of the estate, when he saw a party of eight CTs crossing the river on a raft. Jenkins dived his aircraft at them and flew so low that the CTs took to the water. He repeated this manoeuvre several times, at the same time trying to unstrap his rifle from behind his seat. The CTs by this time had realized that the aircraft was not a fighter or a bomber and began to clamber back onto the raft. Seeing this and not having been able to release his rifle, Jenkins again dived at the party, this time firing his Very Pistol at them as he passed. So successful was his 'beat up' that the CTs took to the water again, this time capsizing the raft and loosing packs and equipment into the river; and then swam back to the southern bank. Jenkins was by this time short of fuel and was forced to return to Sungei Siput airstrip, where he immediately reported the action. As a result of this incident troops on the ground managed to intercept the CTs attempting a further river crossing after dark. A considerable quantity of clothes and equipment were later recovered from the river bed at the spot where Jenkins had used his Very Pistol in anger.

An aerial photograph of Noble Field. From top to bottom, on left side of the runway, are the Light Aircraft Workshop REME, 656 Squadron HQ and the resident flight dispersal area.

The year 1957 would be a momentous one, not only for Malaya, but also for Army Aviation. For 656 Squadron, in the first instance, it would be business as usual. Major Wheeler stood down as OC in June, but 'soldiered on' as 2i/c to the new CO, Lieutenant Colonel Brian Storey. He arrived just in time to receive the full brunt of the administrative work entailed in the changeover from RAF to Army Air Corps. RAF personnel were all slowly withdrawn over a period of several months and replaced by the newly trained members of REME and a few ordinary airmen were replaced by soldiers. The Squadron was retitled 656 Light Aircraft Squadron Army Air Corps, with four flights – 2 Recce, 7 Recce, 11 Liaison and 14 Liaison and for the first time a Light Aircraft Squadron Workshop REME. Dispersal was still the order of the day and small formation parades were held at Kuala Lumpur, Ipoh, Seremban, Taiping and Sembawang on 1 September. The Squadron (and 1914 Flight) had been part of the RAF for fourteen years and nine months, of which, just one year and eight months had been spent in the UK. The day before Malaya had gained full independence – Merdeka – and from that time onwards, the maintenance of law and order would be the exclusive responsibility of the Governments of Malaya and Singapore, who naturally requested the continued assistance of the UK and Commonwealth Governments for the duration of the Emergency. The changeover caused the Squadron no loss of operational efficiency and indeed in October 1958, a fifth flight, 16 Recce, was added and stationed at Kuala Lumpur. Visitors to the Squadron in this period included the Duke and

Duchess of Gloucester and also the Director of Operations, Lieutenant General Sir James Cassels.

There was some discussion about the possibility of trialling the light Saro Skeeter AOP 12 helicopter in Malaya, but this idea was eventually abandoned due to the Skeeter's lack of range and passenger carrying ability, particularly in the hot and humid conditions that it would have encountered.

Two Austers and their crews were detached to Sandakan, North Borneo, from 10 November to 4 December for Exercise Tiger Leg, the object of which was to show the flag and assist troops and police in anti-smuggling and anti-pirate patrols and in jungle training. The detachment was commanded by Major Wheeler. The aircraft were transported by Bristol Freighters of No 41 Squadron RNZAF from Changi, 'wings off and oleo legs tied in and held by a stout jury strut.' Two vehicles and stores went by the LST *Reginald Kerr*. No startling operational successes were achieved, which was to be expected, but the high intensity of flying and splendid liaison merited the praise of all. The aircraft behaved admirably, as did the troops, who, like the officers, were generously entertained by the local residents. All left Borneo with 'a fervent wish to return', which in the light of events which were to occur a few years later, just goes to show that you should be careful what you wish for.

By 1958 the Emergency had improved to such an extent that the States of Johore, Negri Sembilan, Selangor and South Perak were cleared of the CTs. While a few CTs remained in Pahang, the main focus of the bandit war was in North Perak and further north on the Thailand border. The direction of artillery fire or the marking of targets over the border was not permitted; instead, all relevant details were passed to the Thai police for action. This meant a marked reduction in operational flying for 11 Liaison

Aircraft often had to land on the roads to refuel, in this case at Klaung Ngae on the Thai border.

Flight, based at Sembawang on Singapore Island, 14 Liaison Flight at Seremban and 16 Reconnaissance Flight at Noble Field, Kuala Lumpur. However, 2 Reconnaissance Flight at Ipoh and 7 Reconnaissance Flight at Taiping, who had the South Perak area and the border area respectively, were fully committed supporting their Brigades. The continuous high pressure applied by the security forces resulted in successful ambushes, and a large number of surrenders.

The first fatality of the Squadron's new life as part of the AAC, rather than the RAF occurred on 14 February 1958, when Captain P.J.L. Dalley of 7 Flight lost control on approach to Kroh airstrip. Some tricky recovery problems were set when an aircraft made an emergency landing in a paddy field. The occupants were unhurt but the undercarriage was torn off. No roads or tracks led to the field, which was reached only by very narrow banks between the other fields. It was the wet season and all the ground, apart from the banks, was under water. The local Malay policeman kept curious children away from the aircraft and Gurkha soldiers, who could become almost invisible in the jungle edge, supplied the guard against the terrorists. Mechanics, standing knee-deep in water among the young rice plants, removed the engine, which was then tied to a sledge and dragged a mile to a waiting Land Rover. This had been driven as near as possible to the scene, but was finally stopped by a wide stream. The engine was rafted across the stream. The wings were detached and they were carefully manhandled beyond the stream to a waiting Bedford truck. On the next journey the fuselage was moved in the same way.

The undoubted highlight of the following year took place on 28 February 1959, when the Squadron gave a flying demonstration before a number of distinguished spectators at Noble Field, Kuala Lumpur, to mark the achievement of 150,000 operational flying hours. This demonstration, followed by the presentation parade, was the culmination of the Squadron's flying effort over the previous ten years. It opened with a formation fly-past of eight aircraft in two boxes of four, line astern. This was followed by a message drop into a Land Rover, a 'high-speed' fly-past by a single aircraft, message pick up, supply drop by parachute and also by free drop, a target marking demo, a shoot (in conjunction with 1 Federation Battery) and finally, three aircraft of 14 Flight performing the 'Prince of Wales' Feathers.' Immediately afterwards, the Squadron formed up on parade in a hollow square for the presentation of a ceremonial Kris by Lieutenant General F.H. Brooke, CB, CBE, DSO, C-in-C Federation Armed Forces and Director of Operations, on behalf of the Malayan Government. Major General J.A.R. Robertson, CB, CBE, DSO, GOC 17 Gurkha Division, then presented a ceremonial Kukri on behalf of 17 Gurkha Division. Lieutenant Colonel Storey, MC, then replied for the Squadron. As soon as the presentations were made a photograph of the Squadron was taken, and the officers and their distinguished guests then left for the Officers' Mess for the official luncheon. In the evening the officers entertained the sergeants in the Officers' Mess, followed by a Sergeants' Mess Ball: still later, the officers retired to the Selangor Club for a very late dinner. The Squadron then had a two-day standdown and individual flights held their own private celebrations. The speeches made at the presentation ceremony were as follows, firstly Lieutenant General Brooke,

'Your Excellency, Ladies and Gentlemen, the acting Prime Minister and Minister of Defence of the Federation had very much hoped to be here today himself, to attend this very creditable and in fact more than that, unique celebration of your Squadron. Unfortunately, doing two jobs, he is a very busy man and just could not make it at the last moment. He has asked me to deputize for him, a duty which I have undertaken with the greatest pleasure. The Minister has asked me to say these things. First of all, to congratulate you on this wonderful achievement, 150,000 flying hours; this is unique and the first time it has ever happened. Secondly, to thank you all most sincerely for all the work you have done on behalf of the government and the people of the Federation in the last ten to twelve years. And thirdly, to wish you all the very best of good luck and good fortune in the future. If I may add a personal note, I would like to thank the Squadron a great deal for all they have done for the Federation Army. I am sure I may speak for all the security forces of the Federation, including the Royal Federation Malay Police, and many government departments, whom you have helped by reconnaissance and in other ways. I would like to make it even more personal and thank the Squadron very much for the wonderful service they have given in the six years-over six years-in which I have been pretty closely associated with the Squadron. Every demand on the Squadron that I know of has been met not only without delay, but with the greatest efficiency and the greatest cheerfulness. I myself have been carried all over the Federation and I count myself one of the more experienced Auster passengers in the business. So thank you very much indeed, congratulations on your achievement and best wishes for the future. I therefore now take great pleasure in presenting to Colonel Storey on behalf of the government and people, armed forces and security forces of the Federation, this Kris.'

He was followed by Major General Robertson,

'Your Excellency, Ladies and Gentlemen, Officers and Men of the Squadron, there is little that I can add to what General Brooke has already said; except to congratulate you on a magnificent record of which we in 17 Division and the Commonwealth Brigade are very, very proud. I would like to give now a Kukri on behalf of the Officers and Men in token of our very high regard for the work of the Squadron and wishing you the very, very best, in every way for the future.'

And finally Lieutenant Colonel Brian Storey,

'Your Excellency, Ladies and Gentlemen, it is with mixed feelings of pride and pleasure that I accept on behalf of the Officers and Men of 656 Squadron this Kris, presented by the Director of Emergency Operations on behalf of the Prime Minister and people of the Federation of Malaya, and this Kukri presented by the General Officer Commanding 17 Ghurka Division. On this occasion I would especially like to recall the past Officers and Men of this Squadron who, over a period of some ten years, have done so much to make this a memorable day. Let us remember too, that during most of the Emergency the Squadron, although under operational control of both the Imperial and Federation Armies, was in fact a Royal Air Force Unit. Let us recall with gratitude the immense assistance they have invariably given and still continue to give. We have enjoyed and continue to enjoy our task, knowing it to be of such importance to the operations. Our pleasure is complete when our efforts are so handsomely and generously acknowledged. I would like to thank the Director of Emergency Operations and the General Officer Commanding, not only for coming here today and making these presentations, but also for the kind things that they have said about the Squadron and also for the generous thoughts that have been expressed by all of you. In receiving this Kris and this Kukri we in the Squadron are well aware of the very great privilege that is being bestowed upon us and we will honour them and guard them at all times.'

Some facts and figures were also provided in the official programme of the event,

Tasks

Supply Drops	8275
Artillery Observation	2400
Air Search	2350
Leaflet Drops	5250
Photographic	1125
Air-Sea Rescue	1105
Recce of Landing Zones and Dropping Zones	7800
Communication Flying	1800
Total Hours Flown 1948 – 1959	150,265

The Sunday Times journalist, Harry Miller, wrote that 150,000 hours was equivalent to seventeen years of non-stop flying by a single Auster, or 498 times around the world.

The Squadron also flew over 40,000 additional hours on training, air testing, demonstrations, etc., of a non-operational nature.

The results achieved are:

CT Camps found	Over 1750
Supplies Dropped	400 Tons
Aerial Observation for Artillery Fire	3500 Targets
Air Strikes Marked for Bombers	4000 Targets
Leaflets Dropped	150,000,000
Passengers Carried	50,000

Brigadier Peter Mead, who had flown very briefly with 1587 Flight in 1944 and would become Brigadier Army Aviation in 1961, wrote,

'656 Squadron was in Malaya, where the war against the communists was in its eleventh year. Their reconnaissance was widely described as the greatest single factor against the terrorists, and one can say with confidence that in this theatre, Army Aviation had completely sold itself to the Army.'

A further visit was made to Borneo, for a month in the late summer of 1959, by 11 Flight, to 'cover the North territory well; carry out several "casevacs," help to round up pirates and guide home some of our own lost patrols.' Advance notice was given of a remarkable plan being concocted by Captain Mike Somerton-Rayner, the OC of 2 Flight. In October, he had bought an Auster from the Kuala Lumpur Flying Club. It was registered 9M-ALB and had previously been VR-RBM with the club and VR-SCJ in Singapore, where it had been purchased by the Director of Civil Aviation in 1947. However, before that it had been AOP III MT438 and had served with the Squadron in Burma. Somerton-Rayner had decided that it would be much more fun to fly home at the end of his tour, rather than go by ship. The final Newsletter for the 1950s concluded with the following anecdote,

> 'Recently a conversation was overheard at a ground OP during a recent Air OP shoot which may give old and new pilots food for thought: An AOP Officer, "Do you still post air sentries during shooting to safeguard passing aeroplanes?" Battery Commander, "Oh, yes – but of course there is no closed season for Austers, we consider them fair game!'

Before relinquishing command Brian Storey applied for the Squadron to be granted the honour title of "Malaya", but nothing came of what would have been a very appropriate distinction. February 1960 saw Lieutenant Colonel John Cresswell, OBE, assume command, just a few days after the loss of a pilot in the jungle on 20 January, Sergeant W.J. McCammont of 11 Flight, who was carrying Private E.J. Finnerty of the Cheshire Regiment with him in an Auster 9, WZ728, when he disappeared near Kuala Pilah. This time the wreckage was not found for three months, even though the aircraft was on course on its prescribed route and was close to a major highway and also despite an intensive air search carried out by Squadron aircraft, Sycamores, Valettas, Shackletons, Dakotas and Meteors, lasting ten days – such were the challenges presented by the terrain and foliage. In April, a logging contractor found the aircraft about six miles from Seremban in dense jungle. Private Finnerty had died instantly but Sergeant McCammont, though clearly badly injured, had gallantly managed to cover 400 yards of the 800 yards to the main road. The aircraft was eventually brought out of the jungle by Aborigines of the Senoi Prak and Gurkhas for a full investigation. It was established that the most likely cause of the crash was the sticking of one of the engine exhaust valves, leading to loss of power.

During March and April a retraining camp was established on the east coast of Malaya and flights were taken from operational duties for a period of training in the more conventional aspects of war. As the OC wrote, also mentioning an old favourite location,

> 'Flights spent up to one month on basic flying and deployment exercises, recce and layout of ALGs, Flight exercises and finally a Commanding Officer's exercise. This is one of the very few areas in Malaya where it is possible to find suitable landing grounds for training of this nature and is confined to a narrow coastal strip at the northern end of which lies the Beach of Passionate Love. This training proved to be of great value and was the first of its kind to have taken place throughout twelve years of intense flying in support of Emergency operations.'

The old skill of airborne message pickup was still being practiced by the Squadron in Malaya in 1960, in this case by the pilot of Auster 9, XK379.

Largely due to the excellent liaison that existed between 11 Flight in Singapore and the Royal Navy, it was possible to carry out some deck landings on HMS *Albion* in the South Asian Sea off the coast of Johore in May. Intensive training in true naval style in the form of a cocktail party the previous night was a prelude to an enjoyable day's flying. After making the first landing the OC watched from the compass platform while the QFI, Captain F. Legg, took the Lieutenant Commander Flying, 'with a martyred look', to see how landing the Auster compared with his jet aircraft. Each landing was witnessed by astonished groups on each side of the flight deck as a host of cameras filmed each effort, including those of Captain J. Bedford-Davies, Captain D.T. Cholerton and Sergeant G.T. Ryan. As the ship was steaming at nearly 30 knots into a thirty knot wind it was difficult for the Austers, 'with a top speed of 80 knots downhill' to catch up. Captain Keith Bush believed it was the only time he experienced vertical take-offs and landings. A total of ten Austers landed on during the day and each pilot was later sent a certificate from Commander Joe Honywill stating that he had completed his deck landings on the carrier and continued: 'Therefore let it be known that he has joined those beings known as Amphibians, and is now subject to Neptunus Rex, Lord of the Deeps, King of all funny creatures, sea monsters and sailors. This being so, he is wished the best of Luck.'

The Malayan Emergency somewhat petered out rather than ending in any dramatic fashion and was declared to be over, with the lifting of the Emergency regulations on 31

July. At the end of twelve years of sometimes bitter hostilities, over 7000 CTs had been killed and 4000 had surrendered or been captured. On the other side of the balance sheet were the 2000 civilians who had lost their lives, as well as over 1000 Malay Police and 500 British, Malayan, Gurkha, Australian, New Zealand, Fijian and East African servicemen. The advance of Communism in South-East Asia had been halted, but at a considerable price in lives and money. The Squadron took part in the End of Emergency parade in Kuala Lumpur, providing sixteen Austers in four boxes of four flying in close formation. It had flown 171,241 hours and carried out 181,236 sorties. Adding together India, Burma, Java, Sumatra and Malaya, the totals were 179,259.30 and 189,748 respectively. The Squadron further reported that over those twelve years it had uncovered 2140 CT camps, dropped 6675 tons of supplies and no less than 232 million leaflets. It was time to resume peacetime soldiering and flying – for now. It was noted that the deployment of the Squadron remained unchanged: 2 Recce Flight at Ipoh and 7 Recce Flight at Taiping, both in North Malaya, SHQ and 16 Recce Flight at Kuala Lumpur in Central Malaya, with 14 Liaison Flight at Seremban in South Malaya and 11 Liaison Flight at Singapore.

The tempo changed from operations to thoughts on retraining and the allied problems created by a new challenge for the Squadron – airportability. During trials carried out, one factor was foremost in mind, that of the extreme weight and bad design of so much of the equipment.

'Outward Bound' activity had its enthusiasts and an energetic club was formed. Its first major project was to climb the highest peak in Malaya, Gunong Tahan, a 7200 feet mountain in North Pahang in the middle of dense jungle. The trip lasted fourteen days and was led by the Adjutant, Captain R. Horne. In September, Captain John Bedford-Davies set out with his pilots of 14 Flight for a trip to Bangkok. The CO noted, 'It is not clear what training value this flight had, but from an almost closed shop attitude on the details, Bangkok must have produced some excellent training.' Bedford-Davies also had a penchant for formation flying, and the Flight performed at various ceremonies, such as the Sultan's Birthday Parade.

On 4 September, Captain J.H.C. Roberts of 7 Flight was flying a visual reconnaissance in South Thailand when, due to engine trouble, he had to make a forced landing. The only available strip was a short stretch of laterite road on the edge of some paddy fields. The landing was successful with no damage to the aircraft. The recovery operation was carried out by a team from the Aircraft Workshop, supported by Sycamores of No 110 Squadron. Then on 1 October, Mike Somerton-Rayner and his wife departed in their Auster, now rechristened 'The Yellow Peril'. The aircraft had been modified to take a 25 gallon fuselage tank and was also equipped with a Plessey radio and a full blind flying panel. On take-off they were escorted by three of the Squadron's Auster 9s and given a rousing send off. The journey home took six weeks, with thirty-nine stops in sixteen countries on the way. MT438 is still flying as G-AREI and is now based in Devon, resplendent in its original military livery.

As a further example of the desire to return to some sort of civilized normality some fine silverware was bought for use at Mess Formal Dinners,

'It has long been the desire of the Squadron to possess a silver centrepiece of some distinction and value. To this end a fund has been subscribed to by Squadron officers for the past years. The fund, growing slowly, received a most magnificent gift from the Auster Company and associated manufacturers of the Auster 9. This gift made possible the purchase of a centrepiece. The inscription reads, "To commemorate the completion on 28th February, 1959, of 150,000 operational hours by 656 Light Aircraft Squadron in support of the Emergency in Malaya." The plaques on the side of the plinth bear the names of the Squadron Commanders since the Squadron was formed.'

Chapter 5

Malaya (Malaysia), Brunei and Borneo 1961–1969

There were many changes in Malaya during 1961; 28 Commonwealth Infantry Brigade Group had been assigned a new role and would henceforth devote most of its time to conventional warfare training on airportable equipment scales with a view to fulfilling a role as the strategic reserve for the South-East Asia Treaty Organization (SEATO). The Brigade had in fact been on standby for operations in Laos, which was in the grip of a long civil war that had threatened, for a time, to become an arena of superpower confrontation. In the event, its services were not called upon. This change of emphasis particularly involved 7 Recce Flight, which began to concern itself with the air movement of its vehicles and stores at short notice, combined with the potential requirement to fly in support of 28 Brigade. Prior to its departure from northern Malaya, 7 Flight was involved in the first major airportable exercise – Trinity Angel. Henceforth, all light aircraft tasks in support of 2 Federal Infantry Brigade would be carried out by 2 Reconnaissance Flight stationed at Ipoh. This Brigade was by then the only military force campaigning against the CTs in the Border Security Area. The Federation Police Field Force continued to mount operations against couriers and camps in North Malaya and over the Thai border in conjunction with the Thai Border Police. Visual and contact reconnaissance flights continued at a much slower pace than before, which was hardly surprising as there were only an estimated 350 hardcore CTs left. At Sembawang, 11 Flight supported 99 Gurkha Infantry Brigade Group on Singapore Island, whose main task was internal security. Based at Paroi Airstrip, Seremban, 14 Flight remained as 17 Gurkha Division's Liaison Flight and, with 7 Flight, commenced training on airportable scales of equipment; 11 and 14 Flights each took delivery of three DHC-2 Beavers in September and also retained three Auster 9s. The Beaver AL1 was a tough, high-wing monoplane, with a capacity for six passengers or half a ton of freight. It first flew in August 1947, with 1631 being sold worldwide, including forty-six to the British Army. It was a very reliable, robust aircraft and a joy to fly. It was powered by a 450 hp Pratt and Whitney radial engine and had an excellent short take-off capability. Six pilots were converted initially, as well as the CO and 2i/c. The demand for VIP communication flights was increasing, despite what was hoped would be a temporary shortage of spares. 16 Flight, which had been reformed earlier in the year to act as a recce flight for 48 Gurkha Brigade, was in process of being run down prior to its official disbandment in 1 April 1962, only to be re-formed in Aden as one of the four Royal Armoured Corps manned reconnaissance flights. Until then, what remained of the Flight was being run as a Squadron HQ Section.

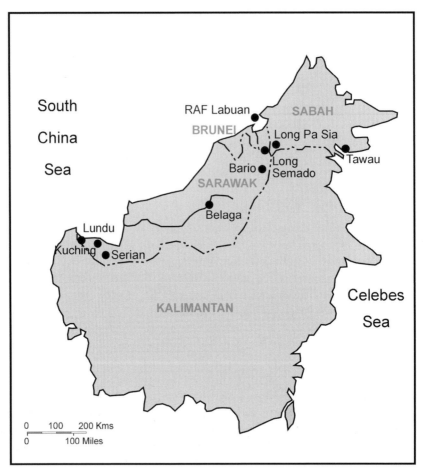

Borneo 1962–1966.

   Squadron exercises were held on the east coast during the year and successful landings were carried out on HMS *Hermes* and HMS *Bulwark* by 11 Flight and several of the pilots from SHQ and the other flights. In conjunction with 2 and 26 Regiments RA, a number of pilots undertook successful shoots at Asahan Ranges and 11 Liaison Flight conducted many shoots with the Royal Navy. Various tasks were described as 'funnies', including the illumination, by flares, of a helicopter LZ for a casualty evacuation by a RN helicopter from the jungle, dropping mail to the C-in-C Far East Station at sea, flour bag bombing of a minesweeper flotilla and numerous casualty evacuations. There was also another close encounter with a large yellow and black striped snake in the cockpit for Captain James Adair of 2 Flight, which hissed at him and slithered about as he banked the Auster and eventually came to rest somewhere out of sight.

   Three major search and rescue operations were carried out in quick succession in October and November. The first was for a Royal Malaysian Air Force Single Pioneer, which crashed in the Bentong Pass with the loss of all five on board. They were looking for a party of seventy schoolboys (and one schoolgirl) who were behind schedule on a

Two Auster 9s at Taiping airfield, Malaya.

7 Flight pilots at Taiping in September 1961. On the wings of Auster AOP 9 XK376 are Captains Chris Roberts and Peter Williams, standing on the wheels, Captain Mike Panton and Lieutenant Mike Monro and at the front are Captains Rory O'Callaghan and Malcolm Fleming, the Flight's OC.

Auster AOP9 WZ677 taking off from the airstrip at the Asahan ranges in Malaya, in 1962.

jungle expedition. The second incident involved a Canberra B.2 of 75 Squadron RNZAF, which took off on a night cross-country from Tengah to Butterworth in October, the period of the North-East monsoon. Of three aircraft taking part, the first turned back severely damaged by hail and lightning; one went missing and one made it. The missing aircraft flew into a cumulonimbus cloud at 40,000 feet. The pilot lost control, and, after repeatedly telling his navigator to eject from what he believed to be an inverted spin, ejected himself at 8000 feet. This was the third occasion on which he had abandoned an aircraft. He walked out of the jungle after a series of lucky escapes, and two days later WO2 Standen, of 11 Flight and his observer, Corporal Goodey, found the wreckage. The navigator's body was found with the aircraft when the jungle rescue team arrived.

The third and final search was for Captain Peter Hills of 2 Flight, who went missing while on a visual reconnaissance from Ipoh over South Thailand on 22 November. His passenger in AOP 9, XK374, was Captain O'Grady, of the Royal Army Dental Corps. In spite of an intensive air and ground search lasting seven weeks, no trace of the crew or aircraft was found – until 1967. The air search was controlled by the RAAF at Butterworth and, besides 656; aircraft of the RAF, RMAF, RAAF and RNZAF took part. The ground search was carried out by units of the Federation Army and Federation Police in conjunction with the Thai Frontier Police Force. Only the latter two forces were permitted to search in Thailand.

It was also noted that two new pilots, Lieutenants R. Andrews and C. Brown of the New Zealand Army, joined the Squadron in December for continuation and conversion training, before an anticipated posting to 7 Flight early in 1962. During 1961 the Squadron flew 9436 hours on Austers and 314 on Beavers.

The major news for the first part of 1962 was very well described in the Squadron's report for the Army Air Corps Journal,

'In the bad old days new arrivals in the Squadron were met by the Flight based in Singapore. They were introduced to the Navy at Sembawang and gradually filtered to SHQ. The great thing about this process was that the newcomers were always well indoctrinated with the big city life before going up country. This happens no more, for this year was movement year and there was no longer a Singapore flight. To the consternation of all, the Squadron not only moved to Kluang, but remained there. Whether this was due to a high sense of military discipline or the advent of the north-east monsoon is hard to say. Nightlife in Kluang certainly had nothing to do with it. Kluang, for those who knew it, had not changed much. For those who have never been to Malaya, it is a small town in Johore, about 60 miles north of Singapore and it is distinguished in that the tourist has the choice of whether he comes to Kluang or not. The Squadron settled in, backed by that well-known, if slightly hackneyed phrase, a "Get-you-in Service." On the works and bricks side, amongst other things, they had a leaky hangar and an almost completed new tower. In fact, they were told that the tower was the first permanent building to be erected in Kluang for many years. The move was not without its humour. The Squadron had all been settled in for many years in their old locations and the efforts to bring their treasured belongings reached fantastic proportions. Someone even wanted to bring the pierced steel planking from Noble Field.'

The Squadron was busy even before the upheaval of the move to Kluang began, as it played a full part in Exercise Trumpeter, probably the biggest exercise ever held in Malaya. 7, 11 and 14 Flights all remained in being, 16 Flight returned from Aden, but 2 Flight was disbanded and the title taken up by an integrated flight in Northern Ireland. There was a considerable changeover in personnel, including the CO, John Cresswell, who had seen the Squadron through Emergency to Conventional Training, then to air portability, and from dispersal to concentration. He was succeeded by Lieutenant Colonel Bob Begbie, the first AAC officer to take command of the Squadron.

November saw the departure of the last three National Service Aircraft Technicians to serve with the Squadron (National Service wound down gradually from 1960. In November of that year the last men entered service, as call-ups formally ended on 31 December and the last National Servicemen left the Armed Forces in May 1963).

Brunei
The Sulu Sea pirates had become a dangerous menace to shipping, so between October and November, 14 Flight deployed a Beaver in support of a joint Service anti-piracy operation on the north-east coast of Borneo, some 1000 miles from Flight HQ. Captain W.P. Duthoit gave chase to the pirates, who, mounting twin outboard motors of considerable horsepower on their craft, could show a remarkably clean pair of heels when challenged. This detachment proved invaluable, as it gave 14 Flight two months of excellent training over ground which was to prove more significant later. It also exercised the Squadron Workshops and Stores Section on maintenance over long distances, as in December the Brunei revolt broke out and events happened fast. The plan to incorporate British North Borneo and Singapore into a Greater Malaysia within the British Commonwealth had not gone down well in Indonesia, where President Sukarno had the ambition of dominating the whole of Borneo himself (as well as Malaya and Singapore if

that became feasible). Revolutionary factions in Borneo had been receiving covert Indonesian support for some time under the umbrella title of the North Kalimantan National Army (NKNA). The rebel forces consisted of some fifteen companies of 150 men, armed with shotguns, parangs, axes and spears, under the leadership of A.M. Azahari. The Squadron was fortunate in having the 14 Flight detachment more or less on the spot (at least in the same country) and in a very short time the anti-pirate aircraft switched roles to become an anti-rebel aircraft and did excellent and timely work in the opening stages of the revolt. Meanwhile, there was furious activity at Kluang. All the tedious air portability exercises paid off and Flights adjusted themselves to operate on light scales. 14 Flight moved first to back up their existing detachment. The Beavers flew direct over an uncomfortably large stretch of shark infested sea, while the Austers were brought by RAF transport. Most things worked like a charm and the Equipment Officer and his loading/lashing teams earned their pay. Little sleep and little food were had by everyone during these initial stages. On arrival in Brunei, the Flight Commander dashed out of his Beaver and smartly reported himself to the Brigade Commander and was 'uncharitably engaged' by a rebel machine-gunner from a roof top while he was in mid salute.

A more personal view of events in Brunei has been supplied by AQMS Len Edgecock, 14 Flight's REME 'Tiffy',

'I was ill in bed when Bill Duthoit turned up upon the doorstep about 2000 hours. The conversation went like this, "What's up with you?"

"I'm ill."

"How about going to Brunei?"

"I'm getting better."

"Good. Can you contact Scouse Lees (Flight Sergeant) and WO2 Red Meaton (Pilot) and bring them to my house about 2200 hours?"

"Will do."

The three of us went to Bill Duthoit's house as arranged and planned the move over a few beers, which was pretty good going as we were gone for eight months. The plan for the move and detachment was fairly simple. We were to go as light as possible to support two Austers and two Beavers, one of which was already out there. We restricted ourselves to four boxes for spares and equipment. Personal kit as light as possible, small arms and ammunition to be carried, water-bottles filled. The Austers were to travel out in a Beverley and the Beaver to fly. We were to be resupplied from Kluang.

Saturday morning at about ten o'clock, we of the ground party moved out to Seletar. The aircraft were to fly later. That afternoon/evening we removed the mainplanes and tailplanes from the Austers and loaded them onto a Beverley, along with our meagre kit. We then wandered around Seletar shopping centre where we came across some pencil torches, the top inch of which were made out of luminous perspex: most of us bought one. On Sunday morning we landed at RAF Labuan [an important staging post situated on a small but pleasant island 20 miles off the coast of Brunei and belonging to Sabah]. Our Austers were unloaded, put together and tested. Bill Duthoit and Simon De La Rue Salter taxied out on to the runway and were given permission to take off. They moved off together when we noticed a Beverley, tail to the runway, running all four engines at full bore. We watched helplessly as the Austers gathered speed, but just before they came level with the Beverley, the throttles were pulled back and our Austers took off. We had very nearly lost half our aircraft before we started – not to mention two pilots.

On the Friday, our fourth Beaver took off from Sandakan on the north-east coast, on an anti-piracy patrol flown by Sergeant Nick Nichols. He was diverted to help against the rebels and never did go back. On the Saturday, he flew 10.55 hours, doing all his own handling, turn-rounds and re-fuelling. During that day he landed at one airstrip and taxied in the middle of a firefight without knowing it until it was too late. Neither he nor the aircraft was hit. He was given a well-earned decoration for that day and had started a reputation for 14 Flight Brunei which was never lost.

On the Monday we moved to Brunei; some by air and the rest by ferry. On arrival, we found that we were to be housed in the Brunei airport building, along with about 400 RAF personnel. Our first real problem quickly became apparent and worsened over the next five days: the water pipes to the airport had been cut. The atmosphere rapidly thickened.

In the meantime we were there to fly, and did we fly? All the hours of daylight we flew, taking out patrols, picking them up, spotting, leaflet dropping and quite often search and rescue. My hat came off to our pilots, who were flying into territory marked 'unexplored' more often than not. One of their main jobs was updating the maps. A number of times when I was with them we would be on finals and I still couldn't see the airstrip. In the first three weeks our four aircraft and four pilots flew 355.55 hours. Some of this was night-flying, dropping flares.

An Auster 9 which had been overhauled at the Squadron Workshop in Kluang arriving at Kuching, having been transported in a Blackburn Beverley freighter of the RAF. This was the standard method of intra-theatre transport practised by the Squadron at that time.

Not every hour was spent in recce and the evacuation of European civilians was a task given to the Beavers on occasions. Captain C.J. Carey was seen to land after one such sortie and four nuns in white habits disembarked.

One casevac worthy of note was completed later on by Staff Sergeant Tony Horsey. When he arrived back the Medics diagnosed his patient as having smallpox. They placed Tony and the Beaver in isolation until both could be fumigated. We fed and watered Tony at a distance. The aircraft was fumigated and had to remain isolated for a minimum of forty-eight hours. The aircraft Form 700 was annotated Ac U/S – suspect smallpox. Twenty-four hours later the Medics were able to confirm that the patient had an advanced case of chicken pox, so the Form 700 now read "Ac now serviceable – was only chicken pox."

Brunei airport at this time was like Gatwick; with Beverleys, Hastings, Valettas, RNZAF Bristol Freighters, Austers, Beavers, Pioneers, Belvederes, Pembrokes, Sycamores, Shell Company aircraft, the occasional Singapore Airline aircraft and weekly Hong Kong Airline aircraft, all trying to use the pans. It was fascinating watching the Austers and Beavers negotiating the obstacle course.'

The detachment was reinforced by several aircraft from 7 Flight in the second week of December, the first to arrive being the ground party under REME Staff Sergeant Jack Greaves. Long-range fuel tanks had been fitted to the three Austers to enable them to fly 800 miles across the South China Sea, from Singapore to Kuching on the coast of Sarawak and onwards to Brunei. The over-water sector was some 450 miles and was escorted by a Shackleton from No 205 Squadron. Also included in the formation were Single Pioneers and Twin Pioneers of No 209 Squadron. This was a calculated risk with a narrow margin of error – with a five knot headwind the aircraft would not have made it. Another factor to consider was that, as the engine was inverted, if the oil loss was anywhere near the maximum allowed, the oil level would reduce below the minimum and a likelihood of engine failure could occur. The weather turned torrentially wet in the New Year and flood relief was added to the growing list of tasks. 14 Flight would spend eight months in Brunei before being relieved by 11 Flight, which was dispatched to Sarawak, where further trouble had flared. The Squadron diary noted,

'The topography was formidable and by comparison even the worst Malayan territory was easy. There were no roads up country; rivers were the sole means of communication, except for aircraft which could operate to existing strips. Mountains towered up and the weather was treacherous. There were no really accurate maps. However, despite this, the Flight pilots soon became familiar with their new environment and their support was much in demand and well appreciated.'

A young RAF officer, Flying Officer 'Jeff' Jefford of No 45 Squadron, had a flight in one of the Austers, which left an indelible memory,

'I did a four-week stint at Brunei as the resident RAF Ops Officer in early 1963. Whilst there, I volunteered to fly as dispatcher on a couple of leaflet dropping sorties in AOP 9s of 656 Squadron. It was an interesting experience for a Canberra navigator, accustomed to pressurized cockpits and assorted mod cons – like an ejector seat – to go flying in what appeared to be a very insubstantial device, made of fabric and lacking even a door! Anyway, having climbed aboard, and been buried up to the eyes in bundles of leaflets, we burbled off and flew over an assortment of villages where I duly disposed of the paperwork. Having dumped the last batch over the side, I glanced back and was somewhat alarmed to see that the tail surfaces were heavily festooned with paper and that some of it appeared to be lodged between the tailplane and elevators and thus likely to interfere with longitudinal control. I alerted the driver to the impending disaster, but he was singularly unimpressed. He just closed the throttle, pulled the stick back and stalled the aeroplane, freeing the trapped paper and leaving us in a cloud of fluttering bumf.'

By the end of February 1963, the initial and localized revolt in Brunei and Sarawak had been put down. However, by the end of the year, 7, 11 and 16 Flights were deployed on operations, with 14 Flight resting and retraining at Kluang. Where possible, a system of reliefs was operated, allowing a maximum of three months on operations and then a break for R & R in Malaya. More than 8000 hours were flown during the year, with nearly half this total being operational. The Squadron's coming of age was celebrated in verse,

We were twenty-one in sixty-three, Twenty-one in sixty-three
We now have the key of the door
To enter into sixty-four
The wind of change is bringing the Scout
The Dragmaster, bless it, is now out
But we've seen it all before.
And while we are breaking into verse
The Squadron is going from bad to worse
So said someone the other day
Who now alas is on his way.

Confrontation

It was, however, only the beginning. The policy of 'Confrontation' instigated by President Sukarno of Indonesia, would commence following the establishment of the independent Federation of Malaysia in September 1963. Two of the constituent parts of the island of Borneo, which lies 400 miles east of Singapore, had joined the Federation as East Malaysia; Sabah and Sarawak, which had together formed the Crown Colony of British North Borneo. Sandwiched between these was the independent Sultanate of Brunei, which was a British Protectorate. The bulk of the island, Kalimantan, was part of the Republic of Indonesia, which deeply resented the establishment of East Malaysia. A frontier of nearly 1000 miles stretched between the four territories, with ground heights up to 13,000 feet, few roads and an abundance of featureless primary jungle. A good description was given by Captain Tim Deane of 7 Flight, which served in Brunei from December 1962 until mid-January 1963, in close support to the Queen's Own Highlanders, and at Kuching in Sarawak from May 1963 to October 1964 as a full or part flight,

'The terrain is characterized by dense virgin mountain jungle in the interior reaching to 9000 feet and more, falling away to a wide strip of coastal swamp. Most of the country is uncharted and no topographical information is given on any map outside the centres of population. Generally, the people fall into two categories: the educated and trading Chinese who have settled in the more developed area, and the Borneo tribes – Ibans, Kyans, etc. – former headhunters who live in the interior. The only lines of communication are the great rivers which dominate the country. Roads are almost non-existent, except within the towns. There are no railways. Rivers are the lifeblood of the country, and the vast majority of the tribes live in community longhouses along the banks of these great chocolate coloured turgid streams. In the thousands of square miles of mountainous jungle separating the rivers, no sign of human life is ever seen from the air. The climate is similar to Malaya and generally conforms to the pattern of fine mornings after the clearance of dawn mist or fog, building up in the afternoon and evening to immense thunderstorms. This pattern, however, may vary considerably, especially during the monsoon period, when the rainfall is more widespread and unpredictable. Borneo has one of the highest annual rainfalls in the world, rivers commonly rising 20 or 30 feet overnight in the rainy season.'

As we have seen, the trouble started late in 1962 with an internal revolt in Brunei, which was rapidly suppressed. Britain was fully ready to meet its obligations to deal with any internal subversion or hostile incursion and to this end appointed a Director of Operations in Borneo, Major General Walter Walker. Indonesian raids on border police posts began in April 1963. Thereafter, the offensive activity by the Indonesians chiefly consisted of incursions along the border, which amounted to an undeclared war. The Army was deployed all along the Kalimantan border in a chain of forward bases from which patrols were made. Helicopter landing sites were constructed every thousand yards or so for the purposes of resupply, troop movements and casualty evacuation. As roads were virtually non-existent, the importance of the helicopter can hardly be overemphasized. Food, water, kerosene and ammunition were supplied to the bases daily. Troops could be airlifted rapidly to border crossing points where incursions had occurred. Flexibility in response to fast developing local situations and central tactical control of the bigger picture were the key factors in utilizing aviation resources efficiently.

The weather was an important factor in dictating the level and intensity of flying activity. Morning mist and low cloud was frequent and tenacious, the afternoon thunderstorms were widespread, regular and heavy. A further factor to be considered was balancing fuel against payload, as refuelling was available at the jungle clearing bases in cases of emergency only. Lieutenant Colonel Begbie provided a very succinct summary of the necessity of air support in the FARELF Army Aviation Newsletter No 1 of 1964,

'The primary role of Army Aviation in Borneo boils down to one thing and one thing only – to give support to the troops on the ground in whatever form they need it most. Without aircraft to provide logistical support and tactical mobility it would be impossible to maintain control over most border areas in Borneo. In the Central Brigade area for example, the infantry battalions and their supporting Scouts and Whirlwinds, deployed in the interior, have no surface L of C (Lines of

Communication) whatsoever and depend entirely on air supply for their existence. In these areas AVTUR, rations, ammunition and other stores are delivered by parachute, while Pioneers, Beavers and short-range transport helicopters are fully committed to the movement of personnel and the recovery of parachutes and containers for reuse. In few forward areas are light aircraft strips capable of redevelopment to accommodate Beverleys from No 34 Squadron [or later No 215 Squadron with the Armstrong Whitworth Argosy]. Distances, terrain and the continuous air support necessary in all battalion areas has led to a general forward deployment of aircraft to minimize response time and the distance to be flown on each task.'

Tim Deane described life at Belaga strip in 1963, some 160 miles up river, where he was based with 7 Flight,

'For the man keen on getting away from it all, Belaga was the ideal spot, being two days journey by boat over treacherous rapids from the nearest sizeable town and surrounded by the dark inaccessible forests of the interior. Supplied by daily Argosy or Hastings drop, the AAC detachment and the Wessex of 845 NAS were completely dependent on air supply. The Belaga section was quartered twenty minutes ride in a powered longboat upriver, at a Somerset Maugham type rest house which served as the local administrative building for the village. Due to missionary influence, the neckline of the female members of this community was high above the waist, but fortunately, in longhouses up and down river, the sarongs of both sexes were worn at their natural waist level. Parties in these longhouses were frequent and popular occasions and the friendly and convivial atmosphere much appreciated by all.

Members of a 7 Flight detachment pose with Iban workers around Auster 9 WZ730 at Belaga in October 1963.

Dancing by the men, to the monotonous chanting of the women, took the place of cabaret, and depicted in lithe and sinuous movements the story of the headhunt. The men were intricately tattooed from head to foot, and many of the women too. Tattooed hands indicated that the owner had taken a head, thus becoming an important man in the community. After the dancing exhibition, we, as guests, were invited to perform our own cabaret. I shall never forget the evening Mike Monro and myself, suitably primed by copious draughts of air-dropped Tiger beer, performed a reel never before witnessed North of the Border, to the strumming of the weird native instruments. The applause for this performance was deafening.'

It was not all so enticing and relaxing however, as Tim Deane explains,

'Flying Austers on sorties lasting four and sometimes five hours, over some of the most rugged and hostile country in the world, took some getting used to after the green fields of Hampshire, with that endless green carpet of mountainous jungle intersected with chocolate coloured torrents. Every change in engine note brought an uncomfortable shifting in the seat, and an anxious glance at the gauges, but there was a definite feeling of the wild frontier when we occasionally discovered completely new river systems and mountain ranges, where the map was a virgin white.'

His arrival in the middle of October had coincided with the mopping-up operations of the Long Jarwi battle,

'Briefly, a sizeable party of Indonesian irregulars had made their way over the frontier, and using river systems, had penetrated to Long Jarwi on the Balui River, a boat and trading station deep in the interior. They had quickly overcome the meagre defence by sheer weight of numbers, and as quickly, started to withdraw back up the rivers to

The airstrip at Belaga in November 1963 – note the Austers parked on the far side of the strip.

the frontier, several days' journey away. Thanks to Auster recce and the quick use of Naval helicopters, Ghurka cut-off parties were positioned on the exit rivers, and the majority of the enemy were killed in ambushes as they paddled back up their escape routes. This sort of battle really underlined the value of the Auster and the helicopter in this type of warfare, and was perhaps a copybook example of the use of both.'

Following this success, enemy activity quietened down considerably and frequent long distance recces, lasting four hours or so, based on intelligence information, now became the general routine,

'The majority of these recces were up to the headwaters of the Balui River, a river so rugged and utterly remote, cleaving through 5000 foot mountainous jungle, the source perhaps 100 miles from the nearest living human being; that every visit sent an involuntary shiver up the spines of those who flew up it. Occasionally, we would catch a glimpse on these long-distance forays of the weird science fiction wildlife of Borneo. Giant hornbills, which flew low over the jungle canopy looking like the great pterodactyls of prehistory. When low flying up the rivers, monitor lizards could be seen basking like crocodiles on the shingle banks, giving the impression that one was viewing a world untouched for millions of years.'

Another member of the Squadron, Captain Bill Morgan of 7 Flight, recalls,

'I carried out some target registration tasks in the border area between Kuching and Lundu. This was to preregister targets that we thought were likely to be used by the enemy as forming up or crossing points. The aim was to be able to quickly call down artillery fire should the troops on the ground need support in any instances of incursion. I think there were a couple of 105 pack howitzers and one 5.5 inch howitzer. This would have been in mid-October 1963. I also remember being shot at during a recce of an Indonesian training camp at Badau, just across the border. I was tasked by the CO of 10 Gurkha Rifles to take some aerial photos of the camp. Some of the Gurkha patrols just on our side of the border heard shots being fired as I was in the area. On returning to base we found the odd hole in the rear fuselage fabric of the Auster, the date was about 15 December 1963. In order to avoid any problems about me being possibly over the border whist carrying out my task, the CO (Lieutenant Colonel Bunny Burnett) and I decided it would be easier to say they were just drain holes and just patch them up!'

With the year of 1963 drawing to a close, Sergeant Dave Thackeray of 7 Flight was involved in a serious incident in the border area in Borneo. He was engaged in dropping mail to a forward detachment when his Auster came under Indonesian fire from the ground. His passenger was a senior RAF chaplain, Wing Commander A.M. Ross. Both were hit and wounded. Thackeray was losing a lot of blood, his passenger's wound seemed serious and he was forty minutes flying time from the nearest airfield, so he elected to land on a space cleared for helicopters. On his first attempt he felt a bone in his left arm break, rendering it useless. He had to take his right hand off the throttle and juggle with the stick in that hand and between his knees, as he made two further circuits.

He judged his final approach so well that the aircraft came to rest with comparatively little damage. Before fainting from loss of blood, Thackeray drew the attention of those clustering around to his critically wounded passenger, who sadly died before he could be lifted out of the cockpit. The pilot was Mentioned in Dispatches and also received a Green Endorsement in his logbook for airmanship.

As it entered 1964, the Squadron could anticipate six major challenges. Firstly, involvement in the Confrontation – during the year nearly all the Squadron's pilots and ground crew would have tours in Borneo, which would evolve into a regular pattern whereby two flights would be in Borneo and two in Malaysia, rotating every three months. Secondly, the introduction of the Westland Scout AH1 helicopter to replace the Auster. Thirdly, reorganization of its structure to provide flights organic to formations and sub-units integrated into teeth arm units (Air Troops or Platoons). Fourthly, planning for the assumption of responsibility by the Royal Army Service Corps for the manning of fixed-wing aircraft, which in the case of 656 Squadron would be 30 Flight with Beavers, and also, fifthly, for REME taking complete control of reorganized aircraft workshops. Finally, there was the plan that the Squadron would evolve into a Wing as part of GHQ of Far East Land Forces. This proposal resembled earlier wartime discussions, which similarly never came to fruition.

In February, 11 Flight set off on a three month tour, with a Beaver and Auster section operating in Tawau in the north-east against Indonesian infiltrations and the rest of the Flight taking over the usual duties from 14 Flight. The Beaver was proving itself to be a very valuable workhorse that everyone came to rely on.

Meanwhile back in England, on 2 March, a formation of sixteen Scouts departed Middle Wallop, the first to be sent to the Far East. The Director of Land/Air Warfare, Major General Napier Crookenden, flew in the leading aircraft. They landed on the commando carrier HMS *Bulwark*, which, four weeks later, arrived in Singapore, also bringing 10 Flight, which had been loaned from 651 Squadron to join 656 at Kluang. The Squadron was faced with the task of re-equipping 7, 11 and 14 Flights with Scouts, acceptance checks, pilot training and rushing them to Borneo 'all by this time yesterday.' The fact that the dates were met reflected great credit on the workshops and the two flying instructors, WO2 Hutchings, and Major Woodbridge, who came out from UK. Moreover, REME was very short of practised technicians and much appreciated the expertise of Joe Clixby of Bristol Siddeley, and Roy Allison of Westland, who worked very hard to get the Flight aircraft off to a good start and to pass on their experience to the technicians. At this stage the Squadron had no indication as to the intensive maintenance effort this aircraft was to require. The five-seat Scout was the first British 'home grown' turbine-powered helicopter. In terms of performance it was a great leap forward. It was fast – over 100 knots – and had an impressive rate of climb, reaching 10,000 feet in less than ten minutes. Pilots, used to the underpowered Skeeter, found it a delight to fly and it would eventually prove to be both rugged and robust; but in its early years it was beset by numerous technical defects which resulted in very poor serviceability, which was a considerable headache for all concerned.

Early in April, 14 Flight was re-equipped with five Scouts and said goodbye to the Austers and Beavers which had undertaken sterling service in Borneo since the Brunei rebellion began. It got down to intensive training to be ready to move to Sarawak in June. Early in May, jungle survival courses were completed and towards the end of the month

845 SQDN.

R. M.   7. FLT. A.A.C.

SIBU
1963

CHRISTMAS DAY

Breakfast
Grape Fruit or Fruit Juice
Scrambled Egg   Bacon   Mushroom
Fried Egg   Sausage   Baked Beans
Omlette   Kidney   Tomatoes
Tea or Coffee

Lunch
Cold Buffet

Dinner
Tomato Soup
Roast Turkey
Stuffing
Cranberry Sauce
Chippolatas
Roast & Boiled Potatoes
Sprouts   Peas   Cauliflower
Christmas Pudding, Rum Sauce
Mince Pies   Nuts
Fresh Fruit   Ice Cream
Tea or Coffee
Beer

Distances may have been great in Sarawak but the 7 Flight detachment was still able to celebrate Christmas in the traditional way.

the Flight spent three days in the Cameron Highlands at 6000 feet, learning all about the problems of handling the Scout in the rarefied air. It was noted that, 'Fresh strawberries and sleeping under blankets were an enjoyable change from the steamy heat of Kluang.' In the second week the Flight had a signal from 28 Brigade, who were on exercise about sixty miles north of Kluang. Their RAF support helicopters had all broken down, they were desperate for water and rations, and had casualties in all three battalions in primary jungle. Four Scouts flew regular sorties over five days and supplied most of the Brigade by landing in very small jungle clearings. The Flight evacuated no less than seven serious casualties to the Field Hospital at Malacca on the west coast. It also carried out Air OP Shoots with 170 (Imjin) Battery RA, using their 5.5 guns on Asahan Ranges. On the way back from the Cameron Highlands the aircraft were refuelled at Kuala Lumpur Airport and created quite a stir when they did a short fly-past. In the same month, 30 Flight, which was staffed by RASC and AAC permanent cadre pilots in the main, the first integrated flight, was formed under Major John Riggall, taking over the Beavers operated by 11 and 14 Flights, with a base firstly at Kluang, but from July at Seletar. The Warrant Officer in charge of the Flight Workshop, which remained at Kluang, was a Chief Petty Officer RN on loan to REME, of whom John later wrote,

'Twenty years of aviation experience and a refreshing attitude to Army methods made an invaluable combination.'

The new Flight undertook its first operation at 0800 on the morning of its formation, in lieu of a far more traditional workup period. The lack of either a clerk or a typewriter provided,

'A first class excuse for not writing letters and HQ FARELF were remarkably courteous about receiving essential correspondence in long hand on a memo pad.'

It would soon find its assets spread across Malaysia and Borneo in four detachments, covering some 1500 miles,

'Distances are huge. If Flight HQ was in London, our Workshops would be in Cambridge; Sibu is as far away as Berlin, Brunei as Trieste and Tawau as Tunis. Brigade areas are vast, five hours of flying at 125 mph showed four Major Generals, the Brigade Commander and a Battalion Commander, a considerable proportion of Central Brigade's area in Brunei recently. One Company Commander has a Company area rather larger than that of the Rhine Army. The airstrips vary from the very frightening to the very good.'

The problem presented by communications from outstations was solved by very creative means,

'By giving a C13 radio to an eighteen year old Driver/Operator straight out of Buller Barracks at Aldershot and not telling him that what he was about to do was practically impossible, we succeeded in working voice communications 800 miles back to Malaya.'

11 Flight returned to Kluang to convert to the Scout. It would have encouraged all personnel who struggled with the Scout in its early days to have learned of this subsequent comment made to OC 656 by Brigadier W.W. Cheyne DSO, OBE, when rotary-wing support had been more fully established,

'I command my brigade with a Scout helicopter. I cannot do it any other way. There is no other way.'

The first to occupy the Squadron's jungle fort at Long Pa Sia in Borneo, was 10 Flight. This initial period lasted from June to August, and during this time the Flight had on its establishment five Scouts, six pilots, twenty-three ground crew (at various times a dog, an owl and a baby deer), and the only hot baths in Sabah! After two months work at Kluang, it had moved by way of the LST *Empire Gannet* to Labuan. There, the aircraft were flown off the deck of the LST, and on in formation to Brunei for three weeks operations before moving out to Long Pa Sia. Long Pa Sia itself was a small longhouse village, or kampong, on the Sungei Padas, tucked into the south-westerly corner of Sabah, about four miles east of the border with Sarawak and eight miles north of the border with Indonesian Borneo, although the Indonesians insisted that the Flight was only three miles north of their border – 'a fact the Flight patriotically chose to ignore!'

The strip at Pa Sia was situated some 400 yards north of the kampong in the middle of dense primary jungle, and was only accessible by air, 'unless one was prepared to accept a three week walk from the nearest civilization!' It was surrounded by mountains on all sides which rose up to 6000 feet, and the runway itself had an elevation of 3275 feet, which made it a very pleasant climate in which to live. Fresh water was permanently available from the Padas which rushed past the strip and although this water was a bright orange in colour, it became quite palatable when, 'diluted with a little of John Haig's taste and colour-removing elixir!' Fresh meat could be obtained by issuing one of the villagers with a couple of twelve-bore cartridges, though this practice could have had its perils, as the locals were apparently fervid pro-Indonesians whose sole interest in the British Forces and Malaysia was one of finance.

The flying task of the five Scouts was to support Central Brigade in any way that was asked, and this involved mostly freight-lifting, resupply, troop-lifting and communications flying.

The camp itself was typical of the jungle forts which dotted the border in Sabah and Sarawak, and was built entirely of wood, bamboo and sandbags, with tarpaulins for the roofs of all the bashas. The initial construction work was to build an Ops Room and this, together with improvements to all the other bashas, a water supply for the Officers'/Sergeants' Mess basha, communications trenches, bunker rebuilding, new latrines, a basketball court and sundry other building projects, 'occupied most of the people for most of the time.'

All supplies arrived at the end of a parachute, and air drop days – normally a Friday – were the highlight of the week. On the whole, the accuracy of the RAF was of the highest standard, and not only had they to hit the strip with the one-ton containers; they also had to miss the camp and the parked aircraft. Apart from the odd one-ton's worth of AVTUR that landed irrecoverably in the 'ulu', the only real tragedy was when the NAAFI supplies and fresh rations free-fell into the jungle one morning, and all that was salvaged were a few pencils and a roll of film. Beer and spirits of course, arrived in this way and thankfully were always recovered. Spirits were dropped in one gallon oil tins to avoid any possibility of breaking the bottles, and it was found that a can of Tiger beer would sustain a fairly hard blow before splitting.

Apart from the excitement of the weekly airdrop, the Flight was often visited by Gloster Javelin FAW 9 delta-wing fighters of Nos 60 and 64 Squadrons which patrolled the border daily, and they were only too glad to use the Pa Sia low flying area when requested over the radio to check the strip. Some of their low flying passes were quite memorable, particularly, 'if it was remembered that there was a 6000 foot jungle-clad alp at the north end of the strip, and a Javelin doing an emergency turn on full reheat was quite a sight!' A typical day's routine on the ground was outlined as follows,

'Stand-to in the mornings was at 0530, followed by a hot mug of tea from the cookhouse and breakfast at 0700. The REME technicians would start work on the aircraft as soon as it was really light to ensure that there was an aircraft ready to go at all times. The morning would be spent in hard manual labour around the camp with everyone taking part, as in a place like Pa Sia, boredom was the worst enemy. Lunch at 1230 and an afternoon either at work or play, a 2400 foot airstrip makes an excellent cricket pitch, until tea at 1730. Then showers were the order of the day until the evening stand-to at 1850. A can of beer, a butty and a yarn over a dim hurricane lamp until 2100, and then lights out and to bed.'

The domestic facilities were also described,

'We had water storage tanks – seven 45-gallon fuel drums standing on an eight foot high platform. The height of these drums produced a strong enough head of water to give showers, and in the case of the Officers' and Sergeants' bashas, to fill their two baths. These baths, which became famous throughout Borneo, consisted simply of a 45-gallon fuel drum with the bottom cut off, the drum being sunk a foot into the ground with a drain pipe attached for ease of emptying it. The drum was filled daily with water and a

No 1 burner placed against the side would produce a hot water bath in about thirty minutes. It was possible to ease oneself into the bath until the water came up to one's neck and although this bathing method was frowned on by all who had not tried it, a quick dip in hot water was all that was ever needed to convince even the seventh person in the water, that the only word that could really do justice was ecstasy!'

Some aerial work did however have to interrupt this life of repose,

'Take-off times were normally 0830 to 0900 as, due to the 3,000 foot-plus altitude of the strip, we were normally encased in eight-eighths cloud at 50 feet until about this time. It dispersed and lifted regularly at about 0815, and the weather invariably remained fine and clear until the daily build-up of cumulus cloud started at lunchtime. This led to storms in the afternoon and early evening, which formed so quickly as to catch out many a pilot leisurely making his way home after a day's work away from base. All pilots very quickly obtained a healthy respect for the weather. The average day's flying would see perhaps three of the five Scouts in use. One might have been involved in a troop lift of forty soldiers over a distance of up to 30 miles; another in flying a company commander and his platoon commanders on a recce for forth-coming patrols and sites for new clearings; while the third perhaps resupplied three platoons of a company from the company base.'

Invariably, a platoon or patrol position, indeed even some company positions, were situated in clearings in the jungle, and these clearings posed many problems for those flying into them. Owing to the altitudes involved, and the fact that the aircraft were always used to the full and were loaded up for every trip, a great deal of the clearing work was done on limited power. The Scout, being small and highly manoeuvrable, enabled pilots to get in and out of clearings that the RAF's Whirlwinds would not consider, and even then it was not always possible to land owing to tree stumps left in the bottom. The height of the trees surrounding these clearings could be more than 200 feet, and more often than not there was only one way into a valley, and the same way out again,

'Still, the Scout always obliged pilots by flying for long periods on 100 per cent, everything, and the standby power check of "the more you sweat, the more weight you lose, thus the more power that becomes available" got most of the pilots out of hot, high clearings at one time or another.'

In June, all five Scouts of 14 Flight were flown down to the Empire Dock in Singapore. They landed alongside the *Empire Gannett*, the blades were folded and the aircraft hoisted on board in no time at all. The pilots would have liked to land on, but the Port Authorities forbade this because apparently the dock would have lost the handling charges. They arrived at Kuching on 19 June and flew off – the first time an Army Air Corps Flight had been launched at sea as a unit. The first few days in Kuching were spent being shown round the area by the OC, Major J.L. Dawson, who had previous experience with 7 Flight, and the Whirlwind pilots of 225 Squadron. The latter shared the Royal Green Jackets' Mess with the Flight and Belvedere pilots from 66 Squadron. The Flight's role was to support West Brigade in Sarawak from Kuching Airfield, about five miles south of the town itself. West Brigade, with five battalions on the border, was responsible for aiding the civil powers in keeping order, not only against the bands of Indonesian infiltrators on the border itself, but also against a large number of the CCO (Clandestine Communist Organizations), Chinese immigrants who lived and worked in the territory. Roads were few and far between, the local population inland consisted of land or sea Dyaks – the Ibans, former headhunters, who 'unfortunately appeared to be returning to their old sport' in parts of Sarawak. This part of Borneo had few mountain ranges, most of the area was, or had been cultivated, so there was a great deal of secondary jungle and scrub. The only recognizable features from the air were the hills and often these were great slabs of limestone with vertical faces, full of caves and stalagmites. A large number of clearings and helicopter pads had been made in the border area; all these were numbered and it took the pilots days to plot them all on their maps, not to mention the inevitable amendments.

Indonesian raids by regular and irregular troops continued in the border areas, on forward platoon bases and even unprotected kampongs. There were occasional diversions, as on 13 July when,

> 'One aircraft was flown up to the beach for a compass swing near an old Japanese fighter airfield. Staff Sergeant Bushby was the pilot and the aircraft returned loaded with ripe coconuts!'

Back in Kluang, the Squadron sustained its first fatal helicopter accident on 15 July, when Captain Daniel Jacot de Boinod and flying instructor WO2 W.J. Hutchings, were killed in the crash of Scout XR596. The cause was mechanical failure and could be directly attributed to the hasty introduction of an unreliable and untried aircraft into an operational theatre. The only positive benefit was that this tragic loss spurred on efforts to improve the Scout. The Army Air Corps Journal reported as follows,

> 'The most tragic news of the last year was the death of WO2 Hutchings, better known as Hutch or Baldy, and Captain Dan Jacot de Boinod. Hutch was known to many generations of pilots, and was greatly liked and respected, wherever he went. Dan was known to fewer people, but he was a fine officer, destined for high position. The loss of both these men was terrible for their families as well as for the AAC, our high regard for them can be but a crumb of comfort for those they left behind, but our real sympathy goes out to them. His father, Colonel Jacot de Boinod, had flown with the Royal Flying Corps in the First World War, and Daniel seemed to share with him the same pleasure and exhilaration in flying really well.'

Needless to say the work of the Squadron carried on. For example, on 17 July, a Scout piloted by Captain L.C. Bond flew forty miles out to sea, touching down on HMS *Bulwark* to collect the pilot of an Auster who had just landed on board, the aircraft was en-route for the Squadron Workshop in Kluang, and on 21 July, a number of gun registration sorties were flown, as well as the air observation of 3 inch mortar shells for the Green Jackets. The AOP shoots took a standard form. The pilots landed at the forward base and collected the Platoon Commander who sat beside the pilot, and he could point out the track, junction or stream from low overhead. The aircraft then retired to a safe fly line to engage the target. This method definitely paid dividends since enemy casualties after one ambush were credited to accurate target registration.

In August, much to the frustration of all, the Scouts were grounded for nearly ten days due to serious Nimbus engine problems. Aircrew spent the time acting as second pilots on the Whirlwind Mk 10s of 225 Squadron, helping them on tasks. The majority of the flying was to forward areas with company and battalion commanders, whose headquarters were between twenty and forty miles from their platoons on the border.

When the Scouts were back in action again, one from 14 Flight was detached to the Royal Ulster Rifles at Serian, about forty miles south-east of Kuching,

> 'Captain Bond was sent there at first, because despite the fact he lives in County Cork, it was thought he could at least speak the same language.'

In mid-August, 10 Flight was relieved by 11 Flight at Long Pa Sia, before returning for its second three months' spell in November. Towards the end of the month, on 27 August, a report from Serian noted that the detached Scout had completed sixteen sorties in one day, which included a mortar and ammunition flight and the seven-man Combat Tracker team and their dog.

At the beginning of September the Indonesians carried out a parachute drop in the area of Labis, about 40 miles north of Kluang. The Squadron was called into operation and 10 Flight, which had, of course, just returned from Borneo for a rest, found that this had been curtailed. In addition, two Austers from 16 Flight were sent down to help out.

Back in Borneo on 11 September, Sergeant Hall from 14 Flight conveyed an assortment of Padres round the Green Jackets' bases – 'It was rather difficult deciding which denomination to put in the front seat.' The engine trouble continued and a Beaver from 30 Flight RASC, flown by Captain D.A. Beechcroft-Kay, was sent to help out 14 Flight, as at one stage it only had one helicopter flying.

On 1 October, 16 Flight officially disbanded and became Air Troop 4 RTR (Royal Tank Regiment), moving their location from Ipoh to Seremban. They would continue to fly Austers in Malaya and Borneo until their Sioux helicopters were available and would be the only formation to keep its Austers throughout the Confrontation, except for a detachment on loan from 20 Independent Recce Flight in Hong Kong. The Squadron was now busily engaged in its seventh major task, the preparation for the arrival of the Sioux and dispatching the unit's flights. The American-designed Westland Bell 47G Sioux light utility helicopter had been purchased by the AAC, supplementing the troublesome Scout. It was produced under licence by Agusta in Italy and by Westland at Yeovil, some 150 being delivered to the Army, the first British built example flying in 1965. The plan was to embed sections of Sioux as Air Platoons, or Air Troops, into individual fighting units within the Order of Battle.

As the New Year of 1965 dawned, the Squadron was:

(a) Preparing a flying training programme of 600 hours (for which flying instructors were flown out from the UK and another brought in from 20 Flight in Hong Kong).
(b) Assembling five newly arrived Sioux.
(c) Preparing for the Administrative Inspection.

(d) Getting the Scouts flying with a modicum of safety.
(e) Administering two AAC Flights in Borneo, which should have been taken over by their respective Brigades in May.
(f) Tackling day-to-day problems.

It promised to be another busy year. The situation in Borneo remained highly volatile with the prospects for a negotiated peace not looking promising. On 13 January, Government authority was given to extend the Claret 'hot pursuit' policy, up to 10,000 yards across the border with Kalimantan, from the previous limit of 3000 yards. This extension of offensive patrolling was not widely publicized, as open and declared warfare was the last thing that the British, Malaysian, Australian or New Zealand governments wanted. The desire was to persuade the Indonesians to desist by maintaining a stance that would convince them any provocation would meet a firm and appropriate response. The incursions would continue by land, sea and in the air, but without any significant effect.

The first Sioux arrived in Singapore in February 1965 and were handed over to the RAF MU at Seletar for assembly. As there was a certain amount of impatience to start operations with these new arrivals and as the MU was hard pressed with other work, scratch teams of technicians were provided by REME from the Squadron Workshops to help. On 10 April 1965, the first Sioux-equipped air platoon was operational at Kuching. When the second batch of Sioux arrived in Singapore Lieutenant Colonel Begbie went down to the dockside to see them being unloaded,

'It was an impressive sight, all those packing cases addressed to me and labelled "For the Commanding Officer, 656 Squadron, Army Air Corps." I have seldom had such a feeling of wealth and importance. I was seized by an overwhelming desire to take them away and unpack them myself. Reason prevailed. I stepped back out of the way, and once again the teams from the RAF and the Squadron Workshops set about their task and in a few days another six helicopters took to the air.'

At a Guest Night at Middle Wallop in February 1965, Colonel Denis Coyle, as the first commander of 656 Squadron, accepted, on behalf of the Officers' Mess, a magnificent silver model of a Scout. This was handed over by Mr H. Winkworth of the Westland Aircraft Company, and was a joint present from Westlands and Bristol Siddeley Engines. The Ceremonial Malayan Kris, given by the Government of the Federation of Malaya to commemorate 150,000 hours of operational flying, was also taken into safe custody by the Mess at the same Guest Night.

Far away in Borneo at more or less the same time, a pilot from 7 Flight found out that it was not only the MT drivers who could collect parking tickets,

'Gumbang Rural District Council, Parish of Bukit Knuckle

Notice of Traffic Offence

Notice is hereby given that (vehicle type): Scout helicopter (vehicle registration number): XP 901 is reported for the understated traffic offence(s).

1. Parking is clearly marked limited parking area for a period of time over and above the specified leave period of sixty (60) minutes, in that on (date) 11/12 February 1965 from (times) 7.15 pm – 6.00 am the above stated vehicle did so park, in contravention of GRDC Byelaw 36(a) (5) (Traffic).
2. Failing to display parking lights of any form between the hours of (times) 7 pm and 6 am, the statutory required hours, in a limited parking area, to the great danger and impedance of parishioners, in contravention of GRDC

Byelaw 36 (6) (1) (Traffic).'

Meanwhile back at SHQ in Kluang, 1965 was described as 'a year of stimulating expansion.' It was noted that,

'The number of Army aircraft flying in the Far East had more than doubled and further increases were due. This number included helicopters on which the ARMY marking has been cunningly altered to RM, as the Royal Marines entered the field for the first time under the wing of Army Aviation – this despite some rather "old-fashioned" looks from the Senior Service.'

The Squadron and the REME Workshops would support the four Air Troops of 3 Commando Brigade, which were each equipped with three Sioux. The deployment of steadily increasing numbers of Sioux was the most important development of the year. Progress was remarkable in spite of obstacles of all sorts, due not only to technical and

Scout XP888 landing at Gunong Sepadang in Sarawak, a hilltop rebroadcasting station code-named Red 267, which was close to the border with Kalimantan.

logistic problems, but also to the fact that Army Aviation was breaking entirely new ground. Raising and training of air troops/platoons was undertaken at Kluang, initially under HQ 656 Squadron and later the Wing Flying Training Element. Throughout the year the hard working flying instructors and fitters worked under considerable pressure to turn out the finished products on time. To launch newly trained air platoons into Borneo, untried and still lacking full technical and spares backing was also something of a risk. After all the difficulties with the introduction of the Scout, Army Aviation could ill afford another setback, but as the situation on the ground demanded more helicopters, so in they went. Battalions certainly had to contend with many difficulties, which were highlighted by the signals which flooded into Squadron HQ,

'One air platoon, remote in north-east Borneo, received an unwanted Land Rover Mk 4 radiator, issued by some mischance in mistake for a precious ARC 44 radio; another had no Air Publications, so how could it answer signals about Part Numbers; others impatiently await the "automatic" initial issue of G 1098 stores [tools and equipment] which, for some reason, seemed to have reverted to manual; and "why can't the Army Air Corps ..." and so on. And still, pushing urgently to the top of the piled-up IN trays in the headquarters, came those ominous signals stamped OP IMMEDIATE and starting off "Scout serious defect," though admittedly there were not so many of them these days.'

In spite of all this the Sioux was a success from the start. Enthusiasm in the air platoons was high, serviceability had nearly always been good and the helicopters were of great value to those regiments and battalions fortunate enough to receive them. Logistic support was now improving and HQ thrashed out problems of control, including the responsibilities of Aviation Commanders, while also making clear which Service commanded the Army's aircraft in the field.

From the start of February, 30 Flight came under the command of 3 Army Air Supply Group. The Flight would be renamed 130 Flight RCT in July, following the creation of the Royal Corps of Transport, but continued to carry out its duties as theatre Beaver flight with detachments in Brunei and Sabah. The Beavers undertook a wide variety of tasks, including the delivery of men and materials, VIP in-theatre transport, casualty evacuation, search and rescue, aerial photography, visual reconnaissance, observation by brigade or battalion commanders, Air OP for artillery batteries and warships, dropping supplies, leaflets and flares and free-fall parachute training. There was even the opportunity for one Beaver to land on the deck of the aircraft carrier, HMS *Hermes*. On one occasion, due to a shortage of Twin Pioneers, the Beavers carried out a full company changeover – 400 troops and a considerable quantity of stores were lifted in the course of 161 sorties over a period of a week in 100 flying hours. In John Riggall's opinion,

'The Beaver is probably the most efficient aircraft the Army has had. Reliability has been one of the main factors in its success. Much of the credit is due to the very long hours of work by the REME technicians, and perhaps most important of all, much thought and planning by the Chief Petty Officer to achieve a good servicing stagger and anticipate trouble before it occurred. None of this would be possible without a basically sound, rugged aeroplane.'

Pilots WO2 "Red" Meaton, Sergeant Barrie Davies and Staff Sergeant Tony Horsey after landing at Sibu in Sarawak, on their way to Brunei, pose for the camera beside Beaver XP804.

In March 1965, 11 Flight moved to its old haunt of Long Pa Sia. During this tour the difficulties of maintenance and a changed tactical picture combined to bring the Flight HQ back to Brunei airfield, leaving a detachment to enjoy the 'relaxing climate' of Long Pa Sia, where the Flight was very pleased to be visited by HRH Prince Philip, Duke of Edinburgh,

> 'He heads a list of VIP, and not so VIP, visitors who came to see us, many of whom expressed surprise at seeing Scouts deployed so far forward, which made us wonder how far some of our tales of unreliability and other forms of woe have reached.'

At the end of May, 10 Flight returned to Borneo for its third tour on the island and was based at Brunei Airport rather than at Long Pa Sia, as in the past. The main reason for this change of base was an attempt to improve the serviceability of the Scouts, the lack of readily available spares, plus the inability to work at night at Pa Sia. It was hoped to overcome these snags by moving to Brunei, '11 Flight had three months and three weeks to put the theory to test.' On serviceability, it took a little while for the improved servicing facilities offered at Brunei to start to bear fruit. The ground crews 'worked wonders through many a long night' and always produced serviceable aircraft in the morning. It became so regular a matter to have four aircraft tasked every day that, 'the Flight pilots started to complain at the excess of flying that had to be done; the first time such a complaint had been heard in this Flight!' The tasks carried out by the Flight during this tour were as varied as before, including, recce, casevac, communications, troop lifts, photo recce, Forward Air Control, freight lifts, plus a small amount of training and a deal of air-testing. The leading statistics showed:

Hours	654
Sorties	1799
Passengers	2744
Freight	182,629 lbs.
Casualties	29

The main tasks were still troop lifting and freight moving, the daily record for both being ninety troops and 18,000lbs of freight. The aircraft also moved several 105mm howitzers with ammunition and personnel, plus other sundry items of freight. Staff Sergeant Overy arrived at Long Banga one day to discover that there was about 10,000lbs of RE plant twenty miles away that was urgently required for the rebuilding of the Long Banga airstrip. The RN had been tasked to move this plant with Wessex HU5s, but had not turned up as yet. Staff Sergeant Overy broke it down into Scout-type loads, hung it beneath his aircraft, and ferried it the twenty miles in nine trips. The Flight also had its moments with 24 Construction Squadron of the Royal Australian Engineers. They were building a road through primary jungle between Kenningau and Pensiangan in Sabah, and on several occasions had cases of appendicitis to evacuate. These never became apparent until late in the afternoon, and it was invariably Major Benthall's lot to go out the odd 100 miles to collect them. The race was then on to arrive back in Brunei before dark; which must have been the only international airport in the world without a single navigational aid. Only once did he return well after sunset (with no landing lamp and two mile visibility in haze). However, the Flight switched the lights up in the bar, and this illumination, together with the light cast by the starboard navigation light, was sufficient for a safe landing to be made. The never ceasing 'hearts and minds' campaign continued, the Flight's main contribution being twofold. First, they carried out many civilian medevacs and casevacs from remote kampongs in Sabah, Sarawak and Brunei States, transporting them mainly to the Government Hospital in Brunei and returning them when cured (or otherwise) back to their homes. The other means, by which the Flight assisted in winning over the locals, was by flying Army vaccination teams around the countryside to immunize local people against a variety of diseases. Two trips of this nature were undertaken, visiting ten villages and injecting some 2000 people. The pilot was an invaluable member of the team, assisting on the production line by swabbing arms or charging hypodermics.

The Flight was visited by several notable people, one of the most welcome being the Commander, Brigadier Harry Tuzo, OBE, MC, 'always a stalwart and knowledgeable supporter of Army Aviation, the Commander visited the Flight on several occasions and always expressed a preference for Army aircraft on all his many journeys around the Brigade, which covered an area about the size of Wales.' The AOC 224 Group, Air Vice-Marshal Christopher Foxley-Norris, spent some time listening to the Flight's challenges in August, as did several Army Aviation and RAF Evaluation and Stores Acquisition teams. It was hoped that the Flight would get all the spares it required as a result; the most important being a comfortable, sensible, up-to-date and efficient form of pilot's microphone, 'one could gauge the popularity and efficiency of the issue throat microphone by the number of pilots wearing home-made and locally "modded" boom mikes.'

During the tour there was not a lot of time for organized relaxation owing to the intensity of the flying effort. However, the Flight found time to visit Muara Beach on

Long Seridan was a typical jungle airstrip, not far from Long Pa Sia in Sarawak. The photograph was taken from a Beaver, XP817.

several occasions for water skiing, and made a visit to the oilfield at Seria. For pilot relaxation, Lieutenant Pyke and Staff Sergeant Overy undertook a river 'patrol' in a longboat. An 18 hp outboard was borrowed from the RE Port Squadron, and in a boat heavily laden with food, petrol, beer and blankets, a trip up the Limbang was achieved.

The major political development during August was the not entirely amicable withdrawal of Singapore from the Malaysian Federation by means of the Separation Agreement which, however, maintained civilized relations, trade agreements and mutual defence ties. Singaporean troops would continue to serve in Borneo.

Meanwhile, 7 Flight spent six months in Sarawak, based at Kuching Airport. Serviceability of the Scout had improved and at one stage in August they had all four aircraft serviceable at the same time. Sergeant Markham was subjected to a very harassing few minutes in July, when, over primary jungle and 4000 feet peaks, his engine stopped. By using great skill and making best use of any available glide, he managed to put the helicopter down in the only small patch of secondary jungle in the area. His four passengers, a major and three subalterns, were uninjured, except for one bruised back. After landing, Sergeant Markham set his passengers to work clearing the area around the Scout in readiness for the arrival of the rescue aircraft. The unit knew the area he was operating in and the search aircraft found them and lifted them out to Kuching. 'Very well done' and 'above praise' were some of the comments made by the passengers. The Scout was recovered later by a Belvedere. Sergeant Markham was awarded a Green Endorsement for his handling of the emergency.

The Squadron suffered another loss on the night of 19 September, when Sergeant D.J.P. 'Doc' Waghorn, of 7 Flight was flying in the Kuching area with a Gurkha and a prisoner in Scout XR599. It is thought that the aircraft crashed into the sea.

Bill Morgan, who flew with both 7 and 14 Flights had very few good words to say about the Scout in its early period of service,

'The Scout was a disaster from day one, the "fracto" Nimbus 102 engine was unreliable and we had two Rolls Royce engineers attached on site to keep things going. They were carrying out major engine rebuilds in the field. Whilst in UK on training we were not allowed to fly over woods, yet in Sarawak it was 99.5 per cent woods in the shape of solid jungle. We never got anywhere near the target 150 hours engine life out of the Nimbus and, to add insult to injury, one arrived flown in from UK, marked "temperate climates" only. The later Nimbus 105 post Mod 664 engine was hardly any better. We also had a problem called lateral shake, whereby the helicopter's tail boom twitched. Damper units were fitted, but this made little or no practical difference. We spent many hours doing flight idle descents from about 10,000 feet to try and adjust the dampers. Much later it was discovered that there was a design fault in the free turbine which caused the vibration.

Scouts were deployed at forward locations with units near the border, crewed by a pilot and a mechanic. The crew stayed forward until the aircraft needed a thirty hour service when they were flown back to Kuching. There were not enough tools to cover these deployments, so we had to go to Kuching Town and buy extra spanners etc out of the PRI funds.

Often, when all the Scouts were grounded, I flew in the second seat in a Handley Page Hastings of No 48 Squadron. The RAF needed two pilots when they flew within range of the Indonesian AA guns on the border. They only came out with one pilot per aircraft, so they offered to basically train any AAC ex-fixed-wing pilot to bring the Hastings back to Kuching and land it in an emergency. For a couple of months I had more fixed-wing hours than helicopter ones!'

11 Flight spent June, July and August back in Kluang,

'Where our long-suffering ground crew found themselves providing first line servicing for a sizeable flying training programme, as the large number of Sioux theatre conversions continued.'

Further reinforcements were added to the Scouts in August when 3 Flight arrived in Borneo, bringing their Scouts out from Tidworth in support of 5 Infantry Brigade in Sarawak for the next year. It was, however, another sub-unit to fall under the aegis of the Squadron and the REME Workshop. As the CO, Lieutenant Colonel P.E. Collins, (who had assumed command in March) wrote in the FARELF Army Aviation Newsletter No 6 of 20 August, that the Squadron was fighting, "a rearguard action to defend its title." In the middle of September, 11 Flight returned to Brunei,

'via a five-hour vibro-massage in a Bristol Freighter of the RNZAF, and the same aircraft returned to Malaysia with 10 Flight. They looked much happier than we did, but I think we were all glad to be here, if only because the journey was over. Marlene Dietrich reclining in her seat of a VC10 should really sample the more rustic pleasures of these venerable flying machines.'

In the aftermath of what was claimed to be an attempted coup by the Indonesian Communist Party in Jakarta on 30 September and its brutal suppression thereafter by the Army, executive power slipped away from President Sukarno. Moreover, the country was beginning to suffer an economic downturn. Slowly but surely the steam began to go out of the Confrontation.

On 1 October 1965, after more than twenty years of eventful service, the focus of Army Aviation in the Far East was changed as the Squadron completed its reorganization to form HQ 4 Wing Army Air Corps at HQ FARELF and HQ Army Aviation, Borneo (which retained the title of 656 Squadron, in Labuan). The event was marked in Kluang with several good causes being supported, the aim being to perpetuate the name of the Squadron in Malaysia. Firstly, a cheque for $3000 was presented as the initial donation to an appeal for funds to build a Christian church in Kluang. Secondly, a cheque for $3000 was presented to the Chinese High School, and this money was used to furnish a new basketball court, which was named after the Squadron, and which had opened officially on 26 September 1965. A plaque at the side of the court bore the 656 Squadron Crest and a suitable inscription. Thirdly, a cheque for $3000 was presented to the Jubilee School, which was an English speaking establishment in Kluang and whose headmaster, the Reverend Victor Samuel, was an officiating chaplain to the Forces. This cheque was presented by Major General Napier Crookenden on 16 December 1965, during a visit to the Squadron. During the final thanksgiving service in the Garrison Church, a memorial plaque was dedicated to the memory of Captain Jacot de Boinod and Warrant Officer Hutchings, who lost their lives in the Scout which crashed on 15 July 1964.

Wing HQ was installed in Singapore as an integral part of GHQ, FARELF, with staff responsibility for aviation affairs throughout the Theatre. The Wing Flying Training Element remained at Kluang, together with the Theatre Flight AAC (a role undertaken by either one of two Flights, depending on which was in Borneo). This Flight was directly controlled by Wing HQ and was locally administered by 75 Aircraft Workshop REME, also based at Kluang and with detachments in Borneo.

The Training Wing reported on its debut with some aplomb,

'Since those overworked days (and nights!) of February/March' when the Woodbridge/Dawson/Eccles/Patrick team did battle with Sioux conversions, aided and abetted by Major Crawshaw who came down from Hong Kong to do some real flying, things settled down somewhat. Day One in the life of the Senior Flying Instructor, FARELF Standards AAC: "What is it that turns a reasonable chap into a devil with horns once he is a QHI?" one rather bewildered Theatre Flight pilot was heard to mutter. But even his check report wasn't too bad. With the Theatre conversions progressing smoothly, it was once again time to think of places further afield; another visit to "the other side," to tales of woe, and in early October, WO2 W.A. Patrick and Staff Sergeant D.E. Ford, were seen climbing aboard a Bristol Britannia at Changi outbound for Labuan. Armed with cholera certificates and newly made questionnaires, the first stop was Brunei to invade 11 Flight AAC and the 4 RTR detachment at Bario. The 4 RTR detachment was involved in a "hearts and minds" campaign, but despite being "out in the ulu" none escaped the net. An hour's hop over an 8000 foot ridge in a Handley Page Herald of 4 Squadron RMAF soon brought Tawau into sight for Act 2. An overnight stop with the Scots Guards rear, a thirty minute run in an Alouette III of 5 Squadron RMAF to Kalabakan, a quick look at the Indonesian border and out come the by now rather grubby and tattered questionnaires. With no dual Sioux, this meant a full ground "trap" for the Scots Guards Air Platoon. Then off to Kuching to be met by Major Woodbridge. Under his wing were to be found 45 Regiment RA, 40 Commando and the QDG Air Troop an hour away at Simmanggang. A quick flip by 20 Flight "plank" to the QDG and an unexpected night trip, saw the end of this tour of the Borneo territories looming into sight. The Training Element of 4 Wing was off to a flying start.'

One of the young pilots visited by Patrick and Ford was Lieutenant John Charteris of 4 RTR Air Squadron. He had a very high regard for them both. It is not recorded what they thought of John's habit of taking two pet companions flying with him in his Sioux, a Gibbon by the name of Shack and a Hornbill called Wilbur. One of Shack's favourite tricks was to jump up and swing from the swash bar as the rotor blades wound down. Meanwhile, the very well received Hearts and Minds Campaign involved bringing doctors or dentists to the native villages.

As always, great and richly deserved praise was reserved for the hard working REME ground crew, in this case those belonging to 11 Flight,

Lieutenant John Charteris picks an unusual landing site for his Sioux in Borneo. (Lieutenant Colonel John Charteris)

'The biggest bouquet of all must be handed to Staff Sergeant Keil and his men. At the end of last year we looked forward, very cautiously, to an increase in serviceability. Initially we wondered at our own optimism, but recently we have begun to feel that we must be, if not out of the woods, at least peering through the bushes. Our operational target has been reached now (in Borneo), for several months, and our November serviceability of over 60 per cent is our best ever, and stands comparison with anybody. This is partly due to the improvement in the spares situation, but the main credit must rest squarely on the shoulders of our Flight Workshops, who have worked very long hours, in extremely unpleasant conditions, to achieve good results.'

Lieutenant Colonel Collins fully endorsed these sentiments and added that it was the technicians who bore the brunt of the frustrations and enormous extra workload arising from the frequent unserviceability and technical unreliability of the Nimbus engine. He mentioned in particular one young sergeant, who had supervised the changing of no less than eighty engines during his two and a half-year tour,

'In doing so he handled £2,000,000 worth of equipment in new engines alone and one can double that figure as each change was replacing one for one. Many times he and his team worked through the night and frequently in conditions of appalling discomfort. They never made a single mistake.'

On New Year's Eve 1965, Colonel David Bayne-Jardine arrived as Commander Army Aviation FARELF, and in due course Lieutenant Colonel Collins set off to form HQ Army Aviation Borneo at Labuan, which had 'the unique distinction of being the only Army Aviation HQ supporting a formation engaged in active operations and separated by twenty miles of sea and ten miles of land from the nearest army aircraft.' Other changes were afoot; 20 Flight in Hong Kong and the Air Troops were brought within FARELF Army Aviation, the Workshops, which had reorganized on to a REME establishment and were now called 75 Aircraft Workshop REME. The title of 656 Squadron and 'virtually nothing else' moved with Collins. So for a while, 656 Squadron existed more in spirit than reality, although that spirit burned bright in the detached flights throughout the region. While the Flights were now all supporting Brigades, it was generally agreed that whichever Flights were in Borneo were under command of the Commander Army Aviation, Borneo. Colonel Collins wrote that,

'The cold English winter drove out the usual migration of visitors to Borneo in numbers so large that at one stage they represented a greater threat than the Indonesians. The Brigadier Army Aviation [Brigadier C.D.S. Kennedy] cleverly chose a quieter moment in the spring and had an interesting but short tour round the main areas of activity. This time we managed to show him some characteristic weather, when his first sight of Kuching airfield was in thick rain from a low-level fly-past downwind at a ground speed of 100 knots, with a large storm closing in around us, and the pilot at the controls of the Beaver murmured "I don't think I'll land here from this approach." An Auster coming in from the opposite direction just made it and so did we some fifteen minutes later.'

He was highly appreciative of the contribution made by the Austers in Borneo,

'The usefulness of the Austers is undoubtedly overshadowed by the more dramatic roles played by the Scout and the Sioux, but there is little doubt that fixed-wing light aircraft still have a major part to play, particularly when flying hours can be had at such a relatively low cost. And where there is no danger from an enemy air force, the fixed-wing light aircraft is probably still the best vehicle to provide continuous surveillance of the battlefield.'

One particularly unusual event took place just before 3 Flight's departure from Borneo in the summer. Their Malayan honey-bear, 'Judy', who had been looked after by Trooper Kent was accepted as a gift by London Zoo who agreed to pay her airfare home. Judy made royal progress, receiving lavish media coverage in Singapore and the UK.

The year followed much the same pattern for 10 and 11 Flights, rotating between Brunei and Kluang. Having been on roulement since 1964, these three-monthly moves held few problems for the Flights, with the average handover time being reduced to about three hours. On the not so operational side, two pilots spent a day flying the Rt Hon. Denis Healey, MBE, MP, Secretary of State for Defence, and Air Marshal Sir John Grandy, KCB, KBE, DFC, Commander-in-Chief FARELF, plus their party and wives, on a series of visits to local longhouses. Owing to the importance of these guests, lavish parties were laid on by the local chiefs, and a fascinating and enjoyable day was had by all. Unfortunately, the two pilots were unable to partake of the customary vast quantities of rice wine because of the 'Don't ask a man to drink and fly' campaign – but this enforced sobriety did not absolve the two concerned from their duty in performing solo native dances for the benefit of the Minister and his friends!

The Scout was a very popular aircraft with RE survey teams and many hours were flown helping to map the country. A lot of this required maintaining a lengthy free-air hover at heights in excess of 5000 feet while the surveyors took readings. The remarkable performance of the Scout in this aspect of flight enabled the job to be completed with relative ease.

For 11 Flight, May brought a flurry of activity, with an incursion of Indonesians in the Bario area,

'Once again, the speed of the Scout demonstrated itself when two Scouts were sent from Brunei, one as the Brigade Commander's personal OP, the other for possible casualty evacuation. Time and again, the Scout had proved itself far superior to the Whirlwind 10 in any particular role in this theatre, carrying at least the same payload, but some 30 knots faster.'

The Flight also carried out FAC training with RNZAF Canberras on several occasions, with varying degrees of success. The main problem always seemed to be communications, but once a mutually satisfactory channel had been found, things proceeded quite well. It also started night cross-country flying, which was very successful and encouraging. It was generally felt among the pilots that, given good weather, night flights into the interior regions were quite possible. It summed up its time in Borneo,

'The Flight was based in Long Pa Sia, a forward jungle airstrip, from August 1964, serving there a total of seven months before the Brigade Flight location was moved back to Brunei, where they served for a total of ten months. In that time they were employed mainly as part of the short-range transport force, flying almost 3000 hours all told – not an outstanding effort, but a worthwhile and satisfying one, reflecting credit on all ranks of the Flight, technical and otherwise.'

Squadron members travelled by both sea and air across the 700 miles of water between East Malaysia and West Malaysia during the course of the Confrontation, including the bone-shaking experience of flying in a Bristol 'Frightener' (170 Freighter) of the RNZAF, which was described as, 'many long hours of shaking, vibrating, sleepless cacophony from Brunei to Changi or vice-versa.' During the course of 1966 the Indonesian Government began to show greater awareness of the worldwide lack of sympathy with its position. Discussions began with Malaysia in July and on 11 August, a peace treaty was signed in Bangkok. For the time being vigilance was maintained, but the peace agreement held and it soon became possible to start withdrawing forces from Borneo.

On 17 September, the day before 10 Flight left Brunei for Malaysia, they were told that they were to move back to UK in November to rejoin 3rd Division on Salisbury Plain. This involved many problems, as the Flight personnel were in Malaysia and all the equipment, aircraft, small arms, etc, were in Brunei with 11 Flight. However, a tremendous amount of hard work on the part of the Flight Sergeant and his men ensured the stores were on the quay ready for shipment on the day before the Flight flew home from Singapore. During its thirty-two month tour in FARELF, 10 Flight achieved the following flying effort:

7471 sorties
3413 hours
10,818 passengers
537,395 lbs freight
145 casualties evacuated

Lieutenant Rob Hills of 7 Flight calculated that it alone flew in excess of 5500 operational hours during the Confrontation, in both Austers and Scouts.

One of the best little vignettes to come out of Borneo that year was an air-to-air conversation which took place between an American strike pilot flying in Vietnam and one the AAC's pilots in Borneo. American: 'Will you get to **** off this frequency; we're fighting a war over here.'

Sharp reply, 'So are we bud, but we're winning!'

20 Flight's experience was rather different. It was decided in June that the Flight would leave Hong Kong and re-establish itself as a Scout flight at Seremban in West Malaysia. The plan was that it would rotate with 2 Flight in East Malaysia. However, confrontation ended shortly after the Flight had arrived at Seremban and neither Scouts nor pilots were made available. By October plans changed and the Flight repacked its stores and other chattels. Meanwhile, the last Auster 9, XK409, was flown from Kuching until October 1966 on surveillance duties, equipped with a listening device to detect radio

transmissions. The remaining Austers in theatre were either sold to the Hong Kong Government for the Auxiliary Air Force, or scrapped by burning at Kuching. After a short period in limbo the Flight finally returned to Kai Tak equipped with Sioux.

Last Years in Malaysia

In November, SHQ left Labuan and joined 17 Division in Seremban, and 'continued to keep the name of the 656 Squadron alive,' closely followed by 2 Flight. The redeployment back from Borneo enabled 4 Wing to have a get-together in Singapore of nearly all Flight and Air Troop/Platoon Commanders in December, where staffs and operators were able to exchange views with 'gay abandon.' A very successful cocktail party was held in the 'Old Folks Home' (Senior Officers' Mess) on the first evening of the Conference.

At the start of the year the Flying Instructional Element was just beginning to find its feet, but by the end of 1966 it had managed to fly 1625 hours instruction and had passed sixty-five new pilots through its twenty-five hour theatre familiarization course. All pilots posted to FARELF, on arrival, first reported to their parent unit for a few days' orientation and personal administration. Then they moved to Kluang for the theatre familiarization course, during which they received not only a period of general refresher flying, but also learned how to tackle jungle clearings, local navigation, the weather and other Far East specialities. It was not a case of 'forget what Wallop taught you', but there were some advanced techniques which differed in detail from those in Europe. After this course, or sometimes before it if a suitable vacancy existed, each pilot attended the two-week course run by the RAF Jungle Survival School based at Changi. The newly joined pilot was then ready to rejoin his unit, having successfully been 'passenger qualified.' Major P.G.C. Child was SFI, WO2 W.A. Patrick, DFM and Staff Sergeant E. Ford, were the helicopter instructors, while WO1 Tapping looked after the Beavers at Seletar. As it was responsible for the flying standards of all Army pilots in the Far East, stretching from Hong Kong in the north, Seria in Brunei, West Malaysia and Singapore – the same area that in north-west Europe would cover UK, the Low Countries and a considerable amount of BAOR – it was kept busy.

In 1967 Air Vice-Marshal Christopher Foxley-Norris wrote, 'The Borneo campaign was a classic example of the lesson that the side which uses air power most effectively to defeat the jungle will also defeat the enemy.' It would have been more accurate to say the side which used air power most effectively in support of ground forces, would be the one which gained the upper hand. And it would certainly be fair to add that no squadron was more versatile and had greater experience of jungle warfare than 656 between 1944 and 1966.

The ending of the Confrontation made it possible, in 1967, to expand, 'the exercise studies of the techniques of counter-revolutionary warfare,' the practical result of which was a series of exercises in West Malaysia and included brief excursions to East Malaysia and Australia. The Wing was able to study the employment of Army helicopters in the tactical troop lift, continuous airborne surveillance and gunship roles against a numerous and well-armed 'opposition.' Also involved were both 7 and 11 Flights and the sub-units of 28 Commonwealth Brigade, a detachment of the Australian Army Aviation Regiment, 182 Recce Flight, which was equipped with three American Bell 47s and the four air sub-units of 3 Commando Brigade RM (Brunei, Dieppe and Kangaw Flights and 95 Locating Regiment Air Troop). As regards HQ Army Aviation, 17 Division (656 Squadron) was now established in Rasah Camp, while 2 Flight had a 'decent hangar' in Paroi Camp. The year was a fruitful one in bringing Army Aviation to the notice of soldiers on the ground in other than an operational situation. The future of the HQ and accordingly of 656 Squadron was, however, undecided in view of impending reductions in Britain's military commitment to the Far East, which had been laid out in the Defence Review of 1966. In the light of the prevailing economic conditions the Government had resolved to cut down considerably on expenditure on overseas bases, a plan which was further reinforced by the Defence White Papers of the succeeding two years. Despite this it can be said that the late 1960s were a pleasant time in which to serve in Malaysia and Singapore, as the economies of both were prospering and relations with Indonesia had been patched up into a state of mutual toleration.

In May, the Commander Army Aviation and a team went into Thailand to look at the wreckage of Auster XK374, which was lost on 22 November 1961, with the pilot and observer (Captain P.H. Hills, RA and Captain D.J. O'Grady, RADC). They were accompanied by a platoon of Thai Border Patrol Police; the wreckage was duly inspected, photographed, and one or two pieces removed and brought back. It was discovered that the accident was caused by the failure of a union in the fuel pipe; the union had been incorrectly wire-locked.

At the end of September, Lieutenant Colonel R.J. Parker, MC, AAC, arrived fresh from Wallop 'full of up-to-date knowledge' to take over from Lieutenant Colonel P.E. Collins RA. His first function was to receive the Waghorn Trophy from Lieutenant Colonel Collins on 1 October, at the Army Aviation Parade, in which the HQ and 2 Flight formed a squad behind the Pipes and Drums of 17 Gurkha Signal Regiment and marched past the GOC, Major General A.G. Patterson, DSO, OBE, MC, while aircraft of 28 Commonwealth Infantry Brigade flew overhead. The Waghorn Trophy, which was a large Royal Kukri mounted on a Malacca wood representation of the Malay Peninsula, was to commemorate the memory of Sergeant D.J.P. Waghorn RAMC, lost in Borneo in 1965. At the same time, the tip of the propeller from XK374 was 'returned' to 2 Flight, duly polished and mounted.

At the end of January 1968, 11 Flight suffered a tragic loss when Scout XT625 had to make a forced landing near Grik after severe engine trouble which was caused by turbine blade failure. On impact the helicopter rolled over, trapping one of the three occupants, Corporal Christopher Galloway REME, who drowned. The pilot, Captain Chris Cross, and the other occupant escaped safely.

The year continued with various unit moves around the theatre, for example; the Royal Engineers Air Troop returned from Thailand, 7th Gurkha Air Platoon moved to Hong Kong, the Air Platoon of 3 Light Infantry spent ten months in Mauritius and in that period flew nearly 1500 hours, while 130 Flight RCT now had single aircraft detachments in Nepal and Laos during the eight month non-monsoon period (for the use of the British Embassy in Vientiane, a role which would last for over seven years up until 1975, though XP821 was officially on charter to the Foreign Office from 1970 onwards). These movements, together with major exercises involving 2, 7, 11 and 14 Flights, kept HQ well occupied. They were delighted to see the new Brigadier Army Aviation, Denis Coyle, and his team in March. In three weeks they visited Singapore -Kluang -Terendak – Seremban – Penang -Thailand and Hong Kong. Apart from disseminating the Army Aviation gospel to all and sundry, the HQ organized Aviation Training Camps, through which all AAC Flights and all Air Troops and Platoons passed once a year, these were mounted with the capable assistance of 2 Flight. The HQ expected only one further year in Seremban and hoped that the 656 Squadron title would be readopted elsewhere to continue to perpetuate its proud record.

In March, 2 Flight gave a display of airborne GPMG night-firing to an audience of senior officers. The target area was illuminated by slow-falling flares, dropped from a Beaver provided by 130 Flight. As the aircraft were blacked out, and, they were told, impossible to see, the effect of 600 tracer rounds fired onto a small target with some accuracy was startling to behold.

In mid-1968 the flights were located as follows:

Kluang 11 Flight,
Seremban (Paroi) 2 Flight,
Sembawang (Singapore) 14 Flight
Terendak (Malacca) 7 Flight.
All those Flights with six Scouts.

Sioux units were:

10 Gurkha Rifles Air Platoon (Penang),
RE Air Troop (Kota Tingii),
6 Gurkha Rifles Air Platoon (Kluang),
Life Guards Air Squadron (Changi),
Commando Brigade Air Squadron Royal Marines (Sembawang),
20 Flight AAC in Hong Kong and 2 Gurkha Rifles Air Platoon in Brunei.
The Air Platoons and Troops had three Sioux each, the Life Guards six, 20 Flight ten and the Commando Brigade about sixteen. There was also, of course, 130 Flight at Changi with six Beavers.

Captain John Charteris was with the Air Platoon at Penang, which was working with the SAS preventing infiltration from Thailand and where Shack the Gibbon disgraced

Gurkha Rifles Air Platoon and Sioux in Borneo 1966. (Lieutenant Colonel John Charteris)

himself by performing his party piece at a Mess Function. All went well at first, as he rotated gently beneath the roof fan, but did not improve as the guests in their finest began to feel a light but pungent shower descending on their heads.

An additional change was the termination of the RAF's presence at Labuan in the middle of June, which was a source of regret to many.

In July, 2 Flight sent a couple of pilots and aircraft on annual AOP shooting with 14 Light Regiment RA, closely followed by deck landing practice on the LSL *Sir Galahad* prior to the eagerly awaited Australia deployment. Exercise Coral Sands, which took place on the east coast of Australia, was undoubtedly the main event of the year. Having departed from Singapore on board LSL *Sir Galahad* the Flight (plus two aircraft and pilots from 7 Flight) spent ten days 'soaking up the sun, food and alcohol' whilst cruising past Indonesia, Bali, Timor and finally the Great Barrier Reef, to their destination at Shoalwater Bay. After 'countless games of cards, darts and "uckers" played on the high seas', they were relieved to get down to some interesting flying in a new country. The training area was certainly no paradise for those being exercised. Both hills and plains were amply covered with gum trees and dry grass and very prone to bush fires at that time of the year. Fortunately, they were based on the LSL for the whole period and enjoyed the good food, air conditioning and hot and cold running water provided on board. Flights to the assault ship HMS *Intrepid* and the Commando carrier HMS *Albion* were commonplace for all pilots and two were fortunate enough to land on board the aircraft carrier HMS *Hermes*, which was at the time cruising some 30 to 40 miles out to sea. However, as soon as they had landed their passengers they were told to hover alongside whilst naval fighter aircraft took off and landed. Some forty-five minutes later they were granted permission to land again to rest their weary limbs. After the exercise

Army pilots could never resist the opportunity to add a carrier landing to their log books, in this case Auster AOP9, XN407 takes off from HMS Albion.

ended the Flight was allowed to go ashore, taking with them four aircraft and twelve members of the Flight. The aim was to fly north and meet the ship at Townsville and whilst there to organize suitable female company for a proposed party on board,

> 'The first night was spent in a small sugar port of Mackay where everyone found accommodation with the assistance of friendly beer-drinking taxi drivers. The pilots got on so well with their taxi driver that they ended up being shown round a sugar refinery at 11.30 pm on a Sunday.'

Townsville was reached by noon on the second day, where they eventually persuaded the RAAF to put them up for two nights, money at this stage running rather short. They soon made their way into the city of Townsville, population 35,000, and 'having purchased the right number of koala bears and boomerangs,' set about the serious business of finding willing company for the impending party,

> 'To say their mission was 100 per cent successful was perhaps not quite true, however, the wardroom rang with the sound of shuffling feet and elbow jostling made by military and ship's officers eager to get to know the six air hostesses and ten university students provided by the apprehensive pilots.'

Most felt it was a good thing when the Flight finally set sail for Singapore, knowing that they had a clear nine days to recover from their Australian entertainment. At the end of the year the Flight had one aircraft on detachment at Grik near Butterworth in North Malaysia in support of troops training there. One pilot reported having flown thirty-four hours in seven days, which the Flight assumed must be a record. Despite technical problems with its Scouts, 11 Flight managed to continue its service for the South of Malaysia which was instituted in 1967. Since then a total of forty-eight serious medical cases were flown to the British Military Hospital in Singapore. Flight personnel considered this to be a really worthwhile task which kept everyone on their toes and provided an added incentive to maintain night flying training.

The Flying Instructional Element reported 'rather a lean year in many ways,'

> 'Not only had both the Sioux and the Scout suffered from periods of debility, but the Element had also been presiding over a contraction of our once large empire. Hong Kong, Thailand and Mauritius all left our mandate. On the other hand the amount of paperwork passing between Kluang and Middle Wallop increased alarmingly.'

Lieutenant Colonel R.J. Parker departed after a year, on elevation to 1 Wing in BAOR. His relief was Lieutenant Colonel Michael Hickey, who returned to 656 Squadron, having served from 1953-55 in 1907 Light Liaison Flight,

> 'Apart from a tendency to reminisce in a high cracked voice about Auster Sixes, Warby, Nanto's Bar, and other joys of the dear dead days, he seemed to be none the worse for starting his sixth tour.'

Following the statement made in the 1968 Defence White Paper, the rundown of forces in the Far East got into its stride in 1969 and a number of Air Troops and Platoons were disbanded or posted. There were a few incidents but these were due in the main to mechanical failure. In February, Captain John Elliot of 11 Flight carried out a copybook engine-off landing into young rubber trees after a Scout engine failure. His passenger, Brigadier Cooper, was the Chief Engineer FARELF, so was well placed to appreciate the problem. Then in May, Captain Christopher Hunt of 14 Flight made a skilful forced-landing after a turbine failure, at 300 feet in a climb. Both pilots well merited their Green Endorsements. Three further incidents were well handled by the pilots in difficult circumstances. Captain Mike Jameson force-landed his Sioux at night at the Jungle Warfare School after his throttle became disconnected and Captain David Stephens, flying a Beaver, finished up on a road in Thailand after an engine failure en route to Nepal; there were no injuries or damage to either case. On 25 November, WO2 (AQMS) Maxwell was lucky to walk away with only seat harness bruises after his Sioux, XT210, suffered complete engine failure over the jungle at night. As was written at the time,

> 'We all dread an engine failure; at night it is unthinkable, and over the jungle unmentionable and yet "Q" Maxwell had it all three ways. His complete survival was miraculous.'

HQ Army Aviation 17 Division/Malaya District (656 Squadron AAC) was determined, if not to go out with a bang, to at least 'keep on pedalling hard, right up to disbandment,'

> 'Although our bicycle was almost chainless for a time, with the virtual demise (again!) of the Scout, events conspired to keep us fully employed.'

The last major 17 Division exercise, aptly named Crowning Glory, in which 28 Commonwealth Infantry Brigade was deployed as a completely Air Mobile Brigade, required 2 Flight to support the Joint Forces Headquarters in the control and umpire role. All Brigade aircraft were centralized for tasking and with six Scout and six Sioux, managed in excess of 400 flying hours in nine days. Paroi airstrip was the scene of dawn to dusk activity, which included single and twin rotor helicopters, Beavers and RAF single Pioneers. Subsequent lower formation exercises such as Dosro Kadam found the Flight engaged on deploying rebroadcast and relay stations on mountain peaks, troop lifting, and in the armed helicopter role.

An Aviation Battle Camp, took place in May, at Ipoh and at Brinchang in the Cameron Highlands. 2 and 7 Flights were stretched by two days of intensive flying training, based on the Perak Flying Club; then a particularly strenuous escape-and-evasion exercise. Six teams of four were dropped by helicopter in the valley of the River Brok, deep in the jungles of Ulu Kelantan. These parties had to cover twenty miles or more to reach safe rendezvous points. None of them succeeded, mainly because they were given an impossible task; but those who, after capture by 10th Gurkha Rifles, were subjected to tactical interrogation by Intelligence Corps experts, 'will not forget it in a hurry.'

LSL *Sir Galahad* took 14 Flight away again to Brunei for three weeks, where the tasking was both imaginative and exciting,

'We flew Commando raiding parties into their positions at night, and later on flew them out, again at night, to the LSL, steaming ten miles out at sea. Towards the end of the exercise tasking became so heavy that we found ourselves supporting both sides, which was confusing to say the least.'

A final battle camp was held at Grik in September-October. This remote airstrip, nearly 500 miles north of Singapore, was chosen for the superb training offered by the deep jungle of the Ulu Perak, and by the presence of the SAS, also there on training. The Squadron had a long-standing association with them, going right back to the early days of the Emergency, and it was fitting that their last outing together was at the scene of old triumphs. The camp was split into two phases; flying and ground training based on Grik, and deep jungle exercises tied in with the SAS programme,

'Our SAS instructors were magnificent, whether at first aid, jungle field firing, or demolitions (they were awestruck by our mania for explosives; in cutting a gigantic LZ near Grik we used 400lbs of plastic explosive in two days). The second phase was even better (or so we thought; after all, we laid it on!). There was a deep jungle Search and Rescue exercise, in which the Sioux units ganged up to find and succour CA Avn, the SFI (Spencer Holtom) and our SAS medic. Once found, the victims required first aid, for they lay amidst a welter of tomato ketchup, painted with all sorts of injuries. Nobody fainted, though.'

The Scouts lifted a large body of men into a deep jungle post, from where they patrolled, 'won the hearts and minds of numerous natives' and learnt how to survive in hostile country. From thence, they made their way by bamboo rafts, thirty-five miles down to Grik over fifty sets of rapids. The units taking part were 11 Flight, 10 Gurkha Rifles Air Platoon, RE Air Troop (FARELF), Air Troop 14 Light Regiment RA, and a detachment of 3 Commando Brigade Air Squadron. Largely as a result of their efforts at this and the previous battle camp, and for a year's devoted work at Kluang, the Flying Instructional Element gained the Waghorn Trophy, for their outstanding contribution to Flight Safety in the Far East over the previous year. After the various accidents mentioned above, the last of which was only ten days after General Sir John Mogg, the Colonel Commandant of the AAC, had presented the Senior Flying Instructor with the Trophy, a nameless instructor was heard to mutter, 'I suppose we'll have to give it back now!'

The Squadron finally bowed out from Malaysia on 17 November 1969, with a final review and fly-past by units of Army Aviation 17 Division and all the AAC Flights. The line of thirteen Sioux and fourteen Scouts stretched the whole length of Paroi strip. The parade was reviewed by the GOC 17 Division, Major General D.G.T. Horsford, CBE, DSO. He spoke to every officer and man on the dismounted parade and pleased the personnel of 10 Gurkha Air Platoon by addressing them in Gurkhali. At the end of the line, the GOC gave the signal to man aircraft by firing a green Very light, and so commenced the fly-past, which, despite minimum rehearsal time, consisted of an immaculate four vics (V formation) at low-level. They flew on over Seremban town, to dip in salute over HQ 17 Division, before landing and retiring to have a party during which General Mogg met all ranks and their families. The Squadron's farewell words were as follows,

'So 656 Squadron flies out of Malaysia's history. We are sad to be closing down, for after all this is the Aviation unit with the longest record of active service; twenty-three out of twenty-seven years have been spent on operations, from the Arakan to Imphal, from Java and Sumatra to the Thai Border and all over East Malaysia – flying a total of over 250,000 hours on operations. All of us who served with 656 in any capacity are proud to have done so.'

It cannot be overstated what an impressive achievement this represents. The Squadron had operated in unforgiving environments for twenty-seven years, with rudimentary aircraft and poor lines of communication. Little did the author of 1969 realize that the record of operational service was to continue with different aircraft and different threats, but with the same Squadron spirit.

In January 1970, 14 Flight disbanded, its Scouts going to Brunei Flight of 3 CBAS; 2 Flight followed in March, becoming the Allied Mobile Force Flight at Netheravon; while 7 Flight was reborn in Berlin in April; 11 Flight soldiered on in Singapore until 1975, forming part of the ANZUK Squadron. On 21 August 1975, Sioux XT516 of 11 Flight took off from Sembawang airfield near the north coast of Singapore and headed northwards. It crossed the Johore Straits into Malaysia, returning some time later. This was the last time a British Army aircraft based in the theatre would set out on a sortie into the Malaysian peninsula, so ending thirty eventful years of Army flying, in which 656 Squadron had played such a proud part.

The Squadron's Scouts and Sioux line up at Paroi, ready for its final fly-past in Malaysia on 17 November 1969.

Chapter 6

Hong Kong 1969–1977

Hong Kong, which had been a Crown Colony since 1841, is situated at the mouth of the Pearl River, some eighty miles from the Chinese city of Canton. As well as Hong Kong Island and adjacent islets, it also comprised Stonecutters Island, the Kowloon Peninsula on the mainland and the New Territories (a portion of the mainland and over 230 islands, which were leased from China in 1898 for 99 years). It covered an area of 404 square miles and had a population of about three and a half million. The

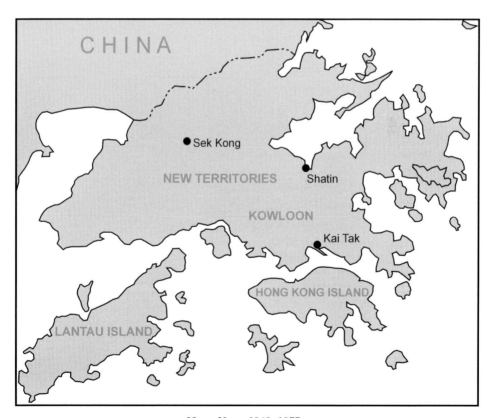

Hong Kong 1969–1977.

greater part of the colony consisted of steep, unproductive hillsides. In the New Territories, almost all flat, low-lying land was intensively cultivated, while valleys and plateaux also contained villages with small areas of farmland. 1903 Flight had served there from 1949 until going to Korea in 1951; 1900 AOP Flight was sent out in 1953, equipped, of course, with Austers Mk 6 and Mk 7 and was retitled 20 Independent Recce Flight in 1957. Typical duties included taking part in range shoots, dropping supplies or mail to infantry patrols, recce flights along the border, providing 'targets' for ship and anti-aircraft tracking radars, tracking practice torpedoes, assisting the Colony's police in public order duties and searching for smugglers, illicit stills or poppy cultivations, plus such one offs as counting the number of sharks and manta rays in coastal waters and flying a Public Works Department surveyor on aerial inspections of possible sites for reservoirs and roads. It was customary for 656 Squadron to provide the pilots for its independent Hong Kong cousin, usually towards the end of their Malayan tours, though normally the Flight Commander came straight from the UK. The flying was a little less pressured and it was not unknown for sport to be had by the pilots aiming toilet rolls to drop down the funnels of the RMS *Queen Mary* when she was in harbour. On 8 January 1961, one of the pilots, Philip Pettyfer, decided to see how high an Auster would fly and took his Mk 9, WZ731 up to 20,000 feet – without the assistance of oxygen. Typhoon *Wanda* wreaked havoc at Shatin in 1962, destroying all the Austers and causing the Flight to move back to RAF Kai Tak. Tragically, three of the Flight's pilots, Flight Commander, Major Peter Richardson, Captain Ian Horsley-Currie and Captain Ian Stevens were killed on 25 July 1963, when Auster 9, XN420, crashed into a hillside. A later Board of Enquiry concluded that the probable cause had been a downdraft or sudden turbulence.

The first Sioux arrived for service with newly formed Air Troop 49 Light Regiment RA in 1965. The remaining Austers were sold to the Royal Hong Kong Auxiliary Air Force in 1966. In the 1960s and 1970s Hong Kong was thriving commercially, business and associated building works were booming. The main security concern was stemming the flow of illegal immigrants across the Chinese border, while the police were greatly exercised by the desire to reduce the level of smuggling. Captain John Charteris was OC 3rd Gurkha Air Platoon at Sek Kong in 1966-67 and recalled such incidents as taking off with two passengers but landing with three, owing to a birth in mid-air, looking into China from 10,000 feet and the mass flight of RN Wessex from HMS *Bulwark* which got a much closer look in February 1967. Ignoring local

Auster AOP9, WZ731, overflies Aberdeen harbour in Hong Kong.

advice, the large formation flew by mistake into Chinese airspace before making a rapid about turn and causing, 'an almighty row.'

The Hong Kong Aviation Squadron had been formed in February 1969, on an interim basis, at Sek Kong camp in the New Territories and was the result of the amalgamation of the four aviation units in the colony. These were 20 Flight, who moved from RAF Kai Tak, to join the Air Platoons of 6th and 7th Gurkha Rifles and the Air Troop of 25 Light Regiment Royal Artillery, all of whom were already operating from Sek Kong.

The Interim Squadron was officially established and titled as 656 Squadron in mid-October. In deference to Army Aviation 17 Division this was not assumed until the end of December 1969, when the final disbandment was completed in Malaysia.

Up to the end of 1969 the Squadron was equipped with twelve Sioux helicopters, which had proven ideal for the Hong Kong terrain. Scout helicopters arrived during January 1970 by ship from various flights in the process of disbandment in Malaysia. For example, all the 7 Flight Scouts went to Hong Kong from Terendak in the LSL *Sir* *Galahad* in January 1970, along with the families, pets, cars and also the 656 silver inside one of the Scouts. The Scouts and the silver were handed over to Major Peter Ralph, the new OC 656 Squadron, by Major Spencer Holtom at Sek Kong on 1 February 1970. Spencer remembers the journey well,

'The families also took their boxes on the LSL and the children got sweets for helping to cover all the orifices on the Scouts - out in the open – to protect them from seawater ingression. Later, they got more sweets for taking off the tape after the four day/night voyage. As we sailed past Vietnam the Americans kept sending out Lockheed Orions to look at us, they were very curious.'

During February some Sioux were returned to Europe and the Squadron's establishment was fixed as two flights of eight helicopters, one of Sioux and the other of Scout. Two reserve helicopters, one of each type, were also held. Second line repairs and major servicing were carried out by a civil aircraft engineering firm located in Kowloon. The Squadron was under the administrative command of 48 Gurkha Infantry Brigade as a HQ Land Force Unit. It also supported 51Brigade, the RN, the RAF and the Royal Hong Kong Police. It was noted, 'Therefore our masters are currently one general, three brigadiers and one colonel in Singapore.'

Peter Ralph wrote an article for the AAC Newsletter in which he described operations in Hong Kong,

'The flying conditions vary with the season but are always interesting. The often strong winds make operations in the mountainous areas reminiscent of North Wales in the later stages of pilot training, except that it is a lot hotter and humid. In Kowloon and Hong Kong the air traffic density is similar to the circuit at Wallop. It is not uncommon to see four or five helicopters of all three services trying to cross the runway of the civil airport with a stream of Boeing 707s landing or taking off. [As well as the Squadron's aircraft, there were also helicopters from visiting RN ships, Whirlwind Mk 10s of No 28 Squadron RAF and lastly the Royal Hong Kong Auxiliary Air Force with Alouette IIIs and Auster Mk 9s] Night flying in the urban areas is an awe-inspiring sight for which tourists would pay a fortune to see. The lights are many and colourful, making London's Leicester Square look like a blackout zone. Landing points are varied, ranging from a jetty surrounded by Chinese territorial waters, to roof tops in the centre of Kowloon, to observation posts a few hundred yards from the Chinese border with Guangdong Province, from whence comes "provocations" and "shows of force" by the million strong People's Liberation Army.'

The first official visitor to the new Squadron in 1970 was particularly welcome, the Director of Army Aviation, Brigadier Denis Coyle. Even more welcome perhaps, was the independence granted to Hong Kong in April 1970 – at least as regards the military chain of command. As a result the Squadron ceased to be part of 4 Wing and 'will deal direct with our masters in Whitehall.' A full report was made on its first year of existence,

'This year has seen a continuing round of exercises during which the Squadron was fully deployed on five and had one flight deployed on a further nine. By far the most interesting were the two amphibious exercises during which operations were partially off the assault ships *Fearless* and *Intrepid*. Operating from the crowded flight deck of these ships – in company with four Westland Wessex HU5 – made a pleasant change from the airstrip at Sek Kong. All pilots are now deck qualified, some by night as well, and a sound alliance has been established with 845 and 847 Royal Naval Air Squadrons. Our other exercises have been more conventional, operating over the hilly and rugged terrain of the New Territories. The helicopter has proved its versatility in this theatre and has in every way justified aviation as a supporting arm. Apart from the more routine aviation tasks we do photographic reconnaissance with conventional and Polaroid cameras, sky shouting on internal security situations, night illumination with flares and searchlights, and water operations with flotation gear. From a flight safety and operational aspect there has been a requirement to fit some Sioux with flotation gear. A protracted trial was completed and we now have two Sioux equipped with floats. Landing on and off water opens a new area of operation which has proved useful and is interesting for the pilots. Engine off landings are now patterned by the QHI in nautical terms "All clear below, no boats," or "Midships, mind the yaw," or "Oops I told you it was a heavy landing if it stays green," were commonplace during the early stages of conversion. It is comforting, though, to be flying one of the "rubber jobs" when over the sea on a two-hour photographic mission and we have used them in earnest once for a sea rescue. Our other major acquisition has been a Nite-Sun searchlight specially modified for the Sioux. This light is by far the best we have seen and its performance in Hong Kong has won itself nothing but praise from pilots and observers on the ground. This light can be remote controlled in four planes from within the cockpit and produces an intense white beam, effective from heights up to five thousand feet above the ground. Pilot reconnaissance is as good as in daylight when at two thousand feet. An observer on the ground can read the evening newspaper with the light four thousand feet above him. It was the biggest single factor in discovering the clandestine landing of troops on Exercise Sea Horse. We understand that eventually we are to be given two on the completion of a confirmatory trial in the United Kingdom.

Life is very good in Hong Kong. The work is interesting and entertainment is full and varied. The Squadron is grateful to the Nuffield Trust for a boat which we will use for water-skiing, which we will put to full use in the next year. Shortly, we shall be part-owners of an island off Lantau, which, with some self-help, is to be turned into a weekend camp for soldiers and families. There is to be an extensive turnover of personnel during the latter part of 1970, so to those of you lucky enough to come we guarantee an interesting and enjoyable tour.'

Captain Rob Welsh arrived in Hong Kong in December 1969,

'The role of the Squadron under the command of Major Peter Ralph was not much different to most other AAC units at that time, in that it was basically reconnaissance and observation, liaison, troop lifting, casevac and aerial AOP. Some of the flying training was new in that we were flying over water a lot and had to take a keen interest in ditching procedures for obvious reasons and practice engine off landings were carried out so as to try and land on an area the size of a paddy field – which would in many cases have been all that was available in a real emergency. Later on and under the command of Lieutenant Colonel A.E. "Alan" Woodford, who became CO in September 1970, we developed a new and additional role of a "Quick Reaction Force," where a Sioux would provide overhead command and control for a formation of Scouts, carrying troops, to enable them to quickly place troops on the ground at tactical locations in the event of an Internal Security situation developing. Roping techniques and rooftop landings were also practised and developed both by day and night until we became quite slick at it. It seemed pretty effective as we could move a small force of men quickly from one place to another as situations required. Thankfully it was never used in anger in my time.'

While the Squadron was not engaged in the dangerous operational flying that had been its bread and butter for nearly a quarter of a century, there were still challenges to be faced,

'The general flying was in some ways quite challenging as we had to contend with hot and high conditions and the various wind effects in and around the many high hills and rocky outcrops. In addition to this the typhoon season produced its own batch of violent storms and strong winds/gales. Some of the HLS locations were more challenging than normal – for instance, Victoria Barracks on Hong Kong Island had a landing platform built into the side of a steep hill and which jutted out towards the sea. There was only one approach which was directly towards the hillside and thus there was no chance of an overshoot! If the approach had been downwind then the take-off was best accomplished by a transition backwards with a controlled right pedal turn into wind. We (the Scout pilots) did quite a lot of troop lifting which worked very well. The requirement was usually to move something like a company of infantry a short distance from the base of a steep hill to some point further up which, in the heat, would be both difficult and tiring to climb, taking many hours with the troops exhausted at the end. It took us only a matter of a few minutes with each load to cover some really difficult terrain. Sometimes the RAF, with Whirlwinds, would work with us and it was weird to see the much bigger Whirlwind helicopters just lifting two or three troops whilst the Scouts were taking four or five soldiers. The downside of flying in Hong Kong and the New Territories was that it is only a small area (about forty miles east-west and thirty miles north-south). The area became so familiar that often there was no need for reference to a map to get to a place and navigation was limited to very short distances indeed.'

The social and family life afforded by a posting to the Colony was enviable,

'There were many diverse attractions for all who lived there. The wives loved the shopping areas of Nathan Road in Kowloon and Hong Kong Island, plus the fact that clothes could be tailor-made to your own specification both cheaply and speedily. Indeed many people continued to buy items from their tailor long after they left. There was plenty of night life with many restaurants, bars, clubs, cabaret and hotel functions. The local sailing club based at "Gordon Hard," close to Castle Peak, had racing every weekend in Enterprise and Bosun dinghies with full family participation along with barbeques on the beach.'

One of the most dramatic events of the Squadron's time in Hong Kong occurred on 9 January 1972, when the former Cunard liner *Queen Elizabeth* (which had been renamed *Seawise University*) caught fire in Victoria Harbour. The OC was actually on board the Star Ferry in the harbour when he contacted the duty pilot and ordered him to get airborne as soon as possible. Within fifteen minutes Staff Sergeant Cox and Sergeant Simpson were overhead in a Sioux, watching the smoke billowing upwards to a height of 1500 feet. An Alouette of the Royal Hong Kong Auxiliary Air Force was already darting in and out over the decks checking to see if anyone remained on board. Back at Sek Kong, three Scouts were made ready with ladders and ropes in case rescue operations were necessary. In the event they were not needed as all those on board had jumped over the side and had been picked up by sampans standing alongside. At 1200 the next day, Sergeant Sharpe reported that the grand old Cunarder had rolled over to starboard but with the Union Jack and Red Ensign still flying defiantly. The ship was completely destroyed by the conflagration and the water sprayed on her by fireboats caused the burnt wreck to capsize and sink in the harbour's shallow water. There was some speculation that the fire was not accidental, as the ship's owner, C.Y. Tung, had bought the vessel for $3.5 million and insured it for $8 million.

By this time the Squadron was providing support to all Hong Kong units exercising throughout the Far East and for the equivalent of a division engaged in limited war training in the Colony. It worked in close association with No 28 Squadron, which was now equipped with Westland Wessex HC Mk2s. They combined to form the Joint Helicopter Force and used a common command net, procedures and tasking cell. It was noted in the AAC Newsletter that,

'Our Internal Security operations range from the normal and well known tasks, such as the reinforcement of police stations by heliborne troops and night surveillance etc. to Vietnam type helicopter assaults, complete with pathfinders and gunships. We practise these regularly by day and night, including live fire-plans from guns and

Major Jim Hailes and Captain Gerry Joyce at Fort George in Korea, 1952.

Leaflet 3530/PK/45 Order 105/55.
Requested by S.I.O. Perak.
Language Chinese.

(Photo of Chong Sze Hoi with cross on face)

Here is a message to Chai Kow, Yoon Thean, Meow Yee and Ah Thai:

Your comrades Chong Sze Hoi, Chong Pin and Kooi Moy have been killed.

They knew as well as you do that they could have self-renewed at any time and begin a new life. They were stubborn and delayed and now they are dead.

Do not wait for the same fate. Over 1500 of your comrades in Malaya have self-renewed and are now living well and earning their own living. If you do not believe this ask the masses - they have seen and talked to self-renewed comrades.

Twenty five of your comrades in the Sungei Siput area have been killed recently. Look at the picture of Chong Sze Hoi and think carefully about this. Contact the masses as soon as you read this leaflet. They will help you to self-renew.

REVERSE:

GENERAL BOURNE'S SAFE CONDUCT PASS.

Date. 7.3.55.

One of the 232 Million propaganda leaflets dropped by the Squadron during the Malayan Emergency.

An Auster AOP 9, WZ706, of 7 Flight, 656 Squadron landing at Sumpitan in North Malaya in 1962 (painting by David Shepherd CBE).

Beaver XP780 taking off from Noble Field, Kuala Lumpur in late 1961.

Corporals Les Rogers and Dick Jones hard at work servicing an Auster 9 of 14 Flight at Brunei Airport in 1963.

10 Flight personnel in the Mess tent at Long Pa Sia, Borneo, in 1964.

One of the Squadron's Scouts, XR602, resting on a raised landing platform at Long Pa Sia. These platforms were constructed from tree trunks and were required due to the swampy nature of the ground.

Beaver XP817 being recovered from Bario, Borneo in early 1965. This fuselage and wings were air-lifted by Scout helicopter as three separate underslung loads 110 miles to Brunei, in hops of 30 miles at a time. This was a unique operation.

The Sioux was introduced into Malaysia in 1965, XT109 is seen here at Kluang.

One of the regular tasks Squadron Scouts undertook in Hong Kong was the resupply of stores to the hilltop radar site at Tai Mo Shan.

A beautifully posed shot of a Squadron Gazelle with an iconic Chinese junk in Hong Kong Harbour.

A Scout flies along the waterfront at Kowloon.

A 656 Scout stands by at Assembly Point Lima in the Rhodesian bush, ready to accept a casualty for transport to hospital. Note the white Kiwi painted on the nose, the handiwork of New Zealander Mike Subritzky, who is standing in the foreground (Mike Subritzky).

Major General Ken Perkins, who was a pilot with the Squadron in the 1950s, inspects a ZANU Patriotic Front guard of honour at Assembly Point Romeo in Rhodesia, during Operation Agila.

On the voyage south to the Falkland Islands, Squadron helicopters were used for transport and liaison duties from ship to ship.

SHQ, groundcrew and elements of the LAD embarked on 12 May 1982 and sailed in the liner Queen Elizabeth 2, along with most of 5 Infantry Brigade.

656 Squadron Falklands CASEVAC at Ajax Bay, 1982 (painting by David Shepherd CBE).

The Squadron's HQ was at one stage based in a cow shed at Fitzroy. Major Colin Sibun is seated on the left, with Staff Sergeant Dave Ward to the right.

On 8 June 1982 Sergeant Dick Kalinski and his crewman Lance Corporal Julian Rigg had to make an emergency landing in McPhee Pond in Scout XR628.

The mountains of South Georgia provide a dramatic backdrop to this picture of a Squadron Scout.

Flying conditions during the Balkan winter in the 1990s could be harsh, as this photograph demonstrates.

In contrast, as more than one Squadron member remarked, you could fly from the heat of Split to the snowy mountains in a single sortie, as is shown in this view of Lynx helicopters at a sunny Split dispersal.

The OC, Major Steven Marshall, beside Lynx XZ653 on a snowy hillside in Bosnia.

A pair of Apaches during training in the UK, 2004.

The Apache is equipped with a very sophisticated and effective suite of defensive aids.

Refuelling an Apache during Conversion To Role (CTR) training at Woodbridge, Suffolk.

An Apache hovering alongside the helicopter carrier HMS *Ocean* (painting by Derek Blois).

Brown-out was a challenge faced by all Apache crews landing in dusty desert conditions.

An Apache lands at Gereshk, Afghanistan.

The Apaches first went to sea in 2005 on board the helicopter carrier HMS *Ocean*.

In 2011 the Apaches were in action in the maritime strike role over Libya.

Burma veterans at the 656 Squadron Association Reunion in 2005, held in the Officers' Mess at Middle Wallop – from left to right, Ray Pett, Jack Hallam, Arthur Maycroft, Bill Peers, Mr Merryweather (Guest), Basil Appleton, Bob Henshaw, Vin Weaver, Arthur Windscheffel, Ted Maslen-Jones, Gwyn Thomas and Peter Andrews.

656 Squadron Association members at the 2006 Annual Reunion at Netheravon.

mortars which have been initially airlifted into their firing positions. The night ops are particularly interesting with flare illumination for two pathfinder Scouts engaged in roping down to the landing point, and the securing troops being provided by another pair of Scout/Sioux stationed above them. During Exercise Eastern Triangle we flew 450 hours, including fifty at night on ten aircraft in ten days. Our friends in the RAF flew just under 400 hours on eight Wessex in the same period.'

Early in 1975, Major David Swan was posted to Hong Kong to replace Lieutenant Colonel Greville Edgecombe in command. Following a Scout refresher course at Middle Wallop, he arrived in Hong Kong in May, just before the Queen, who would be making her first State Visit to the Colony. His official title was not only CO 656 Squadron AAC, but also Commander Aviation Far East, as there were Squadron detachments in Brunei (C Flight) and Singapore (11 ANZUK Flight). 11 Flight closed down in September 1975, so there was only time for him to make one trip to Singapore. The Squadron itself was under the command of 48 Gurkha Infantry Brigade at Sek Kong. At the top of the new CO's in tray was a major re-equipment project,

'It had been decided that all available Scouts would be concentrated in BAOR to boost the AAC's anti-tank capability. There was much prior discussion, some heated, on the suitability of the Gazelle for the Hong Kong operations but, having been involved in that decision in my previous appointment, I had to make it work. The chickens had come home to roost!'

C Flight, at Seria in Brunei, would remain equipped with three Sioux and manned on a six month rotational basis from Hong Kong, later extended to one year. The personnel

In May 1975 Major David Swan assumed command from Lieutenant Colonel Greville Edgecombe.

were looked after by the resident Gurkha Battalion, while the Flight was based in a small hangar close to the beach. As well as carrying out all normal aviation tasks, with observers supplied by the Brigade of Gurkhas, the Flight also provided support to all Hong Kong units engaged in jungle training in Brunei.

Spencer Holtom remembers,

'David Swan was keen to have a spare Sioux as a backup for Brunei and XT546 had just had a Major overhaul, I managed to get it on a Hercules from Tengah and it was delivered to Kai Tak, the other three Sioux I had with 11 Flight in Singapore were sold to the RMAF and taken off to Kuala Lumpur. When I got to Sek Kong in November 1975, I was the only person current on Sioux and it was my job to keep XT546 flying a few hours a month to keep it exercised, all the other aircraft were Gazelles by then; in the event it was never needed in Brunei. It became my personal helicopter and I used to take chums round the colony on photo trips – also, I used it to do a photographic survey of the Royal Hong Kong Golf Club prior to realignment of the Old Course, the Sioux was a perfect platform for this. Happy days!'

One of the Squadron's major tasks in Hong Kong during this period was carrying out patrols along the Chinese border, which were predominantly dawn sorties, searching for and intercepting illegal immigrants seeking their fortune in Hong Kong. The aircraft usually carried three armed Gurkha soldiers whose role was to disembark and attempt to catch anyone spotted by the aircrew. This was not always successful, as the Chinese became very adept at hiding in the undergrowth, crossing the water at night using all sorts of inflatable devices and hiding up during the day. Once they reached the built-up areas they would be virtually impossible to trace by the police. In November 1975, Sergeant Timothy Smith, flying a Scout, had to make a forced landing in the sea off the Tolo Peninsula. Both the pilot and his passenger were given assistance by a local fisherman, Mr So Yat, who took them to a nearby Army camp in his boat. He later received a framed Commendation and a mounted Squadron Crest for his efforts.

David Swan describes the transition from the by now well-loved Scout to the Westland Gazelle AH1, which was manufactured at Yeovil, following the Anglo-French helicopter agreement, which also included the Puma and the Lynx. It was developed from the original Sud Aviation SA340,

'The changeover from Scouts to Gazelles required some major reorganization within the Squadron. The pilots had to return to Middle Wallop for conversion flying courses. In order to maintain our aviation support to the colony, half went at a time, leaving the others to fly the Scouts until the Gazelles were up and running. The REME technicians had to learn about the innards of the new arrival. However, some already had Gazelle experience, which was a bonus. The first three Gazelles arrived at Kai Tak inside a Short Belfast C Mk 1 freighter on 26 November 1975 and the next day the same aircraft took three of our Scouts back to UK. After an overnight stop and a quick check over at Kai Tak, the Gazelles were given clearance for the short formation flight to Sek Kong, where we were welcomed by various dignitaries and the Squadron families. The aircraft were then impounded by the LAD for acceptance servicing and modifications. The remaining three Gazelles arrived in Hong Kong and the last three Scouts departed the same way on 16/17 December.'

To avoid damage to the Gazelle airframes, which were somewhat more delicate than the Scout, walkway strips were fitted on the skids and door frames, and rubber mats in the boot and on the passenger floor. Locally manufactured freight floors were designed and produced before flying began. Eventually, two aircraft reappeared for air testing on 3 December. No problems were encountered and the Squadron work up took place from 3 December to 9 January, 1976. This was followed by a proving exercise (Exercise Swan Around II) in support of a 48 Gurkha Brigade exercise, Exercise Frozen Gleam, where the aircraft were used in support of units for the first time. The Squadron was declared operational again on 19 January 1976.

As David Swan noted,

'As the weather warmed up and the south-west monsoon rains arrived, there was some trouble with separation and holing of the rotor blade leading edges and three sets of blades had to be changed in a short space of time. However, the aircraft proved reliable and popular with passengers and the "extras" fitted (rubber mats and freight floors) kept damage to the minimum. We had some concerns about the possibility of rifles making holes in the canopy but there were no such incidents, mainly through careful training and briefing of passengers and troops. It was amazing how many visitors "required" an airborne familiarization trip around the island and the New Territories.'

Another of the Squadron's activities was the further development of air mobile type operations, deploying Gurkha infantry around the colony in conjunction with the RAF Wessex HC2s. They practised this whenever the time and opportunities arose and Standing Operational Procedures (SOPs) were written. The normal drill was that the Gazelles would carry out the recces and the RAF the troop lifts. These mutual activities attracted the attention of the Joint Warfare Establishment in UK, whose team paid a visit to Hong Kong and were 'quite complimentary about our humble efforts.' One Gazelle was fitted with a Nite Sun searchlight and the capability of installing a Skyshout loudspeaker was also provided.

Later in 1976, Sergeants I.D. Johnstone and D. Clark were awarded Director Army Air Corps commendations for carrying out a medical evacuation in difficult conditions at night. In December, the Squadron passed from the command of Land Forces Hong Kong, to the operational control of the Gurkha Field Force.

There was only one major incident, when in February 1977, a pilot misjudged his approach to a landing site over water at night and ended up in the water. This is described by Captain Simon Fogden,

'During an exercise in February 1977, I was commanding a detachment of three Gazelles from the Flight which was based on the island HLS. A standard NATO 'T' was being used as a night landing aid and the approach to the landing aid was over the sea. At 2305 hours on the night in question, I flew off with the intention of just visiting an alternative HLS, but I was tasked in the air to carry out other sorties, including taking two compassionate cases back to base and then a casualty evacuation (casevac).

By the time of the casevac, it was close to 0100 hours and the ambient light levels were low and there were patches of mist on the water on a windless night. The casualty, who was suffering from stomach cramps, was located at a rebroadcast station high on an isolated mountain and I was reluctant to make an approach direct to the mountain top without more clearly defined reference points. I therefore decided to make an approach to the shoreline from where I hover-taxied up the mountain using my landing light. I managed to land and recover the casualty, but low cloud prevented me from flying over the Lion Rock ridge into Kowloon where I had intended to drop the casualty off at the military hospital. I therefore returned to Sek Kong where I was met by an ambulance which set off with the casualty on the relatively long and twisty journey by road into Kowloon. At Sek Kong airfield I picked up a replacement air crewman as well as a ground crewman to fly back to the Tolo Harbour HLS. By this time it was nearly 0200 hours, with further reduced light levels and a barely discernible horizon. Initially, I found it difficult to locate the HLS but eventually sighted it and set up a right hand circuit for landing. I noted that in the final turn onto finals my height was 600 feet and the speed was 50 knots. At a range of 400 metres, I switched on the landing light and was temporarily dazzled by the reflection off the mist. I adjusted the light down to illuminate the area of the 'T' and still further down to pick out the shoreline short of the 'T'. When I looked up again at the 'T' I realized I had lost height and at the same time the aircraft struck the water. In attempting to lift and fly the aircraft away, the rotor blades struck the water and stopped almost immediately. The aircraft settled into the water and turned over with the landing light still on, illuminating the area. Luckily, we were all able to escape unscathed and with the aid of the dinghy from the aircraft's survival pack we made it to the shore. An RAF Wessex was called and, significantly for me, the pilot also became disorientated on his approach to the HLS when he descended to within 40 feet of the sea, some 300 metres from the 'T'. He was alerted to the danger by his crewman who was monitoring the approach from the rear door. Clearly the still air, the mist and the glass like surface to the sea made the approach to the island more difficult than I had realized, even when using the NATO 'T'. The Wessex picked us up and recovered direct to Kai Tak airport, for the pilot was able to undertake an instrument approach, before then diverting to the military hospital where we were all admitted for observation. The Board of Inquiry came to the conclusion that the cause of the accident was my failure to monitor the instruments during the approach and that pilot fatigue was the main contributory factor to that failure. I was found excusably negligent. It was significant that I had been awake 19.5 hours, on duty for 18 hours and had flown 2.6 hours in the day and 2.1 hours at night, including eight night landings. I had exceeded, by four hours, the maximum crew duty time of fourteen hours laid down in the Squadron's Flying Orders. It was decided that justice had to be seen to be done and I was charged with exceeding Crew Duty Time and was fined two weeks pay, which might have been particularly painful but for the fact that I received a fairly generous Local Overseas Allowance which could not be confiscated as part of the fine. After all the trauma and criticism, I received a Commander British Forces Hong Kong commendation for "showing great flying skill and a high degree of determination" in successfully completing the casevac! On the same day that I was charged, I received a letter of congratulations from the then Director Army Air Corps for being selected to attend

The recovery of Gazelle XX409 from Hong Kong harbour in February 1977 by HMS *Wasperton*.

Staff College. It raised my sagging spirit! When my 'Summary Trial" was reviewed back in the MOD, the punishment was considered too severe and it was amended to read: "To be reprimanded and fined £35". I received a rebate of nearly £300!'

The incident gave the local press some exciting news including pictures of the Gazelle being hauled out of the water by the Royal Navy patrol craft HMS *Wasperton*. It was subsequently rebuilt and flew again in Germany.

David Swan's tour came to an end in June 1977 and at the same time the Squadron's presence in Hong Kong and Brunei also drew to a close. The OC designate was Major Dick Whidborne, but his time in command of the Squadron was brief indeed, as by the start of July, the unit was retitled 11 Flight. The introduction of the armed Lynx to the AAC in Europe allowed representations to be made to bring Scouts back to Hong Kong. This was agreed and the Flight was equipped with six Scouts in Hong Kong, three in Brunei and two Sioux in Hong Kong. The Director Army Air Corps, Major General Tony Ward-Booth, then decided that, 'the unit in Hong Kong was far too important to be a flight and had to be a squadron.' On its disbandment on 1 August 1978, 11 Flight flew a formation of a Gazelle, two Scouts and two Sioux over Victoria Harbour. The Hong Kong unit was again retitled as 660 Squadron, which became the resident AAC unit at Sek Kong, equipped with Scouts and remained there until March 1994 (though it should be noted for the record that Major Whidborne flew what was believed to be the last Sioux, XT546, at the RAF Sek Kong Airshow on 17 November 1978). He has many vivid memories of his time in Hong Kong, of which these are but four,

The Squadron performs a farewell fly-past at Sek Kong for departing Commanding Officer, Major David Swan.

'I was tasked to fly a two-star RAF officer on an aerial tour of the colony. As we flew over the Hong Kong University and towards Tolo Harbour and the Plover Cove reservoir, the Air Vice-Marshall suddenly had convulsions. Luckily, an AAC pilot who was on a non-flying staff tour (Major the Lord Roland Castlemaine) was in the back seat and he was able to restrain the AVM, who was thrashing about and presenting quite a hazard within the small Gazelle cockpit. I immediately set course for the British Military Hospital, Kowloon and landed on the sports pitch, whereupon medics removed the AVM to casualty. It transpired that the AVM had suffered an epileptic or "flicker fit" induced by the stroboscopic effect of bright sunlight passing through the main rotor blades. A frequency of about 12 Hertz is the trigger for such a phenomenon. That evening I received a note from the AVM apologizing for his mishap, saying that "one minute we were chatting away and the next thing I knew was my being in the BMH surrounded by a lot of solicitous medics,"

The primary role of the Squadron was to patrol the border between Hong Kong and Guangdong (Canton) province of China. There were daily attempts by mainland Chinese to enter Hong Kong illegally in a quest to reach "base" in Kowloon, where they could eventually be assimilated into the local population. Many attempts involved a night swim across a narrow stretch of water in the north-east of the colony. A dawn helicopter patrol might find "IIs" (Illegal Immigrants) hiding in the area in preparation for a further covert dash for the south. One morning I was on patrol with my Air Gunner observer and a Gurkha major in the back of the Scout. We searched a small island, and finding nothing continued towards another search area. The Gurkha major tapped me on the shoulder and gave me a "thumbs up" sign. Rather than an affirmation that all was OK, I was later to learn that this indicated the presence of "enemy" and so we returned to the little island to find five "IIs" who had emerged from under the bush in which they had been hiding. The Gurkha major had spotted them, but I had not! They were rounded up and handed over to the Royal Hong Kong Police (RHKP) at their Fanling holding centre. In most case they were returned to mainland China where they met several differing fates. If they were first offenders they were shipped well inland or returned to their villages. Persistent offenders were sent further away or imprisoned. Fleeing "IIs" were often hounded by dogs and/or shot by border guards. One very sad incident involved an "II" who had gained the HK shore but then hanged himself from a tree having lost the rest of his family through drowning in the water crossing.

During this time the colony was the chosen haven for fleeing Vietnamese "boat people". They arrived in a variety of vessels and attempted to smuggle themselves ashore. The squadron was often tasked to photograph such incidents when the boat people had been discovered. At Tai O, I photographed a sampan crowded with refugees, who were only able to stand up because of the density of their crowd, whilst the sampan was close to sinking. They had managed to float across the Yellow River estuary. One significant incident involved the *Huey Fong*, a rust bucket freighter crowded with boat people in the most unimaginable squalor. The ship, from Vietnam, was halted by the Royal Navy on the international boundary and lay there at anchor for several days. The RAF Wessex helicopters ferried food and water and other supplies whilst a solution to the refugees' plight was sought. The squadron Scouts carried out surveillance and photography sorties of this pitiful scene. Eventually the refugees came ashore and were accommodated in huts on part of the airfield at Sek Kong, which was of course the squadron base.

On a lighter note, the Squadron was often tasked to photograph progress on the new racecourse at Shatin, being built on land reclamation by the Royal Hong Kong Jockey Club with every modern facility, including exercise swimming pools for the racehorses. I confidently expected an invitation to the official opening of this impressive racecourse, which supplemented that at Happy Valley, but none came! The Brigadier, Commander Land Forces, was an avid zoologist and ornithologist and so a weekly task was to photograph for him a colony of Egrets in the north-east of the colony. (I won't give his name, but he eventually reached the highest rank in the army!). Similarly, my Scouts in Brunei were frequently tasked by the resident Gurkha battalion commander to collect his moth specimens at night. This consumed an inordinate number of flying hours. I had quite a tussle with him over this flagrant misuse of AAC resources.'

7 Flight returned to the Far East in 1994, to be based at Seria in Brunei, replacing the Scouts of C Flight 660 Squadron. It is still serving there and continues to fly the Bell 212.

With the retitling of squadrons, which paid little respect to military heritage, 656 Squadron's time in the Far East finally – at least in this era – came to an end.

Chapter 7

UK and Rhodesia 1978–1981

On Thursday, 23 March 1978, a Change of Title Parade was held at Jersey Brow, Royal Aircraft Establishment, Farnborough. 664 Squadron AAC, which was under the command of Major Chris Pickup, became 656 Squadron AAC. Farnborough, of course, is one of the cradles of British aviation and had played host to the Army's airmen since the nineteenth century when the Royal Engineers had first flown their 'war balloons.' 664 Squadron had been formed originally in December 1944, as one of three Canadian Air OP units which served in north-west Europe in 1945. 664 Squadron's immediate antecedent was 21 Reconnaissance Flight, which had been based at Farnborough since 1965, and became an Interim Aviation Squadron in 1968, and then 664 Aviation Squadron in 1969. In 1973, 'Parachute' had been incorporated into the Squadron title, as most of the aircrew and LAD were trained parachutists, and everyone wore the Red Beret. With the disbandment of the Parachute Brigade on 1 April 1977, these entitlements were withdrawn. As the 2i/c, Tony McMahon noted,

> 'In March 1977 the squadron exchanged its red berets for the AAC berets on a small parade outside the squadron hangar, with many a tear shed by those who held the para association dear. In fact, there was one REME SNCO who took it so badly that he avoided wearing blue beret whenever he could. I ignored his protest and eventually he came round.'

The Squadron's primary function in 1978 was the support of 6 Field Force and it consisted of two flights; A Flight with six Gazelles (replacing Sioux from 1 April) and B Flight with six Scouts. The SQMS, Ross Skingley, remembers,

> 'The Squadron hangar and offices were situated close to the centre of this large MOD specialist airfield for aircraft and systems testing. There was plenty of room, as the hangar had been designed to accommodate VC10s. During the annual air displays we had a grandstand seat, though it was a little close for comfort should there be a major accident.'

The Squadron was kept very busy during the year, with two Scouts being detached to The Gambia between February and May for exercise with the Royal Anglian Regiment, two Gazelles spending April in Germany, again on exercise, a visit to Canada for B Flight

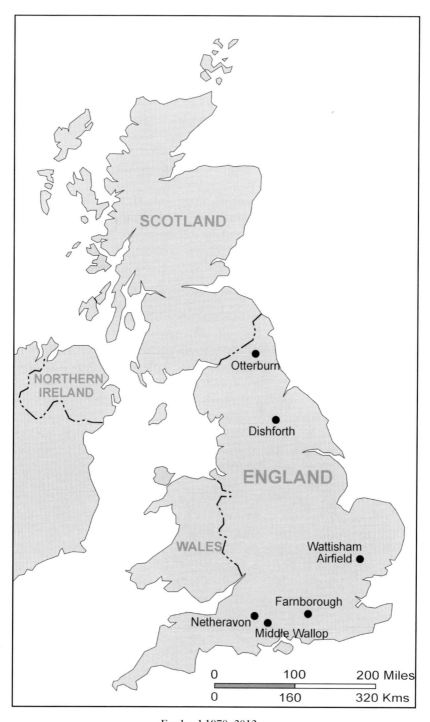

England 1978–2012.

in September to BATUS (the British Army Training Unit Suffield) and between October and November, participation in a main field training exercise in Denmark. Tony McMahon has fond memories of the trip to Denmark,

> 'Exercise Arrow Express proved to be an amazing experience. We self-deployed by air to Denmark, the support elements going by sea. Miraculously we married up over there and proceeded to support the Brigade HQ. As second in command my job was to find a squadron location. I happened upon a wonderful estate and negotiated our occupation with the owner, Ole Molgard Christensen. He made us very welcome, treating the officers to his store of Glenlivet on the first evening and then declared that he would have a dinner party in our honour. He expected that we would have deployed with full mess kit and was very disappointed to discover that we barely had a tie between us. At the end of the exercise he challenged us to a football (soccer) match and our boys were slightly nonplussed to discover that half their local team were girls who were not shy when it came to sharing the same changing room. Nobody remembers the result of the game. Our Danish host subsequently became an honorary member of the Squadron.'

The pattern continued into 1979 with two Scout crews being deployed to Belize between January and April. The colony formerly known as British Honduras was being threatened by its larger neighbour, Guatemala, and a strong British military presence was being maintained to deter any aggressive moves (Belize attained full independence on 21 September 1981). Two Scouts and eleven personnel were attached to 660 Squadron in Hong Kong from July to October, as reinforcements in the prevention of illegal immigrants. According to Sergeant Dick Kalinski, the job consisted mostly of, 'Hovering over the Mai Po marshes while the crewman in the back lent out and pulled them in.' As well as these operational deployments, aircraft were also sent to take part in exercises in Italy, Germany, Denmark, Kenya and the USA. Tony McMahon also recalls receiving some assistance,

> 'Whilst at the Staff College, Camberley, at the beginning of 1979, I called upon 656 Squadron to provide a static display of Scouts with SS.11 missiles and the new Gazelle during the aviation study phase and it impressed even the Commandant, Major General Frank Kitson, if only for the noise they made on arrival!'

Chris Pickup has happy memories of his period in command,

> 'I seem to recall that within a week, during February 1979, I flew over the sea ice around Copenhagen and the primary jungle of Belize. I also took a Gazelle to Italy for a week in the summer of 1978, to fly the Brigade Commander when he went out to recce one of our NATO reinforcement options on the Tagliatmento River. And we were always flying him to Caen to visit Pegasus Bridge. We also forged a link with Bulmer's Cider in Hereford – this through the Chairman, Peter Prior, who set up the Military/Industrial Exchange Scheme. Peter was a free-fall enthusiast – in fact I think he held the world altitude record at one time – hence his interest in what had been the Parachute Brigade. Anyway, he entertained the whole Squadron for a

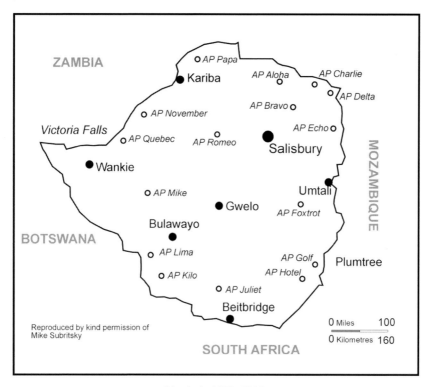

Rhodesia 1979–1980.

weekend at Bulmer's, to include not only a factory visit, but also; a trip in their steam train, a service in the Cathedral and a very smart dinner. As was the case in Denmark [referred to above], at Hovdingsgaard, when the owner invited the whole Squadron to lunch, everyone conducted themselves in an exemplary fashion. I was amazed and really rather proud of them!'

The Squadron also had to maintain a capability to be ready to support the civil power in the UK should an incident arise, eg. a natural disaster or a strike involving essential services. In May, Chris Pickup was succeeded in command by Major Stephen Nathan.

Rhodesia
On 15 November 1979, the Squadron was given five weeks' notice to be ready to depart for Rhodesia, where elections were to be held which it was hoped would bring to an end a dispute which had begun on 11 November 1965, when the government of the British colony of Southern Rhodesia, under its Prime Minister, Ian Smith, issued a Unilateral Declaration of Independence (UDI). Attempts to reach a compromise by personal meetings, held first on board the cruiser HMS *Tiger* and then the assault ship HMS *Fearless*, between the British Prime Minister, Harold Wilson and Ian Smith failed to reach an agreement. Trade sanctions were imposed and a naval blockade was implemented. Rhodesia was declared a republic in March 1970. Then, in 1972, a guerrilla campaign was

begun with scattered attacks on isolated white-owned farms by the military wings of the Zimbabwe African National Union (ZANU) and the Zimbabwe African People's Union (ZAPU), led by Robert Mugabe and Joshua Nkomo respectively, which wished to bring white rule of the country to an end. Mugabe's army was ZANLA (Zimbabwe National Liberation Army) which was largely drawn from the Mashona tribe and received considerable support from China, while Nkomo's was ZIPRA (Zimbabwe People's Revolutionary Army), which was mostly Matabele and obtained weapons and training from Cuba and the USSR. Both peoples were traditionally enemies. Initially, the activities of ZANLA and ZIPRA were contained by the Rhodesian Security Forces (RSF), but it developed into a very nasty conflict with bloody deeds on both sides. However, the situation changed dramatically after the end of Portuguese colonial rule in Mozambique in 1975. Rhodesia now found itself almost entirely surrounded by hostile states, and even South Africa, its only real ally, pressed for a settlement. All attempts made by Smith, Nkomo and Mugabe to broker an honourable peace that would guarantee the rights of the white minority failed. In September 1976, Smith accepted the principle of black majority rule within two years. By 1978–79, the 'Bush War' had become a contest between the guerrilla warfare placing ever increasing pressure on the Rhodesian government and civil population, and the Rhodesian Government's strategy of trying to hold off the militants until external recognition for a compromise political settlement with moderate black leaders could be secured. As the result of an internal settlement between the Rhodesian government and three moderate African leaders, who were not in exile and not involved in the war, elections were held in April 1979. The United African National Council party won a majority in this election, and its leader, Abel Muzorewa, a United Methodist Church bishop, became the country's Prime Minister on 1 June 1979. The country's name was changed to Zimbabwe Rhodesia. While the 1979 election was non-racial and democratic, it did not include ZANU and ZAPU. In spite of offers from Ian Smith, the latter parties declined to participate. Bishop Muzorewa's government did not receive international recognition. The Bush War continued unabated and sanctions were not lifted. The international community refused to accept the validity of any agreement which did not incorporate ZANU and ZAPU. The British Government (then led by the recently elected Margaret Thatcher) issued invitations to all parties to attend a peace conference at Lancaster House. These negotiations took place in London in late 1979. The three month long conference almost failed to reach conclusion, due to disagreements on land reform, but resulted in the Lancaster House Agreement. UDI ended, and Rhodesia reverted to the status of a British colony under a new Governor, Lord Christopher Soames. Some 1500 British and Commonwealth troops (drawn from Australia, New Zealand, Fiji and Kenya) were sent to monitor and supervise the ceasefire between the Rhodesian Security Forces (RSF) and the guerrillas – known collectively as the Popular Front (PF) – with the prospect of an internationally supervized general election in early 1980. This was named Operation Agila and the collective name of the troops deployed was the Commonwealth Monitoring Group (CMG).

Before deploying, the Squadron used its five weeks of grace (while fourteen deployment timetables were considered and rewritten) to study the military and political background; to brief themselves on the climate and terrain; to discuss the technical problems associated with hot and high operations; to study detailed maps, preparing the aircraft; painting them white (which washed off in heavy rain); covering them with

DAYGLO (and removing it again) and finally, adding large white crosses to fuselages and tail fin, then collecting special stores; armour (which in the event was not used); infra-red shields (which were); survival packs, sand filters and SARBE beacons. Ross Skingley comments on the provision of armour,

'The full set of engine and cockpit armour was fitted, but on the test flight the QFI found that it would be too heavy to operate at 6000 feet plus (the altitude at Salisbury airfield) with fuel and four passengers on board. Therefore the only armour was a pan in the seat for protection of rear ends and other essential body parts!'

The initial requirement had been for a detachment of three Gazelles, which were placed on forty-eight hours' notice, with a further detachment at seventy-two hours' notice. Within three days of arriving in theatre it was accepted that another six Scouts should also be sent out (which the Squadron had known all along would be required).

The first elements of the Squadron (and also No 230 Squadron RAF) left Brize Norton on 20 and 21 December 1979, in RAF VC10s and C-130 Hercules, as well as enormous USAF Starlifters and Galaxys, routing via a combination of Cyprus, Egypt and Kenya. It was noted that a single Galaxy could transport three Gazelles, three Pumas and 20,000lbs of freight and still have room for forty passengers. Ross Skingley, who was by this time SSM, recalls,

'After about twenty hours, including a suck of fuel in Cairo, we came overhead Salisbury International at night; however, because of the threat of SAM 7s, the C-5 spiralled down from about 30,000 feet and as there were only about four small windows in the boom, where we were sitting … it was interesting!'

Within two weeks all eighty personnel, six Scouts and six Gazelles had arrived, under the command of Major Stephen Nathan. Maintenance was the responsibility of a detachment from 70 Aircraft Workshop. The Gazelles were based in the capital, Salisbury, with the HQ Monitoring Force and Government House, sharing a hangar with the RAF as well as Rhodesian Bell UH-1Ds and Alouette IIIs (remarkably and somewhat worryingly, all the Rhodesian helicopters had twin waist guns which were left unguarded, loaded with ammunition and belt feeds); while the Scouts were in Gwelo, at the Rhodesian Air Force base, Thornhill. The Gazelle crews covered the north and east of the country, which was twice the size of the UK, while the Scouts looked after the west and south, which was the location of many of the assembly points for ZANLA and ZIPRA guerrillas coming in from the bush. Operations began on Christmas Day, with two aircraft being tasked to fly Brigadier John Learmont, the Deputy Force Commander and some of his staff to Umtali. Brigade HQ was situated in the Morgan High School, Salisbury, which possessed playing fields in which helicopters could land. Many years later General Sir John Learmont wrote,

'Stephen Nathan received all his tasking from the Air Cell in the HQ and I saw him almost on a daily basis. Having such close helicopter access to my HQ was a considerable advantage from my point of view.'

Major Tim Purdon, Lieutenant Colonel Ian Hurley, former 656 Squadron pilot, Major General Ken Perkins and Brigadier John Learmont discuss matters in Rhodesia, 1979.

Tragedy soon struck the RAF, as on 27 December, a Puma crashed after hitting low wires near Salisbury, killing Flight Lieutenant M. Smith and Master Air Loadmaster M.R. Hodges of 230 Squadron and Flying Officer A. Cook of 33 Squadron. The optimum operating height was debated, the Squadron decided to fly at above 2500 feet unless forced down lower by the weather. This initial period was a very tense time; the weather was atrocious as it was the wet season, and moreover, no one knew how the guerrillas would react and if self-defensive force would have to be applied. The ceasefire came into effect at 0001 hours on 29 December. Some thirty-nine Rendezvous Points (RV) and sixteen Assembly Places (AP) were set up across the country. During a ceasefire period of seven days, members of ZIPRA and ZANLA were guaranteed unhindered movement through the RVs and into the APs. Here their names were recorded, together with details of the weapons they carried. They were also provided with food, clothing and bedding. Considerably more people arrived than had been expected, some 22,000. The heavily-armed and ill-disciplined fighters, tended to carry their weapons loaded, cocked and with safety catches off, which did nothing to simplify the operation. The scale of the task created something of a logistical nightmare, which the AAC and RAF helicopters did their best to alleviate with many resupply missions. The OC later commented,

'The guerrillas were never entirely relaxed when we were in the air; at all locations they covered our approach with at least one AA machine gun and, whilst the aircraft were on the ground, with small arms and RPG-7... in the first few days we gave away hundreds of cigarettes... and showed many of them around the helicopters in order to create some kind of trust. What else can you do when armed with a 9mm pistol and a white flying helmet, surrounded by hundreds of rifles and rockets?'

On one flight the OC had to carry a PF officer who had been injured while out hunting buffalo, one of the most dangerous of animals. He had been badly gored and had 'a huge hole in his leg and I had blood all over the cabin.'

The CMG's role was to monitor the activities of the PF and the RSF and report any violations of the ceasefire – it had no powers to intervene in the event of a recurrence of hostilities, nor indeed was it equipped to do so. During the first month of the deployment, the Squadron's twelve aircraft flew 1000 hours in the hot and high local conditions which varied from 1500 to 8000 feet above mean sea level – REME, as ever, worked wonders and ten helicopters were always available for duty. The chief problem areas for the Squadron as a whole concerned the availability of adequate refuelling facilities and of suitable accommodation, the need for better radio sets and of extra means of land transport. It was noticed that the pilots' navigational and map-reading skills improved,

'Some of our better routes were over 100nm of absolutely flat bush with no navigational features at all. You just had to rely on the compass and the clock and then amaze yourself when, at the given time, your destination suddenly appeared.'

Although, by African standards, Rhodesia had a well-developed network of road and rail links, in reality there were thousands of square miles of featureless flat bush to traverse. Off the main tarmac roads transport was restricted to bush tracks which, at the time of the deployment, were considered as a potential landmine hazard. Air support was therefore absolutely crucial to the CMG's mission. The guerrillas were well-armed and before deployment the potential threat had been assessed as quite considerable.

On 5 January 1980, a patrol of two Land Rovers collected about ten guerrillas and was transporting them along a dirt road at the bottom of the Zambezi Escarpment when the first vehicle hit a landmine, seriously injuring the driver and wounding others, including the guerrilla commander. He had been standing up in the back of the first Land Rover, holding on to the roll bar and posing when the explosion occurred and was blasted over the bonnet, landing in a heap on the road, minus his clothes. Staff Sergeant Chris Griffin in a Gazelle and Captain Sam Drennan in a Scout, with a medic each, were scrambled to attend this incident. On arrival they landed beside the road, the situation was tense, but well managed by the three unwounded British ground troops. The driver was in a bad way, with serious injuries to his leg. This was expertly dealt with by the Rhodesian combat medic who had accompanied Drennan, he splinted the leg using a rifle and had the casualty prepared for shipment quickly. The British medic was dealing with the injured guerrilla leader whilst the remaining guerrillas were increasingly panic stricken as their leader was barely conscious and no one else could make decisions. Drennan decided to send Griffin off to hospital with the injured driver; he would then take the guerrilla leader when he could be moved. The remaining guerrillas refused to let the Gazelle go and made their point with wild eyes, shouting and waving of weapons. This situation lasted for a while and the patrol commander communicated their predicament to HQ in Salisbury, who, after an hour or so, produced a ZANU leader (Comrade John) to speak to his men on the HF radio. This resulted in the Gazelle being released, but the Scout had to stay. When invited to help carry the injured driver to the Gazelle, the guerrillas refused, as they had been responsible for planting the landmine and also had put some close to the road, but did not know where they were. The driver was carried to the Gazelle, using the footprints made by the crew on arrival. No explosion occurred and the Gazelle departed. The guerrilla leader's condition continued to deteriorate and his comrades continued to panic. After protracted conversations with Comrade John in Salisbury, the guerrillas eventually agreed to let their leader be taken to hospital. One of the main problems during the long conversations was that the guerrilla doing the talking could not understand that the transmit switch had to be pressed whilst he was talking, which resulted in repeated attempts to communicate. It would have been comical if it hadn't been so unpredictable. Drennan insisted that the guerrillas carry their leader to his aircraft and stood well back in case they rediscovered one of their land mines. This saga lasted for about three hours and had to be resolved by peaceful negotiation as the alternative was to wreck the ceasefire. Sam Drennan recalls another incident which could have worked out badly,

'WO2 Mick Sharp, Colour Sergeant Sean Bonner and I arrived at a refuelling point near a football pitch in SW Rhodesia. One of the British ceasefire monitors (a Lieutenant Colonel) had been tasked with defusing a volatile situation where a group of armed ZIPRA guerrillas had assembled at one end of the football pitch, whilst a group of Rhodesian troops at the opposite end of the pitch were about to dispense summary justice. His plan was to get between them and either prevent bloodshed or get a posthumous medal. Sharp and I conferred and decided that Bonner was the best man for the job and ideally suited for the said medal! He landed the monitoring officer on the centre spot and both sides were so astonished that the situation was controlled.'

In the event there was only one confirmed case of a helicopter being fired at from the ground, this was on 25 February and no damage was sustained. The daily flying task included the movement of men and stores, liaison sorties, casevac, delivery of mail, newspapers and medical supplies, a flying doctor service and the pay office run. A 'milk-run' service was instituted serving each location across the country, which guaranteed (weather permitting) a visit by a Scout or Gazelle every forty-eight hours. The Scout was by this time a much-loved and proven workhorse; however, the Squadron noted with considerable satisfaction that the Gazelle was really good too. Ross Skingley recalled,

'My main role as SSM was to fly with the daily mail delivery Gazelle to Assembly Areas to hand out and collect mail going out from the few Brit Troops who were controlling these sites. Usual delivery times were seven to eight hours a day visiting two to three assembly areas. There were a few tense times with firefights, the odd planted explosive device and in one instance I had a stand-off between a fully armed ZANLA guerrilla and RSF soldiers, who were about to shoot the guerrilla (their arch enemy), who had been wrongly brought into our hangar at Salisbury by one of our British monitoring force liaison officers.'

During its time in the country the Squadron flew 1000 sorties in 2200 flying hours, carried 2000 passengers and 100,000lbs of freight (incidentally finding out that a Gazelle could carry a load of twenty-five empty jerry cans) and covering 250,000 miles (the

RAF's Hercules delivered no less than 1,000,000lbs of stores during the first thirty days – the biggest such operation since the Berlin Airlift). The Squadron was also tasked to fly to Mozambique and Zambia and 'bent a Gazelle doing engine-off landings.' Towards the middle of February tension increased once more and many sorties were flown to the APs to enhance the stocks of arms and ammunition stored in the armouries – just in case the situation turned nasty and CMG troops had to fight their way out. No doubt it felt a little similar to Rourke's Drift. Thankfully, the worst case scenario did not happen and in the last week of the month the Squadron flew members of the Ceasefire Commission, which included Major General Sir John Acland, the CMG Commander, as well as senior officers of both the PF and the RSF, around all the APs. Within a week a training camp had been set up for ZIPRA forces, where British officers and SNCOs began to work with them. A similar camp was planned for ZANLA, while Rhodesia police and soldiers began to take over the administration of the APs. It seemed to a relieved Major Nathan like a minor miracle and just in time in the light of the election results which would, 'shake the whole establishment to its foundations.' The election results were announced on 4 March. ZANU (PF) led by Robert Mugabe won this election, some alleged, by terrorizing those who opposed ZANU, including supporters of ZAPU. The observers and Lord Soames were accused of looking the other way, and Mugabe's victory was certified. Nevertheless, few could doubt that Mugabe's support within his majority Shona tribal group was extremely strong. It is believed that elements in the Rhodesian armed forces toyed with the idea of mounting a coup against a perceived stolen election, to prevent ZANU taking over the government, but this was never realized. On 18 April 1980, the country gained independence as the Republic of Zimbabwe, the Union Flag

Major Stephen Nathan and Brigadier John Learmont with a 656 Squadron Gazelle in Rhodesia.

was lowered for the last time from Government House and the capital, Salisbury, was renamed Harare two years later. Almost as soon as the Monitoring Force had departed Mugabe began to settle old scores, firstly against supporters of Joshua Nkomo in Matabeleland and then eventually against the white farmers, with the unhappy results stretching into the twenty-first century.

However, for the Squadron, its involvement had come to an end on 10 March, when the first return flights commenced, with everyone being back in the UK by 19 March. Brigadier Learmont wrote a letter of appreciation to the OC,

'In the early days you and your pilots were literally the lifeline for the soldiers at the RV points … it was a magnificent performance and will never be forgotten by those whom you supported … As one of your more regular passengers, I would like to record that it is a privilege to have been flown by 656 Squadron.'

In an e-mail to the author, Sir John added,

'I am not sure if my final letter to Stephen did full justice to the Squadron. I can reiterate now that to a man they were magnificent and I have no doubt that but for their heroic performance Op Agila would have failed.'

Back in the UK
Major W.J.H. (Johnny) Moss, 'a forthright officer who managed with style, not forgetting the social side of life,' assumed command in June 1981 and in July, Sergeant Dick Kalinski took part in Airborne Forces Day which was also the 656 Open Day. On that day he had completed 999 parachute jumps and also 999.8 flying hours. He took off from Farnborough with a parachute on his back and the Squadron QHI in the left-hand seat. At 999.9 flying hours and at an altitude of 3500 feet, he said, 'You have control.' As the 1000 hour figure was reached he jumped out, thus accomplishing a remarkable double.

Airtrooper Tim Lynch joined the Squadron in 1981 straight from training at Middle Wallop and has happy memories of a 'fairly relaxed regime'. He recalls one of his regular duties,

'As a signaller, I spent a lot of time on exercise away from the main Squadron sitting on hilltops with an FFR (Fitted For Radio) Landrover rebroadcasting messages to and from the aircraft. Generally it meant a relatively relaxing time enjoying the view but also brought me into contact with the bane of my existence – Don 10 telephone cable. We laid the stuff for miles and then went out and wound it all back in again – perching on the bonnet of the Landrover and frantically winding a reel to collect it all up. In between, we went out to fix the never ending breaks in it.'

He also enjoyed joining the gliding club at Farnborough, a parachuting course organized by Dick Kalinski and exercise deployments to Denmark, Kenya and Schleswig-Holstein, where the RSM at the German Panzer unit which hosted them was very hospitable even to the extent of supplying his guests with homemade cakes. Johnny Moss remembered the NATO exercise Amber Express in Denmark for the following reason,

'The Squadron was based for two days at a Schloss owned by a charming Dane called Ole Christensen. He knew 656 from previous encounters and when the exercise was over, he invited us all back to a party laid on in our honour. To our amazement a coach load of young ladies arrived from Copenhagen in what can only be described as "Night Club attire". Everyone was somewhat shell-shocked by this display of hospitality and, whether it was safety in numbers or exercise fatigue, I shall never know, but absolutely nothing happened. The boys all stood at one end of the Great Hall, with stags heads peering down on them drinking beer, while the girls stayed at the other end, giggling. Call it a missed opportunity!'

Chapter 8

The Falkland Islands 1982

The UK and Kenya

While half of the Scout Flight was in Kenya over the winter, the rest of the Squadron concentrated on night flying. Day was turned into night once a week and all turned up for work at 1800 hours and flew sorties until dawn, then went home to sleep. This training would prove to be of great benefit as events unfolded some months later. In October 1981, part of Scout Flight, commanded by Captain John Greenhalgh, and including Sergeants Dick Kalinski and Ian Roy, had deployed to Kenya with Lieutenant Colonel 'H' Jones and the 2nd Battalion of the Parachute Regiment (2 PARA) to conduct infantry training. John flew 'H' Jones on many occasions including solo to the Masai Mara and around Mount Kenya to Kathendini,

'Some of the sorties were so far that I was unable to take a crewman due to the altitude and high fuel load/all-up weight required. So he used to sit in the front and help with the map-reading or catch up on his sleep. The role of the CO in Kenya was very demanding … socially.'

John returned to the UK to fly the Scout, along with WO2 Mick Sharp and Sergeant Rich Walker, in the filming of the Pinewood Studios feature film *Who Dares Wins*, starring Lewis Collins, while Kalinski, Roy and Captain Iain Mackie spent a further few months in Kenya,

'Based at Nanyuki, just above the equator on the outer slopes of Mount Kenya, providing support for 2 PARA and, on the side, Klink (Kalinski) and his friend Captain Dent took the opportunity to leap out of perfectly serviceable Scouts on a regular basis.'

Iain Mackie adds,

'Another unit we were supporting was commanded by Major Cedric Delves (later to win fame for the raid on Pebble Island in the Falklands War), which was based at a place called Impala Farm, a run-down establishment in the middle of nowhere about twenty miles north-west of Nanyuki. Some were training in the mountain/jungle areas, some practising HALO (High Altitude Low Opening) jumps, some doing the

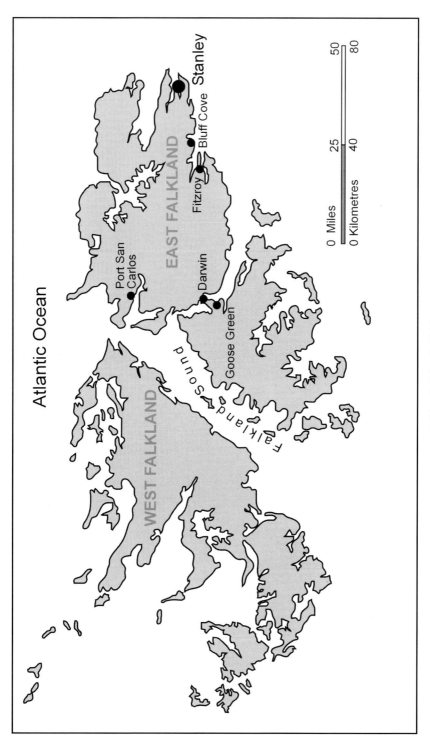

Falklands Islands 1982.

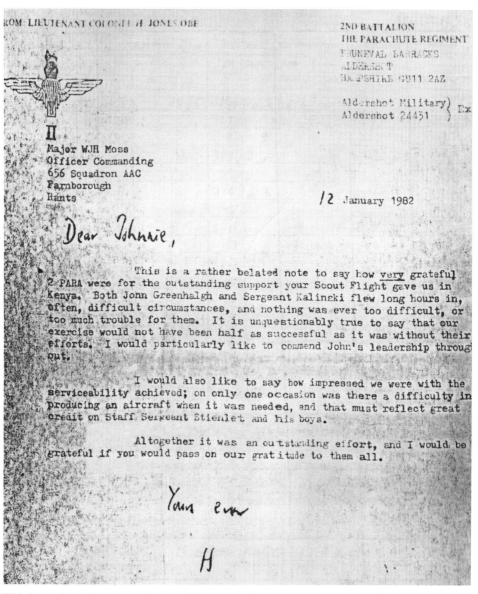

FROM LIEUTENANT COLONEL H JONES OBE

2ND BATTALION
THE PARACHUTE REGIMENT
BRUNEVAL BARRACKS
ALDERSHOT
HAMPSHIRE GU11 2AZ

Aldershot Military⎞ Ex
Aldershot 24451　⎠

Major WJH Moss
Officer Commanding
656 Squadron AAC
Farnborough
Hants

12 January 1982

Dear Johnnie,

This is a rather belated note to say how **very** grateful 2 PARA were for the outstanding support your Scout Flight gave us in Kenya. Both John Greenhalgh and Sergeant Kalinski flew long hours in, often, difficult circumstances, and nothing was ever too difficult, or too much trouble for them. It is unquestionably true to say that our exercise would not have been half as successful as it was without their efforts. I would particularly like to commend John's leadership throughout.

I would also like to say how impressed we were with the serviceability achieved; on only one occasion was there a difficulty in producing an aircraft when it was needed, and that must reflect great credit on Staff Sergeant Stienlet and his boys.

Altogether it was an outstanding effort, and I would be grateful if you would pass on our gratitude to them all.

Yours ever

H

This letter from Lieutenant Colonel 'H' Jones to Major Moss is indicative of the high esteem in which the Squadron was held by 2 PARA.

Long-Range Desert Patrol bit in their Pink Panthers (so called due to the colouring of the vehicles), and others scuba-diving in the Indian Ocean, north of Mombassa. We were required to fly a number of different types of sortie. A lot involved taking people from A to B, sometimes delivering supplies or mail, frequently flying over a training area to ensure there were no lions or other dangerous animals, and sometimes there were! Occasionally we were asked to fly with an underslung load, normally some rations or ammunition which was too bulky to carry inside the aircraft, so had to be flown in a net underneath.'

There was one very unusual load,

'A leopard had been found in the local area, and the National Parks had decided that it would be better if it was relocated to the lower slopes of Mount Kenya. Could we help? As it happened we were due to fly to roughly that area the following day. When we arrived, the leopard had been drugged but was not unconscious. I remember very vividly the very clear eyes watching everything we did. I don't think he believed we were helping him, and I'm sure had he come round a bit more, he would have wasted no time taking a bite out of the person closest. He (and we) survived the trip!'

Another passenger was rather more appreciative,

'We were advised by the High Commission in Nairobi that Lord Carrington, the Foreign Secretary, was visiting Kenya, and we were requested to support his visit and fly him, on a number of occasions, round various locations at the base of Mount Kenya to visit some projects that the UK Government has sponsored. I found him to be a very pleasant person, very easy to talk to and a delight to be with.'

Within a few months Lord Carrington would, of course, be in the public eye, as events in the South Atlantic unfolded. In an act which was both unusual and honourable, he resigned as Foreign Secretary on 5 April 1982, taking responsibility for failures within his department to foresee or prevent the Argentine invasion. Back in Kenya, Iain did not enjoy the HALO training anything like as much,

'The HALO troop definitely made an impact, literally. Nanyuki sits at about 6000 feet above sea level. It is also very hot and the air is much thinner than at ground level. I would take the doors off the Scout, and take the rear seat out. Four parachutists would then sit in the back, with their legs out the sides, feet on the skids. I would then fly up to around 10,000 feet to drop them off. The temperature up there is considerably colder than at ground level. Going up and down all day from boiling hot to very chilly, back to boiling hot etc – my mother would have warned me about getting a cold! The Scout was a good aircraft and could manage this without too much difficulty. A local aviator had advised us that when flying at altitude, to take our gloves off. Lack of oxygen presents a real risk, and it creeps up on a pilot very quietly. However, one of the first signs of lack of oxygen in the blood is when the fingernails start to go blue. When that happens it is time to get back down to a more friendly altitude, quickly. Those who have flown the Scout know that it is a heavy beast, and when all pitch is taken off the blades, it takes on the flying characteristics of a brick. The descent can be impressive! We used to race the parachutists down. They would freefall from 10,000 feet to about 2000-1500 feet above ground level which didn't seem to take much time at all. But then of course their descent slowed down when they deployed their canopy. As soon as they had left the aircraft, and it had stopped rocking violently, I was able to perform a fast descent, and was normally able to catch them up and land near the drop zone at pretty much the same time as they did.'

656 Squadron bids farewell to Farnborough in March 1982 with a fly-past comprised of six Scouts and six Gazelles.

Scout Flight was away on exercise in Schleswig Holstein in late March 1982, while the main focus was the forthcoming logistical challenge presented by the move of the Squadron from Farnborough to the equally historic airfield of Netheravon in Wiltshire, which could trace its association with military flying back to 1913. The Farewell Parade was held on 12 March. Johnny Moss remembered the occasion well,

'The salute was taken by the Managing Director of the Royal Aircraft Establishment and a fly-past of six Scouts and six Gazelles was staged. The guests were seated in front of the Squadron hangar, which was bedecked in Army Air Corps blue flowers. It was a very sad day for all of us as we had enjoyed true independence there. There were no spot visits by Brigade HQ staff, as they had to obtain prior permission and special passes to visit the airfield.'

The Falkland Islands – Preparations
However, the Squadron was not to know that events many thousands of miles away would have a much greater effect on their immediate future. On the island of South Georgia, 800 miles to the east of the Falkland Islands, the seeds of a conflict were brewing that would ultimately cost nearly 1000 British and Argentinian lives. A party of 'scrap-metal workers', accompanied by a force of marines had been landed on the British

overseas territory and had hoisted the flag of Argentina at the abandoned whaling station. On 31 March, John Greenhalgh flew back to the UK and was as surprised as the rest of the country when, on 2 April, Argentine forces invaded and captured the Falkland Islands. It was the Officers' Mess Dinner Night at Netheravon and 656 Squadron was being welcomed to its new home by the officers of 7 Regiment. Naturally there was a great deal of discussion and speculation regarding what would happen and what could be done. They were not impressed when at 2200 hours they found out that Captain Chris Hogan's utility Scout Flight from 658 Squadron had been placed on immediate notice to deploy to the Falklands. By Monday morning, as the first elements of the Royal Naval task force put to sea from Portsmouth, the position had changed. Johnny Moss had been lobbying hard at HQ AAC, UKLF that it would be far more appropriate for the anti-tank Scouts of 656 Squadron to deploy. They had the right equipment, SS.11 missile fits and trained air gunners. Also, Lieutenant Colonel 'H' Jones had called Johnny to specifically ask for the same Scout detachment he had trained with that winter in Kenya. The deal was done and the Flight Commanders were summoned to Johnny's office to be briefed. John Greenhalgh describes the scene at Netheravon,

'We underwent a massive reorganization. Firstly, most of our equipment was piled high in the hangar where it had been dropped by the RCT during our absence in Germany. The G1098 stores [ie. pots and pans, shovels, picks. Every QM or SQMS accounts for these items in his store and is quite often loath to sign them out!] were mixed in with office furniture, REME tools and aircraft role equipment. From this rubbish tip was sifted another pile of equipment that might be suitable for a war in the South Atlantic. Zenith fuel pumps, cargo nets and butane gas cookers were just some of the items. The Intelligence Section came to give a threat presentation on Argentina. They certainly seemed to have a lot of very good kit, including Chinook, Puma, as well as French and American tanks. The presentation was probably the first time that I realized that we were not up against a bunch of third rate troops and it was all a bit frightening.'

By the end of the week the plan had changed again and the Squadron was placed on seven days' notice, so John was able to depart on a pre-arranged skiing holiday in Switzerland but, after a few days, Johnny Moss called him back, as the departure of 2 PARA, with Scout Flight as part of 3 Commando Brigade Air Squadron, Royal Marines, was now imminent. While the main focus at this stage was on preparing the Scouts, John also worked closely with Captain Tony Bourne, the Gazelle Flight Commander. Tony remembers that adequate maps were simply not available,

'Commanders at all levels had to actively seek information. Falkland maps did not materialize, so a last minute rush to the local libraries was made to find and photocopy the most basic of maps – finally copied from a 1960s library book!'

The Scouts were ferried to 70 Aircraft Workshop at Middle Wallop to have radar altimeters (RADALTS) fitted, something that was to prove an excellent decision. John started to assemble and pack his personal kit,

'I had been told on one brief that the weather was varied. A Falkland summer was similar to UK but a winter was more like Norway. The Falklands was about to end its summer so I packed everything. The planning figure was that we would be away for six months and for me that was a lot of clean clothes. Finally, I decided to pack it all into a suitcase, kit bag, navigation bag, webbing and a Bergen, which were all full to capacity. This was mainly due to the large selection of hats I took, from my flying helmet to steel helmet, two colours of beret; light and dark blue, a head-over and an arctic cap.'

He was agreeably surprised that when he placed his order for 550 x 45 gallon drums of AVTUR aircraft fuel, the response of the logistician on the other end of the telephone was, 'no problem, it will be delivered to Southampton,' instead of the usual request for copious paperwork and six weeks' notice. On Tuesday, 20 April, it was decided that deck landing training would be a good idea, so along with Sergeant Dick Kalinski, John flew down to Portland where it was promised that the assault ship, HMS *Intrepid*, would oblige, 'Numerous approaches were shot to her from varying directions until QHI Mick Sharp was happy that we had cracked the black art. It seemed too easy, but of course the ship was at anchor!' Tony Bourne also has vivid memories of the preparations,

'John and I worked closely together to co-ordinate our efforts. Our initial recces of the large orange English Channel P&O Car Ferries, on which the flights were to travel, were invaluable. We began familiarization of the ships in mid-April in Portland harbour and, with the Senior Naval Officers, determined how best to modify the vessels to become Helicopter Landing Ships in the South Atlantic. These modifications ranged from welding large steel plates to reinforce the decks, concreting up the ships deck-drains, to prevent fuel drainage and spread of fire in the event of a crash, installation of night landing aids and preparation of naval Deck Marshalling Teams and AAC deck handling crews. The QHI, WO2 Mick Sharp, was invaluable in his tireless efforts preparing all aircrew for their deck landings and night flights – efforts that were greatly appreciated both before and after deployment. Throughout all of this the REME Section worked tirelessly in integrating aircraft modifications for maritime ops and also preparing themselves for deployment. This included the rapid tailoring of their organization, equipment and spares, to complement the less than precise mission requirements provided by the hierarchy. WO1 (ASM) Pask was notable in his drive and determination to ensure we were ready for operations in all respects – both in soldiering and aviation fitness. Behind the scenes the newly arrived Squadron 2i/c, Captain Bill Twist, was liaising with the Brigade, for whom he would become Aviation Liaison Officer. He was also to act as the link with the many other units and agencies that required major "prompting" to provide the Squadron with the right kit for deployment, ranging from aircraft IFF transponders to Gazelle SNEB Rockets. The Families Officer, Lieutenant Geoff Clark, was also doing a sterling job of preparing the boys with their Wills and briefing the families on what he knew.'

Back at Netheravon there was some discussion regarding the shipping arrangements – it had been suggested by 2 PARA that the Scouts would travel in the hold of the MV *Europic Ferry*, a Townsend Thoresen lorry ferry taken up from trade (STUFT) which had limited accommodation, while the personnel would travel from Hull on the MV *Norland*, a P&O car ferry. Johnny Moss was very unhappy with this and much preferred to have the men travel with the aircraft, keep them on deck, maintain flying skills and potentially provide a useful service. Johnny and John flew down to have a look at the *Europic Ferry*, which they were told was, 'a large orange car ferry parked somewhere in Southampton Docks.' They found it easily and considered landing on the ship but elected instead to land on the dockside between some cranes, which caused a major sand and dirt storm, 'which did little for Army/Merchant Navy relations.' Once on board they found the crew were very friendly, including the ship's captain, Chris Clarke, and there appeared to be no problems putting the aircraft on deck, indeed one of the Second Officers thought that there would be plenty of water to wash down the aircraft on a daily basis, which had been a stumbling block put up to stop the Flight going on deck by Aircraft Branch REME at Middle Wallop. After a couple of phone calls to HQ UK Land Forces the plan was agreed. So the following day three Scouts, XR628, XT637 and XT649, flown by Greenhalgh, Kalinski and Sergeant Rich Walker embarked at thirty minute intervals, to allow time for the ground party to fold the blades and push the aircraft to one side before the arrival of the next helicopter. John returned to Netheravon briefly in a Gazelle to pick up his personal kit and say goodbye to Johnny Moss, to find out that the OC was going to be posted immediately to BAOR to take command of 3 Regiment AAC and that Major Colin Sibun was to take command in his place. Additionally, Captain Iain Mackie, the Squadron 2i/c, was also posted to Germany to be a Lynx Pilot in 1 Regiment at Hildesheim. It seemed a very odd decision indeed to post the OC and the 2i/c just as the Squadron was about to deploy to a potential war zone. The upside was that Iain was replaced by Captain Bill Twist, who would prove to be a tower of strength in the forthcoming months; moreover, Captain Sam Drennan, a very wise and capable aviator, later rejoined the Squadron as a Scout pilot, he had already served as 2i/c and knew the Squadron well. Johnny had been to see the Regimental Colonel at Middle Wallop, Colonel David Canterbury, to plead that he should remain with the Squadron for this operation. After all, he knew the men well, had trained with them and it seemed only logical and right that he should lead them. However, David Canterbury was not sympathetic, quoting 'the interest of the Service,' which required that Johnny spend six months writing a report on Future Officer Manning of the AAC before assuming his command in Germany.

'And in any case,' he added, 'they will only go as far as Ascension Island, get their knees brown and then there will be a diplomatic solution and it will all be over.'

As a result, Johnny spent, 'a miserable two months listening to every news broadcast, wondering how his boys were doing and wishing he was there.' Johnny Moss left the Army in 1986 to pursue a career in banking but continued flying a Cessna 182, which carries the registration N656JM!

Meanwhile, back in 1982, the new OC, Colin Sibun was able to meet and exchange literally a few words with John Greenhalgh before he had to set off for Southampton again in a Gazelle flown by Tony Bourne. Back on board John was somewhat bemused to find that he would be sharing the Bridal Suite with two other officers on the long voyage south – but it did boast two beds and two bunks and a magnificent bathroom with a bath and also looked aft over the flight deck which meant he could keep an eye on flying,

'The activity on the quayside was frantic. A fleet of RCT Foden lorries was busy unloading 45 gallon drums of AVTUR, which would be stored on the top car (flight) deck, SS.11 missiles, pallets of gun and mortar ammunition piled three deep as well as much more. The road party arrived with Staff Sergeant Ross REME, who was to be my 2i/c, and the AMG team from Middle Wallop arrived led by Sergeant Kanek REME. All our role equipment was loaded onto the car deck through the stern. Airtrooper Beets and Airtrooper Coleman arrived with Lance Corporal Angus in the Land Rover, which was at my request put on the top deck with the aircraft.'

The Voyage South

The *Europic Ferry* sailed on a fine morning at around 0700 hours on 22 April, 'no great send off, just a few relatives and one lonely Union Jack.' In the first instance it was a short leg to Portland naval base in Dorset. They passed the time by clearing the top lorry deck in order to turn it into a pristine flight deck, larger items of rubbish were thrown overboard, with the Chief Officer's blessing. John also did a private tour of inspection,

'Around the lower lorry deck to see for myself the vast amounts of stores and equipment we were carrying. The main items were Royal Engineer wheeled plant, 2 PARA's MT vehicles, my aircraft spares and role equipment and hundreds of pallets of ammunition, mostly gun and mortar, but it did include some grenades and small arms. There were also two 20 foot containers with locks on. I discovered later from the Purser that one contained potatoes, milk and bread while the other contained a very large supply of Kestrel Lager.'

The Navy's workup procedure at Portland included drills for action stations, abandon ship, fire practice, damage stations and hands to flying stations. John was issued with 'a massive pile of Royal Navy aviation publications' to read, digest and then pass on to the others. On 24 April, immediately after dawn, the ship sailed from Portland, while the other RN ships all hooted in turn to bid the *Europic Ferry* farewell and bon voyage. The plan was to sail in company with the Cunard container ship, the *Atlantic Conveyor* and *Norland* to Ascension Island. John commented on a smart piece of initiative, which enhanced the on-board entertainment,

'An enterprising aircraft electrician carried out a series of illegal modifications to the Arcade game Pac Man which was situated in the main bar. This allowed free games for all and became the centre of all evening activities. A league led by Dick Kalinski was soon established. This was to end when the machine was badly damaged in a storm when it slid rather too heavily into the bar wall during the night.'

As they were crossing the Bay of Biscay, John spoke with the *Europic Ferry's* Senior Naval Officer (SNO), Lieutenant Commander Charles Roe, about doing some flying at sea off a moving ship, before the weather started to deteriorate. He found that Roe, who had no experience of naval aviation, let alone Army Aviation, was very much against the idea. After 'a series of rather difficult conversations' with the SNO, John approached Captain Chris Clarke, who gave his approval, so the SNO had to concede and allow the Army to fly at sea. John arranged a flying brief for all concerned, which seemed to consist of most of the crew. Then the ship's tannoy piped, 'hands to flying stations, hands to flying stations, no unauthorized movement aft onto the flight deck, no ditching of gash, hands to flying stations.' John flew for over half an hour doing ship approaches and landings; everyone enjoyed it and was surprised how easy it was and this included the SNO. Flying continued and much use was made of the time available to keep in practice,

'The weather was beginning to get much warmer and the ship took on a more holiday atmosphere. The pre-flying brief went well, coordinating the expressions which were to be used to attempt a ship controlled radar pick up and recovery with Clive Arnold the ship's radio officer. The planned training was to include high hovers, max rate climbs to 8000 feet and radar circuits. Unfortunately, the ship's radar would only pick up 10,000 ton ships and not a small Scout and so ship circuits were abandoned permanently. We tried a novel form of dead reckoning at sea with a moving base to work from. Using the Dalton hand computer we devised what we thought was a foolproof method of departing over the horizon and then returning on a different heading to accurately intercept the ship. It was really a failure, even though it did get you roughly back into the parish, it could not take account of the ship altering course, which the *Europic Ferry* seemed to do regularly without informing those who were airborne at the time. In fact it was lucky that the weather was so good with unrestricted visibility, because if you lost the ship all you had to do was to climb until you could see her.'

The next activity attempted was VERTREP at sea (Vertical Replenishment or underslung loads). The session aimed to launch all three Scouts in turn, something which had not been done until then. Once all the Scouts were in the air they approached in turn to pick up a full barrel of AVTUR in a net and then flew away with it. Next came SOATAX (Senior Officer Air Taxi) for the SNO, who wished to pay a liaison visit to the *Atlantic Conveyor* and who was thereafter ever grateful. John flew the sortie as he had not landed away before and thought the idea of lunch on a different ship was irresistible. He had lunch with Captain Ian North and afterwards had a conducted tour of the ship's hold, which he found had much in common with Aladdin's cave, 'Cluster bombs for Harrier, tents for 10,000, loo rolls for six months, G1098 by the ton and lots more.' The next 'hands to flying stations' was a little hair-raising as John described,

'The aim was to take some of the 2 PARA personnel on sea/air experience flights. All three Scouts flew and I ended up on the *Atlantic Conveyor* again, to pick up some kit after the other two had landed back on *Europic Ferry*. The weather deteriorated quickly whilst I was closed down on the *Atlantic Conveyor*. On take-off the *Conveyor* gave me a heading to steer for the *Europic* as she was not visible through the murk. Having flown for four minutes I lost sight of the *Conveyor* and I still couldn't see the *Europic*. I turned back towards the *Conveyor* and asked her to check the heading. She issued an apology and then gave a new heading. Low on fuel I set off again, lost the *Conveyor* and still couldn't see the *Europic*. I was getting alarmed when I spotted the *Europic* about 40 degrees to the right at about three miles. I made a speedy dash towards her, landed on and thanked my lucky stars. Why I didn't go back onto the *Conveyor* for fuel and wait for the weather to clear, or ask the two ships to close, will always baffle me – too proud and stupid to, I expect.'

The only interesting happenings of note during the first week of May were, a brief stop for replenishment at Freetown in Sierra Leone, spotting a Soviet reconnaissance Tupolev TU-20 Bear flying high overhead and a new ship added to the log book, when John flew to the *Norland* for a 2 PARA brief, where, as a bonus, 'the Quartermaster was giving away all sorts of nice warm clothing.' Just after dawn on 7 May they arrived at Ascension Island, where the air was very busy with RN and RM helicopters swapping loads between the ships as well as the shore, in preparation for the coming assault. John added,

'To me Ascension Island just looked like a very hot and rocky island in the middle of nowhere, which was just what it was! I was picked up in a Scout and flown over to the *Norland* for a brief with the Commando Brigade Air Squadron – CBAS Ops Officer. Here I picked up a few more gems on 'aviation in the Commando Brigade' and it was agreed that we would be 5 Flight within the Squadron and would take on that number and call sign. The aircraft were renumbered from A, C and F to DN, DQ and DV for Greenhalgh, Kalinski and Walker respectively. At 2130Z on 7 May we set sail south in company with *Norland*, *Atlantic Conveyor*, RFA *Stromness* and HMS *Fearless*.'

Henceforth, flying was restricted to a thrice daily helicopter delivery service between the ships in the group and some night flying training, including ship-controlled approaches, which enabled the three pilots to become deck qualified in day or night operations. On 10 May, John flew 'H' Jones from the *Norland* to *Fearless* while underway at sea for a meeting. The deck was full and the Flight Deck Officer gave him the wave off, but he managed to sneak on between two Sea Kings and get half a skid on the deck allowing Jones to embark on *Fearless*. As he remembers it, the Flight Deck Officer was furious, but John was more in fear of not getting Colonel Jones onto *Fearless* for his meeting. As a precautionary measure against salt water corrosion the Scouts were flown to the MV *Elk* on 11 May, to be stored below deck for six days. XR627 was taken on charge temporarily from 3 CBAS, which enabled sight familiarization flights to the P&O liner *Canberra* and also *Stromness*. The Scouts returned to the *Europic Ferry* and as they approached the boundary of the Total Exclusion Zone (TEZ) around the Falkland Islands on 19 May, each helicopter test fired an SS.11 missile. Sergeant Rich Walker recalled taking the *Europic Ferry's* master for a flight over his orange and white ship in a successful attempt to persuade him that the crew should make an effort to tone down the colour scheme before closing with the Falklands.

Meanwhile, back in the UK, the rest of the Squadron – three more Scouts and six Gazelles – had embarked in the MVs *Baltic Ferry* and *Nordic Ferry* respectively, at Southampton Docks, departing in the early hours of 9 May. Major Colin Sibun, SHQ and the Main Party joined ship on 12 May and sailed in the liner *Queen Elizabeth 2* along with most of 5 Infantry Brigade. Tim Lynch remembers,

'We sailed later that day to a tumultuous send off with boats accompanying the ship, crowds lining the quays and cars parked on headlands along the Solent flashing their lights as we passed.'

Gazelle Flight, with the assistance of the Master of the *Nordic Ferry*, Captain Roger Jenkins and the SNO, Lieutenant Commander Martin Thorburn, was able to maintain flying currency on the voyage, again as recalled by Tony Bourne,

'Daily routine consisted of early morning PT, under the enthusiastic drive of WO1 Pask, then mixes of individual weapon, map and first aid training, AOP and FAC refreshers, followed by deck flying ops both day and night. Deck operations were not at all easy and had significant risks; the fixed-skid undercarriage on Gazelle and lack of negative blade pitch (as with Wasp naval helicopters) made it essential to have slick and disciplined crews on deck. It was a challenge to manhandle the aircraft from below decks, up car ramps, and fit blades on deck, all in rough seas. The REME were exemplary in their positive attitude to finding solutions and supporting the flying effort. The night flying was demanding and not easy, with the ship navigating without lights and liable to change course at any time (submarine evasion tactics, we were told!). We almost lost an aircraft, but for disciplined double-checks that had been put in place. We were working in a blackout of communications and lights and, whilst life aboard was generally OK, it did not escape our attention that we were extremely vulnerable. Imagination could at times be potentially dangerous to the team effort and this had to be kept in check. As we headed south we studied copies of our library book maps of the Falkland Islands – our Ordnance Survey maps never did arrive! Neither did our promised comprehensive instructions for the SNEB rockets that had just been purchased as an Urgent Operational Requirement. We were promised instructions and instructors on arrival on Ascension Island, but as we never stopped there, we never got them. So initiative took hold. REME fitted the rocket systems to the aircraft and Captains Bourne and Piper, with their rusty Royal Artillery skills and limited ordnance training "inspected" the rockets. A rare signal was received from HQ Aviation (UK) with a half-page "Chinese Cracker" instruction on how to arm and fire – we now had confidence that we could put our act together. The rockets were never used in action but played an important role in boosting our confidence in the knowledge that we had weapons that could be used as suppressive fire, both for self-defence and in support of ground troops.'

The *QE2* and the two ferries called in at Freetown on 16 May, and then sailed on to Ascension, which was bypassed. The standard of service on board the Cunard liner was much appreciated,

'In the evenings the officers fed on delicacies like smoked salmon and washed down with champagne, it was agreed that this was a good way to go to war.'

One of the officers on board was Tony McMahon, who had served with the Squadron only a few years before and was now part of the Task Force as SO2 Light Helicopters on Major General Jeremy Moore's staff. He recalls the voyage with pleasure,

'I joined the bulk of the Squadron on the *QE2* just off Ascension Island in early May and had a jolly pleasant cruise south, dining with the Squadron officers when released from my HQ planning tasks. Colin Sibun looked as though he had been in command for months and he was well supported by Bill Twist and Sam Drennan amongst others. The *QE2* was diverted to South Georgia before 25 May, lest she become a prestigious target for the Argentine Air Force on their national day. This was frustrating for all of us, especially Jeremy Moore, as we all knew that D-Day was likely to be before then.'

Throughout the journey the ORs were also well-treated,

'We had blagged some of the best cabins and settled down three to an en-suite room. Cunard standards did not slip throughout the journey. Although, as we got further south, mess stewards appeared wearing helmets, every night coffee and cakes were laid out for us in a small kitchen near the cabins and when a spotlight bulb burned out, someone came round to replace it.'

Life on board the *Nordic Ferry* was a little less luxurious, as Tony Bourne describes,

'The Southern Atlantic was cold, bleak and rough! The ferry, designed for Channel waters, almost broke its back. Heavily loaded and with sea states that it was not designed for, it was down to the valiant efforts of the Chief Engineer to literally weld up the broken ship's hull to keep us going – a remarkable feat of engineering and determination.'

Operations Begin

Meanwhile, the Squadron's advance element was going to war. Just before dawn on 21 May the *Europic Ferry* made its way into Falkland Sound between East and West Falkland, then proceeded into San Carlos Water. The first two members of the Squadron airborne that day were Greenhalgh and Walker who ferried supplies ashore for 2 PARA and carried out armed reconnaissance. Dick Kalinski was soon in action too and by the end of that first day each had flown some eight hours, including recovering forty SAS troopers to HMS *Intrepid* from Goose Green, where they had been conducting diversionary attacks. John Greenhalgh summed up that first day of operations,

'I watched in horror the devastation of the Leander Class frigate HMS *Argonaut* as it grappled with its bombs and fire. My first casevac was a para with heat exhaustion – which was amazing because it was cold (he had put on too many clothes) – and I put him onto *Norland*. While working up and down the mountain, we initially stopped for air attacks, but it was slowing down our work for no result, so we just continued and observed the McDonnell Douglas A-4 Skyhawks and Dassault Mirage IIIs flying past. On one occasion we were flying down the mountain when we were selected by a Mirage who looked, by his direction and turn, as if he was going to attack us with guns. We followed the drill, which was to accelerate towards the ground, turning to the inside of his turn causing him to tighten further, spoiling his weapons solution. It worked, because he crossed over us with about a 100 foot separation and I could see the pilot so clearly that I almost thought he was going to wave!'

Due to the threat of heavy air raids, the next few days were spent at sea until *Europic* returned to San Carlos on 26 May. John again recalled the prevailing mood,

'We had decided it could only be safer on shore, where you had control of your own destiny. The sea had clearly demonstrated that it was a cruel and unforgiving place both due to the high winds and the various enemy attacks. Chris Clarke – the Captain of the *Europic Ferry* told me after a particularly nasty night that he thought the ship, which had dug the bow so deep into the sea that the bridge was awash, was going to capsize.'

The Flight moved ashore to a temporary Forward Operating Base (FOB) at the foot of the Sussex Mountains near Head of the Bay House. The only unfortunate incident that day was when Staff Sergeant Ross was rendered temporarily insensible, but not by enemy action,

'I was flying solo and elected to jump out with the rotors turning (frictions on) to help remove the SS.11 missile booms and unload the cabin. I removed the top pin while Ross removed the bottom pin. As I got mine out first, the boom rotated and hit him on the head. Even though he was wearing his helmet, he was knocked temporarily unconscious. Picture us by ourselves, him unconscious yet the helicopter was still running with its anti-tank boom half off! Fortunately he came round and was fine, except he was quite mad at me!'

The excitement continued throughout the following day,

'Air attacks on Ajax Bay were coming in at dawn and always from one of two possible directions. Before first light we ferried four Shorts Blowpipe teams out into a saddle where enemy fast air had ingressed before, in order to lay an ambush. Inevitably they didn't come that morning. I flew Brigadier Julian Thompson [Commander 3 Commando Brigade] from San Carlos to Port San Carlos by the most direct route over the hill. He bollocked me as he said Argentine SF might try to shoot us down!'

The breakout from the beachhead was about to commence, with 2 PARA as its spearhead. By 27 May the *QE2*, with Colin Sibun on board, was off South Georgia, and he prepared to cross deck to HMS *Antrim* as part of the Brigade Reconnaissance Group. The transfer was made by ship's lifeboat, in very choppy seas, to the County Class destroyer, which already carried the scars of battle in the form of large wooden pegs hammered into the side of the ship to plug holes inflicted by enemy cannon fire and one very large one where a 1000lb bomb had entered and lodged under the ship's magazine for twelve hours before being removed unexploded. He would go on ahead while the remainder of the Squadron's personnel, under the 2i/c (Captain Bill Twist) also transferred to the *Canberra*. Tim Lynch did not enjoy this part of the proceedings,

'We made our RV with the *Canberra* at Grytviken on South Georgia. One day, we found the ship inching its way into the bay past huge slabs of pack ice and began preparations to cross deck. This was an interesting experience to say the least. Fully laden with personal kit and weapon, you stood in a doorway in the side of the ship and waited for the sea swell to lift a trawler up to a level when you could jump across. Mistiming the jump wasn't really an option. We then transferred to the *Canberra* for the rest of the trip. Having come from a life of luxury aboard *QE2*, *Canberra* was a very different ship and the atmosphere more businesslike. As we arrived, survivors of ships hit earlier were passing the other way. It was clear by now that we were definitely invited to the party and not, as many had thought, simply intended to act as a garrison after everything settled down.'

He noted a few days later,

'One day, a tannoy announcement invited everyone on deck. Spread out over miles of sea were British ships, including the *Invincible* which, according to the BBC, was busy sinking somewhere else. Among the ships, though, was one with a tarpaulin draped over one side where a missile strike had punched a hole in the superstructure. Air warnings started and we all crowded into a ship's lounge as instructed. Crushed elbow to elbow it was clear that if anything hit the ship, we would all be trapped without a chance of getting out.'

On 28 May two aircraft, one crewed by John Greenhalgh with Lance Corporal John Gammon and the other by Sergeant Rich Walker with Corporal 'Jonno' Johns were sent to fly casevac missions arising from 2 PARA's assault at Goose Green and Darwin. John provides an evocative and graphic description,

'The approach was over open terrain, no cover, past the smoking remains of Dick Nunn's Scout towards Darwin Ridge [XT629 had been shot down a mile from Camilla Creek House by a Pucara, with the loss of its pilot Lieutenant R.J. Nunn RM and severe injuries to the crewman Sergeant A.C. Belcher RM]. The gorse was all on fire and smoking which helped the navigation somewhat – there was no doubt where the fighting was taking place. We started a series of evacuations of wounded paras from a number of different finger valleys back to the Red and Green Life Machine [Field Hospital] at Ajax Bay. It was impressed upon me by 2 PARA that they needed more 7.62 link ammunition urgently, so having dropped my casualties at the refrigeration plant, I landed inside the ammo compound at Ajax Bay and sent John Gammon to get the ammo. He was back empty handed, quite quickly, saying that without written authority we couldn't have any ammo! I called for the ammo Warrant Officer who, after being pulled into the Scout through my sliding window for an "interview without coffee," agreed we could have some ammunition – after all there was a war on!'

On 29 May, Colin Sibun transferred from HMS *Antrim* to HMS *Fearless*, 'Another link in the chain of steady deterioration from the *QE2* to a hole in the ground'; while back at the FOB, John Greenhalgh stirred his troops into action, having been aroused from deep slumber at three o'clock in the morning in order to pick up a severely injured para, Captain Young,

A typical CASEVAC mission by a Scout in the Falklands.

'Outside the command post it was very dark and icy cold and I worked my way down a line of frozen sleeping bags waking up half the flight in order to locate Gammon and Walker. I jumped into the aircraft, but the windscreen was just like your car window on an icy morning but with no de-icer spray – I needed to get the engine working to remove the ice. The other two arrived and we departed with Walker and Gammon on the maps hot planning on the move.'

Captain John Young, having being hit by a mortar round at Goose Green, had been lost on the battlefield for ten hours. The return journey with the casualty was frightening, as they entered thick cloud at 200 feet just as they approached the Sussex Mountains. John initiated an emergency instrument climb to avoid the mountains, but as the aircraft was wet it immediately started to freeze and ice over as they climbed through the cloud, holding their heading while Gammon (from the rear) called out the radar altimeter reading. Despite the rate of climb the radar altimeter only registered 40-50 feet. Once over the mountain, they turned through 180 degrees back to the south and flew level on instruments as they watched for the top of the mountain on the radar altimeter. Once it passed they started a rapid descent as the aircraft was vibrating due to the build up of ice on the blades. When they broke cloud they turned north again and descended to ground level using the white landing light. They then proceeded to hover taxi across the mountain top, through the cloud but keeping contact with the ground using the light. When they broke cloud on the north side of the mountain the low-level fuel lights were on and, as John recalls, 'frankly I hadn't a clue where we were or which way to go to get to Ajax Bay.' He called the OC of 3 CBAS, Major Peter Cameron RM, on the radio and explained their desperate plight,

'He was outstanding; he called all the other radio stations and told them to listen for me and amazingly one of the remote operators told me we were to their south and from there we were able to steer to the Red and Green Life Machine. On the final approach we had a very close call with the sea – by nearly landing in it – as we approached Ajax Bay, due to a combination of disorientation, relief at locating the hospital and sheer fatigue – Rich Walker saved the day by pulling hard on the collective after he saw the water out of his side window – what a team effort. We landed with only fumes in the fuel tank. I elected to stay until first light, have a barrel of fuel pumped into the aircraft and then fly back to the Flight for breakfast! In all the casevac took sixty minutes of intense night flying but to me it seemed like just five minutes!'

John Greenhalgh was later awarded the DFC for his actions; in total he recovered fifty-five casualties in the war. The rest of the day was spent moving other casualties, both British and Argentinian and flying Julian Thompson into the centre of Goose Green immediately after the surrender. The next morning *Fearless* sailed into San Carlos Water, Colin Sibun came ashore by landing craft and went to meet the command team of 3 CBAS and also John Greenhalgh, learning that, 'he had done extremely well and that 2 PARA think highly of him.' He also recorded his impressions of his first 'run ashore' in the Falklands,

'Recce Squadron HLS. Beautiful day. Beautiful country. Lovely to be back on dry (?) land. Saw Kelp geese, black with sandy-coloured necks and heads, herd of horses, sheep and cows. Meat hanging outside houses to cure. Smell of peat fires. Walk for five hours and kit gets very heavy. Air raid alert on way back to the beach and I leap into RM slit trench. Big bang – controlled explosion of unexploded 1000lb bomb. Blast damages a Rapier [anti-aircraft missile]. Not very clever. Back on board *Fearless* for supper.'

Tony McMahon remembers Colin Sibun's return,

'Colin came on board HMS *Fearless* soon after our arrival to discuss tasking etc and he was wet, cold and hungry. Over a hot meal I discovered that the Squadron HLS was totally waterlogged and open to the elements. Radio communications were unreliable due to the poor passage of frequency and codeword information and that, in spite of tremendous efforts by HQ AAC UKLF and HQ DAAvn, 656 Squadron's aircraft were not fully modified for the task; IFF equipment was non-existent, missiles were not tested and had been difficult to locate. More worryingly, aviation fuel was in short supply – except on ships – and his aircrew were utilizing captured Argentinian fuel, once checked carefully for booby-traps! Condensation checks on the fuel were impracticable, so the trick had been to fill up and then hover for some moments to see if water had been ingested.'

The urgent task for Colin Sibun was now to reunite the scattered elements of his command. On 1 June the *Baltic Ferry* arrived with the Scouts, followed by the *Canberra* and SHQ the next day. Tim Lynch has interesting memories of disembarking at San Carlos,

'By now I was carrying a Bergen on my back and having to put my backpack radio on my chest. With my helmet on I had a six inch gap through which to navigate and was hauling something not far off my own body weight. I was all set for a John Wayne style landing craft up the beach style assault on the Falklands, but instead found myself on a bright orange and white lifeboat taking a gentle turn around the bay. We reached a jetty at San Carlos settlement and I was helped up the ladder. At the other end of the jetty, two local kids were playing football.'

The six Scouts were now officially reunited as 656 Squadron at Clam Valley and 5 Flight was no more. The day did not pass without incident for John Greenhalgh,

'I was tasked to pick up the Land Force Commander, Major General Jeremy Moore from *Fearless* and take him to Teal Inlet where 3 PARA and the Commandos had yomped to. I was told he would be by himself and as I hadn't been to Teal Inlet before I elected to take full fuel, which was an error, because he turned up with two passengers, including his deputy, Brigadier John "Muddy" Waters. There was a 2–star discussion, which I lost, so I decided to take off from *Fearless* into wind and hope that the descent from the side of the ship would be sufficient to compensate for the load! The General might have realized as we departed and descended towards the water that all was not well, but God was on our side and the Scout at 102.5 per cent torque climbed away without water impact!'

While Colin Sibun was waiting for the *Nordic Ferry* to arrive with the Gazelles, the action continued on 2 June. The morning began with searching for Argentine radars on Mount Osborne at first light. In the afternoon, John Greenhalgh, with five Scouts, was tasked to support 2 PARA as it advanced to occupy Swan Inlet House, which was midway between Goose Green and Fitzroy. Two Scouts were missile armed, while three others each carried four paratroopers apiece. Four SS.11s were fired but only one scored a hit, which did not really matter as Swan House was unoccupied. In the afternoon, Greenhalgh and Kalinski, carrying 2 PARA recce troops, cleared and marked the landing site for the Chinook as it flew two missions bringing 156 fully armed troops thirty miles from Goose Green to take control of Fitzroy Ridge. On the way back to base the helicopters had a close encounter,

'En-route at about 200 feet above ground level and 110 knots, with dusk quickly falling, we were fired upon by infantry – I still don't know whether it was theirs or ours or SF – but they were lousy marksman because we went directly overhead but they still missed!'

Major Sibun was becoming anxious about the non-arrival of the *Nordic Ferry* with his Gazelles, so early on 3 June he 'took a rubber dinghy to go looking for it.' He found the *Nordic* but discovered that the *Baltic Ferry*, having unloaded the helicopters, had sailed out of San Carlos Water with the Squadron's fuel and stores still on board. The six

Gazelles flew off to Clam Valley in appalling weather and the crews were brought up to speed by John Greenhalgh on local conditions. Gazelle pilot, Captain Philip Piper, remembers a detailed brief given by John in a small dugout, in very poor light with the rain pouring down. He noted in his diary,

> 'Everything here (Blue Beach) is an absolute pickle at the moment what with trying to off-load ships and getting 5 Brigade deployed further east. I spent most of the afternoon going from ship-to-shore bringing bods and bits and pieces to wherever they were needed. Last job was to pick up our booms (for the 76mm missile pods) from about a mile away. The whole mission was an absolute disaster and I am lucky to be here in my little Gazelle writing this. The strop length was too short for the load and consequently the booms (in the underslung net) began to swing out of control; the load was dropped from about 100 feet. The REME boys are on their way to recover at the moment. (PS – as the ground was so boggy there was no damage incurred by the booms!)'

The OC spent the next day trying to bring some order after 'the chaotic unloading of the ships which left kit everywhere.' The highlight of his day was sitting in a very wet and muddy trench eating 'delicious steak and kidney pie and spaghetti' cooked by the SSM, WO2 Smith. The possibility of the enemy having sited land-based Exocet missiles was regarded as a potentially very dangerous threat and the search for these occupied John Greenhalgh for much of 5 June,

> 'Search for Exocet missiles to the SE of Goose Green including on Lively Island – 300 square miles – which were supposed to be threatening the move of *Fearless* around to Bluff Cove! Covering huge areas that we had not seen before. At a high state of alert because we didn't know if we found them, what sort of local defence they would have. Carried SS.11 missiles and a rear machine-gunner to do the damage. Nothing found.'

While he was occupied on this wild goose chase both the Scout and Gazelle flights moved to Goose Green, while SHQ and REME's 70 Aircraft Workshop Detachment remained at Clam Valley. Philip Piper noted on 5 June,

> 'Spent most of the day transiting between San Carlos and Darwin/Goose Green. Spent an hour looking for an Argentinian radar site – no luck. We moved out of San Carlos into Goose Green settlement which is simply a couple of dozen houses scattered around a jetty. No roads, no shops, nothing apart from a lot of misused or unused military hardware. The airfield, which is only a grass strip, has two u/s Pucara aircraft on it plus two dumps of bombs. There are still 240 prisoners in the wool shed here in the settlement…We are fortunate enough to have taken over a wee house and although pretty sparse, it's better than living in a grotty trench. The house has only got two bedrooms and it's actually sleeping twenty-eight of us tonight – v cosy!'

In the early hours of 6 June the OC received a report from a Royal Signals rebroadcast station of a loud explosion and two white flashes in the vicinity of Mount Pleasant Peak.

Tony Bourne was standing in the open awaiting the return of the helicopter and as he looked out toward the mountains, suddenly saw a starburst flash in the sky above the mountain range, then a second. Staff Sergeant Chris Griffin and Lance Corporal Simon Cockton had been tasked to fly Gazelle XX377 with Major Mike Forge and Staff Sergeant John Baker, both Royal Signals, as passengers, in order to service a rebro station on the Peak, thereby maintaining a forward communications link between 5 Infantry Brigade and 2 PARA. Chris Griffin was a very capable pilot who had previously served with Colin Sibun in Northern Ireland. It was inconceivable that someone of his skill and experience would have flown into the ground and enemy action was the immediate logical conclusion. There had been no radio contact with the Gazelle and no information other than the report from the rebro station. It had been a clear, cold, moonlit night but was becoming foggy locally and there was also the threat of enemy fire from OPs along the high ground, so the OC decided that he had to wait until first light before initiating a search. He led the search in which four helicopters took part and mid-morning they found the crash site. It was readily apparent that the Gazelle had sustained a direct hit from a missile to the rear fuselage/fenestron tail area and that it would not have been survivable. Tony McMahon was given the task of visiting the site of the crash site to make a preliminary investigation,

'On arrival at the scene, I was dropped off and the Scout flew off to high ground to over watch my activities with its SS.11. We had no idea where the enemy was at this stage. Sadly, all four were lying where they had crashed and had obviously died instantly. The aircraft had been lacerated by some kind of shrapnel and bits of it were embedded in the jerrycan carried by the passengers, presumably in case the generator for the rebro radios had run out of fuel. It was quite obviously not aircrew error and that this had been shot down. As we had no idea where the enemy were and that we knew they had air defence weapons I reported that the crew be listed as "lost in action". This was subsequently challenged and the whole incident clarified in a full enquiry some four years later.'

Tragically, it was a blue-on-blue incident, as the missile was later shown to be a Sea Dart fired from the Type 42 destroyer, HMS *Cardiff* – within the parameters of the existing Rules of Engagement. The subsequent Board of Inquiry recommended that neither negligence nor blame should be attributed to any individual. This was the Squadron's only loss of life during the conflict; made all the more tragic by the circumstances under which it occurred. Towards the end of the day Colin Sibun briefed all ranks on what had happened, with SHQ now moved forward to Darwin, taking up residency in several barns, unoccupied houses and a greenhouse. Once more John Greenhalgh's memories bring an intensely human touch to the reality of war,

'Went to Ajax Bay to collect body bags for Chris Griffin and Simon Cockton and while John Gammon was inside the hospital, RSM Simpson from 2 PARA climbed into the Scout for a chat about who had been killed and injured during the battle for Goose Green. Picture us sitting in a Scout on the ground at Ajax Bay, with me at the controls and the blades going round and both me and the RSM in tears; it was awful, we agreed it was also just not fair. Gammon returned with the body bags, we sorted ourselves out and got on with our work.'

Colin Sibun's diary records a much more positive encounter with Argentine forces on the following day,

> 'Contact in the afternoon. Two Scouts (Captain Sam Drennan and WO2 Mick Sharp), are deploying Gurkha OPs with an SS.11 Scout (Sergeant Ian Roy) escort. Egg Harbour House is approached tactically and appears clear, but at a range of 200m enemy soldiers come out of the house and run off. Scouts land troops and return to collect more. Sergeant Roy remains on watch and is joined by Captain Philip Piper and Lance Corporal L. Berrisford in a Gazelle. Drennan leads in two 825 NAS Sea King HAS2As with troops. Corporal Johns fires a missile from Roy's Scout in the general direction of the enemy who come out of hiding. They are surrounded by the helicopters and taken prisoner. A potentially disastrous task has been turned into a very big feather in the Squadron's cap. Among the weapons captured was a Soviet SA-7 man-portable SAM.'

During the course of this action, Lance Corporal Gammon got out of his helicopter with the Gurkhas and ran forward to take the surrender, but when jumping a fence the top button on his combat trousers broke and they descended to his knees leaving him with his gun in one hand and his trousers in the other – but he still made the capture!

Philip Piper wrote on the 7 June,

> 'We could actually see the countryside, in comparison to yesterday and it is really outstanding. We've been ordered not to fly above 50 feet so one gets a good look at the local wildlife. One of the Scouts had a bird-strike today which is one of the pitfalls of low flying. The islands are well suited to this sort of flying because the only wires around the place are those connecting telephones, which fortunately don't get higher than 10 feet. Spent most of the morning going back and forth to San Carlos with various bods (all flying to date and hereafter with Lance Corporal Berrisford, who was brilliant throughout). Had the opportunity to go up to Fitzroy this afternoon which is closer to where the action is. It's a little settlement on the east side of the island and a mere twenty miles from Port Stanley. Whilst I was there a Para managed to shoot himself in the stomach with a pistol and as I was involved in another task, Captain Tony Bourne had to take him to Red Beach in Ajax Bay – I believe he is quite comfortable. Spent an interesting afternoon looking for Argies fifteen miles to the south of Goose Green. The eventual outcome of the incident was the capture of eight of them. Lance Corporal Long did sterling work with getting the prisoners onto the ground and searching them.'

While the Squadron was preparing to move to Fitzroy on 8 June the devastating air attack on the LSLs *Sir Tristram* and *Sir Galahad* took place. Some of the attacking Skyhawks gave Dick Kalinski and Lance Corporal Julian Rigg in Scout XR628 a very unpleasant surprise; Kalinski immediately took evasive action by getting down as low as possible, bringing the helicopter to a hover a few feet above McPhee Pond. His day did not improve as, when the coast was clear and he engaged power to resume tasking, he suffered a tail rotor driveshaft failure, with the result that the Scout had to make a rapid force-landing in the shallow freshwater pond. The crew suffered not much more than wet feet, using the cabin door as a raft to reach the shore, but it would be several days before the helicopter could be recovered. John Greenhalgh picked up the crew,

'I located the rather wet and bedraggled team on the lakeshore and so I closed down to establish what had happened. While I was being briefed, a Skyhawk flew over us very low and it was being followed by another so we cocked our weapons and prepared to fire at the second as it bore down upon us, when one of the aircrewmen, who was more able at aircraft recognition than the pilots shouted "Harrier!!" So we desisted!'

Tony Bourne describes his very close-up view of the action,

'Landing on *Sir Galahad* for the second time for a rotors-running re-fuel, Lance Corporal Fraser and I were suddenly overflown by two Skyhawks. It was not a good time to hang around and we rapidly departed the ship expecting an attack on us, and so having landed ashore, shut the rotors and left the engine running, we took cover. We waited expecting the worst, but with nothing seen, we then headed back to the ships. Suddenly we saw palls of smoke – we initially thought that the ammunition dump that the LSLs had been offloading was alight, but alas it was *Sir Galahad* and *Sir Tristram* that had both been hit. As we approached the damage became evident and we realized that there were likely to be many casualties aboard the ships. I broke radio silence, and called the RN Sea Kings that I had seen earlier – fortunately they responded and the rest is well documented. It was a bloody horrific day for the Squadron's Scouts and Gazelles, spent ferrying casualties back to the Red and Green Life Machine in Ajax Bay. On one of our many casevac transits we suddenly saw a hospital ship, white with a Red Cross, sitting offshore – it was SS *Uganda*. With her being closer than Ajax Bay we decided to take casualties directly to her. On landing we were efficiently received, too efficiently, as they stripped me of my personal weapon – my SLR was grabbed and thrown overboard – not welcome, but minor in the scheme of things. The very long day over, we recovered Lance Corporal Fraser's pilot seat and our Gazelle doors that we had left on the beach – he had spent most of that day in the back tending to the wounded in transit – applying the saline drips and encouraging the wounded to "hang on in there", whilst desperately hanging on in the back keeping himself aboard. The nasty job of "swabbing out" the Gazelle then fell to the REME that night – not a nice job. It was such sterling work by the REME and ground crew.'

Colin Sibun flew forward to Fitzroy to find that SHQ's new location was a cowshed, with Scout Flight's office being the garden shed. Tim Lynch adds a touch of the typical Army humour which served to keep up spirits,

'I rejoined Squadron HQ, it was fully established in a barn shared with cattle. Although the smell was bad, the cattle didn't complain.'

A defence perimeter had been set up by SSM Smith, with the ground crew and REME Section providing the local defence, sustainment and maintenance that both Flights needed. There were also the dangers of minefields and booby-trapped fuel stocks, but this did not hamper operations. All personnel spent several hours digging trenches against the possibility of further air attacks. Tim Lynch describes the scene at Fitzroy,

'At this point, 5 Infantry Brigade was setting up its HQ in the lumber shed when an "air red" warning came in. These were regular enough and not taken too seriously by now. I had just brewed a cup of tea and was sitting in a corner with my radio headset on. I glanced over my shoulder and saw everybody had taken cover. I started to move just as the blast hit the shed. It was like the slamming of a huge door and dust began to fall. Covering my tea to stop it getting full of bits, I remember thinking it was just like the old war films. Although I don't remember doing it, I was told later that I sent out a contact report immediately. Someone shouted that they were coming again and I ran outside to take cover behind a pile of logs. An officer landed beside me and pulled out his Browning pistol. What he intended to do with that against a Skyhawk I wasn't sure but as the jets passed, he let off a few rounds anyway. A second strike came in later that day and was met with a wall of small arms fire. I read later that an estimated 17,000 rounds were blasted off at them. Certainly the vast amount of tracer seemed to do the trick and they veered off.'

Another small landing craft had been hit that afternoon, the OC's driver, Airtrooper Price was injured, while the Squadron Land Rover, War Diary, radios, tents, the OC's logbook and his entire supply of Mars Bars ended up at the bottom of the sea. The following day Sergeant Ian Roy was delivering supplies to the Scots Guards at Mount Harriet House when their position came under intense mortar fire. After it had ceased he flew two injured Guardsmen to hospital and had a near miss with an Argentine Blowpipe missile. His was not the only lucky escape that day, as Sergeant G.H. Keates and Lance Corporal J.A. Coley very nearly had a catastrophic encounter with a very large, air-portable fuel cell. They had landed a Gazelle on the Harrier strip at Port San Carlos and had commenced refuelling with rotors running. Suddenly Keates noticed the cylindrical fuel cell rolling down the slope towards them. His crewman was standing on the landing skid with the hose, so Keates' choices were limited. He was able to lift off a few inches and rotate the helicopter gently; just enough to let the fuel cell brush past with only very slight damage. The next day, 10 June, WO2 Sharp and Staff Sergeant Ross also had some interesting times, as described once more by John Greenhalgh,

'Move our own fuel to Fitzroy – two drums at a time, refuelling only at Goose Green so that the stocks would build at Fitzroy. WO2 Sharp departed in daylight for a short task and returned after dark and was really quite angry! When he walked round the aircraft after he had landed, he found one hundred yards of telephone wire wrapped around the helicopter tail rotor. Almost immediately we received a complaint from the Royal Signals that someone had destroyed their new telephone link, which they had only just put up sixty minutes before – stringing the wire across the gaps between buildings! WO2 Sharp went to speak to them and to give them back their wire! One of the Scouts wouldn't start after dark and it was assessed that it needed a new torch igniter. There was of course no spare but Staff Sergeant Ross, my amazing engineering officer said there would be one on Kalinski's Scout in McPhee Pond. "Let's go and get it then," I said, but a lack of tools would have precluded progress until the farmer, who we were living with, lent us a pair of pliers. We departed in a Scout with Ross in the back with his pliers; locating the Scout in the dark in the lake. I hovered over it, dropping Ross on to the roof. Unfortunately, Kalinski had not applied the rotor brake when he had egressed. Under the downwash of my Scout the blades started to sail round, requiring Ross, a proud Scotsman, to jump up and down on the roof every time a blade passed – which was frequent – he cut quite a dash with his Scout Highland fling. I departed to the shore to allow Ross some peace and five minutes later, after the flash of a torch (the prearranged come and get me signal) I picked him up again with the torch igniter – hurrah!'

The Squadron also spent a considerable amount of time in preparation for the forthcoming assault by 3 Commando Brigade on Mount Longdon, Mount Harriet and Two Sisters and also on resupply and maintenance visits to the Rapier missile sites around Fitzroy and Bluff Cove, while Ian Roy was tasked to recover a Scots Guards' officer from a covert OP point at Port Harriet House on the far side of a minefield. He flew in 'very tactically' but was engaged by mortar and small arms fire, which caused him to retreat hastily once he had picked up his passenger. Gazelle Flight was primarily involved in command and liaison duties, flying most of the commanders to their O Groups – to the forward dug-in infantry and artillery positions, and the insertion onto high ground of OP, FAC and Rebro parties. Passengers included Major General Jeremy Moore, Brigadier Tony Wilson and the War Artist, Linda Kitson. Tony Bourne's observations are of interest,

'Missions to the forward areas by helicopters inevitably attracted direct or indirect enemy fire. Interestingly, with flying helmets worn, combined with the noise of the aircraft engines, the fear factor of artillery and tracer was diminished. Only when one closed down and took off one's helmet did one realize the seriousness of staying too close and too long.'

Test firing also took place of a Gazelle fitted with SNEB 68mm rocket pods (which in the event were never used). Greenhalgh and Kalinski were attached to B Flight, 3 CBAS for the assault and on 11 June were at Estancia House, 'Living in the back of the aircraft in even more austere conditions than we were used to!' Colin Sibun had also become used to unconventional accommodation, 'Living in a cowshed with several cows is not uncomfortable but is a little cramped. Fresh milk in the morning is a bonus.' He had also persuaded a naval Sea King pilot, by a 'combination of threats, taunts and the promise of a bottle of champagne,' to uplift XR628 from McPhee Pond and bring it to REME, who removed its engine and fitted it to XT649, which was ailing. Philip Piper was also keeping busy as these extracts from his diary show,

'10 June. Day started with Staff Sergeant Emery as an advisor for the test firing of the SNEB rockets (we had never fired them before this!). Went ten miles to the east of Goose Green to see how the things worked. It was great fun – the rockets are not particularly accurate (foresight being a chinagraph mark on the Perspex of the canopy) but they would certainly give the enemy a bit of a scare. Have just returned from a pretty harrowing night sortie. The Scots Guards needed some kit badly and decided they needed it tonight, so a Gazelle (me) was tasked to guide the Scouts in. The night was pitch black and it took us three attempts to actually get down. Anyway the sortie was successful so hopefully the Scots Guards are feeling eternally grateful.

11 June. Spent the morning looking after the Rapier battery – they are located all around Fitzroy and Bluff Cove. The gun batteries have been pounding enemy positions in and around Fitzroy and Bluff Cove for the last three days. Spent the rest of the day taking Major Tim Marsh around the various locations. He is the Deputy Quartermaster for the Brigade; the poor chap has really got a job and a half on his hands as half of its stores were on the LSLs that were hit in the Sound. Managed to pop on board MV *Nordic* this afternoon. She is still unloading her stores. All the ship's officers gave us a very warm welcome when we came aboard. Managed to scrounge some fruit and bread out of the galley and they were kind enough to sell us some beer and whisky.

12 June. It's freezing! Spent two hours yesterday morning sitting in my trench from 0200-0400 waiting for an air raid which never came thankfully. We've just had another one – only half an hour this time. It was thought that four enemy aircraft had taken off from Port Stanley and were on their way to us. We heard their engines but fortunately they didn't drop anything. Must get some sleep – am absolutely knackered.'

Dick Kalinski had another close shave on 13 June, which was observed by John Greenhalgh,

'Daylight casevac from 3 PARA Mount Longdon, mostly artillery casualties. Then Kalinski was leading as we flew into 3 Commando Brigade's HQ pick-up point to drop off some passengers. I was trailing by about half a mile. To my right I suddenly saw seven Skyhawks approaching low from the west, obviously intending to attack the Brigade HQ, which was further to the east. The first thing they saw was Dick in his Scout, XT637, so they attacked him. Several 1000lb bombs dropped on either side of his aircraft and there were several loud explosions. The enemy aircraft departed, Kalinski closed down and a quick inspection by Corporal Ian Mousette revealed shrapnel holes all down the side of the Scout's tail boom, but miraculously no one was hurt.'

Another casualty of the raid was Gazelle ZA728 which had its Perspex bubble canopy shattered. Both aircraft were recovered to the rear echelon at San Carlos for repairs, although the Scout was able to fly immediately after the attack, the Gazelle could not, as it had suffered serious damage to the instrument panel. Shortage of spares meant that it would be some time before they were available again. At one minute before midnight the final offensive of the battle to recover the Falklands began when the Scots Guards and the Paras assaulted Tumbledown and Wireless Ridge respectively. Helicopters from the Squadron were heavily involved in day and night casevac missions over the next twenty-four hours. Greenhalgh and Gammon flew many sorties in extreme weather conditions and under enemy fire, while Drennan and Rigg accomplished a particularly difficult

Goat Ridge, 12 June 1982 – Captain Philip Piper and his crewman, Lance Corporal Les Berrisford, flying one of the many CASEVAC missions undertaken by Gazelles in the campaign.

mission successfully when evacuating three Scots Guardsmen and a Gurkha from a very exposed and inaccessible position on Tumbledown. Tim Lynch was on Goat Ridge manning a rebro post,

'From the top I could make out the Argentine hospital ship in Stanley harbour and a few of the houses on the outskirts. I settled down in the rocks and got to work. My abiding memories of that morning are of Captain Sam Drennan and Corporal Jay Rigg flying in and out of Tumbledown with Captain Drennan's radio stuck on send, allowing me to eavesdrop on his comments as he flew in to what was a very dangerous situation. After picking up the wounded, he would then scoot around Goat Ridge and fly low along the valley floor just below me. It was humbling to hear the determination with which he kept promising the guardsmen he would come back. Himself an ex-Scots Guardsman, I know that he knew some of the men personally and it was clear he would do everything he could for them. I recall hearing the voice of the Squadron Commander telling him he was under fire – again – in what sounded like an exasperated tone as though he was talking to a wayward kid.'

Sam Drennan was later awarded the DFC for his efforts that night in recovering sixteen wounded soldiers in the most hazardous of circumstances and in the course of seven sorties under enemy fire. His thoughts regarding his very busy night are as follows,

'There were casualties scattered all over the mountain. At one point the Scots Guards were firing M79 grenades over the top of my Scout at a sniper 50 yards from us on the side of a hill. I don't know how he could have missed us – probably the grenades landing around were putting him off a bit.'

Colin Sibun and Airtrooper Beets moved up to Tumbledown with a radio to coordinate the casevac tasking. He noted that it was snowing and bleak and that a piper played laments as the dead, wounded, and prisoners, were brought back by three Scouts amid shelling and sniper fire. John Greenhalgh added some thoughts of his own experiences that night,

'Then several night casevacs from 2 PARA on Wireless Ridge back to Fitzroy. Hover taxying forward in total darkness, with no lights except for the continuous tracer fire arcing over the top of us from 2 PARA's GPMG guns in the sustained fire role. Several return journeys in the dark with very poor visibility. Returning to Wireless Ridge about two hours before dawn with Kalinski leading, it just became impossible so we elected to stop on the mountainside and await first light. We didn't really know where we were – Scouts didn't have any navaids – where the enemy was, or anything for that matter. But being British we decided to make a brew and keep our fingers crossed! As it became grey we lifted and returned to 2 PARA on Wireless Ridge who were still consolidating. So we continued to take ammunition forward to the company positions.'

These activities continued on 14 June as the battle for Tumbledown reached its climax and as the enemy retreated towards Stanley, a Scout crew joined in the offensive along with two 3 CBAS crews, again in the words of John Greenhalgh and John Gammon,

'Dawn attack – using SS.11 missiles onto Argentine Pack Howitzer battery, which was dug in just west of the Stanley Racecourse. Major Chris Keeble of 2 PARA was frustrated that the Milan anti-tank missile, which had a range of 1950 metres, would not reach across the water to where the Argentine battery was firing at the Scots Guards who had not yet taken Tumbledown. Keeble asked if it could be done but as we were not fitted for missiles we had to return to Estancia House where we were refuelled, fitted with launchers and then missiles without closing the aircraft down – a first for Scout. We could sense that victory was just around the corner. An O Group was held with two Royal Marine Scouts in front of Greenhalgh's helicopter, which saved extensive radio orders and we departed while the other two Scouts got fitted and ready. I was back with 2 PARA within twenty minutes and conducted a detailed recce and located the target and a suitable firing position and fired two missiles and then returned to the prearranged RV in order to guide in the other two Scouts. [We aligned into an attack formation, flying in line abreast, with the high ground behind us, so it was quite a reasonable firing position. I spotted three bunkers, talked the others in and allocated targets. I fired one of my missiles and it went into the bunker]. We fired a total of ten missiles at a range of 3000 metres, taking out the guns, bunkers and the command post (one launch failure and nine hits). After the first missile hit, you could see the troops running away from the guns in the direction of Stanley. Unfortunately we had been spotted and we were precisely targeted by enemy mortar fire, rounds landing around the aircraft. 2 PARA, who were digging in around our firing position, were not amused that we were attracting enemy fire. As Lieutenant Vince Shaugnessy RM departed from the firing position he still had a rogue missile on the rails, which would not leave. He kept diving the aircraft in the hope that the missile would fall off! 2 PARA later said they had thought that he had been hit and that he was fighting to regain control of his Scout. Then we moved the Mortar Platoon forward to give them better coverage of the 2 PARA area and the deed was done as Brigadier General Menéndez and his troops surrendered at 1630 ZULU! In the afternoon moved back to Fitzroy.'

Philip Piper adds,

'At about 1100 hours today a white flag was seen to be flying over the capital of the Falklands. I was looking after General Moore today and was the first British aircraft into Stanley. The locals were over the moon on seeing us. We seemed to have spent the rest of day shaking hands.'

And Colin Sibun wrote,

'Relief swept over us. I then discover that I have walked through a minefield earlier in the day while working myself forward to find suitable casevac positions. I must have lucky boots!'

However, for Sam Drennan it was not yet all over, as he still had a tricky casevac to fly from Sapper Hill, which was completed in such a heavy snowstorm that he needed to be talked–in to land on a "T" marked out by vehicle headlights. He has vivid memories of this flight,

'We (Mick Sharp and I) landed in a snowstorm in pitch darkness, assisted by the lights of a landing aid and directions on the radio. The weather was so bad that I delayed take-off for a few minutes after the casualty was loaded and Mick remained in the back to comfort the soldier. The snow cleared sufficiently for a safe take-off and as I transitioned forward over the upwind edge of Sapper Hill we were hit by a violent updraft which was so fierce that it caused the main artificial horizon instrument gyros to topple. This coincided with a severe snowstorm which obscured everything outside the aircraft. I reverted to the standby artificial horizon, which is a small instrument about the size of a pocket watch and headed for the sea to avoid colliding with any high ground. My main instrument was all over the place and I was suffering from severe disorientation due to the aircraft being thrown about in the turbulence. The voice from the back, as Mick calmly read out the radar altimeter readings, was very comforting as I struggled to overcome disorientation. It was an almighty relief when the main artificial horizon started working again, but we were still stuck over the sea at 200 feet, flying on instruments, in a snowstorm, in the dark. I felt badly in need of a hug at this time!! Eventually the snow reduced slightly and we found the coast after about fifteen minutes and recovered to base, unscathed but exhausted. Colin took one look at me and promptly grounded me for a day to recover, as apparently I looked a bit rough. Mick was quite outstanding – brave, calm – he contributed greatly to the success of this mission. I had attempted the same mission earlier accompanied by Jay Rigg, in better weather (though there were intermittent snowstorms) but failed due to communication problems with the Welsh Guards and also almost collided with a mountain. Jay Rigg saved my bacon on that occasion. It was pitch black and snowing when in the nick of time he spotted it looming ahead. I switched the landing light on, saw the mountainside and managed to avoid it.'

Once control of Port Stanley had been established the Squadron moved to the racecourse, where several Argentine Bell UH-1H Hueys were found to be in flyable condition. One of these, AE-409, was pressed into service, with the serial number painted out and a large '656' added. OC Colin Sibun and QHI Mick Sharp carried out the initial test flight, as Colin later recalled,

> 'I jumped into the right-hand seat, and Mr Sharp got into the left. We had no experience on that type at all, but just "kept everything in the green" as we taught ourselves how to fly it. It flew very poorly at first (the tracking was badly out), but REME soon sorted that out, and it was put to good use from that point onwards.'

Tim Lynch once more provides memories of this period,

> 'The following weeks were spent in Fitzroy and then in Port Stanley where I worked at Brigade HQ in what had been the old boarding school. The toilets were blocked by the effects of dysentery and the dining room marked by a huge spatter of dried blood. Outside, a pile of bloodied helmets with gaping holes showed how effective the artillery and air strikes had been. We spent the days roaming around, avoiding the booby traps and collecting souvenirs. The Squadron got itself one in the form of a Huey which was used to take groups out to the ships for showers.'

The captured Argentine Huey AE-409, which was renumbered 656 and pressed into service. This helicopter is now on display at the Museum of Army Flying, Middle Wallop.

Philip Piper's diary adds some further details,

'15 June. Again I was looking after the General. Took him to West Falklands in the afternoon which was most interesting. The first port of call was Port Howard. There were over 1000 Argies there having their weapons and ammo being taken from them and then being ushered into a wool shed. Within four days they will find themselves back in Argentina having been taken there on SS *Canberra* or the MV *Norland*. The Argies can't wait. The second port of call was Fox Bay, in which the Argies were even better organized. By the time the RN had arrived there first thing in the morning they had stored all their weapons and were busy clearing the minefields. They numbered about 1000 strong and it did seem a little strange seeing just seven sailors administrating them, and half of the sailors were in the homesteads tucking into tea and shortbread.

I had a hairy trip back to Stanley as the weather had turned really bad with the wind gusting up to 50 mph; the turbulence over the hills was terrible. I was certainly glad to get back to our cowshed (in Fitzroy) this evening.

16 June. Spent the day with the General again; took him to SS *Uganda* to say a fleeting hello to all the poor casualties. The only one we've got is Airtrooper Price who was hit whilst travelling up from Goose Green on an LSL. He had temporary blindness for four days but is now recovering fast. The crew very kindly gave us a stack of eggs, bacon, rolls and butter which really boosted our morale. John Greenhalgh spent the evening with us which was a welcome change. Drank some beer and had a good chit-chat.

17 June. Had my first day off today. The morning was fine but the afternoon dragged. We changed the time back to local, which is three hours behind, so this has been quite a long day. We heard that General Galtieri resigned today which was great news. As yet not all the Argentinians have surrendered to us so we are still on our guard. A Sea King got shot at today; I don't think the aircraft was hit but it certainly gave the crew a fright. Am back on flying duties tomorrow which is good news. As yet we have not heard when we are going home – it ranges from three weeks to six months!'

Over the next couple of weeks replacement aircraft arrived and the Squadron strength was brought up to eight Scouts and eight Gazelles (reduced to four in mid-July) – plus the Huey which was kept in service until 13 July, when it was flown to the *Atlantic Causeway* for return to England and is now, of course, part of the Museum of Army Flying's collection at Middle Wallop. There was just time for another 'first' when on 2 July, Gazelle XX409 began to run short of fuel towards the end of a routine tasking. Captain Philip Piper contacted HMS *Exeter*, which was moored alongside the *Stena Seaspread* in San Carlos Water, and asked for assistance. The ship's Lynx was swiftly removed from the flight deck into its hangar to allow 409 to make what was thought to be the first landing by an AAC helicopter onto the deck of a Type 42 destroyer. Philip describes this period,

A Gazelle and a Royal Navy Wessex over the barren Falklands landscape.

'17 to 30 June was spent on flying duties based at Port Stanley. I then led a small detachment of one Gazelle and one Scout flying from Fox Bay between 30 June and 16 July which was most enjoyable. Then, until 31 July, tasking was again based out of Port Stanley. I flew 170 hours as captain from 4 June to 31 July 1982. None of this could have been achieved without the whole Squadron pulling together and it was an honour to have served with it during this time.'

The Squadron left the Falklands on 2 August, relinquishing its aircraft to 657 Squadron. Tony Bourne's trip home was eventful,

'We departed from Stanley to UK on an RAF Hercules – it was to become an interesting journey. The Hercules had been fitted with a large internal fuel ferry tank for the long leg to Ascension. We had loaded up with our booty of war trophies and took off with great relief. Sitting on top of the ferry tank we suddenly became aware of aviation fuel leaking into the cabin! We showed concern and so too did the Hercules aircrew who also told us that one engine had already been shut down – four months of us being on ops and it had to come to this! Much discussion ensued and we were told that their discussions via HF with Joint HQ had directed us to divert to Rio de Janeiro. However, this could only be permitted if we were to dump our trophies and weapons out to sea. We were reluctant to do this and so much debate was conducted via HF. We eventually landed with our trophies and were immediately put under house arrest on the Copacabana beach, sustained and replenished courtesy of the British Embassy. Thankfully, the remainder of the journey home by RAF VC10 was uneventful. By gum, we were happy to be back.'

Some fifteen Gazelles and twelve Scouts were flown operationally by 3 CBAS and 656 Squadron in the Falklands by forty pilots and thirty-four aircrewmen. The Squadron played a vital operational role, both firing the SS.11 missile and supporting troops in contact. They also played an essential logistic role – particularly in respect of the often critical replenishment of small arms ammunition, rations and water to front line troops and undertook a range of reconnaissance duties. Nearly 400 casualties were evacuated, in all weathers, by twenty-seven light helicopters in theatre of which 195 were carried by 656 crews, it is interesting to note some of the reasons for medical evacuation: wounds caused by gun shot, mine, shrapnel and barbed wire; burns, trench foot, dysentery, shock, exposure, a ruptured ulcer and injury due to a motorcycle accident. At least twenty enemy wounded and several civilians are included in this total. The Squadron also added a further 588 operational flying hours to its record. Some very important lessons were learned, for example, as reported in one post-campaign summary, 'The lack of vegetation made it more difficult for aircraft to see on the battlefield without being seen and engaged. Moreover engine-on refuelling became the norm, which was something not considered necessary in peacetime.' The larger Wessex and Sea King helicopters which could have carried more casualties at a time were often reserved for other duties. The use of SS.11 missiles to attack enemy positions received favourable mention, with an official report stating, 'The problem of deploying artillery resulted in the justifiable misuse of helicopter ATGW in the anti-personnel role. In good visibility it was very effective.'

Royal Marines and Army Air Corps personnel received a combined total of one MC, four DFCs, a DFM and twelve Mentions in Dispatches. Four helicopters were lost in action resulting in the death of six aircrew and four passengers, seven were damaged by enemy action and of these, five were repaired by REME technicians and flown again. One example in particular is quite remarkable, the replacement of Sergeant Kalinski's waterlogged helicopter engine overnight by the 656 REME detachment in temperatures of minus 15 degrees Centigrade, without lights, overhead cover or any protection from the elements. An availability of above 90 per cent was maintained throughout the campaign. Sam Drennan later gave his opinion of REME,

> 'The REME technicians were outstanding at their engineering tasks, but are also excellent, bright soldiers who can be relied on to get "down and dirty" when the need arises. Their military prowess is generally overlooked; many forget that the REME don't just fix things. I have witnessed them as soldiers on many occasions and they are very good.'

The Scout performed as expected, showing its age somewhat, but versatile, tough and 'built like a brick outhouse.' The Gazelle was equally useful, being fast and manoeuvrable, but was rather more vulnerable. Both earned the gratitude of many wounded troops. Yet the official account of Operation Corporate includes scant mention of their deeds, though at least John Greenhalgh was described by Max Hastings and Simon Jenkins in their book on the war as, 'An outstandingly courageous and skilful helicopter pilot.' They might have added that he was one of twenty-six AAC and attached personnel (RA, RE, PARA, RCT and REME) pilots, air gunners and aircrewmen, thirty-nine ground crew and thirty-one REME technicians equally

Left to right: OC 656 Squadron, Major Colin Sibun AAC, SO2 Light Helicopters, Major Tony McMahon AAC and OC 3CBAS, Major Peter Cameron RM, outside Government House, Port Stanley, following the end of hostilities.

deserving of praise. To which may be added forty-eight RN, RM, RA, RCT and AAC aircrew and more than 100 ground crew and technicians serving with 3 CBAS. As John wrote to the author, 'They all did a fantastic job because in total over 350 British casualties were "casevaced" by Scout and Gazelle helicopters.'

Chapter 9

UK, Bosnia, Croatia and Kosovo 1983–2002

Back at Netheravon the Squadron resumed the customary round of exercises in Scotland, Denmark, Canada and Kenya; as well as an operational deployment to Belize from March to July. Captain P.J. Andrew accompanied the family of Staff Sergeant Griffin when they made the long trip to the Falklands in April 1983, via Montevideo, to attend a series of memorial services. In May, fifty-four members of the Squadron were presented with their campaign medals by Major General W.E. Withall, CB, Director Army Air Corps. The next major development would be the arrival of the Westland Lynx AH1 to replace the Scout. In preparation for this the Flight Commander, Captain S.M. Welch and Captain S.D. Jones, attended a Lynx/TOW missile course at Middle Wallop from the middle of September to November. TOW was an anti-tank missile, which had been in service since 1981, the initials standing for: tube launched, optically tracked and wire guided. The first Lynx to arrive were ZD273, ZD274 and ZD275 on 2 October, and were followed by XZ663, XZ613 and XZ221, which had all been delivered by December. The Lynx had been operational with the AAC since 1978 and was proving to be a worthy successor to the Scout, albeit with an inherent vibration problem, and a history of unserviceability which tainted its reputation among REME and aircrew alike.

The new year of 1984 began with a roulement tour to the Falklands. The main party departed Ascension Island in the MV *Keren* and arrived at Port Stanley on 3 February. The Squadron became operational with six Lynx and five Gazelle three days later. At the end of March a TOW live firing exercise was carried out. Meanwhile, back in the UK, the rear party participated in the regular operational deployment to Belize between March and July and an exercise in Denmark. Activities in the Falklands culminated in a field training exercise in May/June, with the final Lynx task on 6 June being a fly-past at a memorial service for those lost in the conflict of only two years before. Back at Netheravon again, the usual round of exercises and training carried on, with the Squadron's role being formally defined as, 'Under command of 1 Infantry Brigade and additional helicopter support to AAC, UKLF and detachments worldwide.' Colin Sibun departed in October 1984 and was replaced by Major John Stirk, who recalls his early days with the Squadron,

'Even though the War had ended in 1982, there remained, quite rightly, a deep sense of pride and exhilaration of what the Squadron had achieved and the experience it

The Balkans 1996–2002.

BELIZE ELEVATION 15ᶠᵀ

A detachment from the Squadron deployed to Belize from March to July 1983.

had been through. Regrettably, at some time the Unit had to be brought back to earth and accept that we were back to peacetime accountability, accountancy and bureaucracy and that our war role was to support 1 Brigade in Denmark or Schleswig Holstein. So, it was time for lots of conventional war training and getting the vehicles up to scratch. There were also a number of stores accounting irregularities to sort out. Somehow the Squadron managed to lose a Land Rover, which only came to light when our neighbouring 658 Squadron asked for it to be returned. On the plus side, we gained an Argentinian Mercedes Benz which, again, required a bit of creative accounting to dispense with.'

He was less than completely impressed by the facilities at Netheravon,

'We were the poor relatives of Netheravon Airfield Camp. The Squadron HQ was "a little house on the prairie" lined in asbestos and with regular power cuts and some distance from the hangar where the majority of the personnel were officed – probably much to their satisfaction! The MT shed was a listed building, being one of the original RFC hangars and boasting one of the largest unsupported roofs in the UK. It was, also, a total disgrace that peacetime soldiers had to put up with such miserable working conditions. Poor lighting and no heating made for a dingy and uninspiring workplace. The only positive element was the ventilation that whistled through the shed, making it necessary for the drivers and mechanics to take regular warm-up breaks as the Salisbury Plain winter winds swept through. Little wonder that they felt like second-class citizens in relation to their flying compatriots in the main hangar; however, their morale was indefatigable and their efforts tireless. Whilst I took every opportunity to point out the MT inadequacies to our many visiting "glitterati," I'm afraid my efforts won sympathy rather than results, as the future of the Camp was always in the balance and it was felt that funding the modernization of the shed would be money poorly spent. Needless to say Netheravon lived on.'

When the Squadron returned to the South Atlantic between May and October 1985, there was no problem filling the spaces, the selection process was very straightforward: volunteers followed by those who had not been on the previous deployment and had no welfare issues. The unreliability of the Lynx made it a non-starter for the Falkland Islands, with a long supply line and a paucity of spare parts making its deployment untenable. This meant that half the aircrew had to refresh or convert back onto the Scout; which as John notes was, 'always a pleasure but a retrograde step.' WO1 Sean Bonner, a very experienced pilot, was brought under command for the tour to bring some added Scout experience.

Pre-deployment training brought some unexpected excitement,

'Following dunker training at Portsmouth we practised deck landings at Portland. We conducted our wet dinghy drills in the North Sea, operating from RAF Boulmer, as I felt that we needed to get a real feel for the Atlantic swell and winter temperatures. The RAF was all too happy to oblige and they, literally, kicked us out of their Sea King Mk 3s. Worryingly we were conducting our drills on an incoming tide and a fresh onshore breeze. The result was that the exercise had to be prematurely curtailed as we needed to be rescued before we were thrown onto the harbour breakwaters.'

John thoroughly enjoyed the tour,

'I was privileged to assemble a wonderful bunch of lads to go south with, who looked after me and maintained the reputation of the Squadron better than I deserved. Morale was high, they were highly motivated, well trained and high jinks was the name of the game. I cannot remember a single disciplinary issue and I can say that I have never enjoyed a tour or a command so much, even accounting for us having the dubious honour of getting three winters on the trot. And what a winter was in store for us. The weather raced over the Islands and it was quite normal to have three or four pressure systems pass in a day. The wind speeds were frightening, making it often impossible to stop the rotors in all but the most sheltered areas. The Gazelles fared well under the prevailing weather conditions but the Scouts showed their age and with a lower cruising speed and less flight endurance it was often touch and go to make the few refuelling sites on the Islands. Fuel and distance computations started soon into every flight and our mental arithmetic improved markedly. On one occasion, with the refuelling site visual but flying into a horrendous headwind, I was obliged to turn downwind and return to the last fuel stop. Much of our work was spent replenishing the radar sites, the radio re-broadcast sites and the men manning the marvellous RAF Rapier sites that had to put up with the most miserable circumstances, but who were always cheerful and utterly professional (they were always our first priority customers). All of these were positioned on the high ground and were often in cloud and covered in snow or ice. It was quite normal practice for passengers to deplane and kneel on the ice-covered helipads before they slipped on the ice. The pilot would then pull pitch and blow the passengers to the side of the pad.'

He was rightly proud that the tour was free of accidents, nor even a serious incident, which he put down to the professionalism of both aircrew and technicians and the close bond between the two that a small unit living under difficult conditions fostered. Though it was not entirely without incident,

'My worst decision was to arrange a night flying sortie that went from bad to worse. We were encouraged to keep night current in case there was a medevac mission. We had strayed into non-currency when we had one of the few beautiful days of the winter. It was 17 July, a cold but consistently gloriously bright day – not a cloud in the sky and such a change to what we had become accustomed to. I had spent most of the day flying and radioed Murray Heights to advise our QHI to arrange a night flying session, with me being the last to go as I would not be back before dusk. The briefing took place and the aircrew were pre-flighting the aircraft as I landed. On receiving my briefing I prepared my maps for what was going to be a straightforward triangular flight to two waypoints and proceeded to take off in the Scout. The first mistake was not switching off the dispersal lights which shone straight into the pilots' eyes and destroyed any chance of night adaptation. The second was to go flying at all – when the snow squall hit the aircraft soon after transitioning away. So, on instruments, in snow, and flying towards the high ground of the Two Sisters with a windscreen that had iced up was not the best of situations and everybody else was having their own moments. The real fear was that this was more than a squall and that the snow was set in, as there was no aircraft approach radar to help us down if we remained in cloud. We had no option but to keep to the plan and, as things worked out, we all got home safe and sound. Needless to say a sheepish OC apologized and "Sir" bought the drinks and promised that we would refrain from flying after "dark-o'clock" for the rest of the tour.'

Socially there were diverse pleasures to be sought out and enjoyed,

'We had a tremendous time, thanks largely to a proposal that was put to me soon after arriving on the Islands. It went along the lines that it was regrettable that you always met the best people when you are saying goodbye. So, if we had our farewell party early then we'd have a good chance of getting to know the right people early on. Consequently, we had our first "farewell" party six weeks into the tour and it was a great success, helped with WO2 "Mario" Clayton's Moose's Milk cocktail. The milk had to be flown in from the "Camp" and it often arrived in open containers. On pain of death from the REME the aircraft were flown with the greatest care in order not to spill a drop. We also rebuilt the crewroom so we had the only "neo-tudor" portacabin in Stanley. Our "Happy Hour" became so popular that the number of visitors had to be reduced to "on invitation only" as there were occasions when

Squadron members couldn't get to the bar. The Squadron fund coffers spilled over. We built up a great relationship with the Royal Navy, fortunately the responsibility of the 2 i/c, as it was undoubtedly the most complex bit of planning of the entire tour. We had ongoing exchanges to give the Navy boys a bit of shore time and for our lot to try their sea legs. Everyone benefitted. My only drawback was to land on a ship to find that my lot was watching my landing and giving me scores for precision and artistic merit – regrettably, I didn't do well on either count.'

One of the delights of a tour of duty in the post-conflict era Falklands was sitting by peat-burning Rayburn stoves, sampling the hospitality of the islanders, who always offered coffee and delicious home-made cakes. One of the pilots (and his Gazelle) paid a visit to South Georgia on the RFA *Olwen*, a fleet tanker of 36,000 tons, with a helideck and hangar aft. The culture shock after experiencing the spartan conditions at the Squadron's base of Murray Heights was immense,

'It was warm! There were no draughts, the food was superb and laundry was cleaned and ironed daily. We had a large, heated hangar for the aircraft, and joy of joys, one's own cabin complete with telephone – and a steward who brought tea in the morning and made the bed. It was beyond belief after braving the Falklands' snowstorms to find a Portaloo.'

All was not completely plain sailing; however, as the weather was rough enough to blow the wheelhouse on the top deck over the side. The ship had to turn into wind for nearly three days to ride out the storm. They eventually anchored off Grytviken and gazed upon South Georgia's austere and forbidding beauty. As the sea was far too rough to launch the ship's boats, the Gazelle earned her keep by flying three passengers or 600lbs of stores at a time to the garrison. In company with a Westland Lynx HAS2 from the Type 21 frigate, HMS *Avenger*, a multitude of other tasks were undertaken – including patrol insertions, route recces and area familiarization trips. Time was taken to pay respects at the grave of the polar explorer, Sir Ernest Shackleton, who made an 'impossible' journey across the island's ice mountains and glaciers in May 1916 to bring help to his stranded crew on Elephant Island. Other memorable sights included thousands of elephant seals, reindeer (introduced by Norwegian whalers in 1909), seals and penguins. Four deployments of this nature were made over the course of the tour. On one occasion, as the helicopters were delivering freight, a sea fret set in out of nowhere and the ship was lost in the fog. Fortunately, at very much the last minute, the ship was found and the helicopters landed safely with 'little more than vapour in the tanks'.

Once the South Atlantic tour was over it was a case of taking part in exercises in the UK and Kenya. Squadron personnel were also detached on individual tours to Northern Ireland, Belize and the Falklands in 1985, while REME Staff Sergeant J.P. Byrne distinguished himself by playing ten matches for the Army rugby team and one for the Combined Services. On 23 October, a Lynx lifted a generator to Flatholme Island in the Bristol Channel, in connection with a Youth Opportunities Programme scheme, turning the area into a bird sanctuary.

In January 1986 there was a five week deployment to Kenya for Exercise Grand Prix in support of 1 Royal Green Jackets, where the Squadron's main function was in the medevac role. John's chief memory of this period concerns a training incident, which could have turned out a lot worse than it did,

'We were accompanied initially by Major Ian Cornall (Senior Flying Instructor UKLF), an exceptionally experienced pilot and always excellent company. His role was to competency check the three pilots and then return to UK. He could be a bit abrasive and intimidating in the air, which resulted in a potentially serious misunderstanding with our least experienced pilot. It was not made sufficiently clear that the exercise being practised was an auto-rotation to a recovery. Regrettably, under persistent pressure, the wrong impression was gained and the throttle was closed, leaving the SFI with no alternative but to conduct an engine-off landing. So, after a tense interchange, a misunderstanding, a lot of quiet, a fast run on, a controlled debrief, the sortie terminated with a trip to the heads and onto the bar in that order. I understand that this was the first time that an engine-off landing had been undertaken so hot and high. Fortunately, Major Cornall's landing was immaculate and the detachment was saved the ignominy of bending an aircraft on day one.'

The final six months of John's time as OC were dominated by the issue of the change of the Squadron's status from 'Independent' to becoming part of 7 Regiment. Fortunately, the CO of 7 Regiment was Lieutenant Colonel Colin Sibun, 'who did not impose too heavy a burden on us, nearly a mile away in RHQ' – John once more recalls,

'A time had been reached when the luxury of independent units was unsustainable. This was precipitated by two unavoidable factors, a shortage of REME technicians and the Lynx helicopter, that was placing an unrelenting burden on those who worked so hard to keep it flying. The maintenance effort required was quoted at being a little under twenty maintenance hours for each flying hour. The best use of resources was to consolidate the REME technicians into a regimental workshop, making it a sub-unit in its own right. Generously, I was given an opportunity to argue against this move and, of course, I did my best for the sake of my successor but the argument for pooling was overwhelming.'

Indeed John concludes his account of his time with 656 with a heartfelt tribute to REME,

'You need to mention the importance that the REME personnel brought to 656 Squadron; as they did to all independent sub units (I was lucky enough to cut my teeth in 665 Squadron and later commanded the BATUS Flight, both independent, but also saw the other side of the equation when I commanded 661 Squadron). They were such a marvellous bunch of individuals; professional, loyal, industrious, rightly ambitious, and with great integrity. They, also, were the greatest fun and brought a balance to those fortunate enough to fly the machines that the REME maintained. The biggest differences emerged when there was a difference of opinion between the "menders" and "benders". Such events were few and far between and when they did the Court would be in session. We would assemble in the crewroom and each side would make its case. Emotion and rhetoric would spill out from the aviator community, whereas the REME fraternity would come with charts, statistics and logic, and, although I felt sorry to have to make the final judgement, the REME did better than average.'

Deployments in 1987 included exercises in Canada, Kenya (twice), Scotland, Denmark and Italy, as well as flood relief work in Wales and an appearance on the BBC children's programme Blue Peter, with an underslung load of lead for the roof of Hammerwood House in East Grinstead. Major Andy Simkins became OC in March of that year and recalled being based in an old hangar of Second World War vintage, with an even older hangar, dating back to the Great War, accommodating the MT section. As for his office, 'It was away from the hangar and looked like a small cricket pavilion. It was perhaps from the early days of the RFC. I would like to think so.' He describes the general circumstances as follows,

'We were well served with facilities, and felt self-contained. The Lynx had Mark 1 engines which restricted us a little, but, except for the odd single engine failure, we suffered no major incidents. We were, operationally, under command of 1 Mechanized Brigade, based at Tidworth. Our operational area was Schleswig Holstein or Denmark. We trained there every summer, which was a good opportunity to move the Squadron assets away from Netheravon and exercise command with the full Squadron. We did not have any Squadron operational deployments during my command. However, I sent aircrew, REME personnel and ground crew around the world during my tenure. I listed the number of countries once and came to nineteen.'

He has very fond memories of one visitor in particular,

'One day, at about 1100 hours, I was in my Squadron office when a gentleman, in his 70s, turned up in his dinner jacket and bowtie. He said he had just come from a Burma Star Dinner in London and had been searching for the present Squadron for some time. His name was Nobby Clark, and he had been one of the original Squadron members and indeed was the radio wizard from the Burma Campaign. During the subsequent discussion I learnt much about the early history of the Squadron and that there had been a very active Association after the war and into the 50s. While I was a little sceptical, I took up Nobby's offer of joining us at our forthcoming Squadron Open Day. He came along with his wife, Claire, and tubs of fuchsias which he grew in his greenhouse; these he sold for a Gurkha charity. Former RAF sergeant, Bill Peers, who had also served with SHQ in Burma, came along with his model passenger train, which was numbered 656 and called the "Burma Star". The contribution of this small contingent from the past proved a success and paved the way for the re-establishment of the 656 Squadron Association.'

Andy was also involved in a flying venture which harked back to the earliest days of Army aviation,

'During my tenure I was encouraged by the then Regimental Colonel, Ed Tait, to form an Army Air Corps Hot Air Balloon Club. The balloon, registration G-OAAC, was built by Bob Pooley's small balloon company. While it was under construction we used another balloon, and a small nucleus learnt how to control a bag of hot air over Southern England. By the time I handed over command we had taken the balloon to many events and participated at the Bristol Balloon Fiesta. After the handover to David Joyce I stepped into the balloon and departed skywards towards Salisbury.'

Major David Joyce began 16 March 1989, celebrating the arrival of a baby daughter at 0635, before driving from Middle Wallop to Netheravon for a handover meeting with Andy Simkins at 1030, which included,

'At 12 o'clock two gentlemen arrived at the office door having travelled from Somerset. Nobby Clark and Bill Peers had come to introduce themselves to me as the new OC and explain their recent founding of the 656 Squadron Association which, at the time of that first meeting, had forty-six members. Over lunch at the Simkins' house, Nobby and Bill's enthusiasm for the whole project was clearly evident, and it is to their eternal credit that the Association has grown into what it is today.'

When he reported to Netheravon a month later to take command officially,

'I found … nobody! The Squadron had deployed lock, stock and barrel to Capel Curig in North Wales to enjoy a week's adventurous training in Snowdonia. It had been arranged that I would join the Squadron in Wales, so after a quick introductory office call with the Commanding Officer of 7 Regiment, Lieutenant Colonel Colin Sibun (who would hand over command to Lieutenant Colonel Nick Hall within a fortnight), I climbed into a Gazelle with the Regimental Second-in-Command, Julian Bourne, and headed for Capel Curig, which was a marvellous way to meet everyone for the first time, and it was good to be able to chat with the officers and soldiers as we dangled on abseil ropes, walked the hills and enjoyed an evening drink.'

Once back at Netheravon, the pace of life changed gear. In early May a recce party from 1 Mechanized Brigade deployed to Schleswig Holstein in Northern Germany to examine its NATO reinforcement role and recce wartime positions in this vital area should Soviet forces be unleashed from their bases on the other side of the nearby Iron Curtain. A small detachment of Lynx and Gazelle spent a week supporting this activity, known as Exercise Bandit Girl 3. Then in June the Squadron deployed to Exercise Burmese Cider on the Somerset Levels and in Devon to practise its role, revise procedures, and undertake small arms training and live firing at Yoxter Ranges.

The following month the Squadron had the honour of preparing to fly Queen Noor of Jordan from her residence near Virginia Water in Surrey, to Felden Grange near Hemel Hempstead, for a reception in support of the Hospital Order of St John. David takes up the story,

'This was scheduled for Saturday, 8 July and required an immaculate Lynx for the flight and another as a standby. It was NOTAM'd as a Selected Flight, and everything seemed to be going to plan during the preparations. On the preceding Friday evening one final starting check was to be made of each aircraft after they had been inspected for cleanliness, the suitability of a padded passenger seat (a sheepskin!) and working passenger headsets. During this process, the standby Lynx had an immediate "heart attack" and refused to start, and the REME couldn't fix the fault easily. Everyone stood in shock as it seemed that all the hard work had been wasted! "Well", said Staff Sergeant Galston, "it looks like we'd better clean another cab". In the best 656 tradition, everyone turned to, and by about 2100 hours, two immaculate Lynx were ready to go as intended. The next day OC 656 and the Squadron QHI, Lieutenant Pete Douglass, flew the sortie, which included a diversion under Heathrow control to take the aircraft straight across the airport at 1000 feet to avoid a localized thunderstorm! Having parked the aircraft at Felden for the night, numerous members of 656 enjoyed the party that was to follow into the wee small hours.'

After summer leave the Squadron turned to its next task, hosting a visit by Dennis Thatcher, husband of the Prime Minister. After receiving a briefing on the Squadron's role and watching Forward Arming and Refuelling Point (FARP) drills, Mr Thatcher joined a sortie on board a Lynx as the Squadron conducted a dummy HELARM exercise to the west of Salisbury Plain, before flying him to the front of the Officers' Mess at Wallop, where he took lunch with Director Army Air Corps, CO 7 Regiment and OC 656 Sqn.

Later that month the Squadron deployed a party of personnel and both aircraft types to Germany to umpire 9 Regiment AAC during a major proving exercise of the operational concepts of the emerging 24 Airmobile Brigade. This was an excellent opportunity for the AAC to demonstrate its ability to conduct rapid engagement of large Soviet armoured forces. But as David comments,

'Times, however, were changing under our feet, and within two months the Iron Curtain had collapsed, the Berlin Wall had been breached and, in the prophetic words of our brigade commander, Brigadier Jack Deverell, we had entered an age where certain threat had given way to uncertain risk.'

Throughout a typically busy year, which also included daily tasking to all parts of the UK, 656 also supported several battlegroup exercises in Canada (Ex Pond Jump West) and Kenya (Ex Grand Prix), and deployed roulement crews to Belize.

It was a stormy start to 1990, in which thousands of trees in the region were felled by winds of up to 100 mph. Netheravon's fragile buildings of 1913 vintage were exposed to the full force of the gales and roof tiles from the neighbouring squadron, 658, were embedded edge on into the tree outside 656 Squadron's office. The 2i/c, Captain Alistair Keith, had a close shave as first, one tree fell across the narrow lane ahead of his car as he drove towards Netheravon, and then another fell just behind him, trapping him, unharmed in his undamaged car, until he could be released by local farmhands with a chainsaw!

After a period of intensive training the Squadron deployed on 2 February as the first AAC squadron ever to undergo the Porton Battle Run, complete with its aircraft, operating in simulated nuclear, biological and chemical warfare conditions for three days at Porton Down Training Area. Exercise Burmese Lexicon included bombardment by simulated multi-barrelled rocket launchers firing CS gas, a nuclear strike in the middle of the night, aircraft decontamination drills, attack by chemical-spray jets, and a squadron HELARM strike to the south of Salisbury conducted in full NBC equipment, including one pilot in each aircraft flying in a respirator. David Joyce recalls,

'This was an impressive catalogue of activities, but things hadn't started so well. The weather was so bad that it was decided to erect a nine-by-nine tent for the guard to shelter in when not patrolling the position. To start with, a couple of soldiers began to put up the tent in the dark in a strengthening wind. More came to their aid, followed by the OC and SSM, and any others who were around. Just as the tent was about to be pinned down the whole thing was caught by a gust of wind and disappeared upwards into the darkness of the night. We had no idea where it had gone, but within seconds everyone was being showered with pieces of tent frame as the poles parted and fell to earth! The sodden canvas was found the next day a couple of hundred metres away. Despite the conditions and the challenge of taking the aircraft on the exercise, we were pleased to be assessed as having given one of the best performances by a sub-unit ever seen on the Porton Battle Run.'

In April the Squadron deployed again, this time to Thorney Island on Exercise Burmese Spring to practise HELARM drills in new terrain. It also gave the ground crew an opportunity to act as airborne infantry, which they always enjoyed, as well as conducting an intensive period of underslung load training by day and night. In late July, the Squadron deployed to Salisbury Plain on Exercise Druids Drake in support of 1 Mechanized Brigade,

'Spending the time in blistering heat, watching all kinds of aircraft, including Concorde and a Vulcan, fly by at low-level en route to the Middle Wallop Air Show which, by dint of the exercise, we missed. Nevertheless, training in this new period of uncertain risk was important, as we were about to learn.'

In August 1990, during Squadron block leave, Iraqi forces invaded Kuwait. At one point 656 was proposed as an option to deploy to the Gulf as part of 9 Regiment, but in the event, 661 Squadron, from 1 Regiment in Hildesheim, reinforced 4 Regiment from Detmold as the aviation force during the first Gulf War in early 1991. Training continued nonetheless and in October the Squadron reinforced 9 Regiment on Exercise Gryphons Flight for a week, centred on Salisbury Plain. This was an enjoyable, fast-moving exercise with the Squadron for once operating within a regimental context.

In late November a visit was made to the Otterburn Ranges to undertake TOW live firing, adopting the concept of Joint Air Attack Team operations whereby TOW was used in coordinated attacks with artillery, mortars and fast-jet strikes to destroy large concentrations of enemy armour,

'The RAF had agreed to supply some Harriers, but after the first day they withdrew for operational reasons and we were left with what we had initially thought would be a second string – the US Air Force's A-10s from Bentwaters and Woodbridge. Since Sergeant Duff had chatted up the Americans to join the exercise some weeks before, they had been warned for operations in the Gulf, they now had endless supplies of cannon ammunition to fire, and were keen to try new methods of attack prior to their deployment. Consequently, Exercise Burmese Snipe was a roaring success (literally) as countless A-10 attacks, controlled by the Squadron's own Airborne Forward Air Controllers, ripped up the North Range with over 60,000 rounds of cannon fire whilst TOW were fired by the Lynx. The Range Commandant came out to see what was happening and broadened the arcs for A-10 directions of attack, allowed vertical dive attacks and gave his final endorsement by saying he would welcome us back to do the same again on another occasion. Most importantly, it gave the American crews the opportunity to work with the Brits before doing it for real.'

In mid-January 1991, airstrikes were launched against Iraqi forces, so beginning the Gulf War. The Squadron continued to train throughout the period, whilst supporting HQ UKLF and other headquarters with numerous sorties to move senior staff between Wilton, High Wycombe and London. In April the Squadron deployed for a short exercise, but after two days the order came to return to Netheravon immediately, as the option to deploy to the Persian Gulf as a follow-on force was being considered. However, in the time taken to recover to base, the plan had changed, and no deployment to this theatre took place after all. A high point in May was the return from another exercise in Yorkshire,

'As an eight-aircraft Vic formation which we could see attracted the gaze of many as we traversed the country.'

David Joyce sums up his time as OC,

'It was a brilliant tour, unrivalled in its challenges both in and out of the cockpit, on 24 May 1991 – and thanks to Nobby's sterling efforts, with a Squadron Association strength now topping 250 – I handed over command to Gary Coward.'

Major Gary Coward took command of six Lynx, six Gazelles (although at least one of each was almost always either in Canada, Cyprus or Deep Maintenance) and 140 personnel assigned as the aviation squadron to the UK Mobile Force (UKMF) and, while still nominally part of 7 Regiment, along with 658 Squadron, was heavily engaged in the airmobile trial, acting as 9 Regiment's second anti-tank squadron. The more mundane routine on Salisbury Plain was well established – day-to-day tasking was mostly providing aircraft to support training around the south of England and transporting senior officers from A to B, mostly from Land HQ at Wilton. The OC remembers,

'One of our standard routines was a HELARM demonstration for JDSC, putting up as many aircraft as we could to "ambush" the course in the midst of a TEWT

(Tactical Exercise Without Troops) at the Hindons, a few miles south-west down the A303. We had a watercolour painted by Gilly Maclaren to commemorate our return to the airfield after one of these demonstrations. Professionally, we spent our time attempting to deliver a more offensive aviation capability.'

Gary Coward explains the concept of airmobility,

'4 Regiment had established the concept of aviation patrols in the Gulf War and so we sought to develop this concept within the context of "airmobility" in Europe. Teamed with 657 Squadron in 9 Regiment, we developed quick orders formats and associated procedures to ensure that we could play a full role within a Combined Arms manoeuvre battle. We trained on our own in the south-west (Exmoor, Bodmin and Dartmoor) all the way down to Lands End, even collaborating with David Hanbury-Tenison attempting to find wild boar from the air with newfangled thermal imaging sights (as they were then). Major exercises took place up near Dishforth, on Salisbury Plain and in Germany, where we were closely monitored by Observer Controllers, ultimately leading to the declaration of a Full Airmobile Capability based on 24 Airmobile Brigade.'

He also has fond memories of Denmark,

'Perhaps our most exciting training event during my tenure was a major test exercise in Denmark – three weeks away from RHQ, as an independent aviation squadron working to both UK and Danish commanders. The Danes were much more adventurous in their use of aviation and so we tended towards them, building up an excellent rapport. And of course there was a little time for R&R and while Copenhagen was not too far away, it was far enough to put off all but the most adventurous, who happily tended to be the best behaved. I seem to recall the aircraft also being reasonably well behaved, although we did leave a small trail of broken helicopters across Germany and Holland on our way home! Our Lynx at the time were Mk1 (GT), halfway to becoming Mk7 – that is uprated engines, but old style main rotor blades and tail rotor. They performed relatively well, especially during the summer.'

Gary noted in 1992,

'The Squadron has participated in support operations following Operation Granby in Kuwait and Iraq and a series of exercises, culminating in Certain Shield, the Multinational Airmobile Division trial in Germany. In the main the Squadron was fully manned and equipped, though suffering a high degree of turbulence due to personnel being posted on roulement tours to Northern Ireland and constant aircraft changes for the Lynx Mk 7 improvement programme. The high point of the year was Exercise Burmese Argonaut, the deployment of a two Lynx detachment on board HMS *Fearless* to Sevastopol in the Crimea between 10 October and 6 December 1991. The RN had run out of Mk3s and so an enterprising skipper requested Army support! Murray Whiteside and his half flight were quickly trained in deck landings and ship approaches, joining the ship on its way past the Isle of Wight. While the skidded Mk1 could not take the punishing deck landings that a Mk3 could, they returned two months later with the RN singing their praises. They were probably fed up of washing aircraft and engines quite so often though.'

He had happy memories of trips to Italy,

'Perhaps the travel highlight of both 1991 and 1992 were the exchanges with 4 ALE (Aviazione Leggera dell Esercito) based in Bolzano, Italy. Each year we would send a couple of Lynx full of intrepid exchangees to Italy for a week and the Italians would reciprocate with a couple of AB-205 Hueys. On each occasion we would attempt to outdo each other's hospitality – it became known as the "European Military Eating and Drinking Competition." In 1992 the QHI, Mick Goss and I led the UK team to Italy, coming a close second to the Italians who outlasted us all, even when flying. Yes, they drank wine (only white not red) prior to flying, on one occasion flying us through the biggest, darkest alpine thunderstorms any of us Brits had ever encountered – scary! On the other hand, when on our way to Edinburgh during the return match, we landed them at Giles Bentley's folks' place in Cumbria and the Italians were suitably amazed to spy a huge herd of llamas, Mrs Bentley's pride and business joy at the time.'

Another highlight was the annual Middle Wallop International Air Show,

'The Squadron was almost 100 per cent committed, certainly in aircraft terms, providing two airborne crash crews and then participating in the famous "Massed Approach" – in those days over 100 helicopters took part and I recall well, sitting at Barton Stacey awaiting the call to rise up and join in the fray. A long trail of helicopters then flew low and slow to the area east of Danbury Hill before rising up in two rather unsteady ranks and approaching the huge crowd. Thankfully, the crash crews were never needed.'

The highlight of the year was undoubtedly the Jubilee celebrating the Squadron's 50th Birthday. This was a splendid occasion and much enjoyed by all present. It was a great privilege for members of the serving Squadron to meet so many of the 'Old and Bold,' complete with an alarmingly large number of medals! One of the most important parts of the Jubilee was the commissioning of the Silver Chinthe. In order to pay for this the Association raised the magnificent total of £2500. This was topped up with donations from the AAC fund and others and the Chinthe purchased.

Gary Coward has happy memories of this event,

'First on the parade ground in front of the Colonel Commandant, General Sir John Learmont and then in the Officers' Mess (it helped I was the PMC at the time), where we held an All Ranks Lunch, washed down with wine brought over from Calais on a booze cruise. Thank goodness we benefitted from a tame Guardsman pilot, Sergeant Tombs, who drilled us sufficiently not to look a shambles in front of the Colonel Commandant and Nobby Clark!

It took me some time to track down enough drawings and examples of a Chinthe for the sculptor; the best figure came from the First Secretary at the Burmese Embassy in London. Unfortunately, I left the small wooden figurine in my office with my mad Labrador for just a little too long – she had decided to give it a good chew – it was a complete wreck! Once I had plucked up enough courage to confess everything to the First Secretary, he let me down very quickly, explaining that it was his birth sign and he had many of these wooden carvings – he would not miss this one and no, I did not need to pay him a King's Ransom for it! This story, when recounted to the assembled masses at the Jubilee Dinner in the Museum of Army Flying caused a few chuckles.'

The main changes during 1993 were the arrival of a new OC and a change of location. The new OC was Garry Key, who took over from Gary Coward in July. In December 1993 a skeleton 656 Squadron packed its bags, bid a fond farewell to Netheravon and commenced the long journey to Dishforth in North Yorkshire to become part of 9 Regiment, along with 664 and 657 Squadrons, under the command firstly of Lieutenant Colonel Pat Lawless, who was followed later in 1994 by Lieutenant Colonel Chris Walch. On arrival they subsumed 672 Squadron and the majority of its new manpower, but not its aircraft. Until this point 672 had been equipped with the new Mk 9 Lynx in support of 24 Airmobile Brigade. This role, along with the rest of 9 Regiment's Mk 9 Lynx was transferred to Wattisham and gratefully received by the newly ensconced 3 Regiment. Six Mk 7 Lynx and six Gazelle, all of which were Gulf War Veterans with plenty of 'character', filled the aircraft void in respect of 656's requirements.

The Squadron became a fully integrated part of 9 Regiment whose role was to support 3 (UK) Division – 'a Division for all seasons, which must prepare for conventional war and sub-conventional conflict. It can expect operations to be joint, probably conducted with allies, quite possibly under a United Nations mandate.' It had three Brigades under its command, two mechanized and one airborne. It was the latter, 5 Airborne Brigade based at Aldershot, to which 656 Squadron now had its affiliation and which the Squadron would be most likely (though not exclusively) to go on operations with. It was, as usual, kept very busy in 1994, with heavy commitments in squadron, regimental, brigade and divisional exercises. This constant workload made a great contribution towards the successful combination of 656 and 672 Squadrons. The OC summarized those early months as follows,

'We embarked upon a series of exercises and training courses intended to "Explore Operational Reach Potential." This involved Squadron helicopters and vehicles being prepared for deployment by RAF C-130 Hercules transport aircraft, two of which landed at Dishforth to test loading procedures. Other vehicles were prepared for deployment by sea using ships of the Royal Fleet Auxiliary (RFA). These ambitions were supported by intensive training activity involving deck landings on the dummy deck and RFAs *Black Rover* and *Gold Rover* and others, the crews of which appreciated the practice marshalling and refuelling. The REME LAD really pulled out the stops to refine aircraft strip down procedures and reduce time for reassembly. NVG (Night Vision Goggle) categorization was an important part of our operational potential. Gazelle Flight all qualified to CAT1 (first of three levels of qualification) and received roof mounted Laser designators. Twelve aircrew qualified in the use of the designators, enabling better ranging and greatly assisting in the control and accuracy of fast-jet support. At this time the Squadron embarked upon an ambitious training programme, which within a year saw it flush with qualified Forward Air Controllers (FACs). Lynx Flight progressed rapidly from Cat 1 to CAT 2 and some achieved CAT 3 at this early stage and demonstrated their capability on Exercise Pegasus Strike.'

Garry goes on to describe this important exercise in some detail,

'We supported 5 Airborne Brigade, with elements of the Squadron deployed by air (two aircraft in a C-130 from RAF Lyneham) and by sea, involving a sail around the Isle of Wight courtesy of the RFA, to provide proof of concept and build knowledge. The remainder deployed from the holding base area and all arrived at Keevil, a disused airfield adjacent to Salisbury Plain. Close cooperation with HQ 5 Airborne Brigade staff, the RAF and RFA ensured that we all arrived on time. After conducting various training events including deployment and retrieval of medical and surgery teams from a Field Hospital (arranged ad hoc the day before); the main event was a long-range night raid by four Lynx aircraft at a creative interpretation of CAT 2. This included a night flight from Keevil to the disused Bodmin Airfield on Bodmin Moor, to be refuelled by RAF parachute-inserted FARP, a return flight to Deptford Down and a simulated TOW attack to cover the tactical withdrawal of Parachute Regiment troops, who had been parachuted in that day to simulate a raid on an HQ in some far flung foreign field. The flight also conducted a live mortar shoot with a PARA mortar platoon. Post exercise the Squadron continued training in NVG, FAC and deck operations as crews left and new replacements came in, placing a heavy strain on the Squadron and Regimental QHIs. We also sent detachments and individuals to Canada, Kenya and Belize.'

Sadly, on 19 September 1994, Captain Julian Pooley, an AAC Territorial Army pilot, who was serving as the Belize detachment commander, was killed in a motorcycle accident while returning from a visit to Mexico. Julian had helped to instruct Andy Simkins in the intricacies of controlling a hot air balloon when serving under his command back in the late 1980s. It was a tragedy made worse by the fact that he was doing so much for disadvantaged children there.

In October, the Squadron returned to the Far East to take part in Exercise Suman Warrior, which took place in Singapore and was part of the Five Nations Defence Agreement (S=Singapore, U=United Kingdom, M=Malaysia, A=Australia, N=New Zealand). The journey by RAF Hercules took thirty-two hours in the air, via Cyprus, Abu Dhabi, Sri Lanka and Kuala Lumpur. Garry recalls that the accommodation 'was terrible, very cramped, no mattresses, no hot water and no air conditioning,' though 'the Officers' Club opposite Raffles Hotel was very obliging.' The exercise was particularly successful; it helped Squadron personnel to gain valuable experience in the kind of multinational operation that was becoming the norm. For many it was the first visit to the Far East. Being so close to 656 Squadron history made the remembrance service held at Changi Cemetery all the more poignant. Wreaths were laid by, and on behalf of, the Squadron and the Association.

Throughout 1995 the Squadron was once again stretched to fulfil its commitments to provide personnel for roulement tours and exercises in Northern Ireland, Canada, Kenya, Belize, and Cyprus – to name but a few. When combined with support to the rest of the Army and maintaining its own training regime to meet the high standards it set for itself, this was to prove a demanding schedule. It continued to make significant advances in night operations, which generated interest Corps wide. Garry Key recalls with gratitude the efforts of all members of the Squadron and in particular,

'I think mention should be made of then WO2, SQHI Mick Galston, who took over from Mick Goss. He was a consummate professional pilot and provider of consistent support to our aims and ambitions, especially in respect of deck landings and NVG. Over and above this I was blessed with a squadron full of vigour and keen to succeed in a climate of warmth of spirit, family and fun. One of our most enjoyable activities was mountain flying in Snowdonia. We carried out underslung load activity for the Snowdonia National Park, lifting pathway materials and tree shoots as well as practising various mountain flying techniques. We usually stayed over in a B&B, courtesy of the National Park service.'

With the deployment of the Rapid Reaction Force in the Former Republic of Yugoslavia and the heavy aviation commitment to this force, the workload again increased. In addition to the normal commitments, personnel were provided to fill temporary posts which had been vacated by regiments earmarked for deployment to Bosnia. Due to its impressive level of training, especially in night flying, the Squadron was the first port of call for those squadrons and regiments who were seeking to boost their own numbers to fill their establishments. The result of the above was a very heavily tasked light Squadron remaining in Dishforth, with the ground crew working especially hard with extra duties on top of normal Squadron tasks. Captain Patrick Logan led a very successful twenty man detachment providing three Gazelles on Exercise Medicine Man in BATUS, Canada, from August to October. Also in October, the Divisional Artillery Exercise was supported with Air OP aircraft provided by the Squadron, and three aircraft with crews participated in a very worthwhile Aviation Reconnaissance Patrol Demonstration on Salisbury Plain for Officer Cadets from RMA Sandhurst. The OC has particular memories of Exercise Pegasus Fury,

'This follow on to Pegasus Strike involved HQ 5 Brigade and a para battalion dropping on Otterburn. Preliminary operations included 656 picking up the pathfinder platoon the day before and deploying them to Carlisle and Otterburn via a FARP at Warcop under NVG Cat 3 conditions, followed by a return there to refuel, then back to pick up the pathfinders from Carlisle and fly to them to Otterburn. The Squadron then conducted live TOW firing, while the Gazelle flight enjoyed doing airborne FAC for 3 x Tornados, 3 x Jaguars and 8 x 8 ship of Harriers, all firing and dropping live munitions. The Gazelles then conducted a live Artillery shoot with Brigade 105s while Lynx flight converted two aircraft to casevac role. The Brigade was flown in by thirteen Hercules, coming in low-level up the valley before popping up to 800 feet over the DZ for a drop in, wind conditions were at the margins to say the least! Following the light drop, aircraft, including RAF and 656, picked up several casualties and evacuated them to hospital. Then came the heavy drop, which as the second Hercules dropped its load, gave a new meaning to FFR Rover – in this case, Free Flight Rover – as the 1 Tonner, carrying live mortar ammunition parted with its load pallet and parachute and proceeded to bury itself into the Otterburn peat. The Free Flight Rover began to cook off and after half an hour or so blew up in front of several hundred visiting environmentalists brought in to discuss road widening for AS90 self-propelled artillery, which had recently been introduced.'

As the main exercising squadron, 656 also played a key role in the Regimental Exercise Eagle Strike in October. This took place on Salisbury Plain and concentrated on night flying, in particular NVG operations. The two weeks provided some difficult and testing situations for both aircrew and ground crew and served to prove their readiness for challenging times ahead. In December, Major Garry Key left the Squadron at the end of his tour in command and was replaced by Major Steven Marshall, who later recalled,

'I was told that the Squadron was warned for deployment to Bosnia to support Major General Mike Jackson's Multi-National Division South-West and I was to lead them on this deployment. I asked when we were deploying and was told that we might just see Christmas at home! I busied myself moving my family and getting to know the people in the Squadron and the wider Regiment. I had only recently completed my Lynx course and was also trying to consolidate my flying, which the winter weather and the demand for hours pre-deployment conspired to make difficult. A memorable difficulty was trying to learn to operate the special equipment that our aircraft had been fitted with for the tour. There was no formal training or documentation and we had to rely on the previous experience of air and ground crews and by "buying in" knowledge from outside of the Regiment.'

The Balkans

The Squadron detachment prepared to deploy to The Former Republic of Yugoslavia and looked forward in the New Year 1996 to the somewhat wintery climate of Bosnia Herzegovina. Some fifty-two members of the Squadron, six Lynx and four Gazelle were sent as part of the 9 Regiment package, with likely duties encompassing the full spectrum of peacekeeping and peace enforcement as part of the multi-national UN force (IFOR), Operation Resolute, supporting the Cessation of Hostilities Agreement, facilitating the development of a durable peace within the Bosnian Muslim/Croat Federation, policing the Contact Line with the Bosnian Serbs and enhancing humanitarian assistance to the people of Bosnia Herzegovina. The start of the operation was not without some difficult moments,

'We did end up spending an anxious Christmas at home, constantly waiting to get the final deployment call. The call finally came at a period of very poor weather with thick fog preventing the departure of our Lynx and Gazelles. We peered out across a freezing and foggy airfield for the next few days, which did nothing for the nerves and morale of our crews and families as we said goodbye every morning and then returned in the evenings to start the same frustrating performance the next day.

I eventually made the decision to leave Dishforth and head south, even if we simply crawled to one of the RAF airfields near to us: we simply needed to make the break and get underway. When we did depart, the weather broke sufficiently for us to get to RAF Manston on the Channel, where we spent two nights. Reports from Bosnia told us that the mobility which we provided was much anticipated by the Division and the pressure was on for us to get to Split in Croatia and join the Regimental advance party who had flown out by RAF transport.

The next morning we crossed a claggy English Channel and made our way slowly and steadily through France. At every fuel stop we checked the increasingly poor weather which lay ahead of us. The Alps simply could not be crossed at altitude, and poor stormy weather south of the Alps would make that route long and difficult and we were constantly being made aware of the importance of getting into theatre as quickly as possible. Our navigation was made easier by the use of personal GPS units jury-rigged into the aircraft to make up for the poor and intermittent performance of the systems on the Lynx.'

However, the Squadron pressed on,

'We were struck by strong winds and torrential rain throughout our journey through France and at one stage my Lynx had inches of rainwater sloshing around in the foot wells which caused the radios to degrade. Good teamwork and initiative kept the group in communication with ATC, and slowly, we proceeded via Reims to overnight at Lyon.

The next day we made our way to Nice. At times, flight at ultra-low-level was required and we found ourselves making use of our pylon crossing techniques and our mountain flying as we negotiated our way, finding a route through the valleys. The following day saw us going via Pisa to Ancona. Here, sea fog infuriatingly prevented us from making the final leg across the sea to Split. We arrived at Ancona, just as the RAF mounting unit (which had been staging RAF units into theatre) was just leaving. They literally threw us the keys to their office, gave us their airfield entry passes and left! Two frustrating days later we made the crossing to Split, the longest sea crossing that most of us had ever undertaken: it was amazing how many "new" noises and vibrations we felt as we stared out over nothing but miles of empty sea!'

Once in theatre the Squadron settled in and got to work,

'We arrived in Split to a largely "miffed" regimental HQ who had for some reason expected us the previous day and had arranged the defence press to be in attendance! We then began the normal painful process of induction into the new theatre and the signing over of various stores and documents. This process took a day, so our move from Croatia "up-country" to Gornji-Vakuf (GV) in Bosnia was delayed. When we did get to GV, we found a ramshackle collection of Portacabin type huts called CorriMecs, after their Italian manufacturers. The HLS was in a dreadful state due to its location in a low lying muddy field and to the ravages of the winter weather. That very day we began the soldierly tradition of improving accommodation for our aircraft and ourselves. We also immediately began the movement around theatre of the GOC, Major General Mike Jackson, who I knew from being my Company Commander for a while in 2 PARA. From there the work just spiralled and we slipped into a rostered duty approach to life.'

The flying was very demanding: high altitudes, appalling wintry weather and only a rudimentary infrastructure for men and machines. The locals generally had it much worse. The country had been ravaged and there were still sporadic instances of inter-ethnic violence happening,

'It was heartbreaking to see the conditions and suffering that the locals had had to endure. During the first few months we experienced armed Mil MI-8 "Hip" helicopters breaking the no-fly embargo, anti-aircraft cannon fire from disgruntled factions whilst making IMC (Instrumental Meteorological Conditions) approaches into Sarajevo airport directed by laissez-faire French military controllers and several near and actual wire-strike incidents caused by the locals jury rigging power supplies back to rural communities and stringing power lines without notification, sometimes by rocket line!

We survived the winter and enjoyed the beauty of the Bosnian spring and early summer. Towards the end of our tour, the MND HQ moved from GV to Banja Luka and we were left in the camp with an infantry battalion that filled the gap on reorganization left by the HQ. Both the Squadron and I enjoyed the greater freedom and responsibility created by the HQ's departure.'

Back in the UK (again)

The Squadron left Bosnia in June 1996 and returned to Dishforth, which was in the view of the OC rather an anticlimax. They returned to very poor aircraft availability due to spares shortages, particularly for the Lynx and struggled to keep aircrew current and aircraft fit and healthy. It was a major engineering and administrative undertaking, to scrape together the resources to support formation exercises. The most important operational development was the Government's announcement concerning the creation of the Joint Rapid Deployment Force (JRDF), which was formed on 1 August 1996, with the Squadron being nominated as the Lead Aviation Squadron. What this meant in practical terms was that several vehicles were kept packed and ready to go, while Squadron members' interest in the news and in particular foreign affairs intensified. With each flare-up of violence somewhere in the world the possibility of having to deploy as a part of a British response became very real.

Garrison life in late 1996 and 1997 also included: Squadron members and detachments supporting Army training and operations in Belize, Bosnia, Canada, Cyprus, Germany, Kenya and Northern Ireland, all in addition to the ongoing support provided to the Army in the UK. It was difficult to find a time when a significant number of Squadron personnel were actually at home rather than abroad. However, there was one particularly enjoyable event,

'We were directed to support training with the Italian Army in November/December 1996 and I took some of our Lynx Flight to Bolzano in Northern Italy where we swapped experiences and seat time on the AB 205s of the unit we were exchanging with. The Italians, used to the much less spirited and somewhat plodding AB 205, relished the power and responsiveness of the Lynx. Their first take-offs were always amusing however, with the aircraft shooting skywards from the hover and then plunging down, as they tried to rapidly come to terms with the Lynx's very different characteristics.'

Major Tim Sharp arrived in November 1997 to assume command and his first impressions were of,

'A sense of belonging to a family which everyone was proud to be a part of. I remember looking up at the board which held the names of previous OCs and felt somewhat in awe.'

It was not long after his arrival that the Squadron was warned of a deployment as a formed unit to BATUS in September 1998. This was a first for any AAC unit, as previously, only the Gazelle crews had ever deployed to fly aircraft that were pre-positioned to support the 'Square Battle Group' training. They would be taking an additional two Gazelle aircraft and four Lynx, plus 'all the trimmings' – to Alberta in Canada. Tim recalls,

'Fortunately, I was blessed with probably the best 2i/c in the (somewhat round) form of Alex Willman, who was still sporting a gunner cap badge, who sorted out the logistics. These were not inconsiderable and involved hiring a couple of Russian Antonov An-124s and a slack handful of Fat Alberts (C-130J) to get the kit over there, whilst a couple of fuel bowsers were shipped across the Atlantic and taken by train across Canada.'

One of the pilots, Gazelle Flight Commander Paul Hayhurst, retains vivid memories of the flight, in formation, of the six helicopters across the prairie from Calgary to Medicine Hat. The whole experience was made even more challenging, as the Squadron was to undertake the 'Deep Operations Battle' in conjunction with the Blues and Royals, led by the larger than life character, Lieutenant Colonel Barney White-Spunner. Tim continues,

'If BATUS was a sausage machine for churning out Battle Groups ready to go to war, we broke the machine and threw it away. The only "Blue" forces on the vast expanse of what is the BATUS prairie, were 656 and Barney's Medium Recce vehicles – the rest of the tanks and APCs were "targets" or "Red" forces. During the planning, we soon realized that even BATUS wasn't big enough for us, so we used another training area at Wainwright as either a FOB or a FARP to stretch the range equivalent to what Deep Operations was meant to represent. We knew, as we were planning the training, that the Squadron was going to be the first to receive the Apache, and so, in effect, we were preparing the crews for the type of missions they would undertake with the Apache, albeit with a now rather aging airframe – the Lynx.

We had a brilliant time; lots of challenges, many records broken, plenty of hours and loads of missiles down the range. We broke the mould, developed new doctrine on the hoof and demonstrated to the Armoured Corps that they had better watch out. I think the funniest moment for me was watching the exasperated SQMS, Staff Sergeant Stokes, who was trying to keep us supplied with water whilst out on the hot and dusty prairie and all he had was a Land Rover and an extremely leaky water trailer which was more like a sieve. Needless to say, it was topped up when he left Camp Crowfoot but usually arrived without enough water to boil an egg, when he found us. This activity kept him occupied for days, whilst the prairie turned green again!'

Paul Hayhurst also remembers a remarkable first accomplished during exercise, the first targeted 'kill' using an unmanned aerial vehicle (UAV), as he says, 'a sign of things to come.' The RA was trialling the Phoenix UAV, which searched for a formation of Warrior armoured fighting vehicles (AFVs) at night and in adverse weather conditions. Surveillance tapes were collected in the field by a Gazelle and brought back to HQ, where a brief was prepared for the Lynx crews, who then took off, found the AFVs and 'destroyed' them with simulated TOW missile strikes.

Tim reported back to the CO of 9 Regiment (then Lieutenant Colonel Tim Goble) that,

'We were like a blade that had been honed to fine cutting edge and that if the Antonovs and C-130s wanted to turn left at the end of the runway and deploy us on operations, rather than turn right to bring us home – that was fine with us because we were ready for anything!'

As it was a twelve hour trip by Hercules to Goose Bay and a further twelve hours of noisy boneshaking across the Atlantic, it might even have been preferable.

On 1 September 1999, as part of the Strategic Defence Review, 9 Regiment was moved from 3 (UK) Division to 16 Air Assault Brigade and its role was changed from anti-tank to air assault. Later that month a very enjoyable and successful exchange visit was made to Bolzano in Italy by two Lynx and thirteen personnel, the Squadron having hosted a party of ten Italian airmen at Dishforth. Mountain flying training and absorbing the local culture were both accomplished. Two Lynx and two Gazelles participated in the 16 Air Assault Brigade Opening Parade at Wattisham Airfield in the same month. In October, an exercise was held on Salisbury Plain, in which four Lynx and four Gazelles from the Squadron took part, this was the first 16 Air Assault Brigade exercise. Paul Hayhurst recalls that a memorable part of this event was the sight of an entire Brigade's worth of transport occupying the car parks at South Mimms Motorway Services and where the only sustenance available was frozen Cornish Pasties.

The Balkans Once More
During the first part of 2000 the Squadron was very well occupied with its pre-Bosnia training. This included the regulation UNTAT (United Nations Training Advisory Team) course and a highly successful week spent mountain flying in Wales. The move to the Balkans on Operation Palatine as the UK Aviation Squadron was spread out over several weeks, but all eighty-six personnel, under the command of Major Alex Tucker, had finally arrived in theatre by 22 April. Bosnia experiences its rapid change from

winter to summer over the month of April and those in the first move were lucky enough to experience temperatures in the 20 to 30 degrees Celsius range, whilst still having large pockets of snow on the ground. The terrain was stunningly beautiful but potentially hazardous for flying. There was much to do on handover, from inventory checks to driver familiarization and theatre qualifying the pilots. The purpose of the mission was to support Multi National Division (South-West) (MND (SW)) which had its Headquarters in Banja Luka. The Squadron initially deployed to Gornji Vakuf in the Vrbas Valley, which was its Main Operating Base for the first three months of the tour. It also manned two FOBs at Banja Luka and Sarajevo, as well as a logistic detachment in Split.

The main tasks were to provide one Lynx AH9 in support of the Deputy Commander Operations of the Stabilization force, Major General Philip Trousdell, one Lynx for the GOC of the MND (SW), Major General Robin Brimms, and one Gazelle undertaking observation tasks for the National Liaison Team. All aircraft were at an hour's notice to move day and night. This was achieved on all but a few days when the weather or unserviceable aircraft intervened. Bosnia was found to be much changed from its turbulent days in the mid-nineties. Although there were numerous uninhabited villages and many parts of the country were still mined, the general attitude seemed to be one of rejuvenation. On the drive up country from Split, new plastering and fresh paint could be seen gradually replacing the once familiar bullet ridden houses. In Sarajevo, where one of the Lynx was normally based, there were houses with satellite dishes, but no windows. The once proud television building stood ruined in the centre of a thriving metropolis. The local people were generally friendly towards SFOR (Stabilization Force) personnel and though troop levels were being reduced, there was a feeling that much had been achieved and there was still a worthwhile job to do.

At the end of June the Squadron moved its Main Operating Base from Gornji Vakuf to Split. To say goodbye to Gornji Vakuf an international heli-meet was organized, which included participation by Americans, Canadians, Dutch, Czechs, as well as the RAF and RN, with a variety of aircraft types including Chinooks, Apaches, Blackhawks, A109s, Cougars and MI-17s. The evening started with a memorial service for the crew of the Lynx that crashed at Gornji Vakuf just before Christmas in 1998. (On 22 December 1998, Lynx AH.7, XZ610, of 669 Squadron, suffered mechanical failure and crashed with the loss of all three crew.) The crew bar at Gornji Vakuf had already been named the 610 to preserve its memory and was a popular venue for unwinding and socializing, with weekly quiz nights being a star attraction.

The Burma Challenge was the Squadron's charity fund raising effort during the tour. This took the form of a sponsored run/row covering the distance from Dishforth to Burma (the location, of course, of its first operational deployment in 1943). All personnel logged their running and rowing mileage to gain the grand total of 8716 miles. Over £6000 was raised towards books for two Bosnian schools and Action Against Breast Cancer. The 2i/c, Paul Hayhurst, came up with the idea of selling out of date oil and lubricants to a local dealer, thus saving the MOD the disposal costs and also raising a considerable sum of money for charity. During the tour, Springfield HLS at Banja Luka was rebuilt (complete with hangar) and handed over just in time for the new independent Gazelle Detachment to move in. As the Squadron left, the new Lynx Detachment was looking forward to moving into Sarajevo airport by the end of November. In summary, the Squadron flew 826.7 hours Lynx and 525.1 hours Gazelle, whilst closing down the base at Gornji Vakuf and drawing down the aviation commitment from a squadron to two independent detachments of two Lynx which operated in support of the Deputy Commander and two Gazelles for special tasking. Flying conditions had often been challenging due to rapidly changing weather, the smoke caused by massive heathland fires and the abundance of overhead power cables. Crews gained experience in mountain flying in hot and high conditions.

Home Again

After a long break, that included post operational tour leave for many and Christmas block leave for all, the Squadron regrouped on 8 January 2001. With a large influx of new Airtroopers and changes in virtually all the key positions, the first priority was a shake-out exercise. It therefore moved to a FOB in Driffield for thirty-six hours. This provided the opportunity to practise basic drills that needed to become second nature by the time the Squadron deployed on the Tactical Engagement Simulation Exercise Druid's Dance in March. It also helped everyone to get back into the air assault mindset after nearly a year away from it. Having got rid of some of the rust, the next challenge was the Brigade Exercise Eagles Flight. This was a chance to do some Squadron training, rounded off with a live firing raid on Castle Martin. Unfortunately the weather was to curtail much of the training. By the end of the first day, only two helicopters had made it to the FOB on Salisbury Plain. The rest were strewn out across the country as Aircraft Commanders and Patrol Commanders had rightly listened to the old saying, 'it is better to be on the ground wishing you were in the air than in the air wishing you were on the ground.' By the end of the next day seven of the Squadron's ten aircraft had managed to reach Salisbury Plain. With four Lynx TOW and three Gazelles there was enough combat power to do the raid. However, the forecast weather was again marginal. After a five hour delay whilst waiting for the fog to clear the decision was made to give it a go and the raid was launched. It was possible only to get to within about twenty miles of the target location where they were again frustrated by fog and had to turn round. With the weather closing in around them, they only just made it back, arriving at the same time as the missing three Gazelles. With better weather forecast, they needed to make the most of it before handing over the aircraft to 664 Squadron around midday the next day. Following some hasty planning a very concentrated scenario that practiced most aspects of the Squadron's role was put together. After the disappointment of the previous day, this was just the tonic that was needed and the Squadron was able to return to Dishforth satisfied with having achieved something despite the weather. The highlight of the second week of Eagles Flight was an escape and evasion exercise for the aircrew. The hunter force consisted of the ground crew, a troop from the Queen's Dragoon Guards and three tracker dogs. The weather was suitably cold and wet. After a search of their kit to ensure no contraband was taken, the aircrew were dropped in pairs at different locations around Catterick training area. The wet weather proved to be a blessing in disguise as the dogs were unable to pick up the scent of the evading aircrew. Despite the best efforts of the hunter force, only two of the escaping teams were captured. All the aircrew were then picked up by a Lynx the next day. The cost to the OC in bottles of champagne for those who managed to evade was considerable!

The Squadron also paid tribute to Burma veteran, Nobby Clark, the founding member of the reformed Squadron Association, who passed away on 20 March, at the age of eighty-two. The OC represented the Squadron at the funeral held at St Mary's Church, Huish Episcopi in Somerset. A Gazelle from the Squadron and an Auster V flown by 656 Association member, Eric Downing, conducted a fly-past as the mourners emerged from the church.

The focus of the Squadron's efforts shifted to an operational deployment to Kosovo and three overseas training exercises. A detachment of two Gazelles departed to Kenya in April, commanded by Captain David Wilkins. As soon as they were up and running they found themselves tasked to search for a missing soldier on the slopes of Mount Kenya. This tested both pilots and aircraft alike, as the majority of this task was completed at night, operating up to 10,000 feet above sea level, using NVG with a handheld thermal imaging camera. The detachment flew over six hours per day for six days during the search, to no avail. Fortunately, the missing person, a Royal Engineer explosives specialist, was found on the mountain at 8000 feet on the morning of the seventh day, none the worse for wear.

9 Regiment was tasked to support Operation Agricola in Kosovo for a ten month period and to achieve this it was decided to split the tour into four detachments. Captain Simon Hill, the Gazelle Flight commander, was selected to command the initial deployment by 656 Squadron. They deployed to Pristina and began the Theatre Qualification training and formally took over responsibility from 847 Naval Air Squadron on 18 May 2001. The tasks undertaken during the initial period were mainly in support of the Multi National Brigade (Centre) and were a mixture of command and liaison tasks and limited overwatch using the Nitesun. The nature of the tasking did however change shortly after this and they found themselves operating from a FOB in the south-western area of Kosovo known as the Bootleg. Here they supported the efforts to check the flow of military materiel from Albania into Macedonia. In conjunction with this they were also required to support specialist tasking. This rapidly began to account for the majority of the hours flown by the detachment, with the flying being, in the main, a solo pilot with an observer in the left-hand seat.

Later in the year, two more Gazelles were earmarked for detachment to Canada and a further two in support of an exercise in Kenya. Meanwhile, back in Dishforth during the period of May and June, the Squadron supported the efforts to control the spread of Foot and Mouth disease, which included taking fly epidemiologists working for MAFF around the infected areas of Cumbria and the Pennines. The use of aviation in this manner was thought to be of great value to the epidemiologists and vets, who were attempting to predict the spread of the disease and implement containment measures to prevent further outbreaks. In July the Squadron focus was again split. At home it supported Exercise Phantom Bugle, an exercise that takes place on Salisbury Plain three times a year to train the next generation of Squadron and Company commanders. It deployed with four Lynx and four Gazelle and an enhanced ground crew element for a week in the field. This provided an opportunity for personnel to test themselves against a live 'enemy' force in their primary role as an anti-tank squadron. Having not had a chance to test these skills for some time, some valuable lessons were relearned and by the final battle run, helicopters were once again proving decisive to the Battle Group Commander's Plan. It was during this exercise that the Squadron hosted a film crew from Carlton Television, the makers of *Peak Practice*. The storyline involved both ground and air elements of the Squadron with Airtroopers Robinson and Rolfe taking a starring role as extras. Just prior to the Squadron taking some well-earned leave over the summer, Captain Alex Rogers took another Gazelle detachment to Canada to participate in Exercise Iron Anvil. This differed from normal due to the restrictions on training imposed due to Foot and Mouth in the UK. They therefore ended up supporting 12 Mechanized Brigade, the first time that an AAC detachment had supported a brigade-sized force at BATUS. They spent forty days on the prairie prior to a brief adventure training package, returning to Dishforth in early October 2001, when Major Neil Dalton assumed command and who recalls,

'The start of my tenure in command seemed to be very indicative of what was to come. Some two days into the job the Squadron deployed on a Brigade FTX chasing the enemy all over Scotland in the type of weather that one would expect up north at that time of year, so testing us in the cockpit and out. But we were determined to maintain the pace and in January 2002 we subsequently deployed for a Squadron live-firing exercise at Otterburn, achieving some excellent TOW firing by day and night and testing the ground elements of the Squadron to provide support in extreme conditions.'

The following month the Squadron was the lead element of 16 Air Assault Brigade participation in a joint, multinational air exercise at RAF Leuchars (Tactical Leadership Training Night Exercise), acquitting itself well. Additionally, a further detachment was sent to Kenya early in the New Year, whilst the Squadron as a whole, was also warned for potential operational deployment to Afghanistan, which in the event did not happen but provided useful stimulus for planning activity and preparation. However, to facilitate support operations the CO, Lieutenant Colonel David Short, directed the Regiment to reorganize from mixed Lynx/Gazelle to single type squadrons. Consequently, the Squadron undertook three long-term operational commitments concurrently, these being a two Gazelle detachment to Kosovo on Operation Agricola (one year), a two Gazelle detachment to Bosnia on Operation Palatine (six months), and a two Gazelle detachment, UK-based, at twelve hours' notice to move on Operation Salvage (one year). In addition to the exercise and operational commitments, the Squadron had other challenges heaped upon it. Firstly, the restructuring demanded much from the command, SQMS and ground crew elements, while at the same time also being tested by the start of planning in respect of yet more restructuring in anticipation of the arrival of Apache in 2003. A significant commitment for this was a project to develop tactical scenarios for the Apache simulator located at the airfield that took Neil away for one week every month throughout the latter half of 2002 until his departure in February 2003. He could, however, celebrate the Squadron winning the Boroughbridge Sword (the inter-Squadron sports challenge), the first time that it had ever been won by a flying squadron. As Neil notes,

'We held an excellent BBQ to celebrate and were fortunate enough to be presented the trophy by General Sir Michael Walker, the Corps Colonel Commandant and Chief of the Defence Staff.'

Another item high on the agenda from late 2002 onwards was preparing for the Squadron's 60th Jubilee. Much time and effort was given over to make the day very memorable. The Jubilee was celebrated in style at Dishforth Airfield on 21 June 2003. The day commenced with a brief introduction from the Squadron to the assembled guests. The Acting OC, Captain Andy Gilks, gave a brief outline of the Squadron's history and splendid achievements over the previous sixty years. Burma veteran Arthur Windscheffel then unveiled a bespoke display cabinet, made from Burmese Teak, the Association's gift to the Squadron. This was from a design by Nobby Clark and was dedicated to his memory. After the group photograph Association members then visited various exhibits or took the opportunity to fly in a Gazelle. In the afternoon there was a buffet in the WOs' and Sergeants' Mess, where a second presentation was made to the Squadron of two new paintings by Lieutenant Colonel David Joyce and Peter Elliston. The day concluded with a dinner dance at the Crown Hotel in Boroughbridge, presided over by Lieutenant Colonel Andrew Simkins.

WO2 (SSM) Jim Lyons had been with the Squadron three years in 2003, having been promoted from Staff Sergeant. He had witnessed the transition from a Lynx and Gazelle equipped anti-tank unit to Gazelle only, as the arrival of the Apache drew closer. He recalls a period of considerable upheaval as a series of exercises for the mostly inexperienced ground crews were laid on to develop cohesion and field skills. It was his aim to make sure that the spirit of 656, which was an elite unit always at the forefront of events, was maintained. The following chapter will show just how successful the Squadron was in achieving this goal.

Chapter 10

The Apache – UK, Afghanistan and Libya 2003–2012

I t should be noted that it is utterly unavoidable to write about the Apache and indeed modern warfare in general without a plethora of acronyms and abbreviations. These have been provided both in the body of the text and at the start of this chapter for ease of reference:

AGM	Air-to-Ground Missile
ALPC	Arming and Landing Point Commander
AMTAT	Air Manoeuvre Training and Advisory Team
Avn BG	Aviation Battle Group
Berm	A man-made mound or wall of earth or sand
BSN	Camp Bastion
bSSFI	bespoke Small Scale Focused Intervention Capability
AH(A)	Apache Ground Crew Advanced Course
AH(B)	Apache Ground Crew Basic Course
CATT	Combined Arms Tactics Trainer
CCA	Close Combat Attack
CIFS	Close in Fire Support
CLT	Command Liaison Team
COMAO	Composite Air Operations
CTR	Conversion to Role
CTT	Conversion to Type
DROPS	Demountable Rack Offload and Pickup System
EW	Electronic Warfare
FAC	Forward Air Controller
FARP	Forward Arming and Refuelling Point
FET	Force Establishment Table
FHT	Final Handling Test
FIBUA	Fighting In Built-Up Areas
FLIR	Forward Looking Infrared
FOB	Forward Operating Base
HALS	Hardened Aircraft Landing Strip

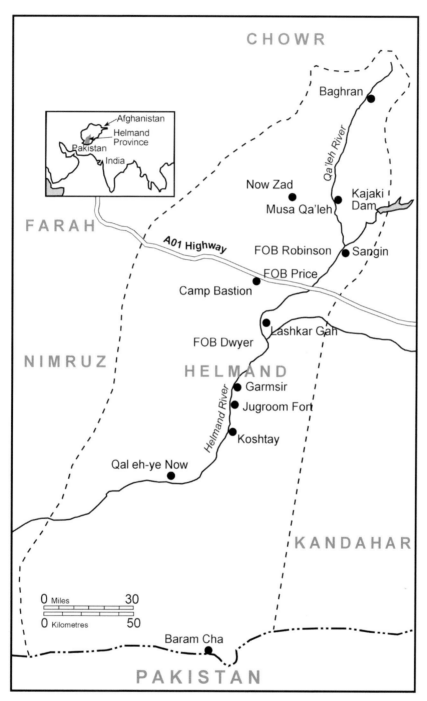

Afghanistan 2006–2009.

HCR	Household Cavalry
HIDAS	Helicopter Integrated Defensive Aids System
HRF	Helmand Reaction Force
IED	Improvised Explosive Device
IEFAB	Improved Extended Forward Avionics Bay
IOC	Initial Operating Capability
IRT	Incident Response Team
ISAF	International Security Assistance Force
ISTAR	Intelligence, Surveillance, Target Acquisition and Reconnaissance
JHF(A)	Joint Helicopter Force (Afghanistan)
JHSU	Joint Helicopter Support Unit
JTAC	Joint Terminal Air Controller
KAF	Kandahar airfield
LCR	Limited Combat Ready
LPH	Landing Platform Helicopter
MAOT	Mobile Air Operations Team
MPS	Mission Planning Station
NVG	Night Vision Goggles
OCF	Operational Conversion Flight
OEF	Operation Enduring Freedom
OPTAG	Operational Training and Advisory Group
ORBAT	Order of Battle
PJHQ	Permanent Joint Headquarters
PNVS	Pilots Night Vision System
RIP	Relief in Place
RPG	Rocket-propelled grenade
SAM	Surface-to-Air Missile
SQHI	Squadron Qualified Helicopter Instructor
TADS	Target Acquisition and Designation Sight
TIC	Troops in Contact
TQ	Theatre Qualification
TSW	Tactical Supply Wing
UAV	Unmanned Aerial Vehicle
VHR	Very High Readiness

Background

Originally designed by the Hughes Helicopter Company, the YAH-64 prototype took to the air for the first time on 30 September 1975. It was not until eight years had elapsed that the much changed first production AH-64A Apache emerged from the factory at Mesa, Arizona and it would be a further three years before the Apache would achieve Initial Operating Capability (IOC) status with the US Army. Following its operational debut in Panama in 1989, the Apache won its spurs in the 1990-91 Gulf War against Iraq, where it proved to be a formidable airborne weapons system.

Following an invitation for bidders to tender their product, in September 1993 at the Farnborough Air Show, 'Team Apache', consisting of GKN Westland, McDonnell Douglas, Martin Marietta and Westinghouse, announced that it would be submitting a design to the British Government, which would be based on the advanced AH-64D Apache Longbow. Bids were also made for the Eurocopter EC-665 Tiger, a version of the Bell AH-1 SuperCobra, the wholly US-built AH-64 Apache, the Boeing-Sikorsky RAH-66 Comanche, and the Agusta A129 Mangusta. However, it was 'Team Apache' which was successful in satisfying the British Army that this was the bid which would best meet the AAC's requirement for a sophisticated attack helicopter, and on 25 March 1996 the contract was signed for the production and delivery of sixty-seven of the WAH-64, which would be designated as the Apache AH1 (Attack Helicopter) by the Ministry of Defence. The contract also included simulators at Middle Wallop, Dishforth and Wattisham. The initial eight production Apaches were constructed in the USA, with the first one, ZJ166, flying on 25 September 1998. In October, the Army Air Corps gave a ground presentation to the press at the new Joint Helicopter Command base at Wilton, where an Apache was put on static display. The first aircraft to be assembled by Westland at Yeovil was ZJ172, which made its first flight on 18 July 2000. The British Army Apache is powered by twin 1850 shp Rolls-Royce RRTM-322 engines, which give it a maximum speed of 182 mph and a range of nearly 300 miles, depending upon the weight of weapons, ammunition and fuel carried. It can be armed with a combination of AGM-114 Hellfire missiles and CRV7 rocket pods, carried on stub-wing pylons and the formidable Hughes 30mm M230 chain gun. It also has an advanced Longbow Fire Control Radar and Electronic Warfare (EW) capability called the Helicopter Integrated Defensive Aids System (HIDAS). To these may be added a suite of highly sophisticated day and night sensors, the Target Acquisition and Designation Sight (TADS) System. As a whole the Apache is without doubt the most capable, complicated and demanding weapons system that the AAC and REME have been called upon to operate. It was vitally important that the AAC, and for that matter the Army hierarchy, grasped the enormity of the task ahead of it. Vested interests in the RAF were ready to criticize the whole process and comment on whether the AAC was up to the task with such a taut establishment, lack of breadth of technical expertise and untested, young non-graduate NCO pilots. It was certainly a huge leap forward from the TOW armed Lynx. The story of the Apache's introduction into AAC service has been told in the author's previous book *First in the Field, the History of 651 Squadron.*

Preparation

Major Andy Cash took command of the Squadron in August 2003 and noted that the past year had been a period of considerable turbulence for the Squadron as it prepared for the Apache era. Personnel were busy supporting operational and training deployments worldwide. The Squadron undertook major restructuring and 're-manning' as personnel were posted in and out to ensure that it had the best team possible to field the Apache, with a more robust SHQ and Ground Support Flight. Captain Keith Millsom arrived in September into a new ground-based appointment, just after the final Lynx had been relinquished. He had been appointed as the AAC's first Forward Arming Refuelling Point (FARP) Commander. It was his responsibility to ensure, along with the FOB Commander, Captain Lee Tinley-Beets, that the ground staff would be ready for the arrival of the first Apaches, with all necessary dedicated ground sections in place: Apache specific ground crew, Signals, Mission Planning Station (MPS) planning and MT, all of whom would require extensive training. To assist with this transition the ground crew were trained and guided by the contractor Aviation Training International Ltd (ATIL) and the military Air Manoeuvre Training and Advisory Team (AMTAT), senior instructors in multiple disciplines, who were at hand to ensure that the Apache was worked up to its full fighting potential, as the Squadron prepared for the Conversion to Role (CTR) training package at Dishforth. They represented the AAC's most experienced instructor cadre of Apache qualified pilots, many of whom had served in 651, the Attack Helicopter Fielding Squadron. These included Major Al Whittle, Major David Meyer, AFC, Captain Paul Mason, Captain Matt Roberts and Lieutenant Commander Sean Dufosee. Additionally, Major Bill O'Brien, DFM, Major Tim Peake and Major David Amlôt, MBE (who went on to become OC 656 Squadron 2006-9) had also spent nine years collectively, serving with US Cobra and Apache units on exchange appointments. Captain Chris Hearn and WO2 Tom O'Malley, the Squadron QHIs were also seconded to AMTAT for the duration of CTR. The ground element of AMTAT was headed by Major Barry Ince and Captain John Weetman. This was intended to ensure that the ground crew were both competent and confident to refuel, rearm, provide logistic, technical and communications support and assist with mission planning – in particular the Mission Planning Station (MPS). Initially, the MPS was the size of two PCs encased in a green environmental cover, but in 2009/10 a laptop version was introduced. By programming the MPS in advance, key data can be entered and then transferred to the helicopter's computer, allowing the pilot to fly a sortie without having to worry about route following, fuel planning, aircraft performance, C of G and a host of other tasks.

One of the Airtroopers learning how to operate a FARP was Matty Rogers, who had been with the Squadron since 2001. He remembers having to absorb a huge amount of knowledge and being impressed by the sheer scale of a FARP capable of supporting two Apaches and the number of vehicles required to supply sufficient quantities of ammunition and fuel. There were seven members in each arming team and five teams in all. There was a great deal of friendly rivalry between the teams to see how quickly and efficiently a full upload could be achieved, but Matty chiefly recalls the spirit of a 'band of brothers' who helped each other, and still hark back to being part of the first CTR with pride. He feels that they had the same sense of teamwork as a Formula One pit crew and a very similar level of efficiency was developed during a hard but satisfying year. He pays tribute to the OC for his leadership and also to Captains Millsom and Tinley-Beets, whom he describes as 'soldiers' soldiers' who earned the respect of their men.

Conversion to Type

The aircrews' Conversion to Type (CTT) course at Middle Wallop was very demanding; learning the new skills required the ability to fly the aircraft while operating the Pilots Night Vision System (PNVS) and utilizing the aircraft's sensors and weapons to best effect. This also took six months, which left the aircrew dislocated with the Squadron up at Dishforth. The night flying element of the programme was particularly daunting as, due to problems with the weather and unserviceability, by early February the course was three weeks behind schedule and each student was faced with completing twelve night sorties in less than three weeks. The aircrew tasks are divided between the front-seater, whose main responsibility is engaging the weaponry and fighting the aircraft, and the rear-seater, who concentrates on flying and navigation. The key differences between flying on the PNVS and NVG (Night Vision Goggles) were the lack of depth perception due to the monocular vision and the rather poor Forward Looking Infrared (FLIR) picture. Students expressed the disorientating impact of the volume of instruction they had to absorb as like 'drinking from a fire hose.' The instructors had to work equally hard as they had to fly using the Target Acquisition and Designation Sight (TADS). The Final Handling Test (FHT) required each pilot to lead a formation trip to an area outside the local low flying region, nap of the earth, flying into battle positions and achieving a set time on target. Once away from the bare expanse of Salisbury Plain they became all too aware of the hazard presented by wires and cables. The weapons phase was conducted in great detail at ground school and in the simulator, before live firing at Otterburn in March. Otterburn was highly suitable as regards its location in reasonable proximity to Dishforth and also Carlisle Airport. Andy Cash has fond memories of the ground crew on a snowy day on the ranges, who, despite being chilled even further by the Apache's downdraft, were always ready with a smile and a cup of tea for the OC.

The training at Otterburn included the first live firing of CRV7 rockets and 30mm cannon on the ranges, which was also the first time that the Squadron's aircrew had been supported by their own ground crew in the Apache era. After the dispersed nature of the initial training phase, the Squadron reformed at Dishforth as a complete sub-unit in April 2004, on the completion of the aircrews' CTT.

Conversion to Role

Then began the six month CTR course at Dishforth, as a Squadron, under the guidance of AMTAT, which 'occupied our every moment, day and night.' One of the young aircrew taking part in CTR was Captain Piers Lewis, who had joined the Squadron as a Gazelle pilot in 2002. He regarded the Apache CTR as a 'real change in gear, going from 2nd in a Gazelle to 5th in the Apache.' A considerable portion of the training was carried out in the simulator and, as a whole, CTR was very demanding. Another feature of this period was the massive increase in curiosity from the general public. The A1 trunk road, which ran alongside one edge of the airfield, became a viewing platform for interested civilians.

The OC noted,

'The difficulty of undertaking, what is in effect, a full-time training course, while also dealing with the demands of Regimental life cannot be understated. As you would expect, everyone pulled out all the stops and despite fatigue and frustrations, managed to maintain good humour and achieve the training objectives.'

Keith Millsom recalls,

New to the ground crew was the introduction of a new qualification and appointment – Arming Landing Point Commander (ALPC). This soldier would need to complete the Apache Ground Crew Basic Course (AH(B)) and then the Apache Ground Crew Advanced Course (AH(A)) before progressing onto the ALPC course. All these courses were to be taught to personnel by the contractor ATIL at Middle Wallop. Selection for this position was made by Captain Lee Tinley-Beets and myself, who had also been commissioned from the ranks and was the Forward Operating Base

(FOB) Commander. We selected the soldiers who had shown a higher level of aptitude on the two preceding courses, were already a minimum of lance corporal rank and had at least four years' service remaining. Each Arming Point team would have two ALPCs and an AH(A), the remaining four must be at least AH(B) qualified. As the FARP Commander I then selected team members for further training, this included DROPS wagons (Demountable Rack Offload and Pickup System) and the Moffet Mounty (all terrain fork lift trucks). Each Arming Point team had to be self-sufficient and capable of being able to deploy with fuel and munitions at any time in support of advancing Apache aircraft. This had to be taken into account during training, exercises and operations. At the same time as the manpower increase was taking place, there was a steady trickle of new vehicles, stores and requirements. Our hangar was converted from being Lynx and Gazelle capable, to being able to take the much taller and wider Apache.

Working days of over twelve hours in length were all too common, filled with ground school, pre-flight preparation, mission briefing, simulator and flying sorties, ground runs and air tests. The ground and air crews discovered that they would be operating as a much more interdependent team than hitherto, with the MPS operators actually planning the missions with the aircrew, plotting corridors in the air along which the helicopter would fly, programming its computer and 'taking away a lot of the donkey work in the cockpit.' The technical burden was high for both technicians and aircrew, but the team worked well and few sorties were lost due to technical failures, at least six aircraft per day were made available, which was a very creditable achievement. The weather was less forgiving and significant numbers of sorties, and indeed entire exercises, were lost due to bad weather and were also exacerbated by aircraft release limitations and by the Squadron's own understandable caution when dealing with marginal weather and inexperienced Apache aircrew operating with an unforgiving night thermal imaging system. The ground crew had, of course, undertaken a vast amount of training as well, covering all aspects of supporting the Apache at base and in the field.

Then a Lance Corporal, Giovanni Morini remembers the intensity and high tempo of CTR, with it not being unknown for soldiers to sleep in the guardroom instead of going home in order to fulfil all the necessary tasks. There was great self-motivation and a desire to be the best, from the youngest FARP No 7 airtrooper upwards.

A significant milestone was reached on 17 June, at BATUS in Canada, when Major David Meyer and Captain Paul Mason, the crew of ZJ230, fired the first live Hellfire from a British Apache. There followed the development of the Close in Fire Support (CIFS) procedures, latterly known as Close Combat Attack (CCA) a method to provide AH firepower directly in support of, and on call from, ground forces, down to the lowest level of an infantry section. Running fire procedures and skills were also developed.

Back in Yorkshire, by June the training had progressed so well that the Squadron deployed out of Dishforth to Elvington, an old WW2 Bomber Command airfield which had a 3000 metre runway and a huge tarmac area alongside it (This location later hit the headlines in September 2006 when Richard Hammond from *Top Gear* had a high speed crash in a jet powered car). The area was ideal for the movement and training of the ground crew, with the increased amount of Squadron vehicles and the area required to set up an arming point. Training also took place at Otterburn again, with convoys being sent on a regular basis, taking up practice 30mm ammunition and 70mm CRV7 rockets which could be fired on the ranges. Once again in the words of the OC,

'For the ground crew, they practised deploying, setting up and operating, initially, two point FARPs by day and night and progressed to the more complex (for Command and Control) four point FARPs [The first ever AAC four point FARP – four AH refuelling and then rearming simultaneously – was a very significant milestone. The Squadron Order of Battle (ORBAT) would require five teams, four from MT manning and one from SHQ, each consisting of seven personnel]. The aircrew undertook progressively more involved tactical formation flying by day and night, leading up to reasonably complex night operations in an Electronic Warfare (EW) threat environment. The operations, both in the air and on the ground, have been very exciting and have given a real sense of coming of age for the AAC. We're in the "big boys' league" now; when we visit RAF bases it is now *them* that come over to look at our aircraft, rather than us theirs!'

SSM Jim Lyons was very gratified to find that the entire Squadron was pulling together so well. It seemed to him that there was a much greater degree of integration between aircrew, ground crew and REME than he had ever experienced before. It was undoubtedly stressful but it was, 'an experience I am glad to say I was part of, though I was ready for a rest at the end of it.' Andy Cash much appreciated his contribution, particularly as it allowed him the time and space to concentrate in getting to grips with the Apache during CTT and CTR. There was, of course, no special dispensation for the OC, he had to pass through the training to the same exacting standards as anyone else – but if he had failed there was no other trained OC in the pipeline. After the completion of CTR the real burden of additional responsibilities for Squadron administration fell on him, such as report writing, discipline, routine inspections and so on. The further development of doctrine, not only for the Squadron but also for the Regiment as a whole, also loomed large. The OC pays tribute to a great team of self-motivated experts around him who provided him with their highly detailed knowledge and advice – including Captain James Murrell from 9 Regiment, Ops Officer, Captain Andy Gilks and WO1 Kev Goddard concerning EW matters, as well as the two QHIs (Captain Hearn and WO1 O'Malley) and a very good set of Flight Commanders. A good relationship with REME's technicians was also crucial and Andy has particular memories of WO2 Parsons and Staff Sergeant Twinn, a real character, who 'would give it to you straight, whoever you were but with good humour.' The REME was also feeling its way with the AH but was working just as hard as the rest of the Squadron team to achieve the common goal.

Towards the end of July came the first 'exam' to pass as a Squadron. The 9 Regiment Battle Group put the Squadron through its paces on Exercise Lightning Dawn. It performed very well, achieving all the tasks it was set, in difficult circumstances. Three missions were conducted; a screen, a deliberate attack and an advance to contact and exploitation. However, as Andy Cash later wrote,

'We achieved much more than just that. We proved that we can talk to and operate with the Household Cavalry (HCR) recce screen and the Parachute Regiment, providing ISTAR (Intelligence, Surveillance, Target Acquisition and Reconnaissance) and close-in fire support. We can operate with the Boeing E-3D of No 8 Squadron and our own Lynx from 672 Squadron. We can plan complex missions involving joint and all arms assets, support them and execute them. We can make a sustained effort for suitable periods and still provide flexibility to respond to changing circumstances. We can rely on our people, especially our JNCOs, to come up to the mark when it is demanded of them. Obviously, we were far from perfect and we continued to learn, but, we are getting there and the advances since we began CTR, only four months ago, have been substantial.'

He later noted that one of the keys to success was that the Squadron's personnel had developed and encouraged a very open and honest culture – being prepared to accept constructive criticism and also being self-critical, but all within a friendly (if pressurized) environment,

'Our approach was based on humility and integrity; we couldn't afford not to learn lessons from each other.'

He could not recall any disciplinary incidents of any significance and felt that a light hand on the tiller was all that was needed; everyone was committed to the task and in any case was too busy and too tired at the end of the working day!

The Squadron returned to the Otterburn Training Area towards the end of August to conduct very successful CTR live firing with 30mm cannon and rockets; deploying with ground crew, REME and aircrew, as well as other Regimental assets. Running fire procedures and CIFS skills were further developed and honed. This period proved the efficiency of both the rocket and cannon weapon systems. However rewarding this period was proving, there were stresses and strains as described by Keith Millsom,

'Many more exercises followed over the coming months, which included an increased amount of time away from home. The aircraft is primarily a night time beast, and as such, meant that we were operating on a reverse cycle for much of the time. There was a fear that this would affect home life because some of the soldiers had lived in North Yorkshire for many years. Many had married and had children, some partners worked at night so their children would be cared for, whilst they were out, by the soldier spouse. This was new to all of us. An acronym was used to cover this situation that was a very serious concern for some and was formally recognized in the early 1990s by the US Army, AIDS (Apache Induced Divorce Syndrome).'

Further Training
Attention then turned, in September, to Composite Air Operations (COMAO) training, which was quite an eye-opener for the Squadron as a whole, and especially the planning teams, who had to adjust from their usual six to eight hour planning cycle to one of three hours. The purpose of the week was to operate with others and understand their planning processes and operating procedures. This resulted in the award of Limited Combat Ready (LCR) status for the aircrew, which was a major milestone for the programme. The exercise itself was very valuable – operating as part of, and in command

of, mixed formations of fast jets and helicopters, e.g. Tornado, Jaguar and Chinook, supporting a ground commander; as well as working with ISA (Intelligence and Situational Awareness) assets such as E-3D Sentry AEW1 and Sea King ASaC 7. It was all undertaken within a high air defence and simulated electronic warfare threat environment, Andy Cash commenting once more,

> 'One of the most challenging aspects of the process was solving issues of logistics support, particularly with regard to adequate fuel and communications. Despite a steep learning curve and a high workload we had great fun, learned a lot and still managed to pull together a seven-ship formation recovery back down the A1 from RAF Leeming to Dishforth, on 16 September 2004, which certainly caused a few heads to turn!'

One week later, the aircrew and the planning staff went to the Combined Arms Tactics Trainer (CATT) at Warminster – a warehouse housing state-of-the-art simulators for Challenger II tanks, Warrior fighting vehicles, Scimitar recce vehicles and a number of others. Despite a low resolution generic simulator representing the Apache, the all arms training was very worthwhile. Planning and fighting alongside 'virtual' armoured recce and other forces and using simulator firepower (Apache, artillery and fast air), they were able to very effectively replicate a genuine battle, demanding integration of assets and firepower to destroy the enemy, which definitely had a mind of its own. There was just a week to draw breath before the climax of the year's Apache conversion training; 16 Air Assault Brigade's Exercise Eagle's Eye, which took place in October. This exercise was designed to prove the Attack Helicopter Initial Operating Capability (IOC) and covered much of the UK, from Warminster to Dumfries. Starting at Keevil airfield, there was an opportunity to run through procedures and rehearsals along with Infantry Battle Groups, Armoured Recce, as well as a wide range of rotary-wing assets: Chinook, Puma, Merlin, Lynx and Gazelle. Once complete in the south, the entire effort moved north for several assaults in the West Freugh area. The rest of the exercise consisted of high tempo operations based around two airfields near Carlisle and West Freugh, conducting missions across the north of England and southern Scotland. The exercise was due to culminate in a final all arms dawn attack, however, the night before the attack, the Battle Group was hit by winds up to 60 knots, blowing away a number of tents (including one housing the Squadron's MPS), and damaging several aircraft. Come the morning, the wind was still gusting too strongly and unfortunately, the final assault never happened. Nonetheless, the Squadron had done enough and IOC was declared as having been tested and achieved, which was a really big first, not only for the Squadron but also for the AAC and UK Defence as a whole. This would enable four Apaches to be deployed in a 'semi-permissive environment' for reconnaissance and strike missions, but not to sustain prolonged operations. The Squadron had worked immensely hard over this period of training, the ground crew, aircrew and REME personnel had been pushed to the limits almost consistently throughout. Following a short breather and a celebratory party the next stage was for Squadron personnel to undertake individual maritime training, as well as some to Forward Air Control and career courses.

Chris Hearn's overall impression was of a really taxing period of eighteen months, with twelve months of seemingly non-stop exercises following the six months of CTR.

Quite a lot of time was spent sleeping under canvas, which was not a great deal of fun when the temperature fell to minus 11 degrees Celsius one night. Much of the time on exercise he believes was spent on the very worthwhile and important task of convincing the 'green Army' that the Apache was a good acquisition, as it had undoubtedly cost a lot of money. The pressure was on to deliver and prove the concept. He feels that the efforts of the entire Squadron, from the most junior airtrooper to the OC, were focused on this aim. One ongoing task of particular importance concerned expanding and developing the performance envelope and so reducing the limitations which had understandably been imposed on the operational parameters, thereby making the effectiveness achieved only a year or two later in Afghanistan possible. He was delighted, as a QHI, to be working with a group which was not only receptive to ideas and instructions, but also contributed a great deal by way of feedback. The overall aim was to develop the Combat Ready syllabus and turn it into a training programme, with a more important exercise planned for 2005, including maritime training on board HMS *Ocean*.

In the spring of 2005, the OC tasked the Ops Officer, Captain Andy Gilks, Regimental Maritime Ops Officer, Captain Steve Tapp, Keith Millsom and Lee Tinley-Beets, to investigate the requirements for operating at sea – this was a reasonable challenge as the Apache had not been designed with a maritime role in mind, nor was it used by the Americans in this capacity. Keith takes up the story,

'After many briefs and discussions the ground crew deployed to HMS *Nelson*, a land base, to carry out ship training and sea drills. We all had to be trained in fire-fighting, ship evacuation drills, daily life at sea and also how to operate the aircraft from a moving platform.'

The next major milestone for the achievement of the Apache's fully worked-up capability came in May 2005, with the establishment of an Attack Aviation Battle Group (Avn BG) based on 9 Regiment (with 664 joining 656 as the two lead Apache Squadrons) during Exercise Eagles Strike. This was a significant test for the entire Regiment. It started at St Mawgan in Cornwall, moved to Merryfield and culminated on Salisbury Plain. The exercise was a great success, justifying all the hard work over the past year or so and proving that given sufficient technicians and the right spares priority, over 90 per cent serviceability could be achieved. On 26 May, the Squadron took part in a fly-past by the whole Regiment over Middle Wallop. 656 then took on the first ever Very High Readiness commitment for an Apache squadron, as the Lead Aviation Squadron from 1 June 2005, which meant that it was at five days notice to move anywhere in the world for operations. In effect it could now be said that the new AH-equipped 656 Squadron had arrived and was ready for business.

Maritime Initial Operating Capability

However, there was no time for complacency, as a mere five days later, on 6 June, the Squadron was off again; to embark in the helicopter carrier (Landing Platform Helicopter – LPH) HMS *Ocean* at Sunderland, which was under the command of Captain Tony Johnstone-Burt, who, along with his crew, gave the Squadron a very warm welcome. This was the beginning of the process of delivering IOC (Maritime) support to the RN and RM with regard to both amphibious and littoral operations. Individuals had been attending specific maritime training courses since October 2004, but this was Army Aviation's first ever Attack Helicopter Squadron embarkation – though it should be remembered, of course, that 656 crews had taken off from escort carriers as long ago as 1945 and over the succeeding years few Army pilots ever resisted an invitation to land on a moving platform at sea. The primary aim was to complete deck landing qualification for all aircrew, the secondary aims were to prove the procedures for embarkation and practise the complex ground and technical support procedures to support Apache when embarked. It was, in effect, the dress rehearsal for the major maritime Exercise Pyxis which would take place later in 2005. It was the start of a very special relationship with HMS *Ocean*. Once more Keith Millsom supplies some details,

> 'The Squadron joined the ship's crew in Newcastle and loaded all the stores that were going to be required to support the Apache whilst at sea for the forthcoming two weeks. We began with well planned day missions without munitions and then progressed on to "bombed up" day and night missions. We had a few problems from the ground crew perspective that we had to adapt to. One was due to the fact the Apache does not have automatically folding rotor blades, so each time the aircraft had to be taken on the lift and placed in the hangar, we had to manually fold the blades. This was a very slow process and very manpower intensive. The time taken was reduced by fifty minutes. The other problem was that due to the amount of movement the ship does at sea, everything on deck had to be lashed down, which could be very time-consuming.'

For crew chief Corporal Morini, the main learning experience was adapting the existing FARP procedure to make it work and be safe afloat. For example, at a land-based FARP the Apaches would be side-by-side 40 metres apart; this was impossible on a ship, so the helicopters had to be set out one behind the other. On land all hands gathered around on either side at the same time; at sea they worked from the ocean side inwards. Ammunition stowage on deck was also a major issue. He found his naval colleagues to be really helpful in working out practical answers to problems and so a workable system evolved. There was also a very harmonious atmosphere in the messes after work.

Chris Hearn, Tom O'Malley and Sean Dufosee had the task of ensuring that all nineteen pilots would gain a qualification in deck landing by day and night. Sean Dufosee did the lion's share in terms of staff work and development (then teaching Chris Hearn and Tom O'Malley what to do). His effort was 'frankly incredible' in the view of a very experienced contemporary. Qualification involved no less than a total of 320 deck landings over a period of ten days. At the end of the month Chris took Apache ZJ227 to Portsmouth and was on board HMS *Ocean* for the Trafalgar 200 celebration and review by Her Majesty the Queen. While in July, Captains Piers Lewis and Jake van Beever flew an Apache to Fairford to take part in the static display at the Royal International Air Tattoo.

As a reward for all the hard work, the Squadron then embarked upon a programme of adventurous training. This consisted either of windsurfing in Italy, sailing across the English Channel, or a multi activity week in the Lake District and was followed by well-deserved summer leave. On return from leave the Squadron deployed immediately to Plymouth to join HMS *Ocean* again for Exercise Pyxis, operating with 3 Commando

Brigade RM as part of a full Tailored Air Group alongside Sea King, Lynx, and Chinook helicopters, with Jim Lyons as its Sergeant Major. Piers Lewis has vivid memories of flying off the coast of Devon for an exercise mission on Dartmoor and then returning to the ship in poor weather with one Apache above the clouds and one below. He also noted the landing technique which all aircrew practised 99 per cent of the time, flying alongside the carrier and then flying sideways to land, with running landings being for emergency use only. It was a refreshing experience with a strong emphasis on aviation operations and the range firing of rockets and 30mm, though the Squadron disembarked earlier than expected, and before undertaking Exercise Joint Warrior from HMS *Ocean*, because by this time it had been tentatively warned that it might have to begin planning for a possible deployment to Afghanistan in 2006. Nonetheless, IOC (Maritime) was duly achieved.

Afghanistan Pre-deployment Training
Meanwhile the Regiment, back at Dishforth, was working hard to prepare a suitable Afghanistan training package, with the full support of HQ Squadron. Squadron personnel were informed that on top of all the normal weapons training, all soldiers would be trained and tested in fire and manoeuvre tactics, advance to contact and withdrawal under fire drills. Anti-ambush drills for those who could be required to move by convoy whilst on deployment would also be taught. The Afghanistan theatre OPTAG (Operational Training and Advisory Group) training covered theatre briefings, intelligence, Afghanistan customs, basic introduction to useful phrases and mine awareness, amongst other subjects. Running concurrently with this military training was the selection and preparation of the vehicles and aircraft, as well as all stores for the four month deployment. A comprehensive issue of personal clothing had also to be organized. Because the Squadron was going to be deploying in the winter and returning in the summer, clothing to cater for both extreme climatic conditions was required. This resulted in a huge amount of kit having to be packed. Overall, the planning effort was intense as the Apache was going on operations rather sooner than had been anticipated. In the meantime Andy Cash had been to Afghanistan as part of the 16 Brigade Recce party. He flew to what would become the site of Camp Bastion and which at that time consisted of,

'A berm, a few vehicles and a couple of tents. On my return I briefed the Squadron on what I had seen – mostly sand.'

Exercise Herrick Resolve at Sennybridge with the Parachute Regiment took place at the end of the year, followed in January 2006 by mountain flying from RAF Kinloss, under the direction of 664 Squadron, which was taking the lead in this aspect of training, and then by Exercise Herrick Eagle around the Wattisham area, which included other air assets and ground-based call-signs to try and replicate the types of missions which could be expected in theatre. This included live firing and, naturally, sleeping in the field, where to keep warm, two sleeping bags were desirable. In order to prepare more fully for the 'hot, desiccated and mountainous' conditions to be expected in Afghanistan, the Squadron deployed to Thumrait Airfield in Oman, in February 2006, for Exercise Desert Eagle. Here they could practise dust-landings, where the storm of sand kicked up by the helicopters' revolving rotor blades would render a pilot totally reliant on the data projected on the monocle in front of his (or soon her) right eye. Much time was also spent on firing ranges working with Forward Air Controllers, so that they could familiarize them with the Apache's weaponry and capability. A third reason was the opportunity given to each pilot to fire two Hellfire missiles, thereby covering a multiplicity of scenarios. Piers Lewis remembers, with almost equal relish, not only sleeping in a poncho out in the desert but also the one second delay followed by a huge 'whoosh' as a Hellfire was released.

Afghanistan – Operation Herrick

The conflict in Afghanistan has been described by the former British ambassador in Kabul, Sir Sherard Cowper-Coles, as 'a multi-player, multidimensional, multi-decade civil conflict, the origins of which go back many years.' This is perhaps understating the complexity of the operation. He added, 'Our servicemen and women have conducted a counter-insurgency campaign of unending valour and increasing professionalism.' The Chief of the Defence Staff, General Sir David Richards, gave his views in an interview with *The Times* in November 2011,

> 'I have every expectation that we will all agree in ten years time that it was a necessary war and we've come out of it with our heads held high. While I am the first to concede that we have made mistakes, collectively and individually, the fact remains that there has not been a terrorist attack launched from Afghanistan in this time. If the Allies had not gone into Afghanistan we should have expected more 9/11s.'

Since 2002 all British operations in the war in Afghanistan have been conducted under the codename Operation Herrick – the British contribution to the NATO-led International Security Assistance Force (ISAF). Operation Herrick increased in size and breadth to match ISAF's growing geographical intervention in Afghanistan. After nearly three years of training and preparation, in the spring of 2006, the Squadron would be a part of Operation Herrick 4. As the OC noted, this was,

> 'Nothing new for the Squadron; but a totally new world for the Apache attack helicopter. SHQ, three flights, ground crew and REME technicians now look forward to putting into practice the teamwork that has been honed in training.'

As has been noted, this was the first operational tour with the Apache Longbow; once more the Squadron was paving the way for the AAC. Joint Helicopter Force (Afghanistan) (JHF(A)) consisted of RHQ 9 Regiment, with 656 Sqn providing the Apaches, 672 Squadron the Lynx and 1310 Flight from RAF Odiham the Chinooks, along with the Tactical Supply Wing (TSW), Mobile Air Operations Team (MAOT), and Joint Helicopter Support Unit (JHSU) elements. It was based on Kandahar airfield (KAF) in the south of the country.

The British Government's aspiration with regard to increased UK military participation was expressed by the then Secretary of State for Defence, Dr John Reid, at a Press Conference in Kabul on 23 April 2006,

'We're in the south to help and protect the Afghan people to reconstruct their economy and democracy. We would be perfectly happy to leave in three years' time without firing one shot.'

With hindsight it can certainly be said that Britain's involvement in Afghanistan was paved with good intentions. Be that as it may, what is not in doubt is that 656 Squadron prepared as thoroughly as possible and that none of the training was time wasted in preparation for what would be a very testing tour of duty. This author can well recall a conversation a few years ago with a very experienced military pilot, who told him to,

'Think of a really bad day in Northern Ireland at the height of the troubles, multiply that by a hundred and then you have some idea of the situation in Iraq...but Afghanistan...that's different again...that's a real shooting war.'

There was enough time to get a few days leave in before all the troops were bussed to RAF Brize Norton for their military flights out to Kandahar (KAF). Corporal Morini was given his Acting Sergeant's tapes on the bus and told he would be the Ammo Sergeant. Essentially his job would be to ensure that sufficient munitions were in the right place at the right time, with adequate stocks being maintained. The advance party was already in theatre to pave the way for the arrival of the aircraft that would have to be rebuilt and test flown before the Theatre Qualification (TQ) package could begin. Captain Chris Hearn and WO1 Tom O'Malley were the Squadron Qualified Helicopter Instructors (SQHIs) and were very busy ensuring all pilots were ready for operational flying and had been out to identify the FOBs. A period of acclimatization had to be taken into account too. All the initial training was conducted from Kandahar but the bulk of the Squadron would move out from there to Camp Bastion (BSN) as soon as they were trained and acclimatized and Bastion was ready for the aircraft. Remaining at Kandahar would be the Regimental HQ element and one complete Arming Point team. The Arming Point team would rotate throughout the tour between the two locations, to allow for a period of relative rest for those that would be operating at a higher tempo from Bastion and also for experience. The pilots would also do the same. The main REME element would remain at Kandahar with a detachment supporting the aircraft being based at Bastion. All major servicing and maintenance would take place at Kandahar with the test flying being carried out by pilots on the 'rest' cycle.
Captain Piers Lewis later wrote,

'The Squadron was based in Kandahar for the first month as Camp Bastion was not ready to receive the Apache. This didn't seem too bad with the creature comforts of the "Green Bean Coffee House," the gym, welfare centre and other attractions, however, with a severe lack of transport, it soon got wearing having to walk everywhere (Kandahar, or KAF is a big place).'

He did not mention the huge cesspool, the smell of which was a constant presence and which bore the satirical sign, 'Swim at your own risk. No lifeguard on duty.'
The forward base at Bastion was set up for up to four Apaches (rising to six on occasions) and two Chinook (sometimes four) and which would also be capable of

operating visiting Lynx. This purpose-built UK Military base in Helmand province, housed not only the helicopters but also 3 PARA, 7 RHA and a host of other units and enablers. For the Squadron, Bastion became its main focus, as the majority of its operations were in support of UK forces in Helmand. The first shock to get to grips with in theatre was the heat. The temperatures would rise up to, and occasionally exceed, 50 degrees in the shade. This was just about acceptable for the aircrew in their air-conditioned cockpits; however, the ground crew, strapping Hellfire missiles and rockets to the side of the aircraft, found the temperatures a real challenge, given their thick protective clothing requirements. Piers Lewis described Bastion as follows,

'It wasn't long before the emphasis switched from operations based out of Kandahar, to operations from the brand new Camp Bastion in the middle of the desert. Most of the Squadron much prefer it there due to the proximity to, and focus on, pure operations and the big team spirit. Unfortunately, there were no coffee houses at Bastion, only dust, dust, and more dust!'

In this initial phase of operations from Bastion the base was still in a fairly rudimentary state and it was not until July that a Hardened Aircraft Landing Strip (HALS) was constructed. The provision of this short metal runway would allow the Apaches to make running take-offs and landings, instead of disappearing in a cloud of dust when using the landing pads made from builder's rubble. The search for viable pads resulted in something of a nomadic existence within the perimeter. Andy Cash remembers it as a large building site with a stream of lorries arriving every day, checked by a heroic sniffer dog and his handler. JHF (A) Forward HQ was an empty tent, for which the ground crew made a map table from scrap wood, which proved very durable. Furniture arrived, and when Andy enquired as to its origin, was told, 'Don't ask sir.' Some of the tents had air-conditioning, which worked some of the time. Washing and shaving facilities could have been described as sparse or perhaps austere. To begin with the OC shared a twelve-man tent pod.

Soon the names of towns and villages in Helmand would become very familiar to those watching the news and reading newspapers back in the UK – Sangin, Musa Qa'leh, Lashkar Gah, Now Zad – these were all within the Squadron's range of activity. Chris Hearn comments on this period of focus, on the intensity of the learning process, establishing the rules of engagement and developing proficiency in the precision use of the range of weapons carried. He notes,

'Our biggest concerns were to avoid a "blue on blue" incident or to cause civilian casualties. It was better not to fire if there was any doubt whatsoever. We also worked hard on expanding the operational parameters through the proper channels and in paying due regard to flight safety.'

Although the first UK Attack Helicopter mission was flown from Kandahar on 10 May, the Squadron's first taste of real action was on 17 May, with an aircraft being engaged from the ground by an RPG. The first use of a Hellfire missile was three days later, and was an equipment denial task of an abandoned French vehicle (following an ambush). It was flown by Captain Lewis and Staff Sergeant Ebdon, with WO1 Mulhall and Staff

Sergeant Bird in support. This naturally spawned comments like, 'The first time the British Longbow has been used in anger against the French since Agincourt!' It was not long before the Apache was conducting engagements very frequently. Tasking was described as, 'varied and complex.' Most tasks required escorting Chinooks, but the Apache also provided surveillance and reconnaissance, ground convoy protection, and a lot of support to Troops In Contact (TIC), working with 3 PARA, US forces, Canadians, Dutch and others. The Squadron also worked with fast jets, both UK and US, providing complimentary fire and, at times, control of all the air assets in a particular area or engagement. This is all now a matter of routine, but back on that first deployment it was part of a succession of ground breaking achievements. Every day saw Squadron personnel learn and develop something new. The learning curve was indeed steep. They also had had a good relationship with, and co-operated with, US Apaches and their crews. Chris Hearn recalls three events of particular significance, firstly, hearing a Joint Terminal Air Controller (JTAC) at Now Zad say to a Harrier pilot, 'You can go back to base now I have the Apaches here.' Secondly, being given the 'cold shoulder' by Harrier pilots at Kandahar when he called in with Tom O'Malley, only to find a few weeks later it was the Harrier pilots seeking out the Apache crews to see how they could integrate on missions. And finally, the very helpful advice given by the pilots of Taskforce Nighthawk, who flew the US Apache,

'The main hazards in Afghanistan are weather, terrain and enemy action, in that order. But do not underestimate the Taliban, they will learn quickly what you do, how you do it, the way you continue to do it and will react accordingly. Do not fall into a routine and stick to it.'

The Apache certainly surpassed the expectations of both its crews and the forces being supported. The Squadron was establishing procedure and doctrine as it carried out its many tasks over a wide operational area – virtually everything was a 'first' for the British Attack Helicopter Force. They were involved in a significant number of missions where troops were being engaged by the Taliban, in which the aircraft performed extremely well, apparently more or less unaffected by the heat, height, and weights being carried. A number of deliberate operations were conducted and in the first, by the name of Mutay, which was supposed to be a 'non-kinetic' cordon and search operation (to use the prevailing jargon), the Apache earned its spurs, and, in the words of many of the private soldiers and officers of the ground forces involved, in what became a major kinetic operation (or firefight to be more exact), the Apache 'saved their lives' and was 'frankly awesome,' which was very rewarding for all involved to hear, both aircrew and ground crew. It provided accurate and timely fire support, very close to friendly force locations, either killing or suppressing the enemy and allowing the ground troops the time and space to regain the initiative. Piers Lewis describes two engagements,

'The Squadron took part in a number of deliberate operations alongside the Chinooks of 1310 Flight, and members of 3 PARA Battlegroup (and their attached elements), not least, two notable operations called Op Mutay and Op Augustus. Mutay was the first real air assault operation by the UK and marked the real emergence of the aircraft on the scene when a 'non-kinetic' operation went against the grain and turned 'fully kinetic', proving the old adage that "the enemy always have a vote." AH supported elements of 3 PARA, notably the Gurkhas and the 3 PARA Patrols Platoon as they became decisively engaged even before the H Hour had arrived. The result of the AH being on station was that a number of Taliban, who had ambushed the ground forces, were engaged by AH, and no British lives were lost. This was incredibly fortunate considering the weight of firepower the ground forces were subject to. The only damage suffered by an Apache was to two small areas of ZJ173's tail boom where, upon return, bullet holes were discovered. Op Augustus, on the other hand, on 14 July, was predicted as being fully kinetic, and epitomized the essence of "Air Assault" with the sheer number of aircraft involved in the mission. The OC was the Air Mission Commander and WO1 Mulhall was the airborne JTAC. Eight Apache and Chinook were airborne at the same time, inserting a sizable force into an area north of Sangin. This included a number of other air assets including B-1B Lancer, Predator, AC-130 gunships, and A-10s to name but a few, and constituted a full, multi-national COMAO. This operation saw the Chinooks take their first battle damage as they inserted members of 3 PARA. The AH fired 30mm and a number of Hellfire missiles. The lessons learned formed the basis for all subsequent AH ops in Herrick.'

Chris Hearn also has vivid memories of Op Augustus. He was flying with the OC who was under pressure from the BG and Brigade Command to confirm if the HLS was safe to land on. Just as he was going to give the 'LS clear' message, they observed a group of people moving towards the HLS. A Hercules AC-130 gunship was all ready to fire when the Apache's crew was able to discern that they were in fact women and children moving around the objective. The crew stopped any engagement and their timely intervention prevented a tragic incident. It should be added, however, that when the Chinooks did land they were shot at heavily from three sides, 'with tracer fire everywhere and an airburst RPG close to the Apache.' This was also the occasion when WO1 Chris Mulhall won a Mention in Dispatches for his role as an airborne JTAC controlling a wide range of Coalition aircraft.

Apache soon came to be considered essential for UK operations in Afghanistan, being a 'go / no go criteria' for many missions. Brigadier Ed Butler, 16 Brigade's Commander was particularly appreciative and described UK Apache as a 'Mission essential piece of equipment.' The insurgents moved in small groups using the ground, which they knew every detail of, very well; sniping at times and places of their choosing, fighting hard and fearlessly. Their main weaknesses were probably their leadership and basic skills, but they proved to be an enemy that demanded respect, who would capitalize on any mistake or weakness. They were armed with small arms, automatic weapons, heavy machine guns and RPGs, with the looming threat of ex-Soviet anti-aircraft guns and surface-to-air missiles, some of which had been given many years before to the Mujahideen by the USA. In reply, the Apache mainly fired 30mm cannon because it was discriminate, effective and accurate. Hellfire was employed twice to destroy abandoned Coalition Force vehicles (one French, as previously mentioned and one UK) and on 16 July 2006, to destroy a suspected anti-aircraft gun site in Now Zad. During Operation Snakebite in early August, the relief and resupply of the District Centre at Musa Qa'leh, the four Apaches of 2 and 3 Flights mounted continuous Relief in Place (RIP) for over fifteen hours, tracking down and destroying a Taliban sniper team, which had just killed a soldier. The capability of the Apache was recognized by the enemy forces and there was ample evidence that the mere presence of the aircraft was an effective deterrent to their activity.

Serviceability proved higher than expected due to the excellent work of the REME detachment at both locations, which was especially evident when the aircraft returned for refuelling and rearming whilst involved in TICs. The ground crew and technicians responded quickly and effectively, checking the aircraft for battle damage (of which there had been two instances in the early weeks of the aircraft sustaining minor damage due to enemy action), providing rapid refuel and rearm, water and food for the crews, and also new video gun tapes to replace the full tapes which recorded the engagements. They also provided NVG equipment if the mission was likely to be prolonged into night. The three years combined training had resulted in a close-knit team, which was proving its effectiveness on operations. Matty Rogers, by then a lance corporal, remembers flying with two airtroopers in a Chinook to Garesh to rearm an Apache with 30mm ammunition; living and working in a dustbowl, loading missiles weighing 45 kilograms in 45 to 50 degree heat, while wearing fireproof suits. There was huge pressure to rearm and refuel the aircraft speedily, knowing that lives depended upon their efficiency, with the time achieved on CTR, while training in England, being halved when necessary. There was a great bond of trust and mutual respect between the pilots and the ground crew. Sergeant Morini recalls the lack of shade and the need to drink up to ten litres of water a day – most of which was sweated away. Between breakfast and dinner he lived on a diet of biscuits and crisps. Living in a hot, crowded 300 man tent at Kandahar was no picnic either. Incoming rocket fire was frequent but thankfully mostly inaccurate. He praises Major Cash and Captain Tinley-Beets for the support which they gave to the teams working away in these difficult conditions. Lance Corporal Marcus Sharpe was equally busy with the Signals Operations Staff, spending less time setting up the MPS and more on manning the communications relay in the Ops tent, where sixteen hour days were not uncommon, as well as editing the vital gun tapes for review. On 2 August a brief ceremony was held at Bastion to name the flight line Chinthe Lines, in tribute to the Squadron's badge and its history. It is of interest to note that according to Burmese mythology, Chinthes almost always travelled in pairs as they protected their pagodas – so too did the Apaches.

Towards the end of the tour the Apache crews were organized with each flight on a 12 day cycle: three days in the Ops Room to assist with communications and paperwork and also planning future missions; followed by three days flying pre-planned sorties, including tasks such as escorting Chinooks dropping off supplies to outlying bases, providing top cover to patrols or supporting a major operation, though it was common on the way back from one of these trips to be retasked in response to a request from a ground call-sign. Next came three days on Very High Readiness (VHR), able to respond at any time day or night. One VHR Apache would be designated the Incident Response Team (IRT) cab, responsible for escorting a medical evacuation Chinook and its medical team for the immediate recovery of personnel, say in the case of a road traffic accident, a mine strike or a compassionate case, though if the location was considered hostile then it would be joined by the Helmand Reaction Force (HRF) cab. A typical HRF task would be bringing swift, urgent reinforcement to TIC and would also require both helicopters.

The last three days of the cycle were spent on Testing and Maintenance, at Kandahar, flight-testing aircraft which had just been serviced. The Apache is a labour intensive machine in ideal conditions and Afghanistan was very taxing on equipment and the personnel required to maintain it, with some thirty-two man-hours of work in gruelling conditions of heat, cold, wind and sand on the ground being required for each flying hour.

Many members of the Squadron paid tribute to Andy Cash's outstanding leadership under a huge amount of pressure and with a vast quantity of administration to process. It is believed, not without justification, that he did not get the official recognition which he deserved. His style of command and care for his personnel was very much in the mould of the Squadron's first OC, Denis Coyle, and in many ways he faced similar challenges in terms of the responsibility resting on his shoulders and in proving a concept. The OC himself felt mentally drained as the Squadron's first tour at Bastion came to a close. He was the only officer who could give the launch authority for the Apaches or Chinooks from Bastion – day or night – and spent many long hours in an Ops Tent full of people and with the temperature baking all inside. He developed a very close relationship with 3 PARA and has high praise for its CO, Lieutenant Colonel Stuart Tootal and his 2i/c, Major Hum Williams, with whom he had to share some very difficult decisions. He also greatly appreciated the skill and bravery of the RAF's Chinook crews. The air assets at Bastion were a small footprint covering a large area and worked on the principle of, 'If we can we will.' Looking back Andy summarizes his thoughts,

'We were pathfinding and laying down the basic seed corn. When I returned two years later as CO of JHF (A) the situation was just recognizable. The AH Squadron remained the backbone of JHF (A), soldiers from the AH Force were key figures in all the main departments, even the ops table in the BSN JOC that had been built by 656 Sqn signallers remained in use. The quality of personnel at all levels was outstanding. We went from zero knowledge to a long way up the scale in the course of the first two or three AH deployments. It is one of my great regrets though, that as my departure from theatre was delayed due to operational requirements in 2006, when I returned to Dishforth, the Squadron had already gone on leave, I was posted and never had the opportunity to say a proper farewell to a great team.'

During the course of this deployment some 7305 cannon rounds, eighteen rockets and eleven Hellfire were expended. The Squadron's first tour in Afghanistan lasted from April to August, handing over to 664 Squadron who, in turn, were followed by 656 again from November 2006 to February 2007, this time with Major David Amlôt, who, having flown various types of Apache over the last ten years as an exchange officer with the US Army and then back in the UK, slotted in quickly at the helm of 'a first class team who all pulled together.' He noted that at no point in his career, before or since, had he worked in a squadron that was so truly integrated between the ground crew, aircrew and technicians, which he directly attributes to the leadership of Andy Cash and their shared collective experience of the preceding four years. This was quickly reaffirmed with the fact that, by the end of week two, he had fired every weapon the aircraft was able to carry. One of his early contacts even appeared on Sky News the following day. Another newcomer was Britain's first female Apache pilot, Captain "Charlotte Madison". Captain Duncan Short deployed as the FARP Commander and Captain Keith Millsom stepped up to deploy as the FOB commander on the second tour, commenting,

> 'The basics of the deployment didn't change much but the place changed a lot. The Taliban were still very active and our flying had increased to ensure that all RAF rotary flights has armed cover and many of the patrols on the ground were afforded top cover from the Apache too. I was based at KAF and along with the FOB Commander role I was also the Motor Transport Officer for JHF(A). I had an Arming Point Team with me and a small MT section, which included Army Air Corps personnel and a few RLC drivers as well as TA soldiers. With Duncan Short I was responsible for planning the AAC's first austere FARP. There was a planned operation that involved the infantry, with fire support from Apaches, at considerable distance from Camp Bastion. This was Operation Chrystal and a FARP was required to allow the aircraft more time on target and a faster response time for rearming. It needed an area that had to be large enough to receive two Apache at a time and have a refuel capability. The fuel was going to be stored in huge pillow tanks that would be flown forward, empty, and then once sited would be filled with aviation fuel via a transfer from the on board fuel tanks of an RAF Hercules transport aircraft that would visit the FARP. The operation was a great success and the FARP was run by Corporal Kev Blundell, the Squadron's senior and most experienced ALPC.'

The first 'austere' AAC FARP was established on a dry lake bed in Southern Helmand, seventy kilometres from the nearest source of water. The ground crew lived in shell scrapes for five days among the wild camels and then suffered torrential rain, which at least eliminated the problem as regards the lack of fresh water. They much appreciated the Pizza Hut takeaways handed out on the flight back to base as evidence of their return to home comforts.

The Squadron was again based at Bastion with major servicing being carried out at Kandahar. There were now sixteen pilots and four flights, SHQ, 2, 3 and 4, each with two aircraft. Bastion by this time contained some 2000 soldiers and was growing into the largest British overseas military camp to have been built since the end of the Second World War. Helmand province was largely in the hands of lawless drug barons, who co-operated with the Taliban to resist any attempts to bring any form of central control to the area. The poppies grown in Helmand amounted to some 75 per cent of the world's total production of opium in an area almost half the size of England. Most of the terrain was either mountainous or desert, apart from the fertile Green Zone, a lush habitation of irrigated fields, hedgerows, trees and small woods on either side of the Helmand River. The aim of the British forces was to combat the Taliban and to support the building of a stable civil society. There were three tiers of Taliban: the senior commanders who were the ideological hardcore, many of whom were based in Pakistan, next came the mid-level commanders and foreign jihadis, mostly young idealists and ideal candidates for suicide bombings, finally there were the rank-and-file, the 'ten dollar Talibans,' who were simply in it as an alternative means of employment after the poppy crop had been harvested.

Towards the end of the tour aircrew and ground crew alike would suffer extreme fatigue. As the very experienced pilot and later best-selling author, 'Ed Macy,' wrote,

'Our Apaches needed REME avionics and airframe technicians, armourers, arming and loading teams, drivers, refuellers, signallers, IT specialists, Intelligence officers, clerks and storemen – ninety-eight people in total; more than six of them to each pilot and every one an expert in their own field.'

Early in this tour the Squadron changed its original Herrick callsign of 'Wildman', which was too similar to other US call-signs and chose its 'Ugly' call-sign, eg 'Ugly Five Zero, Ugly Five One'. As well as having a bit of fun on the ground with carefully selected individual nicknames, it was a boost to everyone's morale.

The job was essentially the same but it was a continual game of cat and mouse as the Taliban changed tactics, 'They learned, we learned; then we had to learn again.' Moreover, the longer the campaign went on the more complex the Helmand battlespace became. The workload for everyone in the air and on the ground at Bastion and back at Kandahar was intense and unrelenting.

Piers Lewis was now the Ops Officer and spent long days in the Ops Tent, often sixteen hours at a time. He still, of course, also took his share of flying duties and remembers escorting a helicopter carrying President Karzai and, on another occasion, a leaflet drop by Dutch AS532 Cougars as part of Op Baaz Tsuka in Panjwayi immediately before Christmas. Instead of gently fanning out over the landscape, the leaflets, still bundled together, fell like a stone. He enjoyed Christmas, which the OC had tried to make as pleasant as possible in the circumstances. Gifts from 656 Squadron Association were appreciated, as well as cigars and Duchy Original biscuits from the Colonel-in-Chief, HRH Prince Charles. Other impressions which remain fixed in his memory are of the awesome power of the canon fired by a US A-10 Thunderbolt II providing suppressive fire support, observing the pattern of life in Kajaki change from the first tour, achieving his 1000 hours escorting a compassionate case CH-47 back to Kandahar in very low dust visibility, a visit in September from Prime Minister Tony Blair and working with the French, Americans, Danes and Dutch,

'I also recall walking back from the BSN JOC (Bastion Joint Operations Centre) to the accommodation on New Year's Eve (after midnight) and having a quiet moment in the cold watching the ground troops fire off flares in festive celebration. On getting back to the pod, I briefly celebrated the New Year with Acting Major Simon Barr (who was COS JHF(A) Forward at that time) whilst listening to some classical music, which was quite surreal after the day I had had.'

David Amlôt recalls two very unusual encounters in November, firstly he was flying in the Kajaki area when he realized that the Harrier GR.7 from 800 NAS with which he was operating was being flown by Lieutenant Commander Toby Everett, an ex-AAC Gazelle pilot, who had been on the same initial Army Pilot training course as David, fifteen years before. And if this did not bring home to him the fact that it was indeed a very small world, only a few days later he was able to patch a direct radio communication from the cockpit of his helicopter and speak to the guests at the Annual Apache Pilots' Dinner, which was being held that evening in the White Hart Hotel, Salisbury.

It had been decided that a major effort would be made early in 2007 to disrupt the Taliban's southern logistics supply chain. This was named Operation Glacier. The

Squadron was heavily involved in the first mission to strike and destroy a command post near the village of Koshtay, just under an hour's flying time from Bastion, which was a reception area for all new recruits coming from Pakistan. On 11 January, two Apaches of HQ Flight followed up an attack by a US B-1B bomber, with cannon, rockets and twelve Hellfire missiles. This was the Apaches' first deep raid and was made much more memorable for the OC by the fact that when on the long transit across the desert, in the earliest hours of the morning, he was able to pick up Beethoven's 5th Symphony on the ADF equipment. Returning to the scene in the early dawn, after rearming and refuelling, it was eerily still.

Ten days later a remarkable action – Glacier II Bravo – took place at Jugroom Fort, which was the next point north on the supply chain and was the Taliban's main forward operating base in southern Helmand. In the course of fierce fighting the Royal Marines sustained several casualties and one marine, Lance Corporal Mathew Ford, was missing in action. He was found, apparently unconscious but still, it seemed, alive, by an Unmanned Aerial Vehicle and confirmed by a Nimrod reconnaissance aircraft and the Apache crew flying overhead (the third wave of support during the mission). The Chinook helicopters were recovering the initial wave of casualties and a second group of five critically injured casualties elsewhere in Southern Afghanistan. It was decided to mount a daring and never-before-attempted rescue mission by landing two helicopters from HQ Flight beside the Royal Marines command post in the desert nearby. Four volunteers, Captain Dave Rigg RE, WO1 Colin Hearn RM and Marines Chris Fraser-Perry and Gary Robinson, attached themselves to grab handles on the sides of each Apache and flew at low-level and much reduced speed towards the fort. There, in the teeth of heavy enemy fire and the smoke and confusion of battle, they landed as close to Marine Ford as possible, hauled him over and strapped him to the side of ZJ224. Meanwhile, two further Apaches from 3 Flight flew overhead and engaged the enemy, expending almost all their weapon loads in the process. As "Charlotte Madison" later wrote,

'Watching our gun tape again, I'm shocked to see how many RPGs and volleys of tracer fire miss our aircraft by inches. It's a small miracle that, of all the aircraft that left Bastion that day, not a single one came back with a bullet hole in it. No physical damage was sustained, but the emotional battering was enormous.'

The rescue was successful in that Marine Ford was recovered but sadly he had been killed instantly during the initial contact. Corporal Matty Rogers remembers it as 'a surreal day' at Bastion with aircraft rolling and in and rolling out for hours and 'all hands on deck' to rearm and refuel them. But under intense pressure he takes pride in the fact that 'the machine worked.' Sergeant Morini was equally satisfied by the ground crews' performance but also remembers the vast amount of paperwork which had to be completed due to the volume of stores expended. For the OC and his Ops Officer too, the time spent on the ground by the Apaches at Jugroom was the longest four minutes and thirty-three seconds of their lives. Some months later, two Squadron members were invested with the DFC, a Joint Commander's commendation and two with the MC in recognition of their great skill and bravery. This is the first time that a 656 pilot had been awarded an MC since 1944. The intensity of the fighting of the Squadron's second tour was notable in the significant increase in total ammunition fired, over five times more Hellfire and a significant rise in 30mm and CRV7, though this was by no means any measure of success.

An interesting reflection on 'coming down to earth' after such a demanding tour, was shown by Giovanni Morini. He noted that, for about the first fortnight at home on leave he was reluctant to make a decision about even the simplest matter – simply due to the fact that having made so many in Helmand, he wanted his wife to tell him what to do. During the summer of 2007 the Squadron backfilled 3 Regiment's Operation Herrick commitment with all serving aircrew completing short tours as flights of four, during six week long rotations in Afghanistan from August through until early November. As the OC noted,

'Whilst in "tour interval harmony" terms, deploying between your own Squadron tours cannot be seen as a good thing, everyone involved considered it relatively painless. It was extremely interesting to see just how much the theatre had changed in only six months. Whilst there were many situations where we found ourselves back in the thick of fighting, the frequency was certainly down from our previous tours. Significantly it was an almost entirely 656 Squadron Flight that flew on the longest range vehicle intercept to date. At the end of an already long duty day the Flight was tasked, at short notice, to support an operation that resulted in a successful vehicle intercept capturing key enemy personnel and equipment.'

In order to generate the requirement for a period of continuous service in Afghanistan, it had been announced in July 2006 that the AH Force would be concentrated in one location. In mid-2007 the Squadron moved from Dishforth to join 4 Regiment as part of the Attack Helicopter 'Super-Base' at Wattisham Airfield in Suffolk. The AH force at Wattisham now consisted of 3 Regiment, with 653, 662 and 663 Squadrons and 4 Regiment with 654, 656 and 664 Squadrons. After the move, Squadron strength plummeted from ninety-eight personnel to only thirty-seven as individuals were posted to the other squadrons to ensure full manning was achieved in time for their pre-deployment training, in the case of 664 Squadron and for 654 Squadron's forthcoming CTR.

"Charlotte Madison" returned to Bastion in August for a short tour, along with Captains Rich Webb, Piers Lewis and Sergeant Nick Cole and noted,

'Even in a short space of time the ground can change unrecognizably: new patrol bases; new enemy firing points; fresh nicknames for scattered buildings, deep wadis and dirty alleyways.'

In October the Squadron was chosen to support the Staff College Land Combat Power Demonstration, by live firing over one thousand 30mm target practice rounds as part of a combined arms firepower scenario, which was a resounding success as well as invaluable live fire training. Throughout the flying demonstration the ground crew manned a static demonstration of an AH FARP. The soldiers, some of whom were only weeks out of basic training, did an excellent job in answering some very tricky questions from some very senior officers. Not long afterwards there was the opportunity to complete the conversion to Bowman, the Army's new communications suite.

By the spring of 2008 the Squadron was back to full strength as it acted as host squadron to CTR 8 and also started its training year prior to deploying again on Operation Herrick in January 2009.

As part of the collocation of all Apaches at Wattisham a number of functions were centralized. The movement and start of all aircraft was now conducted by a Station Airfield Troop (SAT) made up of ground crew from across both 3 and 4 Regiments. Pre-flight planning (using the MPS), authorization and briefing were conducted in a central briefing facility manned again by ground crew from across the two regiments. REME support was no longer carried out by units allocated to individual squadrons, but in three hangars known as Flight Line, Maintenance 1 and Maintenance 2. Fitter Sections were renamed Red, Yellow and Gold and rotated through each of the hangars on a three month cycle. Finally, the flying programme itself was now centrally run by the Station and for which the crews made bids for hours, several weeks in advance. The OC once more commented,

> 'Whilst I cannot say that this has helped Squadron ethos and has certainly meant a step back in the excellent relationship we enjoyed with REME in Dishforth, the centralization has been taken out of necessity in order to provide us with aircraft to fly and ensure that we could maintain currency.'

The Squadron also achieved another first in receiving the AAC's initial Sandhurst Direct Entry (DE) Officer in the role of Ground Support Flight Commander, who was therefore responsible for almost seventy members of the Squadron. Second Lieutenant Héloise Goodley was the first officer in what promised to be a full career stream aimed at providing promotion and command opportunities in areas such as Squadron 2i/c, Adjutant, Squadron Command and beyond, allowing aircrew to remain in flying appointments longer before returning to the inevitable desk job, thereby allowing for a greater return of service in the cockpit for the amount of time and money invested in their training.

CTR training began in January and followed the established pattern; first with the ground crew, who were allowed a week to get on top of their FARP training; then the aircrew to occupy the FARPs. Second Lieutenant Goodley, Staff Sergeant Darren 'Daz' White and Sergeant Morini worked closely together to ensure all ran smoothly on the ground, carrying out site recces, making sure all the vehicles were ready and the necessary documentation was completed, ensuring that adequate stores and rations were available and in place, planning for any foreseeable contingency that might arise and problem solving when, as expected, the unforeseeable happened. The start of CTR was also the start of life in the Field Army for many, with a large percentage of the ground crew and pilots having spent most, if not all of their careers to date in the training system. For some of the officers this amounted to three and a half years. This was not the case for all, there were four QHIs on the course with a wealth of experience and a number of personnel who had remained in the Squadron with previous CTR and operational experience. A little bit of history was made early in CTR, when on 1 February, one of the crews flew the first Apache ab-initio pilot mutual sortie, the significance being that neither pilot was an aircraft commander and the Apache was their first type. The Mission Commanders' Course – a two week Squadron deployment to Middle Wallop – was an important part of every CTR. The aim was to test the Squadron's planning cycle and subsequent command in the execution of a mission. All of this was conducted in the Aircraft Command and Tactics Trainer, a bank of computers which simulated eight aircraft. Another important element of CTR was Exercise Lightning Force, in May 2008, on the Spadeadam Electronic Warfare Ranges near Newcastle,

'Here, our crews trained with live chaff and flare, the first time most had flown with live munitions. They also learnt the art of fighting modern anti-aircraft systems, or at least had an introduction to it. The ground crew benefited from valuable training loading live munitions day and night, another first for many. In all, the eight Squadron aircraft and crews flew 200 hours in two weeks, which was more than the two previous months put together.'

The completion of CTR was in sight, but before that could be achieved, at the end of July, there was a two month deployment to Arizona, along with the Lynx helicopters of 847 NAS, which would provide opportunities to exercise in a very demanding desert environment at the height of summer. The Squadron was based at WAATS (Western Army National Guard Aviation Training Site), with a FOB at Gila Bend. The weather made life interesting with monsoon-like rain at 1700 every day, dust storms and microbursts. The training provided was extremely realistic and was excellent preparation for Afghanistan. A little time was also found for R&R in Las Vegas, San Diego and the Grand Canyon. The newly promoted Staff Sergeant Morini was full of praise for the Arizona experience,

'It is a fantastic exercise putting everyone under as much pressure as it is possible to simulate without actually being in theatre. It is there that everyone hones their craft and comes back with their professionalism enhanced.'

Another aspect of the Apache's capability was explored on exercise in Scotland as the final phase of the Qualified Helicopter Tactics Instructor Course, when, whilst playing the enemy, a simulated air-to-air missile strike was made from a pair of Apaches, hovering stealthily close to the ground, on a formation of Chinooks and Pumas, all of which were 'destroyed.'

The Squadron entered January 2009 with an early start, on a freezing morning, in which personnel arrived with bulging bergens to board the coaches that would take them to RAF Brize Norton for the start of the long journey to Afghanistan once more for Herrick 9. The base for the four month tour was Bastion again, supporting 3 Commando Brigade RM, with a small detachment at Kandahar. There had been many changes, not the least of which was the improved standard of the accommodation at Bastion and the fact that the camp was now also supported by more than 2000 locally employed contract staff. Thousands more troops occupied FOBs across Helmand, with the increased use of mines and IEDs (Improvised Explosive Devices) being a major factor. "Charlotte Madison", who was now the Squadron Ops Officer, noted,

'Things change so quickly here that my two previous tours are almost irrelevant in terms of knowing where I'll fly and where the troops are now concentrated.'

There was one very familiar face in theatre, however, as the commander of the Joint Helicopter Force Afghanistan for the first three months was Lieutenant Colonel Andy Cash. One of the largest operations during this tour was Shahi Tandar, a series of actions by Coalition troops including 42 Commando RM, in Central Helmand and Kandahar, targeting Taliban strongholds, bomb-making factories and stores of opium. Another very significant air assault took place in February – Operation Diesel – the largest Commando raid at that time since the Second World War, with 670 troops accompanied by more than twenty air assets and with the purpose of disrupting narcotics production in the Upper Sangin Valley. This was followed by Aabi Toorah which extended the reach of Coalition forces into the 'Fish Hook,' 100 kilometres south of Garmsir. In order to support the three week operation the Squadron once again deployed a FARP team to a Forward Operating Base – FOB Dwyer. Both aircrew and ground crew were deployed forward, which became the highlight of the tour for many, with up to four aircraft at a time being supported. The REME did an outstanding job in conducting the first engine change in such an austere location following a very rare occurrence of an engine failure in flight. Sergeant Morini remembers the first few days in Dwyer well, his team of fifteen showing tremendous versatility and skill in dealing with between thirty and forty underslung loads, all brought in by Chinook. The FOB was very close to the Green Zone, which certainly concentrated the mind, as did a storm of 'biblical proportions.' Two of the ground crew went out to ensure the Apaches were secured safely, when an overly enthusiastic sentry began shooting off flares and live rounds over their heads. One of them suggested, 'Should we shoot back so that he knows we are friendly,' but they decided instead to request, in rather robust language, that the sentry should desist from firing, which he did. The aircrew were in awe of the terrain, sighting a number of Alexander the Great's forts carved out of ancient volcanic plugs and which abutted the Helmand River. David Amlôt noted that during this tour the Apaches' ability to deliver Hellfire missiles with pinpoint accuracy really came into its own as the Rules of Engagement surrounding its use were modified and that all aircrew spent quite a considerable amount of time working with UAVs, speaking to their 'pilots' many thousands of miles away at Nellis Air Force Base near Las Vegas, Nevada. Such teaming has now become commonplace on the modern battlefield.

Another significant change from previous tours was the amount of time spent operating in the Hindu Kush Mountains in support of other nations. A FOB was maintained on two occasions for five days at the Dutch base of Tarain Kowt. The final important operation of the tour saw the OC as the Air Mission Commander of an air assault supported by twenty-three aircraft into the Northern District of Marjah – until that point an untouched Taliban stronghold. Four days of intense fighting followed with the Apaches spending hours in the overhead expending significant amounts of ammunition, often under sustained anti-aircraft artillery fire. In April 2009, 656 handed over to 662 Squadron. A total of 1985 hours was flown during the tour. Former Chief of Defence Staff, Air Chief Marshal Sir Jock Stirrup, summarized the Apaches' contribution in Afghanistan,

> 'You do not need to ask them about their contribution, you need to ask those on the ground who depended on them, day after day, to provide the crucial military edge over the enemy. They will leave you in no doubt about what the Apache achieved and the praise of the praiseworthy is beyond measure.'

On return to the UK and following a month of post tour leave, the Squadron welcomed HRH Prince Charles and the Duchess of Cornwall to Wattisham in July, when they presented personnel with their Operation Herrick medals. By this time David Amlôt had been followed in command by Major Mike Neville, who was new to the Apache. Having completed CTR and training in Arizona, towards the end of the year he was advised by the CO of 4 Regiment AAC, Lieutenant Colonel Andy Cash, that the Squadron had been earmarked for a new role and would not be returning to Afghanistan.

A Change of Role

The Squadron would become the AH Operational Conversion Flight (OCF). This meant that it would train all Apache pilots in fighting with the aircraft during CTR. It would also take on responsibility for the regeneration and development of Very High Readiness Contingent Operations capabilities, including Land and Maritime bespoke Small Scale Focused Intervention capability (bSSFI). Running CTR was a demanding schedule with long and busy days, but according to the new OC, it 'pretty well ran on rails.' However, the second part of the brief represented a considerable intellectual challenge. Only about 5 per cent of the Squadron had previous experience at sea, mostly at a much lower rank. All personnel were required to undergo mandatory sea survival courses and a lot of other training which occupied about six months. This would provide an opportunity to re-engage with the seagoing skills initially achieved by the Squadron and also to develop enduring and flexible capability beyond the prevailing operational focus of the last few years, which had, of course, been concentrated on Afghanistan. First the aircraft had to be 'marinized' to prepare them for sea service, which required a detailed programme of work.

In August 2010, the Air Manoeuvre Training and Advisory Team (AMTAT) was subsumed into the Squadron to become the Operational Conversion Flight (OCF). Then in the autumn, aircrew from across the entire AH Force, attached to 656 Squadron, embarked on HMS *Ark Royal* to 'reinvigorate the Apache maritime capability.' This was the first significant embarkation of Apaches for five years and involved three weeks of highly concentrated and demanding training for ninety personnel in a 'tough, unforgiving environment.' The aircrew had to obtain their deck landing qualifications, which involved long days and nights of hard work. Mike Neville pays tribute to two naval exchange QHIs, Lieutenant Commanders David Westley and Chris Raynes, who combined considerable experience flying the Apache with a huge amount of maritime knowledge. He also notes that the Apache has a high centre of gravity, a narrow track undercarriage and armour plating just where you would like to see out when landing in a confined space, such as the deck of a carrier. The embarkation was planned to run alongside the annual multi-national maritime exercise Joint Warrior, in which fifteen nations participated with surface, sub-surface and a wide variety of air and aviation assets. Operating off the west coast of Scotland provided rough seas, high winds and a platform which pitched and rolled enough to make deck handling and aircraft maintenance a real challenge – which was met by the arming teams and REME so well, that an availability rate of 95 per cent was achieved. More than sixty sorties were flown, 320 deck landings were made and some 6000 rounds of 30mm ammunition were fired on the Cape Wrath range by day and by night. Other sorties flown included attacks on shore targets, counter shipping and counter fast inshore attack craft, which could involve returning to the ship after a five hour, multi-task mission up to 100 miles from the original take-off point. The importance of this training was, of course, highlighted by the early retirement of the Harrier Force, which meant that Apache became the UK's only flying maritime strike capable platform. A proud but sad duty followed soon afterwards when *Ark Royal* celebrated twenty-five years in service and a visit from Her Majesty the Queen, only to have the announcement made that the ship was to be prematurely retired.

In November, Mike Neville and David Westley went to Afghanistan for two months as line pilots. This gave them an invaluable opportunity to discuss the nuances of operations at sea without any other command distractions. When he returned Mike knew that a major exercise in the Mediterranean would take place within a few months and that he needed to find several pilots to add to the five he already had – OC, 2i/c, Ops Officer, QHI and QWI. He was also aware of the international developments which began in December 2010 and came to be known as the Arab Spring. In late April the Squadron embarked on board HMS *Ocean*, ten pilots with eighty ground crew and engineers. The plan was to exercise for six weeks.

In what was a significant milestone in proving the capability of the Apache to strike from the sea, some 550 30mm rounds and nine radar-guided Hellfire missiles were fired against seaborne targets during an exercise near Gibraltar on 3 May 2011, achieving a 100 per cent strike rate. This was the first time these had been launched by any nation in a maritime environment. Little did the crews know that one month later to the day, they would be firing them for real. During the intensive period of training serving on *Ocean*, aircrew and ground crew from the Squadron practised operating by day and by night. Mike Neville commented that the Squadron had proved that the Apache could operate effectively from *Ocean* as a fully integrated part of the ship's company; drawing munitions from the magazine, uploading these to the aircraft, launching, firing and recovering to the deck. *Ocean's* commanding officer, Captain Andrew Betton, noted that all of this was a considerable achievement; understanding ship borne life and learning new procedures for the preparation and movement of ammunition efficiently and safely. The Squadron was supported by an AH Command Liaison Team (CLT) including MPS operators on the Flag Ship HMS *Albion*, led by former OC, David Amlôt, now the Regimental 2i/c.

Libya

As events turned out this was a timely and fortuitous development, as, the decision having been taken for military intervention in Libya, the carrier needed to be replenished with ammunition, equipment and extra aircraft. This was carried out off the coast of Cyprus with tons of stores being embarked. Another first was the delivery of an Apache to *Ocean* by RFA *Fort Rosalie*, a Fleet Support vessel, being the first time an Apache had flown from a ship of the Royal Fleet Auxiliary. This made a total of five Apaches embarked. There was also much work being done to assess the anti-air threat level, as even a cursory glance on *Google* would have revealed that the pro-Gaddafi forces were well equipped with a large variety of weaponry. In early June, the Squadron commenced operations off the coast of Libya as part of the UK's contribution to the multi-state coalition's military intervention to implement United Nations Security Council Resolution 1973, which formed the legal basis for its intervention in the Libyan Civil War and the protection of civilians from the depredations of the Gaddafi regime.

4 Regiment's new Commanding Officer, Lieutenant Colonel Jason Etherington, joined HMS *Ocean* fresh from rounds of planning at the UK Permanent Joint Headquarters. The AH CLT deployed to the Combined Air Operations Centre in Poggio, Italy, to ensure that the missions were integrated into the Air Component Campaign and supported by the wide-ranging capabilities of other nations' air and maritime assets. The first mission was flown by the OC on the night of 3–4 June and resulted in the destruction of a coastal radar site, as has now been seen by many on *YouTube*. Shortly afterwards the Apache was engaged by an anti-aircraft gun mounted on a pick-up truck, which was a mistake on the part the gunners as the subsequent engagement proved.

In December 2011, writing in *The Times*, Rear Admiral Guy Liardet summarized the contribution of the Apaches,

'AAC Apache gunship helicopters joined the force embarked on the helicopter carrier, HMS *Ocean*. The Air Group Commander, Jolyon Woodard, said, "The challenges of integrating the Apache into the naval air group and *Ocean* were fewer than we anticipated. With an outstanding team of detachment commanders combined with a well-drilled ship's air department, we faced down pretty much everything that came our way. Thus I could relax, look busy and take all the glory." Accompanied by FAA Sea King ASaC Mk 7s, Apaches attacked 110 targets in twenty-two sorties, hitting military vehicles, installations and communications equipment, flying as far as 40 miles inland, averaging about an hour's flying time per target, firing ninety-nine Hellfire missiles and over 4000 rounds of 30mm cannon. Here once more is the well-worn argument, a moveable deck in international waters does not need the proximity of a friendly country, basing rights, overflying rights, Status of Forces Agreements, "boots on the ground" sensitivities and hugely expensive in-flight refuelling.'

One of the pilots, WO1 Jon Lane, who received a Mention in Dispatches, described the operational environment,

'We faced a significant threat from surface-to-air missiles and small arms fire. We came under contact quite frequently and when the enemy attempted to engage us we fought back immediately, destroying their position. I have served in both Iraq and Afghanistan, but the combat in Libya was much more like traditional warfare. It was risky flying with a high threat from the ground.'

Lieutenant Colonel Jason Etherington added,

'We did everything from attacking coastal targets to flying 60 kilometres inland to strike at different locations. We had to launch with certainty and ensure that we were targeting pro-Gaddafi forces. If there was any chance of collateral damage, or if there was a risk to civilians, we were in no doubt about what we should do.'

The OC of 656 Squadron, Major Mike Neville, commented,

'The typical mission saw us fly across the sea and over the land to targets allocated to us by NATO for the protection of Libyan civilians on the coast and inland. This was demanding aviation, but the Squadron was well furnished with very experienced pilots (the average crew had 4560 flying hours at the controls and 310 deck landings). Add to this the professional dedication of the REME, AAC soldiers and RAF safety equipment support technicians who worked twelve hours on, twelve hours off for the majority of the embarkation and one can begin to appreciate the professional application required. The operationally focused and tireless Ship's Company maintained a continually ready platform.'

As regards the particular unique elements that the Apache brings to the battlefield, he noted,

'Attack Helicopters are menacing, they manoeuvre in and out of sight and sound at any time of day and in almost all weather. They create uncertainty and deep unease in the mind of the enemy and they are precise with their weapons; with the additional element of surprise by launching from a floating platform capable of moving hundreds of miles a day. Several missions were flown in concert with Tornado GR4 and Typhoon, with coordinated targeting and weapons effect.'

On a nightly basis Apaches operated with an extraordinary variety of assets, from French and UK submarines, to the last operational flight of the UK's Nimrod MR2. On one occasion they took the UAV teaming concept, which had been well proven in Afghanistan, to the next level by launching Hellfire after Hellfire to destroy armoured vehicles hidden in a palm grove – out of sight of the Apaches – but laser designated by a UAV positioned overhead. One of those experienced pilots, mentioned by the OC, was Chris Hearn, who passed 1000 hours on Apache alone while on board *Ocean*. He recalls being woken at 1400 hours for night operations, flying over the dark sea towards the Libyan coast with his heart fluttering, into a potentially very dangerous environment, as Gaddafi's forces were very well equipped with a large variety of anti-aircraft artillery. Chris was most impressed by the sight of a SAM being launched from the shore and was equally gratified by the effectiveness of the Apache's countermeasures. Even such a well-qualified pilot found the deployment, 'challenging, thought-provoking and exhilarating.' One of the ninety servicemen and women from 4 Regiment who served on *Ocean* during the operation, REME WO2 Craig Peaple commented,

'The hangar was 40 degrees Celsius with 85 per cent humidity, so the guys were sweating all the time, but we achieved 100 per cent serviceability for every mission. We were in the hangar throughout the day and when we came on deck it was dark, so we didn't see any natural light for a long time.'

Sergeant Matty Rogers pays tribute to the planning of Lieutenant Gavin Bosher and Sergeant Dan Bonner, with whom he worked to ensure that the loading of fuel and armament went smoothly. They had an excellent relationship with *Ocean*'s crew, who were in turn impressed by the efficiency of the Ground Support Flight and REME personnel. Matty again remembers another 'surreal moment, straight from the film *GI Jane*' – sitting in the Petty Officers' Mess on the ship and watching it being announced on the television news that British Apaches were being sent to operate off Libya. Gavin adds,

'Working aboard HMS *Ocean* left one with no doubt that aviation operations afloat are uniquely demanding; standards mustn't just be monitored but scrutinized daily, training and supervision were vital. The SNCOs and NCOs repeatedly came to the fore and were supported by outstanding demonstrations of resolute working practises by even the most inexperienced airtrooper. The full measure of the achievement has now sunk in – that we were the first and as yet only AH enablers to have conducted, successfully, the Ground Support Flight role at sea operationally.'

The last mission was flown in August and *Ocean* withdrew from the theatre in September. If the operation had continued, another squadron had been readied to take over having worked up on board HMS *Illustrious*. *Ocean* and 656 returned to port in October, six months after departing for a five week exercise! 656 Squadron had completed the first operational maritime deployment of the Apache helicopter of any nation, since first coming into service in 1984. This was a Joint operation in purest sense, the Apache operated in its traditional air manoeuvre role launching from a ship in support of air operations. Following the end of the operation *Ocean* received a visit from the Chief of the Defence Staff, General Sir David Richards, who addressed the ship's company,

'What you did in Libya and the way you have responded over the last few months have been in the best traditions of the Service; not only have you done great work operationally but you have broken new barriers professionally, particularly with the Apache. The name of HMS *Ocean* is held in high regard back in the UK and you should be proud, and deservedly so, of what you have achieved.'

Conclusion

The outstanding versatility of the Apache may be further gauged from a brief report in *Defence News* of June 2011, which summarized five years of service by Apache in Afghanistan, describing it as the platform of choice when fire support was requested by soldiers on the ground – for close combat attack, ISTAR, escort and support to other operations. It noted that in many cases the mere sight of an Apache at the scene of a contact was sufficient to persuade the enemy to make a swift retreat and added,

> 'The most sophisticated weapon system currently in service with the British Army, it carries a fire-control radar and radar frequency interferometer [a passive radar receiving device] providing an integrated surveillance and attack system. The Apache can operate in all weathers, day or night, and detect, classify and prioritize up to 256 potential targets in a matter of seconds.'

Another interesting comment was made by WO2 Giovanni Morini in conversation with the author. He has had eleven years of experience with the AH force, firstly with 651 Squadron and then with 656, rising steadily through the ranks,

> 'The professional standards of the entire Army Air Corps have risen over the last decade and this is due in no small part to the experience we have all had in introducing and operating the Apache. We are like three sides of an equilateral triangle, aircrew, ground crew and REME, all needing each other and sharing mutual respect and trust. I have a great respect not only for my three OCs, Majors Cash, Amlôt and Neville, but for all Squadron members who have strived to be the best they can and who have made the Squadron what it is today.'

His words are echoed by Colonel Andy Cash, now the AH Force Commander who believes that the AAC was given a helicopter and associated equipment that was second to none, a training package of the highest quality and very demanding operations to fulfil. The Corps has risen to the challenge outstandingly, with teamwork the key to this success,

> 'The confident and capable ALPC who effectively takes charge of the aircraft on the FARP, the signallers at the MPS and the REME technicians are all just as much a part of the crew now as the pilots.'

It was apposite that, in December 2011, personnel from the Apache Force 'cleaned up' at the annual Guild of Air Pilots and Navigators awards ceremony. This included a Master's Commendation to 656 Squadron for its work on board HMS *Ocean* and the Sir Barnes Wallace Medal to former OC, Major David Amlôt. This was richly deserved and demonstrated that the wider aviation community recognized the professionalism and brave determination of Squadron personnel.

As the research for this book is being concluded in 2012, the Squadron's task (under its latest OC, Major Piers Lewis, the first 'home grown' AH OC) is to train for its role as Contingent Operations Squadron, ready for deployment operationally anywhere in the world at short notice. The Squadron is still leading the way as the AH Force as a whole prepares to adapt to a post-Herrick world. The immediate future for the Squadron is likely to be based on close cooperation with HMS *Illustrious*, 3 Commando Brigade RM and 16 Air Assault Brigade, as both the maritime and land-based contingency requirements are developed. The learning process never stops.

An Operational Conversion Flight (OCF) is currently embedded within the Squadron with the task of providing CTR to all new AH pilots who have completed CTT at Middle Wallop. Within this training role the Squadron has seen soldiers of all hues pass through its ranks, from airtroopers to royalty.

In April 2012, two Apaches from the Squadron fired one Hellfire missile each at a training target that was positioned by HMS *Illustrious*, in the sea off Northern Scotland, where the ship was taking part in the multinational Exercise Joint Warrior. This was the first time that the pilots had fired live missiles in the UK. As well as training the Apache pilots themselves, the firings also allowed the ship's crew to practice safely delivering the missiles from weapon magazines to the helicopters on the flight deck. Piers Lewis, commented,

> 'The Apache crews are comfortable operating in all environments and this has once again demonstrated our ability to fire Hellfire from sea, having launched from HMS *Illustrious*. We forged excellent links with HMS *Ocean* last year – and are now making similarly strong links with *Illustrious*.'

Much has changed in the last seventy years, the complexity and capability of today's Apaches would have been far beyond the imaginations of the pioneer Auster pilots, fitters, signallers and drivers who took part in the Burma campaign. Moreover, instead of directing ground-based artillery from the air, 656 Squadron now constitutes airborne artillery itself, being directed from the ground by FAC/JTAC. Yet much remains the same, the Squadron is still on call for operations far away from home, with small numbers of aircraft and personnel giving a level of support far beyond that which could reasonably be expected of a single squadron. Back at base, technicians and other specialists still labour tirelessly to keep the aircraft and equipment ready for combat. The skill, dedication, courage, comradeship and good humour of all Squadron members, either in the air or on the ground, remains a constant factor. This is a quite remarkable unit with a history to match and at times surpass those of any squadron in British military service.

Appendix 1

Roll of Honour

Kohima Epitaph
When you go home,
Tell them of us and say,
For your tomorrow,
We gave our today.

Burma Campaign

222097	Captain A.W. Cheshire	RA	Aged 24	29 Nov 1944
1153979	Gunner W.C. Cherrington	RA	Aged 21	1 Dec 1944
115434	Lance Bombardier D. Gibbons	RA	Aged 21	25 Jan 1945
1085616	AC2 H.E. John	RAF	Aged 23	25 Jan 1945
1642931	AC2 R.J. McCauley	RAF	Aged 24	25 Jan 1945

Hong Kong and Korea – 1903 Flight

229636	Captain K.G.W. Wilson	RA	Aged 27	29 Aug 1949
5/7003	Captain B.T. Luscombe	RAA	Aged 24	5 Jun 1952
22307090	Gunner A. Bond	RA	Aged 20	9 Dec 1952
4087544	LAC K. Goodfield	RAF	Aged 19	12 May 1953
134761	Major W.G. Harris MC	RA	Aged 36	2 Jun 1953

Malaya and Borneo

190944	Captain J.F. Churcher	RA	Aged 28	27 Oct 1949
14191865	Gunner F.R. Houghton	RA	Aged 22	11 Nov 1951
57370	Staff Sergeant W.D. Gay	RASC/ GPR	Aged 29	13 Mar 1952
860875	Sergeant J. Perry	RA/GPR	Aged 41	21 Jan 1954
407989	Captain M.R. Mather	RA	Aged 25	29 Apr 1955
407833	Captain L.P. Griffiths	RA	Aged 25	7 Jun 1956
407797	Captain P.J.L. Dalley	RA	Aged 29	14 Feb 1958
22577658	Sergeant W.J. McCammont	Cameronians	Aged 28	20 Jan 1960
437085	Captain P.H. Hills	RA	Aged 27	22 Nov 1961
23680614	Gunner G.M. Russell	RA	Aged 20	15 Jun 1963
14084626	WO2 W.J. Hutchings	AAC	Aged 36	15 July 1964
453506	Captain D. Jacot de Boinod	Coldstream Guards	Aged 26	15 July 1964

| 23396474 | Sergeant D.J.P. Waghorn | RAMC | Aged 27 | 20 Sep 1965 |
| 23995742 | Corporal C.S. Galloway | REME | Aged 22 | 30 Jan 1968 |

Falklands War

| 24075845 | Staff Sergeant C.A. Griffin | AAC | Aged 33 | 6 Jun 1982 |
| 24398996 | Lance Corporal S.J.G. Cockton | AAC | Aged 22 | 6 Jun 1982 |

656 Squadron Association pays its respects at the Cheras Road Military Cemetery, Kuala Lumpur, during a reunion visit in 2006. Burma veterans Ray Pett and Peter Andrews are shown here with Colonel Paul Edwards MBE, Military Adviser, South East Asia, who kindly accepted an invitation to lead the ceremony.

Appendix 2

Honours and Awards

Burma Campaign

MBE, DFC	Major D.W. Coyle
MBE	Captain I.N.R. Shield
MC, DFC	Captain J.B. Jarrett
MC, DFC	Captain E.W. Maslen-Jones
DFC	Captain W.R.A. Boyd
DFC	Captain M.F. Gregg
DFC	Captain S.N. Harrison
DFC	Captain P.J. McLinden
DFC	Captain F.J. McMath
DFC	Captain R.I. Walton

Java and Sumatra

MBE	Captain M.J. Cubbage
MBE	Warrant Officer A.E. Calvert
DFC	Captain R.F.N. Eke
DFC	Major H.B. Warburton

Korea – 1903 Flight

DSO	Major J.M.B. Hailes
DFC	Captain The Hon. L.R.B. Addington
DFC	Captain D.J. Browne
DFC	Captain J.A. Crawshaw
DFC	Major R.N.L. Gower
DFC	Captain J.E.T. Hoare
DFC, US Air Medal	Captain D.B.W. Jarvis
DFC	Captain G.W.C. Joyce
DFC	Captain W.T.A. Nicholls
DFC	Captain K. Perkins
DFC	Captain A.G.E. Stewart-Cox
DFC	Captain P.J.A. Tees
BEM	Sergeant R.V. Patterick

Korea – 1913 Flight

DFC	Captain P.A. Downward
DFC	Captain P.F. Wilson
AFM	Sergeant R. Meaton
DFM	Sergeant J.W. Hutchings (for service in Malaya and Korea)
DFM	Staff Sergeant J.C. Rolley
BEM	Sergeant P.O. Carr
US Air Medal	Sergeant H. Jermy
US Air Medal	Captain R.M. Begbie (for service with 3rd US Light Aviation Section)
US Air Medal	Lieutenant W.P.R. Tolputt (attached US Forces)

Malaya and Borneo

OBE	Lieutenant Colonel B.B. Storey
MBE	Captain J.B. Chanter
MBE	Major R.W. Daniel
MBE	Captain K. Perkins
MBE	Major J.S. Riggall
MBE	Major F.C. Russell
MBE	Captain H.B. Warburton
MBE	Major L.J. Wheeler
MBE	Captain R.D. Wilkinson
DFC	Captain M.G. Badger
DFC	Captain I.E. Bell
DFC	Captain J.F. Campbell
DFC	Captain H.G. Crutchley
DFC	Captain T.N.W. Lacey
DFC	Captain M.P.E. Legg
DFC	Captain V.K. Metcalf
DFC	Captain L.B. Molyneux-Berry
DFC	Captain P.T.A. Musters
DFC	Captain J.E. Nunn
DFC	Major D.P.D. Oldman
DFC	Captain C.H.C. Pickthall
DFC	Captain F.C. Russell
DFC	Captain J.P. Sellers
DFC	Captain D.W. Smith
DFC	Captain J.M.G. Stenson
DFC	Captain R.P.F. Warner
DFC	Captain D.H.G. Wisdom
DFC	Captain R. Woodbridge
DFC	Lieutenant D.T. Young
AFC	Captain J. Chandler
AFC	Major A.C.S. Holtom
AFM	Staff Sergeant P.J. Myatt
DFM	Staff Sergeant R.W. Bowles
DFM	Staff Sergeant J.I. Ford

DFM	Sergeant B.A. Horsey
DFM	Warrant Officer 2 G.D. Jenkins
DFM	Staff Sergeant K.A. Mead
DFM	Sergeant M.R. Nichols
DFM	Sergeant W.A. Patrick
DCM (Perak)	Captain S.M.W. Hickey
DCM (Selangor)	Captain K. Perkins
BEM	Chief Petty Officer G.L. Fielder
BEM	Corporal D.N. Gibson
BEM	Sergeant D.G. Goddard
BEM	Flight Sergeant G. May
BEM	Bombardier F. Merrigan
BEM	Flight Sergeant R.D. Reynolds
BEM	Corporal P.R. Rickard
BEM	Sergeant J.A. Roberts
BEM	Staff Sergeant J.N. Sanderson
BEM	Corporal A. Wainman
BEM	Staff Sergeant G.B. Warner
BEM	Sergeant F.R. Williams
BEM	Corporal J.P. Wrench
BEM	Staff Sergeant R.G. Wright

Falklands War

MBE	Warrant Officer 1 N. Pask
DFC	Captain S.N. Drennan
DFC	Captain J.G. Greenhalgh
BEM	Sergeant D. Collier

1985–1989

BEM	Corporal H. Little
BEM	Sergeant P.J.S. Mowlam
BEM	Staff Sergeant P.A. Pile

Afghanistan

MC	WO1 Ed Macy[1]
MC	Staff Sergeant K.J. Armitage
DFC	Captain N.P. Barton
DFC	Captain D.G. O'Malley

Libya

DFC	Captain N. Sierens
QCVS	Major M. Neville

Note
1. Ed Macy is a pseudonym

Appendix 3

OCs

December 1942	Major Denis Coyle
November 1945	Major Frank McMath
June 1946	Major H.B. 'Warby' Warburton
January 1947	Captain Russell Matthews (1914 AOP Flight)
June 1948	Major J.R.S. 'Jack' Elmsley
November 1948	Major Stuart Gates
March 1950	Major David Oldman
July 1952	Major L.J. 'Banger' Wheeler
June 1953	Major A.F. 'Sandy' Robertson
January 1956	Major L.J. 'Banger' Wheeler
June 1957	Lieutenant Colonel Brian Storey
February 1960	Lieutenant Colonel John Cresswell
July 1962	Lieutenant Colonel Bob Begbie
March 1965	Lieutenant Colonel Peter Collins
November 1967	Lieutenant Colonel R.J. 'Dickie' Parker
November 1968	Lieutenant Colonel Michael Hickey
October 1969	Major Peter Ralph
September 1970	Lieutenant Colonel A.E. 'Alan' Woodford
January 1973	Lieutenant Colonel Freddie Legg
August 1973	Lieutenant Colonel Greville Edgecombe
April 1975	Lieutenant Colonel David Swan
June 1977	Major Dick Whidborne
April 1978	Major Chris Pickup
June 1979	Major Stephen Nathan
June 1981	Major Johnny Moss
May 1982	Major Colin Sibun
October 1984	Major John Stirk
March 1987	Major Andy Simkins
April 1989	Major David Joyce
May 1991	Major Gary Coward
June 1993	Major Garry Key
December 1995	Major Steven Marshall
November 1997	Major Tim Sharp
October 1999	Major Alex Tucker

October 2001   Major Neil Dalton
September 2003   Major Andy Cash
October 2006   Major David Amlôt
May 2009   Major Mike Neville
October 2011   Major Piers Lewis

From left, two Squadron OCs, Major Denis Coyle MBE, DFC, and Major 'Warby' Warburton MBE, DFC, with Major Claude Surgeon and Captain John Tippen, look over one of the training helicopters at the US Army Primary Helicopter School, Camp Wolters, Texas, in December 1957.

Appendix 4

Squadron Aircraft Types and Representative Serial Numbers

DH82 Tiger Moth	T6897
Auster AOP I	LB379
Auster AOP III	MZ122
Auster AOP IV	MT159
Auster AOP V	NJ739
Auster AOP 6	VF647
Auster T7	VX929
Auster AOP 9	WZ670
DHC-2 Beaver AL1	XP817
Westland Scout AH1	XR595
Westland Bell 47G Sioux	XT210
Westland Gazelle AH1	XZ329
Westland Lynx AH1	ZD273
Westland Lynx AH7	XZ183
Westland Lynx AH9	ZG921
Westland Apache AH1	ZJ173

Should any interested party wish to carry out further research with regard to Serial Numbers of Squadron aircraft, the 656 Squadron Association archive material at the Museum of Army Flying, Middle Wallop, hold a considerable amount of information on this subject.

The Spirit of 656 in 1944

Something of the very special spirit of 656 Squadron may be gathered from the Daily Routine Orders for Christmas Day 1944 in Burma, which were presented thus:

SPECIAL CHRISTMAS NUMBER
DROs   (Darned Ridiculous Orders)   by ERK

Date... Christmas 1944

1. DUTIES   ORDERLY OFFICER   DUTY NCO
   25 Dec 44   Santa Claus   A Good Fairy (where's that fairy)

2. MUSTER PARADE
0700 hrs. Any man found out of bed will be liable to 'naik markaro' (corporal punishment). Parade will be taken by the Adj with Sgts (bless' em all) in support; the Adj will carry the bucket. Dress : Pyjamas. Men will fall-in in a horizontal position. No swearing permitted. The services of the Accts Sgt will be rendered free and will not be deducted from Credits.

3. BREAKFAST
Personnel rising between the hrs of 0800 and 0830 will be lucky. Special dish – Soyas (not chocolate coated) will be supplied on demand – limit one tin per man. NOTE: Breakfast is being prepared for about nine men.

MENU: Fruit, tinned, Grape	(Grape Fruit)
Kellogg' au lait	(Cornflakes and milk)
Unda a l'Anglais	(Egg(s) and bacon)
Burnt offering	(Toast)
Redskins	(Tomatoes)
Char (with sugar)	(French for tea)

4. DINNER
With every faith in the ability of our cooks we present the following list of fare :-

Potage a la Bebagie	(Soup)
Calcutta Bibi	(Roast Fowl)
Jungle dewdrops	(Green peas)
Pomme de terre a la Nolmes	(Just potatoes)

Veg au Butch	
You too	(Stuffing)
Mystery Rollers	(Sausage balls)
Noel Kanner	(Christmas Pudding)
Liquer Cover	(Brandy Sauce)
Mince Pies	(No recipes given)
Coffee (Let's be posh) or Char.	
Beer	(If you bring your own)

TOASTS

THE KING, EMPEROR OF INDIA
THE CO and his minions
THE COOKS

To the sufferers of Blighty
To the Girl I left Behind Me
To the Happy Jungle Boys
To the kids who play with toys
To the fast decreasing Japs
To us hardworking chaps   (rpt working)

JOE (tum ho eck, tum ho – you are a one, you are)

5. TRAINING

1400 hrs.   Horizontal Drill (in bed or out of barracks)

6. THE LITTLE YELLOW PILL

1730 hrs. It is regretted that owing to the over increasing popularity of the Little Yellow Pills, it is not possible to supply more than one per man.

The Mosquito Rajah has expressed his wish that personnel refrain from imbibing intoxicating liquor as this has been the cause of several prangs amongst his subjects. In one particular instance, one of his members was seen falling out of control after an attack upon one Sergeant of this Squadron.

We intend to ignore this appeal for the following reasons :-

1. Before 2359 hrs we are too drunk to feel a mosquito bite,
2. After 0001 hrs they are too drunk to bite.

7. SMOKEY JOE'S SNACK BAR

There will be a cold buffet which opens at 1800 hrs until cleared out. Take what you want it's on the house – don't shove just push, plenty of room for you and me.

The excellent range of dishes will include :-

Pot Luck Layers	(Asstd sandwiches)
Tarts – Savoury, Mince & Apple	(All except the right tart)
Kuchnai Soya	(Sausage rolls)
Squeaky buns	
Firpo's Special	(Fruit Salad)
What's left over	(Trifle)
Smokey's Masterpiece	(Christmas Cake)
Whatisit	(Fruit Cake)
Drinks	(As for para. 4 above)

and anything else Bruiser Bill Butch can concoct.

8. DISCIPLINE

It is requested that any songs sung during the evening be kept as pure as possible, to avoid embarrassment to the local girls (black) of the village. It was noted that several were seen to be blushing after the last jam session. I.e. Ram Sammy Safkaro (keep the party clean).

9. MISCELLANEOUS

1. It is hoped that the 0700 hrs fatigue party will NOT rpt NOT sing Christmas Carols.
2. Personnel will NOT be served with breakfast at 1230 hrs, but will be first in the queue for dinner.
3. No gratuities or adverse comments will be passed to the waiters during dinner. Any complaints will be ignored.
4. Training is an essential part of Army life (para.5 above refers).
5. The evenings entertainment will NOT include Postmans Knock or its equivalent.
6. Visitors to the Orderly Room will, for a change, be treated with civility, with the exception of one, a certain LAC Foster (alias 'Peachy').
7. Keep smiling – the Postal Orderly (Vish) is doing his best but he don't write the letters to you.
8. Message to Tac HQ and Flights :-
   "Keep smiling – we're right behind you."
9. Message to the TROOPS :-

'The Orderly Room Staff wish to take this opportunity of wishing all friends, and others, a very Merry Christmas and lashings of DROs in the New Year. They would also like to point out that, with the true Yuletide Spirit, they will be pleased to drink anyone's health if asked.'

10. No Follower will wear a black look on Christmas Day.
11. FLASH – The Orderly Room Staff, as a special privilege, will cease work (?) at 1630 hrs on Christmas Day.
12. A consignment of Knickers (WAC[I]), in lieu of Drawers Cellular have been received by the Eqpt Section. These have been reserved for issue to Dvr Ops of SHQ only.

(Original signed)
(ERK)
The Democrat,
656 Sqdn RAF.

AFTER ORDER

Drink lime juice and be happy on Boxing Day.

Appendix 6

Memories of Peter Short – Malaya 1952–1955

EVACUATION BY AIR

I graduated from the Air OP School at RAF Middle Wallop in February 1952. I requested a posting to BAOR Germany and was sent instead, along with Captain Ken Bath, to 656 Air OP Squadron RAF in Malaya. We had a fairly uneventful voyage to Singapore. Ken was a senior gunner captain, having spent most of the war as a POW in Italy. We immediately struck up a good and lasting friendship. In fact I was his best man when he married his long-time girlfriend, Daphne, in the military chapel of HQ Malaya.

At that time 656 Squadron was stationed and headquartered at Noble Field HQ Malaya. We had four flights:

1907 flight was stationed in Singapore at the Royal Naval Air Station at HMS *Simbang*, in Seremban, overlooking the causeway and naval dockyard and the southern state of Jahore. This was our operational area.

1902 flight was stationed at Benta in Pahang covering the central and east coast.

1911 flight was stationed in Seremban covering the central Malaya area.

1914 flight was stationed at Taiping in the state of Perak in the north.

It was generally accepted that newly arrived pilots should spend about a week of acclimatization before going out to the flights – this did not always happen.

One episode which stands out in my mind of my early days in Malaya is as follows:

I was in the Intelligence Officers' office, located in a wooden hut at Noble Field, next to the OC's office, when I heard Major David Oldman, calling, 'Peter, come here,' in a very urgent tone.

I went quickly into his office and he said, 'Go up to Bidor. The Royal Worcesters have suffered casualties on patrol and one soldier has to be flow to the military hospital in KL (Kuala Lumpur) for urgent treatment.'

I asked, 'Where is Bidor.'

He responded, 'Get a bloody map and I'll show you.'

I saw on the map that Bidor was about fifteen minutes flying time south-east of Ipoh and approximately ten minutes off my track.

The navigation was not difficult as the railway line from Siam to Singapore was a wonderful guide to follow. When I got in sight of Bidor I first observed that both ends of this temporary runway were clear – that is, not covered by high trees, as many runways in Malaya were at that time. As soon as I landed the MO got out of a jeep that was parked next to the waiting ambulance. After initial greetings he said to me, 'You know this is a stretcher case don't you?' I responded that I didn't know but it was okay because we could make room for the stretcher by taking off the starboard door and removing the

Army 62 wireless set. This was done quickly as I inquired regarding the wounded soldier. He said that this National Serviceman was an eighteen year old on his first patrol and had been shot through the eye and part of his brain was exposed. The left side of his face and head were covered in bandages. As the casualty was strapped in and I replaced the aircraft door, there was no room for the Army 62 wireless set, which I ended up leaving behind.

On the way to Bidor I had seen the clouds building up along the mountain range and thought it would be a pretty close thing to get back to K.L. before the storm set in. The MO gave me two small injection syringes and said, 'If he begins to wake up or move give him a shot right away as he must be kept absolutely still.' I told the MO to give our ETA to Noble Field and to alert the British Military Hospital in Kinrara that we were on our way to Noble Field with the casualty.

The nearer we got to K.L. the more concerned I became regarding the storm coming down the mountain and covering K.L. and Noble Field. When I got over Batu Caves I could see clearly that the storm would be covering Noble Field and RAF K.L. before we got there and there was no way we could land in those conditions. I thought I should notify them of my plight, completely forgetting that I had to leave the Army 62 wireless set behind in Bidor. I looked at my map and my petrol gauge to try to work out how long I could stay airborne before going in to land. While looking at the map I saw there was an emergency strip at BMH Kinrara, made up of two or three football fields which could be used in an emergency. I flew to Kinrara and saw that the storm had not yet reached the BMH and that soldiers, who had observed my approach, were frantically pulling down the goal posts.

I went in low to have a look at the surface, which did not look too bad, and in quick time an ambulance stationed itself alongside the playing field. The wind was coming in

Captain Peter Short, his OC Major "Banger" Wheeler and an unknown visiting officer, in front of Auster AOP 6, WJ356, in Malaya in the early 1950s.

strong from the east with the storm. Ideal conditions for landing; if I could get the aircraft down before the storm arrived. I said a silent prayer and went in on my final approach, just as the leading edge of the storm was less than 400 yards away. By the grace of God I 'greased her in' and made a perfect landing. I stayed put until the ambulance arrived and the casualty was transferred to the ambulance as it was pretty bumpy for taxiing.

I called the IO from the ambulance radio, giving him a run down on what had taken place and estimated that I would be back at base in one and a half hours.

I followed-up on the progress of the National Serviceman and found that he stayed in intensive care for many days and had lost his eye but was making a good recovery. I later learned that he was invalided out of the Army and returned to England.

BREAKING THE RULES

There was a policy in 656 Squadron that to qualify to command a flight one must have at least six months remaining to serve in Malaya before returning to the UK. I readily agreed to serve an additional six months and was given command of 1902 Flight, at that time stationed at Sembawang – the RNAS at Singapore. This for me was an ideal situation as my wife Ann had given birth to our son, Walter, who was born at BMH Kinrara. This was before independence and there was no emergency in Singapore and I was lucky to get the rental of a small wooden bungalow, with no electricity, in the 'cabbage patch' on a rubber plantation at 11th Mile Nee Soon – five minutes away from my base at Sembawang

1902 Flight had the difficult task of covering the very Terrorist-active area of Jahore: despite a very efficient SWEC (State War Executive Committee) which was chaired by the Sultan of Jahore, or his nominee. The Committee depended greatly on the information provided by 1902 Flight on the location of terrorist clearings and camps from which the terrorists grew food and operated. There were many interesting and challenging times, almost on a daily basis, but one operation particularly stands out in my mind and memory.

The 1st Fijian Regiment (1st FIR), under the command of New Zealander, Lieutenant Colonel Lowe, was stationed at Malacca, right in the heart of terrorist activity. After flying Colonel Lowe around the operational area a few times I got to know him fairly well and we developed a good rapport. He said to me, 'Why don't you leave one aircraft here in Malacca to save the down time of flying back to Singapore every evening during the operation.' This suggestion made sense to me so I told him I would recommend it to HQ. This was done and accepted on the condition that 1st FIR provided the necessary security at the Malacca airstrip.

One of the most difficult tasks that a flight commander in Malaya had was arranging the flying programme for the next day and putting it up in chalk on a blackboard in the operations room. I decided to do the detachment to Malacca myself as I knew the area better than any of the other pilots. It was agreed that the detachment to Malacca was not to last longer than three days.

On the late afternoon of the second day I was returning to my temporary base at Malacca and the sun was very low, when I flew right over a terrorist camp. There was a pig fence around it under the trees and the 'bashas' were quite visible. I could not believe my eyes, as it was located only about ten minutes from the base. I decided to turn the aircraft around and have another look – and there it was. Then suddenly I felt the whole aircraft shake and I reckoned that I had been hit by gunfire under the engine. I flew back to base at Malacca without difficulty and let my ground crew, an engine mechanic and an airframe mechanic, know that I would make a low flying pass over the runway with flaps down and asked them to check the undercarriage. After doing the slow fly-past they reported that no damage could be seen and suggested that I carry out a normal landing, which I did with no difficulty. I was also told that Colonel Lowe was waiting to see me. I got out of the aircraft quickly and went straight to have a look under the engine. In a matter of minutes the airframe mechanic called out to me, 'Come and have a look at this sir.' We all converged at the tail of the aircraft and saw five bullet holes in the tail fin. The jarring that I had felt was in fact the relayed impact on the rudder pedals under my feet. The bullets must have missed the rudder pedal cables by a couple of inches.

While we were chatting about my close escape, the airframe mechanic was quickly patching the holes, clearly made by bullets from a Bren Gun. The Colonel, in the meantime, was speculating as to how we should respond and informed us that all his troops were committed and by the morning the CTs (communist terrorists) would have broken camp and disappeared. Then he said, 'I know, why don't we drop some grenades on them? We can't just sit here and do nothing.'

I responded, 'That is a very dangerous exercise and completely against regulations.'

He said, 'To hell with the regulations! This is a war and we have to respond in a positive way'.

He repeated that he could not send in any troops as they were all committed, and in any case, tomorrow would be too late. We discussed the possibility of an air strike, but this would take too much time to mount. The Colonel was adamant that action had to be taken urgently. Uppermost in my mind was the fact that flight commanders were told to inform all pilots that they, the pilots, were in command of the aircraft and were not to give in to pressure from senior officers, particularly regarding weather and light. The pilots were the sole judges and would have to make the decision if, for example, the weather was good enough to take off.

I agreed rather reluctantly to the Colonel's idea, giving way to pressure and ignoring common sense logic, in the full knowledge that if this got back to HQ I would be for the 'high jump'. We had to hurry as the light was fading fast. We took an empty Fraser and Neave orange juice crate and put twelve fully charged hand grenades in it. I took off the aircraft doors, which was standard procedure for dropping small supplies, and told the Colonel to use the starboard door space while I would use the port door area from which to drop the grenades.

When we were about five minutes away from the terrorist camp I saw a small column of smoke from the area to which we were heading. I said to the Colonel, 'They're marking the target for us.'

I flew in as low as possible without endangering the aircraft, which was a bit sluggish with the doors off. We dropped three grenades each on the first flyover. I did a sharp 180 degree turn for the return attack and we dropped the remaining three grenades each. I could not say how effective the grenades were as I was fully occupied flying the aircraft and sorting out the grenades. The whole operation took twenty-eight minutes before we were safely back at the Malacca airstrip. The Colonel was overjoyed and delighted with the operation which had been accomplished successfully, in good time, and just before night set in.

The Colonel asked me to dinner in his Officers' Mess, but I said I would come over for one drink only (we did not drink when we were flying). He sent his chief for me along with a security escort. When I got to the Mess the Colonel was at the bar with some of his officers and two men in civilian clothes who I did not recognize. The Colonel stood up and came over to me. He put his arm around my shoulder and said in a very loud voice, 'Gentlemen, this is my bomber pilot.' I quickly cautioned the Colonel, who appeared to have already had a couple of drinks, about the confidentiality of the operation. My worst fears where confirmed when I discovered that the two civilians were reporters from *The Malay Mail* and *The Straits Times*. It turned out that the Colonel had already given his version of the operation that day. I politely as possible avoided the questions of the reporters, had a quick drink, and departed.

After my encounter with the media men I felt pretty sure that within a couple of days the 'news' would be in both local newspapers in Malaya and Singapore. I did not have long to wait. The *Malay Mail* headline, in bold print, announced 'Airborne grenades send "reds" fleeing.' I cannot recall the wording of the report in *The Straits Times*, but it was given full coverage.

Later that morning I got the not unexpected phone call, from the OC of 656 Squadron, Major Sandy Robertson, who asked me if the reports were correct, to which I replied, 'Yes, substantially so.'

He said, 'Look Peter, you're in some trouble and the GOC Malaya, Major General Sir Hugh Stockwell, would like to see you forthwith – and I can tell you he is not pleased. Drop everything and fly up here immediately.'

This I did, fearing the worst but hoping for the best. I landed at Noble Field and was met by Sandy Robertson, to whom I gave a detailed account of what had taken place and accepted full responsibility.

He said, 'My advice to you is to tell the truth as you have told me, say a prayer and hope for the best.'

Within half an hour of my landing I was standing at attention in front of the GOC Malaya, General Sir Hugh Stockwell. I gave him the story while he listened attentively. Then there was what seemed to me a very long pause before the General responded. He gave me a tremendous dressing down, telling me what a serious matter this was and how I endangered the life of Lieutenant Colonel Lowe, my own, and risked destruction of the aircraft. He let me know how very stupid I had been.

He then said, 'You can go now.' The words that I had prayed to hear.

I think I said, 'Thank you Sir, it certainly won't happen again.'

Before I could leave his office he called out, 'Peter, come back here, take off your cap and sit down.' All of this in a very different tone of voice. Then he continued, 'Bloody good show! I would probably have done the same thing myself. I have told your OC that this must not appear on your Confidential Report.'

Then he added, 'By the way, how is your cricket?' The General had seen me make seventy-two runs for the Army against Oxford University at the RMA Sandhurst when he was on the staff there in 1950. We chatted for about another five minutes and as I was leaving, Major Sandy Robertson's parting words were, 'You're a damned lucky young man.'

Bumph 1954

It is often contended that one of the curses of modern times is form filling, just to show that there is indeed nothing new under the sun, the following heartfelt contribution comes from a Flight Newsletter of 1954,

BUMPH

The paper war seems to increase daily, and we feel that a former Squadron Commander of 652 was perhaps right in many of the views expressed in the RA Journal. In the last twelve months the number of letters etc, in and out of SHQ has doubled. Flight Commanders are finding the position no better and it has been found necessary to ask for a second Flight clerk (a retrograde but necessary step it is felt).

Someone in an Air Force HQ decided that we hadn't completed a small detail in our Forms 540 and 541 in the manner approved and laid down in AP 3040. Admittedly, we hadn't sent them in duplicate to SHQ, so we didn't complain about producing another copy, but, just to satisfy ourselves that we had in fact created a grave error by not completing the form in exactly the right manner, we rang up the gentleman at HQ FEAF who is responsible for seeing that these particular forms are completed and collected from all the units in the Command and for sending them on to the Air Ministry. As we suspected, he said that he saw no reason for us to revise our original efforts but that it might help in years to come, when someone was writing of our stupendous efforts, if we followed the instructions implicitly. Being meek by nature we decided to do what the someone in an Air Force HQ had told us to do, but perhaps he could be reminded, by the Adjutant, that in addition to his 540s and 541s, we are an operational unit, working regrettably on peacetime administration and accounting, who also have to deal with the following returns :-

Daily Conspectus & DSR to SHQ.
Weekly Ops Returns to SHQ
Weekly I Summary to SHQ.
Monthly Ops Return to SHQ.
Monthly Ops Return to Div HQ & Bde HQ.
Monthly Form 4218 to SHQ.
FEAF STATS 25A weekly to SHQ.
Monthly Summary of Flying Hours/Sorties to ATC Simbang.
W.O.C.S., Arms – Ammn State Return monthly to SHQ.

Monthly, Living-in–State to Bk Stores.
Monthly, Newsletter to SHQ and Flts.
Quarterly, Certificate of Correction of Stores to SHQ.
Quarterly, Certificate of Accn. Stores State to Bk Stores.
Quarterly, Audit of P.S.I. Account to SHQ.
Monthly. MT Serviceability Return to SHQ.
Monthly. POL Vouchers to Command Secretariat.

Doubtless there are other forms we complete, in fact its certain there are, and doubtless any moment now we are going to be told to add some more returns to this vast list – all just to administer approx. thirty men.

If at the end of a Quarter, anyone should ever be so foolish as to ask the Flight's new Adjutant, Gunner Williams, why he doesn't sign on as a Regular he would doubtless be given an adequate answer.

It is hard to remain meek when we were threatened with having to keep a log of our outgoing trunk calls and submit a monthly Locstat (Flights changeover every nine months).

Appendix 8

Malaya – a view from REME 1958–1961

Craftsman/Corporal Derek Walker, now retired Major, recalls some of the technical background of the time:

Arriving at RAF Kuala Lumpur (KL Main) in September 1958, I joined 656 Light Aircraft Workshop, REME, supporting dispersed flights at SHQ, Noble Field (the other side of Kuala Lumpur); 2 Flight, Ipoh; 7 Flight, Taiping; 14 Flight, Seremban; and 11 Flight, Sembawang, Singapore; each with a REME servicing section, and five aircraft. The workshop OC was Major Bunting, and the ASM Frank Penfold. All mechanics had to undertake 1st and 2nd Line, Theatre Continuation Training, in their first three months. My 2nd Line Continuation Training was on a minor inspection of an Auster Mk 9. Others went to the RAF component overhaul bays and departments, used by the workshop on the RAF base.

For my 1st Line Continuation Training, I moved to 14 Flight, which covered flight, primary and primary star servicings, maintenance of aircraft ground support equipment, refuelling, cleaning, picketing of aircraft, and night flying procedures. Aircraft problems at the time were engine starter misfires, hydraulic defects, sticking valves and fuel evaporation and aeration, the latter two being alleviated with cowling air scoops and painting fuel tank covers white. Engine oil gulping, was also experienced and overcome by introducing a scavenge filter mod No.1022. Airframes suffered oleo and flap actuator decompression and fabric deterioration. Radio mechanics were kept busy retuning HF 62 Sets and VHF Set crystal changes, also replacement of trailing aerial cones lost on landing and the effects of moisture on instruments via the pitot/static system.

We also recovered Auster XK375, which force-landed on a dirt track near Malacca, for investigation to KL Main. Preparations at SHQ, Noble Field, for the workshop relocation occurred during December and January, raising canvas aircraft hangars for the workshop and tin huts for the bays. The workshop moved in February 1959, and was responsible for the technical support of thirty-two Auster AOP 9, aircraft. Tasks included minor, minor star and major servicings, engine changes and major component overhauls, also work beyond the capability of the flights. Due to the departing RAF, at KL Main, this meant various component overhaul facilities were now needed. The requirement was for ten separate bays, each involving much work in setting up. AQMS Southon, was the maintenance supervisor, whilst ASM Frank Penfold, supported by a Sergeant and his Tech Clerk, ran engineering technical control. There was also a G1098 technical tool store, an OC's driver and eight repair crews, consisting of an NCO and three aircraft mechanics. In January, the new OC, Major Storey, took command of the

Left to right, Gunner Geordie Foster, REME Corporals Barry Rogers, Mick Gavin and Derek "Chunky" Walker at Batu Arang, during Exercise Trinity Angel.

Workshop. The WEME (Wing Electrical and Mechanical Engineer) on the SHQ Staff, initially Major Whitehead, changed to Major Dennis Weatherhead.

It was during February that the Squadron celebrated its achievement of 150,000 operational flying hours in support of the Malayan Emergency and the workshop was on parade. 14 Flight contributed the Prince of Wales' Feathers in the flying display and afterwards an AAC Colonel addressed us and prophesized a future Army Aviation servicing unit and light blue berets for all aviation personnel.

The First Class Trade Test for Air Mechanics was introduced in March 1959, the first in the new Corps, very necessary due to the shortage of First Class Mechanics at the time. A spares-chaser post was initiated, providing twice daily liaison for collection and delivery of aircraft spares to the shop floor crews. One day I heard a helicopter overhead and suddenly the noise stopped, looking up I saw a large section parting from a helicopter, the RAF at KL Main were quickly alerted. It transpired that a Sycamore helicopter on air test had lost the main rotor head. All on board perished. Later, I had to appear in front of a Board of Inquiry at KL Main, as a witness.

During April 1959, a detachment from the workshop was sent to 7 Recce Flight, to support the servicing section, which already had detachments at Grik and Kroh. In September, engine firewall 'panting' occurred, which, on inspection, revealed severely worn fuselage cross tubes. To determine whether local repair by inserting fibre anti-rubbing strips was necessary, or tube replacement at HAEC (Hong Kong Aircraft Engineering Company), all Squadron aircraft had to be inspected. A stripdown and inspection programme, of four aircraft a month was agreed upon. This required the loan of mechanics from each of the flights to enable planned workshop tasking to continue. Beverley aircraft flew the tube replacement fuselages to HAEC, at Kai Tak Airport, in

Hong Kong, returning two months later. Locally, the strip downs continued and local repair (fibre strip) rebuilds began, creating a high learning curve. Some of the areas giving concern I remember were, the engine air intake, flight control cable adjustment and setup, soft aircraft floorboards, and the replacement of many, top, centre and rear canopies. Fabric had rotted in the sun on fuselages, mainplanes and control surfaces, which needed replacement and the effect of humidity and temperature, during doping and re-spray, was severe. One aircraft, reported flying port wing low on arrival, was found to have three engine APs (Air Publications) in the wing tip, which had worn the cross strut. After each rebuild, full fuel flow checks, engine ground runs and air tests were required, usually flown by a QFI, with the crew chief alongside. There was a need to bolster rebuild supervision; RN (Fleet Air Arm), CPOs and POs; RAF Flight Sergeants, and later a supplement of Leading and Naval Air Mechanics, achieved this. On rebuild completion, in March 1960, the mechanics returned to their respective Flights. I was posted to 7 Flight.

April 1960, brought "Technician Day", when all aircraft mechanics remustered as technicians and being qualified Class X2, were promoted to Corporal. Overnight there was a glut of REME corporals.

The workshop was involved in several aircraft recoveries. In particular, an aircraft from 7 Flight, Auster 9, WZ706, went down with a severe oil leak near Yala, forty miles inside the Thai Border. It landed intact on a track. A recovery party from the workshop, with ASM Penfold in charge, arrived at Grik, near the border and departed after lunch for Yala, collecting a Thai Police escort at the border. The recovery took place the next day, after a long trip involving a river crossing and then a walk to the aircraft. The cause was sheared attachment studs for the oil scavenge pipe union connection, resulting in total engine oil loss. The mainplanes and engine were removed and fuselage jury rigged, intending to carry and wheel them to the river. However, the WEME and an RAF Engineering Wing Commander arrived by Sycamore helicopter, deciding to undersling the engine, fuselage and mainplanes separately back to the vehicle. The first two lifts went well, but the mainplanes, lifted individually, then as a pair, spun, causing the helicopter pilot to jettison them. Finally the mainplanes, by now damaged, were manhandled to the river and then the vehicle. By lunchtime recovery was completed. We bade farewell to the villagers and police who had helped us and at the border debussed our escorts, heading for Taiping to drop me off, before returning to the workshop with the aircraft for repair. A very interesting experience indeed!

Later, 28 Commonwealth Brigade was put on standby for Laos, and technicians were drafted in from the workshop to support the ten aircraft 7 Flight now had. The Brigade was later stood down and in August 1961, Air Portability training was completed in the form of the first major Brigade Exercise Trinity Angel, reflecting a 1000 mile move over water to deal with insurgents, insignificant at the time. Later the Commonwealth Brigade moved to Terendak Camp, at Malacca, but that was after my departure in September 1961.

Bibliography

National Archive
Operational Record Books 1942–57 in the series AIR/27 and AIR/29
War Office Historical Monograph – Army Air Support and Photographic Interpretation 1939–1945 (WO277/34)
Report of a Board of Enquiry into the loss of an Army Air Corps Gazelle over the Falkland Islands on 6 June 1982 244/1/63.W dated 6 November 1986 (Names of authors redacted)

Museum of Army Flying – 656 Squadron Archive
Squadron and Flight Diaries, Newsletters 1943–1968
Correspondence and reports concerning 1587 Flight 1944–1945
Squadron Association Newsletters 1950–2011
Air OP Officers' Association Review 1947–1957

Unpublished Manuscripts
Anon, *Memoirs of a Decrepit Aviator*
Anon, *Outline of Events – Operation Corporate Royal Marine and Army Aviation Participation*
Bailey, Reginald, *Personal Experiences in the 7th Div "Admin Box"*
Barker, Ralph, *The night a young wife was told – your husband is lost*
Begbie, Bob, *Letter of October 1977 to Brigadier Peter Mead concerning Air OP in Korea*
Boys, Captain Rex, *Prelude to Action and its Outcome*
CJC, *Hong Kong Memoir 1963*
Collins, Lieutenant Colonel P.E, *656 Squadron Army Air Corps. A Digest History of Army Aviation in the Far East*
Coward, Lieutenant General Gary, *656 Squadron AAC – 1991–1993*
Cross, John, *The De Havilland (Canada) Model 2 Beaver AL Mk 1*
Deane, Captain T.M., *Austers Over Borneo*
Downward, Major General Sir Peter, *1913 Flight in Korea*
Edgecock, Len, *The Brunei Rebellion A personal memory*
Fogden, Simon, *Hong Kong December 1974–July 1977 "I Learned About Flying From That"*
Gower, Colonel Ronald, *Letter of October 1999 to John Bennett concerning 1903 Flight in Korea*
Greenhalgh, John, *Falklands 1982, the Journey South*
Greenhalgh, John, *Falklands 1982–May 21 to August 1*
Groom, Harry, *Morse was my Catalyst*
Hammond, Lieutenant Colonel "Wally", *Letter of December 1997 and enclosures to Ted Maslen-Jones*
Harris, Peter, *Return to Korea*

Harrison, Tom, *Background to a Revolt. Brunei and the Surrounding Territory*

Hickey, Colonel S.M.W, *The British Army and the Battlefield Aerial Vehicle*

Howard, Alfred, *Memories of 656 Squadron in the UK, India and Burma*

Howe, Clive, *1903 Independent Air OP Flight RAF*

Joyce, Lieutenant Colonel David, *656 Squadron AAC April 1989–May 1991*

Joyce, Sarah and Jeremy, *Captain G.W.C. Joyce DFC – With 1903 Flight in Korea*

Key, Major Garry, *656 Squadron*

Leetham, L.A, *Introducing the AOP Mk9 to Far Away Places*

Marshall, Colonel Steven, *656 Sqn AAC – OC's Notes*

Matthews, Russell, *Medan Muses 1946 'A' Flight. A Flight Commander's Memory*

Matthews, Russell, *"Jock" An appreciation – The Eulogy to a loyal friend*

Matthews, Russell, *Farewell Medan 'A' Flight's move back to Malaya*

McKenzie, George, *Borneo – The Final Curtain*

McMath, Major Frank, *The Jungle Lay Beneath*

Morgan, Bill, *Memories of Sarawak 1963–64*

Moss, Colonel John, *Babes in the Jungle*

Musters, Captain Pat, *A Close Encounter with a Snake*

Nathan, Major S.R, *Operation Agila 1979–80 656 Squadron AAC Report 25.4.1980*

Pengelly, Martin, *The History of Auster MT438*

Perkins, Major General Ken, *Letter to the Editor of The Chinthe Spring 2006*

Rai, Manbahadur (as told to Kufus, Marty), *Fighting Nature, Insects, Disease and Japanese. The Chindit War in Burma*

Simkins, Lieutenant Colonel Andrew, *My time as OC 656*

Smith, Ernest, *Early Days How 656 Squadron drove across India and stood fast at the Battle of Chota Maungnama*

Stewart-Cox, Major General Arthur, *Letter of September 1999 to John Bennett concerning 1903 Flight in Korea*

Stirk, John, *656 Squadron AAC History 1984–87*

Subritzky, Mike, *Rhodesia – Operation Agila the British Empire's Last Sunset*

Swan, David, *Hong Kong 1975–77*

Warburton, Major H.B, *656 Squadron in Java and Sumatra 1945–46*

Ward, Ron, *7 Reconnaissance Flight 1961–1964*

Welsh, Rob, *Memories of 656 Sqn AAC in Hong Kong – Dec 1969 to Oct 1971*

Windscheffel, Arthur, *Diaries 1943–1946*

Books

Anon, *Java Handbook for Servicemen* (SEAC 1946)

Arnold-Foster, Mark, *The World at War* (London 1989)

Ashworth, Chris, *Avro York in RAF Service 1942–1957* (Berkhamsted 1983)

Burden, R.A; Draper, M.I; Rough, D.A; Smith, C.R. and Wilton, D, *Falklands, The Air War* (London 1986)

Catchpole, Brian, *The Korean War 1950–53* (London 2000)

Dowling, Wing Commander J.R, *RAF Helicopters – The First Twenty Years* (London 1987)

Farndale, General Sir Martin, *History of the Royal Regiment of Artillery. The Years of Defeat 1939–41* (London 1996)

Farndale, General Sir Martin, *History of the Royal Regiment of Artillery. The Far East Theatre 1939 – 1946* (London 2000)

Farrar-Hockley, General Sir Anthony, *The Army in the Air* (Stroud 1994)

Fowler, Will, *Britain's Secret War: The Indonesian Confrontation 1962–66* (Oxford 2006)

Hastings, Max and Jenkins, Simon, *The Battle for the Falklands* (London 1983)

Hastings, Max, *All Hell Let Loose – the World at War 1939–1945* (London 2011)

Hickey, Colonel Michael, *The Unforgettable Army. Slim's XIV Army in Burma* (Tunbridge Wells 1992)

Hickey, Colonel S.M.W, *The Army Air Corps Past and Present* (Middle Wallop 1986)

Hobson, Chris, *Falklands Air War* (Hinckley 2002)

Jackson, Robert, *Army Wings – A History of Air Observation Flying 1914–1960* (Barnsley 2006)

Jackson, Robert, *The Malayan Emergency and Indonesian Confrontation* (Barnsley 2008)

James, Derek N, *Westland – A History* (Stroud 2002)

Jefford, Wing Commander C.G, *RAF Squadrons* (Shrewsbury, 1988)

Keegan, John, (editor) *Churchill's Generals* (London 1991)

Ketley, Barry, *Auster A Brief History of the Auster in British Military Service* (Ottringham 2005)

Lee, Air Chief Marshal, Sir David, *Eastward – A History of the RAF in the Far East 1945–1972* (London 1984)

Lewis, Damien, *Apache Dawn* (London 2008)

Macy, Ed, *Apache* (London 2009)

Macy, Ed, *Hellfire* (London 2010)

Madison, Charlotte, *Dressed to Kill* (London 2010)

Maslen-Jones, E.W, *Fire by Order* (Barnsley 1997)

Mead, Peter, *Soldiers in the Air* (London 1967)

Mead, Peter, *The Eye in the Air* (London 1983)

Palmer, Alan, *The Penguin Dictionary of Twentieth Century History* (London 1979)

Parham, Major-General H.J and Belfield, E.M.G, *Unarmed into Battle* (Chippenham 1956)

Postgate, Malcolm, *Air Transport Support in the Malayan Emergency 1948–60* (London 1992)

Potter, John and Barnes, Murray, *The Twelve Miles Snipers* (Belfast 2011)

Ripley, Tim, *British Army Aviation in Action From Kosovo to Libya* (Barnsley 2011)

Robertson, Bruce, *The Army and Aviation* (London 1981)

Scurr, John, *The Malayan Campaign 1948–60* (Oxford 1982)

Several authors, *The Royal Artillery Commemoration Book 1939–1945* (London 1950)

Several authors, *The British Pacific and East Indies Fleets "The Forgotten Fleets"* (Portsmouth 1995)

Smurthwaite, David (Ed), *The Forgotten War* (London 1992)

Terraine, John, *The Right of the Line – the Role of the RAF in WW2* (Barnsley 2010)

Thompson, Julian, *Forgotten Voices of Burma* (London 2009)

Van der Bijl, Nick, *Confrontation: The War with Indonesia 1962–66* (Barnsley 2007)

Whitnall, Frank, *Wings over Westley, The Story of a Suffolk Airfield* (Bury St Edmunds 2004)

Periodicals

The Army Air Corps Journal 1959 to 2010

Anon, *656 Squadron Army Air Corps* (AAC Journal 1968)

Anon, *656 Aviation Squadron – Hong Kong* (AAC Newsletter 1970)

Anon, *The End of an Era* (AAC Newsletter 1972)

Anon, *656 Aviation Squadron in the Far East* (AAC Newsletter 1973)

Anon, *11 Flight AAC* (AAC Newsletter 1975)

Anon, *The Laos Beaver* (AAC Journal 1979)

Anon, *656 Squadron AAC – Falklands Tour '85* (AAC Journal 1986)

Anon, *Appreciation Brigadier Denis Weston Coyle* (AAC Journal 1996)

Anon, *Appreciation Major "Warby" Warburton* (AAC Journal 1999)

Anon, *HMS Defender in Malaya* (Auster News Volume 5 No 2 1954)

Anon, *The Falklands: Army Air Corps Operations* (Airplane 1989)

Anon, *9 Regiment AAC Roundup* (AAC Journal 2007)

Anon, *4 Regiment AAC* (AAC Journal 2008)

Anon, *4 Regiment Army Air Corps* (AAC Journal 2009)

Anon, *Obituary: John Merton* (Daily Telegraph February 2011)

Anon, *Apache Fires First Hellfire Missiles at Sea* (Hawkeye Issue No 20 September 2011)
Another Old China Hand, *More Austers in Honkers*, (AAC Journal 2006)
Ballantyne, Iain (Editor), *Several articles* (Warships IFR Guide to the Royal Navy 2012)
Barton, Lieutenant Nick; Ebdon, Staff Sergeant Tony; Goddard, WO1 Kev and Langford, Staff Sergeant "Bonnie", *Onwards and Upwards – A brief students' account of Apache conversion training* (AAC Journal 2004)
Bennett, John, *656 Squadron Association* (AAC Journal 2001)
Bonner, Captain Sean, *Army Flying Profile* (AAC Journal 1997)
Bush, Keith, *Flying in Malaya* (AAC Journal 2002)
Caplin, Major N.J, *Operation Grapple – Army Aviation in the Balkans* (AAC Journal 1995)
Collins, Lieutenant Colonel P.E, *The Front was Everywhere* (RUSI Journal 1967)
Condon, Captain Mark, *HMS Ark Royal Celebrates its 25th Anniversary of Commissioning with the Queen and two Apaches* (AAC Journal 2010)
Cowper-Coles, Sir Sherard (Article in The Sunday Times 22 May 2011)
Crawshaw, Lieutenant Colonel J.A, *The War in Korea Part 1* (AAC Journal 1972)
Draper, Michael, *AOP Squadrons 1942 – 1947 656 Squadron* (BARG Roundel September 1982)
Draper, Michael, *1587 (Air OP) Refresher Flight Deolali, India 1944/5* (Auster Quarterly Vol 1 No 6 1977)
Fleming, Malcolm, *Two Recce Flights in Malaya 1959–1962* (AAC Journal 2008)
Grevatte-Ball, Richard, *Appreciation Major Frank McMath* (AAC Journal 2003)
Hamilton, Leigh, *Apache in Afghanistan* (Defence News June 2011)
Heyes, John, *A Sprog arrives in 656 Squadron in Kuala Lumpur (*AAC Journal 2005)
Hicks, Major J.D, *The War Korea Part II* (AAC Journal 1975)
Hunt, Wing Commander Bryan J, *Air Power and Psychological Warfare Operations – Malaya 1948 – 1960* (RAFHS Journal 47 2010)
Kalinski, Staff Sergeant Dick, *Army Flying Profile* (AAC Journal 1996)
King, H.F, *The Sharp End – Britain and Australia in the Korean War* (Flight Magazine July 1953)
Liardet, Rear Admiral Guy, *How the Navy helped to stop Gaddafi's brutal regime* (The Times 10 December 2011)
Long, Richard, *Mission Accomplished* (Soldier Magazine December 2011)
Longley, Tim, *More Malaya 656 Sqn Wksps – KL – 1960/61* (AAC Journal 2008)
Maslen-Jones, E.W, *An Unusual Task for Air OP* (AAC Journal 1995)
MGB, *Appreciation Major Mike Somerton-Rayner* (AAC Journal 2002)
Miller, Harry, *No 656 Sets a World Record* (The Sunday Times March 1959)
Moss, John, with Coyle D.W, McMath, F.W, Warburton, H.B, *Air OP Austers: Eyes for the Army* (Aeroplane Monthly March – May 1993)
Nathan, Major S.R, *Operation Agila* (AAC Journal 1980)
Neville, Major Michael, *656 Squadron on Exercise Joint Warrior* (AAC Journal 2010)
Nunn, Jimmy, *Malaya Remembered* (AAC Journal 2003)
Pettyfer, Philip, *Austers in "Honkers"* (AAC Journal 2003)
Ralph, Major Peter, *Army Aviation in Hong Kong* (AAC Newsletter 1968)
Richards, General Sir David (Interview in The Times 24 November 2011)
Riggall, Major J.S, *RCT Light Aircraft Operations in Borneo* (RCT Review March 1966)
Russell, John, *Austers at War* and *Forgotten Force: Austers in Korea* (International Auster Club News Volume 24 Number 2, Summer 2001)
Sibun, Major Colin, *Falklands Diary* (AAC Journal 2003)
Sturtivant, Ray, *Air Observation Post Flights 1947–1957* (Aviation News 9–22 August 1985)
Wheeler, Major J.H, *What was Belize?* (AAC Journal 1981)
Wheeler, Major L.J, *Letter to the Editor* (Auster News Volume 4 No 8 1953)
Whidborne, Major Dick, *Hong Kong Revisited 2007* (AAC Journal 2007)

Index